Endorsements

DAVID SHIBLEY
Founder of Global Advance

Why Apostles Now? is a landmark book that deserves to be read by every devoted follower of Christ today. From the dual perspective of both a thorough researcher and a veteran practitioner Ernest Gentile calls today's church to powerful, rapid advance through apostolic leadership. Your life and ministry will be forever enriched by absorbing the insights of this timely book.

DAVID CANNISTRACI
Lead Pastor at GateWay City Church, San Jose, CA
Author of *Apostles and the Emerging Apostolic Movement.*

With his usual blend of solid scholarship and rich insight, Ernest Gentile delivers again! *Why Apostles Now?* is a remarkable contribution that advances the discussion of apostolic ministry in a balanced and inspiring way. I love this book.

C. PETER WAGNER
Vice President and Apostolic Ambassador, Global Spheres, Inc.

As the apostolic movement develops, the literature continues to increase both in quantity and quality. I am delighted that Ernest Gentile has stepped up to the plate, and, drawing on his well-honed research skills, has given us a superb textbook on apostolic ministry. An outstanding feature of *Why Apostles Now?* is the presentation of the different views of those who have addressed each of the major issues along with a fair analysis of the strengths and weaknesses of each. I strongly recommend this book.

DOUG BEACHAM
Vice-Chairman, International Pentecostal Holiness Church Ministries,
Executive Director, IPHC World Missions Ministries

Ernest Gentile has given us another excellent book dealing with the spiritual leadership gift of "apostle" in the body of Christ. In his easy to read style and stellar use of sources Gentile offers fresh perspectives on the emerging role of apostles as the 21st century church. His chapter on "Spheres and Cultures" is worth the price of the book. This is a must-read book for leaders sensing an apostolic anointing in their lives and for those who serve with such leaders.

RONALD E. COTTLE
Founder-President of Christian Life Educators Network

Ernest Gentile is himself an "apostle extraordinary" which he describes in this book. One line...shows it is what we need today...."I contend for a balance of the fire of the Spirit, the reality of the Scripture, the wisdom of experience, and just good Christian thinking." These are the qualities that have defined Gentile's writings over the years. This book is no exception. It is vintage Gentile and a must read for all interested in the emerging Apostolic Church.

FRANK DAMAZIO
Lead Pastor of City Bible Church, Portland, Oregon
Chairman of Ministers Fellowship International

One of the great leaders of today's church, Ernest Gentile has given us a balanced and biblical perspective on the sometimes-controversial subject of the ministry of apostles today....a well thought-out book with solid insights. I recommend it for all leaders.

JIM GOLL
Encounters Network • Prayer Storm • Compassion Acts, Author of *The Seer*

With the back drop of a history tour of the early church...Ernest Gentile gives us a thorough, scholarly and yet connectable read in...*Why Apostles Today?* Do apostles exist today? What are the qualifications? How do apostles relate to culture and various spheres of life and ministry? How ...commissioned? ...pertinent questions are asked and definitive answers given by this humble and wise father in the faith. I highly recommend this book to those who love the truth of God's word and desire to see a victorious church emerge!

RAJU THOMAS
Senior Pastor of Poona Faith Community Church, Pune, India
Apostolic Overseer of Numerous Churches

... the Church today needs Apostles as much as the Church of the first century. *Why Apostles Now?* is a compelling book born out of a long ministry experience and deep Biblical convictions. Those who buy into the proposition that we need Apostles or leaders of apostolic gifting today to produce Churches of spiritual maturity and fruitfulness will greatly benefit from the teachings of this book. All one needs to know about Apostles and apostleship is presented in this one volume with lucidity and sound scholarship.

STEPHEN M. STELLS
Pastor of The House of Prayer, Chesterfield, VA
Church Planter, MFI Apostolic Team Member

... masterfully articulates key reasons for the current stalemate of the church in the western hemisphere...offers solid solutions garnered from sound biblical theology and exegesis, solid research, historical and contemporary perspective, as well 65 years of life experience as a pastor, teacher, mentor and author....is comprehensive in scope, easy to read and compels the reader to action....will serve the serious seeker from seminaries to pastor's private libraries and help to shape a more glorious church for years to come.

MIKE HERRON
Prophetic Worship Ambassador to the Nations, Author of *Heart of a Psalmist*

...a convincing argument for modern day apostolic ministry...stands alongside *Your Sons & Daughters Shall Prophesy,* his parallel work calling for present-day prophetic people....extensive research, accurate exposition and engaging literary style...takes the reader through the genesis and fulfillment of the meaning of the apostolic office....particularly impressed with his understanding of the "ascension gift" apostles that are so sorely needed in the church today....a "banner text"...every student should begin their journey here!

DAVID SELL
Dean, Northern Calif. Bible College, Pleasanton, CA

Having served with Ernest Gentile for the past 40 years I have come to appreciate his Christian character, prophetic influence and ability to clarify the meaning of Scripture. *Why Apostles Now?* presents . . . a new cutting edge insight. Many realize there must be modern day apostles, but ... that every believer must also become *"apostolic"*... is a brand new thought! I recommend this book to every pastor and Christian leader who anticipates the day when the Church will have reached the measure of the stature of the fullness of Christ!

GLENDA MALMIN
Instructor & Dean of Women, Portland Bible College, Portland, OR
Author of *Woman, You Are Called & Anointed*

Ernest Gentile has a gift for writing with spiritual insight and intellectual acuity....takes that which is complex to many and makes it simple to all....This text...is a must-read....sound Biblical understanding of apostolic ministry...inspires the reader to be an active participant in an apostolic church today....From the vignettes to the charts...saturated with sound Biblical hermeneutics....thorough and insightful...worthy of digesting, quoting, and using as a teaching resource.

DICK STARK
Pastor of Faith Temple, Alexander City, AL

Scholars will appreciate the thorough research...while laymen will be grateful for its readable style....a great book which kept me thinking, evaluating my ministry, evaluating our church and promising myself I am going to do a better job. That's what I think a good book is all about....a valuable tool to affirm the church's New Testament commission.

IV

DONALD L. PHILLIPS
Licensed Marriage Counselor, Author of *Healing Broken Lives and Relationships*

This timely book will assist you to more clearly understand God's purpose for the fivefold ministry, especially the apostolic ministry and its significance for these "last days." You will discover a scholarly, strategically balanced approach to deal with a rather controversial subject. I highly recommend this book, written by my friend and pastor whom I have known for the past 42 years. He has faithfully demonstrated what a modern day apostle looks and acts like.

MICHAEL DE WAYNE PIPER
Senior Pastor of Comunidade Cristã de Curitiba, Brazil
President of MFI-Brasil, Missionary to Brazil for 41 years
Apostolic Oversight to Many Churches

The author really cares about this subject, sensitive to the point of showing us the humanity of apostles, objective enough to show this sacred path as a 'natural progression' where proficiency, fruitfulness and peer approval confirm God's call. You find yourself paging through different chapters looking for the answers to your unanswered questions. Thank you Ernest for this work of love.

KEN WILDE
Pastor of Capital Christian Center, Meridian, ID
Founder and Exec. Director of National Prayer Center, Wash. D.C.

As followers of Christ we have been entrusted with the kingdom message and its treasure. Unfortunately, many of us have opted to represent a Christianity that has become watered down and no longer adequately describes the kingdom message of the Bible....Ernest once again reminds us of the biblical truths that are necessary for the church to function properly in the last days. Apostles are necessary for the church to build a proper foundation and thereby influence a world out of control. His wisdom and research shine through as he lays out how the church, its leaders, and apostles should function....should be required reading for every Christian leader.

Why Apostles Now?

A fresh look at the vital ministry of both apostles and churches apostolic

To Linda —
a friend & encouragement
for many years.
God bless !
Ernest Gentile

By

Ernest Gentile

Why Apostles Now?
2011 by Ernest Gentile
BT Johnson Publishing
PO Box 1247
Moses Lake, WA 98837
btjohnsonpublishing.com

Visit the author's web site: www.ernestgentile.com

List of Abbreviations

ALF	Alford
AMP	The Amplified Bible
ANCHOR	The Anchor Bible
BER	Berkeley
CEV	The Contemporary English Version
JNT	Jewish New Testament
KJV	The King James Version of the Bible
KNOW	Knox
LB	The Living Bible
LXX	The Septuagint
M	The Message
Mof	Moffatt Translation
NASB	New American Standard Bible
NEB	The New English Bible
NIV	The Holy Bible, New International Version
NKJ	The New King James Version
NT	New Testament
NLT	The Holy Bible, New Living Translation
OT	Old Testament
Rhm	Rotherham Translation
TEV	The Good News Bible, Today's English Version
W	The New Testament in the Language of the People (Charles B. Williams)

Dedication

To the members of the
Ministers Fellowship International
and the Apostolic Leadership Team
whose camaraderie I have shared
for two dozen eventful years

Table of Contents

Vignettes, Tables, Charts 1

Foreword 3

Prologue 4

Part I – Our Apostolic Heritage

Chapter 1 – Are Apostles Among Us? 9
   • *Why apostles now?* • *What? I can be apostolic?* • *Is a new Church arising? What should it be like?* • *Four questions that demand an answer*

Chapter 2 – Marks of an Apostolic Church 25
   • *Spurgeon's powerful "river" statement* • *Seven marks of an apostolic church* • *Discovery of the "one, unassailable truth"* • *Every local church should be an apostolic team* • *A lesson from Charles E. Finney and E. M. Bounds*

Chapter 3 – The Church Needs Apostles 44
   • *A shave and haircut opened Inland China to the gospel* • *"Apostle" needs an upgrade* • *"Ambassador in chains" can have two meanings* • *Amazing Scriptures about Jesus The apostle* • *Meet Sunday Adelaja, "The Unlikely Ambassador"*

Part II – The Apostolic Momentum

Chapter 4 – He Chose Twelve . . . Apostles 62
   • *Why "Twelve" apostles?* • *What made the Twelve appealing to Jesus?* • *Good reasons cancelled out other candidates* • *Why was ministry time in Galilee so important?*

Chapter 5 – Paul, Apostle Extraordinary 82
   • *Visited by an angel, then shipwrecked!* • *Did Roman citizenship help Paul?* • *Terrible Terminator stopped dead in his tracks by*

Merciful Messiah • Impressive portfolio: Paul's fourteen-point resume

Chapter 6 – Validation for Additional Apostles 103
• *Some scholarly support for our thesis • What? A possible 25 more apostles in the New Testament? • Three primary "proof texts" reinforced by seven compelling reasons • Who's the foundation – Jesus or the apostles and prophets, or all three?*

Chapter 7 – Reasons for More Apostles 121
• *Five more reasons validate our claim • Were the authors of Luke, Acts, Mark and Jude apostles? • Why "test" visiting apostles? • How do "Living apostles trump dead tradition"*

Part III – A New Kind of Apostles and People of God

Chapter 8 – Four Apostles Save the Gentile Mission 140
• *Three great events launched the Church • What and why was the "Council at Jerusalem" • The bottom line of the Pharisees' opposition • Peter's story recorded three times! • Irrefutable evidences that God had invaded history again*

Chapter 9 -- An Open Door to the Gentiles 159
• *Challenging the Jewish "status quo" • Oh! The wonderful, lavish grace of Jesus! • Let's rethink the traditional four qualifications of an apostle • Has the Body lost an important member?*

Chapter 10 – The Macedonian Crusade 175
• *Macedonia, here we come! • Whoa! A "Python spirit" in Philippi? • "Vantage ground" is important • Paul's most receptive "target group" • Lessons from the Macedonian adventure for Apostolic Christians*

Chapter 11 – The Word to All Asia 191
• *Alone in a decadent Asian City! • Superstition and demonism were concentrated in Ephesus • Why so many Jews in such a worldly place? • Paul's amazing advice to the Ephesian elders*

Part IV – Apostolic Ministry Today

Chapter 12 – Leadership in Christ's Church.................................207
    • *Is Paul our example of what an apostle should be?* • *Six key signs* • *Three charts explain how apostles lead* • *The Fivefold Expression of the Church* • *How one "apostolic" church is reaching its city* • *An activity chart for "God's Generals"*

Chapter 13 – Spheres and Cultures...223
    • *Paul uses "sphere" to explain ministry calling and placement*
    • *God's continual reaffirmation of Paul's call and mission*
    • *The parallel ministries of Peter and Paul* • *The importance of everyone knowing his/her "sphere"* • *Culture is a "many splendored" thing*

Chapter 14 – Definitions and Illustrations 237
    • *God doesn't make cookie-cutter apostles* • *Apostles facilitate momentum* • *How are apostles acknowledged?*
    • *Definitions of and descriptions of modern apostles*

Chapter 15 – Activation and Motivation..................................257
    • *The Apostle's number one priority* • *How should an apostle relate to a local church?*

Part V – Apostolic Church Function

Chapter 16 – The Metamorphosis of "Church".............................262
    • *Find out what the LXX is and where it came from* • *Discover why the "church" at Ephesus got in an uproar* • *Examine an unusual chart showing all the local churches* • *Why did the people of Antioch coin the nickname "Christian"?*

Chapter 17 – Full Coverage Ministry for the Local Church 275
    • *Monitoring the Fivefold Ministry* • *Apostolic* • *Prophetic*
    • *Evangelistic* • *Pastoral* • *Teaching* • *Challenging Questions*

Chapter 18 – Women in Apostolic Ministry 294
    • *The amazing roll call of women in Scripture* • *Seven approaches to women ministry: which is right?* • *The Church's "Magna Carta" verse on freedom* • *The success secret of the world's largest church*

Appendices

Appendix A – Use "Apostle" Appropriately 312

* *Two extreme views exist* • *Do apostles need recognition and affirmation?* • *The importance of a title* • *Jesus' attitude about His titles* • *Jesus' advice about titles* • *Jesus' emphasis on humility* • *Comments from 10 thoughtful authors* • *"The Law of Unintended Consequences"*

Appendix B – A Woman's Role in Church 322

* *Analysis of the two most frequently quoted texts*
* *The context of 1 Timothy 2:11-12*
* *The context of 1 Corinthians 14:34-35*
* *How 1 Corinthians 11:2-16 blends with 14:34-35*

Appendix C – Team Ministry 332

* *How Jesus used teams* • *Teams mentioned in Acts and epistles*
* *Four objectives of team ministry* • *Husband and wife teams*

Bibliography 340

Other Products 348

Vignettes

Chapter-Page

- David Yonggi Cho: Impacting Australia   1   13
- Reg Layzell: Apostle of the Latter Rain   2   35
- Hudson Taylor: Opening Inland China   3   43
- Tony Kawalsingh: Ambassador to Trinidad   3   50
- Sunday Adelaja: The Unlikely Ambassador   3   56
- T.L. Osborn: A Legacy of Faith   9   167
- David Shibley: Missions Addiction   11   197
- Wendell Smith: Reaching a City   12   217
- Kayy Gordon: Ambassador to the Inuit People   13   225
- David Minor: Oversight of Local Pastors   14   251
- Jackie Pullinger: Chasing the Dragon   18   297
- Amy Carmichael: Let the Little Children Come   18   304
- World's Largest Church: The Secret   18   306

Special Charts

- 7 Distinguishing Marks of an Apostolic Church   2   27
- Listing of the Original Twelve Apostles   4   73
- How Paul "Ravaged" the Church   5   87
- The Physical Sufferings of Paul   5   90
- Other Apostles   6   106
- Foundation Metaphors   6   109
- Timothy's Connection with Paul   7   127
- How the Pharisees Presented Their Argument   8   145
- Elements of the Yoke of Bondage   8   146
- The Third Epochal Interpretation of God's Word   8   151
- Paul's Good News for Gentiles   9   160
- Lessons from the Macedonian Crusade   10   187
- Paul's Personal Creed   11   202
- Why Discuss Apostles Today?   12   209
- How an Apostle Leads   12   211
- Leading in World Harvest   12   212
- Leading in Planting Churches   12   214
- The Fivefold Expression of the Church   12   215
- How an Apostle Leads in …   12   221
- Apostolic Similarities between Peter and Paul   13   231
- Defining Culture   13   232
- Values of a Spirit-driven Church   13   235
- Definitions of "What Is an Apostle?"   14   243
- Local Church Locations in the NT   16   228

- Other Descriptions of Local Churches   16   269
- General References to Local Churches   16   270
- 14 References to the Universal Church   16   270
- 27 Descriptions of the Church   16   271
- Full Coverage Ministry for the Local Church   17   277
- Notable Women in the Old Testament   18   294
- Notable Women in Gospels   18   299
- Notable Women in Acts and Epistles   18   301
- Teams Mentioned in Acts and Epistles   Appendix C   334

Foreword

It is with great joy that I recommend Pastor Ernest Gentile's book on Apostles. My late husband, Wendell, would have been deeply honored and humbled to have his biographical sketch included in such a great volume. He lived the concepts presented in this book and would have applauded Bro. Gentile for writing what only a lifetime of study and prophetic insight could produce.

For nearly 40 years both Wendell and I leaned upon the pillar of strength, integrity and insight that Bro. Gentile provided for us not only in his preaching ministry, but in authoring many books. These volumes on prayer, systematic theology, worship and the end times have become deep reference wells that we have drawn from over and over again.

And now, this thorough, timely and insightful book on apostles is amazing in that it is broad in historical scope and prophetic implications, while being incredibly practical at the same time. This valuable resource imparts a new type of believing, which will provide a framework for faith to grow and develop churches!

I am so excited for a new generation who will now read, embrace and imitate the principles in this book and will be privileged to be a part of a great, global apostolic movement. The principles in this book should be read, digested and taught in every Bible-believing church around the world!

Gini Smith,
Founding Pastor of The City Church, Seattle, WA

Prologue

An ominous cloud drifted over the Christian Church of Rome in the 60s A.D. The crazed emperor Nero initiated a purge of Christians as retaliation for their supposed burning of Rome. Many Romans shared his hostility, and -- acting as Caesar's bloodhounds -- hunted the Christians down. The followers of Jesus died valiantly, giving new meaning to the Greek word *martyr* (witness). Some Christians, especially those considered ringleaders for the sect, were thrown into the escape-proof, Mamertine Prison to await execution.[1]

The very name of the prison struck dread in the hearts of the Roman populace. The hellish place was hewn out of the solid rock of the Capitoline hill, as if dug-down into the bowels of Sheol itself. Condemned prisoners were lowered by ropes into the murky depths, and then, as though all hope had not already been extinguished, chained to the walls or heavy blocks. Many never saw the light of day again. Yet . . . thank God . . . the stone fastness of the awful place could not extinguish the light of Jesus nor stifle the ringing testimony, prayers and worship of the redeemed.

Two of Christendom's greatest leaders were apparently interred there. Awaiting death, the duo encouraged the crushed believers with Scriptures of hope and prayers of faith. Finally released from that foul place, they were led away. Some say it was probably on that same day their emaciated bodies were hoisted up from the lightless depths of Mamertine and taken off to their respective places of execution.

Both men were Jews, but one was also a Roman citizen. The two men boldly professed Christ, refusing either to offer incense before the image of Caesar or call him Lord (the name of their beloved Savior).[2] Clemency was no longer possible, but they could care less: they served a higher order, belonged to an eternal kingdom, and *it was graduation day*. They knew Rome's action would merely release them from pitiful surroundings to the glorious City of God!

Certain tradition says the executions were in different parts of the City, and Christians who watched the awful death march wept openly, as did some of the guards. The two chained prisoners were Christianity's greatest ambassadors: Peter, beloved apostle to the Jews, and Paul, battle-scarred apostle to the Gentiles.[3]

The guards parted them, leading each away to his place of execution. The two felt warmed by the deep love they shared for each other and Jesus. Peter, they say, was crucified on the Vaticanum, his bloodied body (after scourging with the leaded whip) nailed upside down by his own request. Paul was decapitated on the via Ostiensis, saved from scourging or crucifixion by his citizenship. With eyes bound shut, Paul saw Him who is invisible. His head was placed upon the block – and the sword of Rome quickly granted his spirit instant flight into the presence of his beloved Lord.[4]

What a grand reception when the spirits of these two great apostles entered the portals of heaven accompanied by the spirits of multitudes of other newly made martyrs. A vast throng of shouting believers welcomed and escorted them into the very presence of Jesus.

*   *   *   *   *   *   *   *   *

It would seem Satan and his minions had triumphed gloriously. After all, snuffing out the lives of the two great generals of the army of God – as well as a great host of other Christian and Jewish martyrs – was no small accomplishment. Surely, this would be the deathblow to the beleaguered Church.

The message of Jesus the Christ was surely smoldering down . . . and finally would just burn out! The Church was finished! In spite of Jesus' promise, the Gates of Hades had not buckled but triumphed instead! The great leaders were dead, the Church was undergoing barbaric persecution, and the Jewish Temple in Jerusalem would soon be demolished. "Mission accomplished!" the adversary must have chortled gleefully.

But wait! Much to his dismay, Satan discovered the Church *did not die that day*! In spite of such devastation, the joyful, worshiping martyrs were far from the last of Jesus' living witnesses. Their blood became the seed for a Church spread throughout the entire world.

The people of God march on and the early apostles did not die in vain! They laid a foundation that weathered the test of time. Now, modern apostles and ministers reapply the great truths which insure to the last-days Church the experience of a final, glorious revolution of New Testament Christianity. What a great day in which we live!

Prologue Endnotes

[1]*The Zondervan Pictorial Encyclopedia of the Bible* (Grand Rapids, Zondervan, 1975), p. 655, shows a picture of the "Plaque at the entrance to the Mamertine Prison in Rome, where both Paul and Peter were imprisoned before their execution according to traditions going back to the 5th century." The wording says: "According to tradition, during Nero's persecution of the Christians both Peter and Paul were held captive in Rome's Mamertine Prison. The lightless interior cell of this prison was 12 feet underground and as originally designed it could be reached only through a hole in the ceiling. Prisoners were so often chained during confinement that *publica vincula* ('public chains') was a synonym for 'jail.'"
The death of Peter is not recorded in Scripture, but Jesus did tell Peter that he would be a martyr (John 21:18-19). All the records of early church history confirm his crucifixion. The testimony of Clement, cited by Eusebius, "says that before Peter was crucified he was forced to watch the crucifixion of his own wife." John MacArthur, *Twelve Ordinary Men* (Nashville: Thomas Nelson, 2002), p. 60.
Admittedly, the account as presented here is based on various traditions and may not be entirely accurate, but how it all happened would certainly be similar. The executions seem well documented.
[2]Kenneth Scott Latourette: "The antagonism was particularly marked, since Christians, revering Christ as *Kurios,* or lord of the whole earth, often looked upon the Emperor, for whom the same claim was made, as Anti-Christ, while the imperial authorities were hostile to them as those who gave allegiance to a rival of the Emperor." *A History of Christianity, Volume I: to A. D. 1500* (NY: Harper & Row, 1975), p. 84.
[3]A hundred years later Irenaeus referred to these two martyrs as "the two most glorious apostles, Peter and Paul" (*Against Heresies,* III, 3; c. A. D. 180).
[4]Various traditions surround the last days of the two apostles. F.F. Bruce comments that the tradition that Peter was crucified and Paul was beheaded "is very likely to be true."

The Spreading Flame, Vol. 1 (Grand Rapids: Wm. B. Eerdmans, 1958 (from 1973 reprint), p. 146. Latourette says: "Tradition, probably reliable, reports that both Peter and Paul suffered death at Rome under Nero, although not necessarily at this time," p. 85. Sholem Asch tells the story in a most believable and fascinating way: *The Apostle* (NY: G.P. Putnam's Sons, 1943), chapters 20-21. *1 Clement 5:5-7* also affirms that both apostles died in Rome.

Part I – Our Apostolic Heritage

Chapter 1 – Are Apostles Among Us?

Chapter 2 – Marks of an Apostolic Church

Chapter 3 – The Church Needs Apostles

Chapter 1
Are Apostles Among Us?

In This Chapter

- *Why apostles now?*
- *What? I can be apostolic?*
- *Is a new Church arising? What should it be like?*
- *Four questions demand an answer*

If you are *not* an apostle, or do not see yourself in that way, why would or should you read this book? Most people see apostles as a select few – "so, why would I want to be one anyway? Aren't they the sent-out ones? Suppose I don't feel called to be sent out?" Reasonable questions – but with surprising answers.

Perhaps you feel yourself a dedicated member of the Body of Christ but have no aspirations to be an apostle -- or even meet an apostle. Still, this book has something for you, because in these last days God wants His whole Church to be "apostolic" *in the sense that all of God's people are filled with the Holy Spirit, captivated by Christ's vision to build and maintain strong community churches characterized by a culture of love and Spirit-filled activity.*

Purpose of This Book

This book has a dynamic, dual purpose:
- *explain, establish and promote the importance of apostles,* and
- *recruit all Christians to a Spirit-filled life-style, using their ministries to insure that the local church functions in a truly biblical, apostolic culture.*

I wish to pull the wrappings off Christ's gift to the Church, that is, take a close, thoughtful look at apostles -- and explore how such awareness can upgrade *all of our spiritual lives.*

Why Apostles Now?

The plain, direct answer is threefold, and I can give that here and now, but the logic and proof will require the information in the rest of the book.

1. *The Bible teaches that there should be apostles in the Church.*

Paul, God's *architect* for local churches, taught that the Body of Christ cannot attain maturity or fulfill God's ultimate intention without apostles. Every sincere Bible believer embraces the great vision of the Church being the Body of Christ, but let us also include every Christian being a functioning member in particular, with apostles as welcome members.

2. *Apostles release God's people to their full "apostolic" potential.*

Apostles, along with prophets and other functioning ministries, will release every member of the Body of Christ to perform the Spirit-filled activity that made the churches of Bible days "apostolic." We Christians need the influence of apostolic leaders, and each one of us need to be "apostolic" -- even if we are not actual apostles!

3. *Only an apostolic Church can meet the demands of our time.*

The Church faces, along with all society, desperate times; but, for the churches it will be their finest hour because only God can supply the necessary answers and solutions. Think of these last days as a great "window of opportunity" in which God can manifest His power through His people. Imagine most communities with at least one local church having *not only* the belief system, *but also* the loving, spiritual culture, of the New Testament.

All Christians Apostolic

The times require genuine apostles and also churches made up of real, Spirit-filled, apostolic members – people of God in our communities following the pattern given by the Church of Bible times, every Christian being a vibrant, functioning member of the Body of Christ in today's society.

Said in a more focused, practical way, a local church membership needs to be a dynamic "apostolic team" which is led or influenced by apostles and shepherded by pastors and teachers who are part of the same team. David Shibley has wisely said:

> In recent years, not only has God been restoring an apostolic *company;* He's been restoring an apostolic *church.* Let's remember that the restoration of the fivefold ministry is not the point [Ephesians 4:11]. That is the means to an end. The end result God is after is a full-grown church that is ministering in apostolic authority – believers who are equipped for ministry.[1]

You may or may not be called by the Lord to be an actual apostle, but you are special, called to be a ministering member in His Church, the Body of Christ. It is important to define and discuss apostles, but there is absolutely no inclination to downgrade pastors, teachers, evangelists or any other ministry, including yours! Consider this good comment by Doug Beacham:

> While most of us are not apostles in the strict sense of the word, we are all called to be "apostolic." That means we are faithful to the *message* handed down through two thousand years of church history. It means all of us recognize that the *message* is more important than any of our titles or gifts.[2]

Your calling, gifting and spirituality will be unlocked by association with apostles in the Church and other believers who share the vision of New Testament living. Later we will discuss how all this can take place and you can share in such a great adventure. My prayer is that you will be one of many who press into all that God has for you.

Why More Apostles?

God's people are destined to finish this age triumphantly, but absolute success hinges on apostolic ministry. *Without apostles, the Church cannot become all she is meant to be.* God's health plan requires these unique members to be functioning in His Body, releasing other members to function more effectively and efficiently.

The Ephesians 4:11ff statement about fivefold ministry – which includes apostles and prophets – does not have apostles as the primary focus. The object of apostles and other fivefold is *to enable the whole Church to become spiritually mature and truly functional as representatives of Christ's kingdom.*

We must seek to understand apostleship in a practical, nuts and bolts way – not just as a matter of academic interest. We will not ignore the academic, but let us update our focus to the effective life-force of the early Church. Apostolic propulsion imparts and maintains spiritual life, lifting our churches from stuck-in-the-mud traditions to the solid highway of accelerated action. Many accept apostles theologically and historically, but are mentally boxed-in by a tradition that allows no room for such ministry today.

Not to Replace the Twelve

Contemporary apostles do not replace the Twelve Apostles and Paul. Those great ministries of the past are properly established in Christian belief and history. Remember, however, the Twelve were handpicked to perform a specialized ministry to a unique group during a particular time in history, which they did magnificently. They opened the gospel age and launched the Church; they were given a window of opportunity and responsibility in history, and they were faithful to their commission. Chapter 4 will review those original apostles.

Later, Paul and others (including the far-ranging Twelve) broke loose from the *status quo* of Jerusalem's legalistic Jewish Christianity, throwing open the gates of God's kingdom to people everywhere (discussed in Parts II and III). The Great Commission of Jesus to go and disciple all nations and communities moved into high gear – *continuing today* as a mandate of highest importance.

Today's Status Quo

Today the Church does not battle an insidious legalism, but rather a barefaced indifference to the Bible, the Holy Spirit, and dynamic church life. Apostles help correct such problems, being the spiritual efficiency experts and power initiators of the Church. Apostles upgrade serious Christians to a new life of devotion and service. How we need apostles among us! What a joy for the people to be released into Spirit-filled living and activity.

Lack of concern about apostles is traced to an insufficient grasp of New Testament Christianity, a Christianity that seems far removed from Paul's dynamic missionary journeys and church planting efforts. How do such things even have relevance for modern city dwellers and our electronic sophistication?

Today's Situation

We Christians must face the fact of societal and cultural change. 2,000 years have made a difference! Peter and Paul would be overwhelmed at our big cities with the multitudes of people and fast cars. They would not be able to comprehend the internet.

Apostolic Impact of Dr. Cho on Australia

"we pray most earnestly that we may see you again and supply what is lacking in your faith."[3]

David Cartledge writes "If ever this kind [referring to above Scripture] of impartation has been replicated in the modern Church, the ministry of David Yonggi Cho to the Australian Assemblies of God in 1977 would be a case in point. He came to a Movement that was polarized into two distinct groups, with very different values and ministry style. It took just a few days of his dynamic faith filled ministry to produce a dramatically different direction in the pastors and churches."[4]

Cho's apostolic ministry to the 1977 conference helped redirect the entire movement, enabling it to become united and effective. He presented an active and specific faith that enabled vision to be generated. Picking up on the negativity and conservatism that had come to characterize the ministry, Cho strongly challenged their stagnated "status quo" thinking. His approach worked, for a new openness to change and a willingness to accept living by faith and generating vision for their people became much more common in the churches.

David Cartledge, one of the leading church leaders, organized a tour of pastors and leaders to go to Korea and visit Dr. Cho's church. The visible evidence of faith seen by the 208 visitors literally overwhelmed them. During their visit in Korea, Cho's church attained a membership of 50,000 members – a church size far beyond the thinking of any on the tour.

Cho imparted to the Australians a new type of believing, providing a framework for faith to grow and develop churches. The Australians were enabled to bring their faith out of the theoretical or mystical realm. They began to focus their faith on souls being saved and adding people to their congregations. A new corporate faith was birthed into their movement.

> Cartledge comments: "His influence on my life and ministry has been profound, and this could be said for a number of the other Australian Assemblies of God leaders. The strong emphasis of Cho on prayer, and his courage to receive goals from God and declare them, was highly motivational. He urged us to preach the threefold blessings of 3 John 2."[5]
>
> Cho emphasized that sermons with only theology, reasoning or philosophy will create ineffective Christians. He exposed the legalism and fear rampant in many Pentecostal churches at the time. Urging the ministers to cultivate a strong faith relationship with God, he showed how they could eliminate negative preaching. Cho's teachings demonstrated how to live in the invisible reality of God's promises (and a flourishing church helped cinch his argument!).
>
> The Australians visited Korea in 1978, and three of their National Executive members were appointed to Cho's Church Growth International. As the next 20 years passed, the Korean church grew to 750,000 members, providing even more ongoing inspiration and motivation.
>
> Cho exemplifies the power of an apostle's influence: impartation of his faith and relationship with God. Cartledge says: "It is now clear through this example alone that the ministry of one apostle has the ability to reformat and redirect an entire movement, and change the spiritual landscape of a nation. There is proof positive of this in Australia."[6]

Imagine their surprise when visiting today's church services! The need for biblical Christianity is absolute. There is no reason to change the core belief system of Christianity, but the need for awareness of the secular culture and the skill for reaching the modern unbeliever must be paramount.

Today's Serious Need

Things are serious in the world and in the Church! Let us upgrade our thinking and utilize apostles who are true to the Scripture, contemporary in approach – and, above all, truly filled with the power and overflowing with the fruit of the Spirit! The question, "Why more apostles?" should be obvious from the religious scene. Certain hard facts scream for solution:

- The faith-community has declining impact on its surrounding community. Christianity is no longer a dominant force in Western culture. How can the average person relate to a Christianity that has practically no influence in our culture?

14

• Many churches are in decline, pastors and leaders are close to burnout, and the surrounding culture is looking for anything spiritual with which to connect.

Today's Solution

Modern day apostles and prophets, properly recognized and functioning, associated with local church communities walking in the ways of the Lord, can tip the scales for genuine renewal. Because religious leadership has lacked responsibility, governance and accountability, the one Church of Jesus has fragmented into many parts, each claiming to be the best available. Today's cluttered leadership has rendered the churches anemic for impacting the world, acting like rudderless boats, drifting at the mercy of prevailing winds.

Today's religious movements have powerful potential, but the numerous eddies (groups, streams, movements, fellowships, denominations, organizations) have sapped our strength, and their circuitous currents are comedic in the eyes of the average citizen.

Many believers desperately yearn for apostolic Christianity. In a day when the Christian market is flash flooded with books geared to renewing, redoing, rejuvenating, redefining, reviving and reforming the Church, the following strategy is appealing, simple, biblical, inspiring, challenging … and *daringly doable*:

"Utilize Apostles and Reap Church Growth, Church Renewal, Culture Penetration and World Harvest."

Is a New Church Emerging?

The inundation of renewal/change books has aroused great interest, fresh insights, renewed research, and restless spirituality. Church leaders and people everywhere realize that cultural trends are making fatal impact on irrelevant, non-appealing churches. Where can answers be found?

Is Change Inevitable?

Be cautious about saying the Church does not need change. *The Church is already in its greatest change-mode of the entire Church age.* The remarkable innovations of the cyber space revolution have impacted society, advanced secularism, changed moral concepts, and challenged every religious institution. Change is everywhere, even in the churches!

Here's the good news: this fluctuating climate presents God's people with unprecedented opportunity to exhibit God and His plan to a desperate world. This is the Church's greatest hour!

Successful churches must address meaningfully the cultural trends that captivate the masses; but – *also -- let the churches come alive with Holy Spirit cultural power!* Honest signs and wonders must again assume rightful prominence in the churches; love and concern for people must characterize our churches. Apostles and prophets can set the pace and lead the way in such apostolic revolution, winning the world to Christ, and maturing the churches.

Consider the New Books

The following forty-plus recent-book titles (a mere sampling) illustrate what various authors are emphasizing:

> *Equipping Church, Breakout Churches, Prayer Saturated Church, Five Star Church, Externally Focused Church, Emerging Churches, Church Next, Emerging Church, New Apostolic Churches, Gate Church, Passionate Church, Eternal Church,* Disciple-making Church, *Changing Church, Emotionally Healthy Church, Purpose Driven Church, Simple Church, Naked Church, Spirit-Driven Church, Living Church, Domestic Church, Open Church, Impact Church, Connecting Church, New Church, Hip Hop Church, Church in Emerging Culture, Church on the Other Side, Church for the Twenty-first Century, Church of Irresistible Influence, Missional Church, Transformational Church, Incomplete Church, Multi-Ethnic Church, Comeback Churches, Deep Church, Multi-Site Church, Blogging Church, Sim Church, Significant Church, Church Shift, American Church, Giving Church, Vintage Church.*

Whew! Who can handle this tsunami of ideas? Need we adopt every new innovation? These and other books present forceful, thought-provoking concepts, daring ideas and relevant materials on a weary Church, already mired in the *status quo.* Some authors, it does seem, are more polemic than practical, and some choose to by-pass biblical patterns for trendy things for reaching more people. Yes, we do need the good ideas, but ideas are relatively fruitless in bringing maturity to Christ's Body if Ephesians 4:11ff is ignored. *Is it not a shame to revive and reshape churches while ignoring and eliminating apostles, prophets, the miraculous and true biblical culture?*

Yes, But What About . . . ?

Resistance to apostles today is *not* based on Scripture. Such arguments result from not knowing what the Bible teaches or how to implement it, observing the failures and cultic pride of some claiming to be apostles, and lacking any hands-on experience with authentic apostolic activity.

We also acknowledge that church leaders sometimes see the Scriptural need for apostolic ministry in the local church program, but organizational structure and tradition is too tight, squeezing out the apostles and prophets.

Author's Unique Perspective

A Spirit movement began in the Holiness churches, flowed on into the Pentecostal Movement, the Charismatic movement, the Latter Rain Revival, the Toronto Blessing, manifesting now in other dynamic streams of life flowing throughout the Church. Having experienced and observed firsthand the efforts, frustrations and effects of promoting apostleship in churches, I hope my cautious-but-enthusiastic approach will be a blessing and stimulus to every reader. I contend for a balance of the fire of the Spirit, the reality of the Scripture, the wisdom of experience, and just good Christian thinking.

Revivalistic movements throughout Church history have contended for the Church to be restored to her former vibrant life and power. Even those who have not experienced spiritual renewal can appreciate what restoration activities contribute to the Church: without such emphasis, the churches settle into comfortable forms and beliefs, which then harden into cement-like traditions.

Evelyn Underhill, well-known authority on worship, gave us this insight over 70 years ago:

> Whenever the institutional life stiffens and becomes standardized, there is a [positive] reaction towards that primitive group enthusiasm and prophetic ministry which is described in the New Testament and – even though it sometimes oversteps the bounds of good taste and common sense – is a true part of the church's Godward life.[7]

Thank God, we are now in a time of positive reaction to the apostolic and prophetic ministries of Bible times. Let us move forward with the guidance of the Holy Spirit and the cooperation of every dedicated believer.

Questions that Demand Response

Some readers may wish the Church would have apostles, doubting, however, that it could ever happen. This book pursues a worthy goal:

> *Persuade serious Christians that Christ wants His local churches to be apostolic, with functioning apostles influencing those churches, and the church members caught up in an aggressive quest to impact their communities for Christ.*

Four direct questions identify and justify that apostles are essential in the Church – past, present and yet to come. (The rest of the book will showcase the accuracy and results of the following direct answers.)

Question 1: Who is the Architect of the Church?

Jesus -- of course! -- *is the chief architect!* He said, "I will build My Church" (Matthew 16:18). Paul said, "you are God's building" (1 Corinthians 3:9). Solomon said, "Unless the LORD builds a house, the work of the builders is useless" (Psalm 127:1, NLT). The prophet said, "And He [the Christ] shall build the temple of the LORD" (Zechariah 6:12).

"He alone is its Architect, Builder, Owner and Lord" (MacArthur).[8]

Question 2: How will Jesus build His Church?

The Holy Spirit now works individually in the lives of God's people. Additionally Christ provides a fivefold, directional leadership ministry that equips, edifies, brings to the unity of the faith and produces spiritual maturity.

> And He Himself [Christ] gave some *to be* apostles, some prophets, some evangelists, and some pastors and teachers, for the equipping of the saints for the work of ministry, for the edifying of the body of Christ, till we all come to the unity of the faith and the knowledge of the Son of God to a perfect man, to the measure of the stature of the fullness of Christ" (Ephesians 4:11-16).

Paul was used of Christ as a "wise master builder" [*architekton*] of the Church at Corinth (1 Corinthians 3:10), working directly under Jesus the *Chief Architect.* Appointed by the Head of the Church, Paul and other apostles founded, grounded and grew the churches of Bible days. This is our need today!

Question 3: Should apostles and prophets be disjoined from the Body?

Apostles are vital to the health and life of the Body.

> "Now you are the body of Christ, and members individually. And God has appointed these in the church; first apostles, second prophets… " (1 Corinthians 12:28).

Those who believe in pastors, evangelists, teachers, and all the other ministries, must consider that Jesus places apostles in primary position (and prophets second) for the total Body's development. This is a poor time to dismember the Body!

Question 4: Should we do something about this tragedy?

With fasting, prayer, humility and open discussion let devoted Christians in every fellowship reexamine its ways, seeking to make every church an active apostolic team – as well as a loving Christ-centered community.

- *contend earnestly* for the faith which was once for all delivered to the

saints" (Jude 3).
- *continue in the faith,* grounded and steadfast... (Colossians 2:23).
- *Look to yourselves,* that we do not lose those things we worked for, but that we may receive a full reward" (2 John 8).

Are Apostles "Surfacing"?

During the 1990s, apostolic activity and information surfaced rather dramatically in various charismatic circles. At the same time "an emerging church" movement began making appearances with various streams of thought and activity, some of which has had meaningful application in people's lives. Obviously, not all movements (and splinter groups) say and do the same things or seek the same objectives. We must define terms, for meanings change quickly.

A growing number of charismatic groups espouse the concept of modern apostles, and an increasing general acceptance of apostles is taking place.

This growing interest is illustrated by the 2004 "Fivefold Ministries Focus" series in *Ministries Today* Magazine. After devoting four issues to the other five ministries of Ephesians 4, the November/December issue focused on Apostles. A lead article, after introducing five apostles who "are transforming their nations for Christ," stated,

> We hope that as you read, you'll agree: Apostles *are* among us today. And their ministry is crucial for the equipping of the body of Christ and the evangelism of the nations in the 21st century."[9]

Senior Editorial Adviser Larry Keefauver, in a companion article said: "Their sacrifices and achievements are irrefutable: Apostles are alive and well in the 21st century...."

Exciting renewal is happening around the world, causing many to feel we are in the midst of an "Apostolic Revolution" or "Apostolic Reformation." This surge of interest, confidence, information and prayer about the restoration of apostles in the Church is heartening and does affirm that a new awareness and increased activity is taking place.

We contend that apostolic reformation must have as major objectives the establishing in every community of local churches that sustain the culture of New Testament Christianity, including both outward secular community impact as well as healing and good personal relationship within the church community.

Renewal movements contend for the restoration of the New Testament Church with the attendant supernatural signs and spiritual gifts. Simultaneously there must be true devotion and relationship among the Christians. Leadership for such churches has been sparse, but it now appears that some apostles are coming into view and others may be expected to show up in many places during this generation.[10] As will be shown later, actual apostles may appear differently than some of us expect, and some may be functioning with God's help without a whole lot of fanfare. Regardless of titles, local churches need pastoral direction through leadership teams that are dedicated to producing biblical culture.

If denominational and independent churches can learn to identify, help, and cooperate with such ministries (within our own ranks and outside our ranks), and those with apostolic ministries can humbly work with other pastors and leaders, great things are possible in affecting positive change in today's church and secular cultures. A formidable challenge, exciting possibilities!

The ideal would be for the churches to embrace what should be standard operating procedure. Imagine if a united Church would state without apology: "*Apostles are expected and wanted in Apostolic Christian churches!*"

Recent Books on Apostleship for Our Day

A variety of 39 authors in the bibliography (noted by *) endorse apostles in today's Church. Valuable insights can be gained from their writings. There are, of course, some differences of opinion. I am grateful, nevertheless, for all the sincere effort to understand what God is initiating in our time.

D. A. Carson in his 2005 book about "the emerging Church" and "understanding a movement and its implications" wisely said:

> Whenever a Christian movement comes along that presents itself as reformist, it should not be summarily dismissed. Even if one ultimately decides that the movement embraces a number of worrying weaknesses,

it may also have some important things to say that the rest of the Christian world needs to hear.[11]

Seek a Productive Approach

Books, commentaries and materials on apostleship seem to be at one pole or another, either *very academic* in their approach (i.e., scholarly, historical) or *extremely practical* (urging apostleship now). The first group focuses on the Twelve Apostles and Paul (indicating they did a good job of getting the church going), leaving the reader content and satisfied with Church history.

The second group gives a strong focus on Ephesians 4:11ff, stressing so forcefully the immediate need for contemporary apostles that readers are sometimes shaken up and left wondering what is going on.

Today's leadership should strive to present a balanced, reasonable, practical, Scriptural basis for more apostles and apostolic believers, but also seek and research realistic ways of implementation, including the benefits of fasting and prayer. That is the aim of this book, and why contemporary illustrations are scattered through the text.

I will not advocate the abolishment of denominations or religious organizations, nor will I endorse every restorationist group promoting apostles. I am asking for – pleading for – an updated evaluation of church leadership in the light of Scripture. Every serious Christian fellowship needs to align with the Bible and what the Spirit is saying to the world-wide Church in this hour. Apostolic leaders – that is, pastoral, fatherly, directional leaders with true vision and concern -- will give our churches the winning edge. Be warned, however, that their arrival and the development of Spirit-filled saints does have a way of eliminating *dead-wood traditions.*

If churches, fellowships, denominations and movements want to be apostolic and have apostles, they must first set their minds on what the culture of a Holy Spirit-led church is like. Then, with much prayer and openness seek God and talk with each other about what the culture of New Testament living would be like. It will involve more than recognizing some people as apostles; it will require serious evaluation of personal life styles and the transformation that Jesus can bring. The culture that Jesus would promote in His Church will change our relationships, and open us to the awesome guidance of the Holy Spirit.[12]

We need world-changers to start churches, awaken God's people and reach our generation, apostles on fire for God with a passion to reach the world for Christ. Spiritual lethargy and famine must end! We dare not minimize the Church of New Testament times. Survival today requires prayerful diligence and faith for New Testament reality!

Every serious church and leadership group must consider how essential apostolic activity is for the Body of Christ! Since apostles and prophets laid foundations for the early churches . . . *does it not seem terribly wrong to neglect such major ministry in our discussions of modern Church renewal?*

Reminisce

Did the deaths of the two greatest apostles, Peter and Paul, end "The Apostolic Age"? If we could ask the opinion of these beloved martyrs, their enthusiastic challenge would be for the Church to forge ahead in the power of the Holy Spirit with dedicated apostolic leaders. They would exhort us to grasp and run with the baton, finishing the race with strength and confidence.

Hastening forward, we face an ideal setting:

- The world is a global village with increased information and technology
- God's Spirit is awakening the Church
- Intensified prayer is greater than ever
- A great response of youth to missionary recruitment is taking place
- World problems abound which can only be solved by spiritual renewal

Have we come to the kingdom for such a time as this (Esther 4:14)?

All factors portend a great work of God in our day. Like a tender-dry forest, global conditions are ideal for a sweeping revival of spiritual fire – driven by the Pneuma-Wind of God's Spirit.

Will the emerging Church of the last days be a Spirit-inspired company of faithful believers, or will she merely blend with an increasingly secular community? My hope is pinned on a biblical, victorious Church!

Chapter 1 Endnotes

[1] David Shibley, *The Missions Addiction,* p. 175.

[2] Doug Beacham, *Rediscovering the Role of Apostles & Prophets* (LifeSprings Resources, 2003), p. x.

[3] 1 Thessalonians 3:10.

[4] David Cartledge, *The Apostolic Revolution: The Restoration of Apostles and Prophets in the Assemblies of God in Australia* (Chester Hill, Australia: Paraclete Institute, 2000), p. 93.

[5] Ibid., p. 96.

[6] Ibid., p. 97.

[7] Evelyn Underhill, *Worship* (Harper & Bros., 1937), p. 89.

[8] John MacArthur, Author and gen.ed, *The MacArthur Study Bible* (Thomas Nelson, 1997), p. 14223.

[9] "Apostles Among Us," *Ministries Today* (November/December, 2004): 25-31.

[10] "[T]imes are changing. A growing number of Christian leaders now recognize, acknowledge and affirm both the gift and the office of apostle in today's churches. The Apostles have surfaced!" C. Peter Wagner, *Apostles Today* (Ventura, CA: Regal, 2006), p. 7.

[11] D. A. Carson, *Becoming Conversant with the Emerging Church* (Grand Rapids: Zondervan, 2005), p. 10. Carson added, "So I have tried to listen respectfully and carefully; I hope and pray that the leaders of this 'movement' will similarly listen to what I have to say." Good advice to remember in these times of renewal.

[12] An outstanding book to help today's church leaders would be *Culture Shift: Transforming Your Church from the Inside Out* by Robert Lewis and Wayne Cordeiro (San Francisco: Jossey-Bass, 2005).

Chapter 2
Marks of an Apostolic Church

In This Chapter

- *Spurgeon's description of an apostolic church*
- *Seven "marks" (distinguishing characteristics) of an apostolic church*
- *Dr. McBirnie discovered the "one, unassailable truth"*
- *E. M. Bounds describes "a fallen church"*

Charles Spurgeon (1834-1892), the great London preacher and pastor of the world's largest church of his day, nostalgically dropped this thought into one of his sermons, perhaps exposing a hidden heart's desire:

> . . . I have a third thing to say, which will strike home to some of us: that is, that WE HAVE NOT APOSTOLIC CHURCHES. O! had you seen an Apostolic church, what a different thing it would appear to one of our churches! As different, I had almost said, as light from darkness; as different as the shallow bed of the brook that is dried by summer is from the mighty rolling river, ever full, ever deep and clear, and ever rushing into the sea.[1]

Serious Christians like to be part of a real "apostolic church," yet, defining (or finding!) such a church is not easy. Tacking a sign on a church building is not enough: *words don't make it so.*

Comparing the shallow, dried-out bed of a trickling brook with a mighty, rolling river, deep and clear, provides a graphic contrast for our discussion. The "marks" of a powerful river are quite overwhelming. I recently traveled along the Columbia River Gorge Highway in Oregon that runs beside the great Columbia River. The current's flow was awesome. In the evening, my wife Joy and I stood outside our motel at Hood River and watched amazed at the undulating mass of water pressing onward to the sea: the river's movement clearly pictured God's power. I assume,

25

like me, you would prefer a "flowing river" church to a "trickling brook" church whose stream bed is drying up.

Christians through the ages have longed to see "apostolic marks" in their churches. The primary source book for such renewal has always been the Acts of the Apostles, and many in our day are reexamining this source. Without apology, Scripture remains the guiding star – in spite of vast changes in our global world.

What distinguishing characteristics indicate the dynamic spiritual realities of yesteryear? And, another question naturally follows: how can we retain and maintain such biblical marks while relating wisely to our modern setting?

Many ideas have been given about what a church should be, reflecting societal distinctives, denominational biases, numerical successes. The focus of this chapter is *seven biblical signs*, performing like the city building codes which safeguard construction in a city. As you know, buildings may have very different outward embellishments, but if a building is "built to code," the building will pass inspection, be safe, and be serviceable for a long time.

The "marks" are briefly stated in the following chart and amplified in the text that follows. Here are the basics of the kingdom's building code.

Seven Distinguishing Marks of an Apostolic Church

1. *Biblical Leadership*

The people are committed to the Lordship of Jesus Christ. Christ is head of The Church, and the believers are each members of His body. The local church is served by elders and deacons, receiving spiritual direction from apostles, prophets, evangelists, pastors and teachers. Lead Pastors direct the local churches.

2. *Spiritual Reality*

The Presence of Christ in the Person of the Holy Spirit is experienced: people have meaningful, vital religious encounter with God, an intense, satisfying relationship with the guidance and blessing of the Holy Spirit.

3. *God's Message*

The full Bible is believed and presented with thoughtful and meaningful application, enabling the people to live with hope and faith in the secular community. Prophetic ministry brings present application to the biblical message.

4. *Charismatic Community*

Each member is an activated, joyful, gifted participant in the organism of spiritual body life, participating in inspirational worship and fervent prayer, Holy Spirit activity and community outreach. Ministries evolve and develop within the local church from this inward focus.

5. *Great Commission Focus*

The guiding priority of the church is to reach people everywhere with the "Good News" of Jesus Christ. This outward focus enables each Church to be dedicated to the life and growth of Christ's Universal Church.

6. *Caring Ministry*

An apostolic church is characterized by great concern for the welfare of people, finding needs within the church and secular community and meeting them. The church is driven by vision and values; finances and faith are proactive; the church is a people on a mission. Giving and generosity characterize this kind of people.

7. *Nonsectarian Mentality*

While maintaining the local vision, there is nevertheless an appreciation for and cooperation with all dedicated Christians of good will to impact our community and world. A "cultic attitude" should not characterize an apostolic church.

First Sign: Biblical Leadership

The people are committed to the Lordship of Jesus Christ. Christ is head of the Church, and the believers are each members of His body. The church is served by elders and deacons, receiving spiritual direction from apostles, prophets, evangelists, pastors and teachers. Lead pastors direct the local churches.

Jesus is Lord and Master of churches apostolic, every believer striving to be obedient to His will -- guidance coming through His inspired Word, His quickening Spirit and His anointed leaders. Every "member" of the church body recognizes and subscribes to the leadership of Jesus as head.

Churches in Bible days kept things simple, workable and aligned with the objectives of Jesus the founder. Laymen rather than professional clerics were recruited to lead small groups and even local churches. The emphasis was simple, yet profound -- helping one another and recruiting more people into the kingdom of God and blessing the community. Buildings, although helpful, were secondary to the people who, after all, were the actual church.

A community of Spirit-filled believers was a treasury of diversified spiritual giftings. Twenty of such gifts are mentioned in the New Testament, but the eight lists are obviously not meant to be final and conclusive. Patterns of function in these listings can be seen, causing the local church to be effective and efficient. Paul's teaching was that *the church was a living organism (a body) as opposed to being a static organization (a business),* every person an active body part.

The need was to start and maintain churches and reach more people, so apostles, prophets, evangelists, healers, and so on, were utilized to form teams to accomplish the basics of church planting and maintenance close to home and farther abroad. The home community of believers, functioning as local citizens and family units in a town or city, found it essential to have elders (that is, shepherds or spiritual guardians) to give guidance, teachers to instruct the various ages, people of prayer to maintain the spiritual base, helpers to do the tasks menial and spiritual, and so on.

Some leaders cared for people, watchful like shepherds tending sheep. Some were particularly skilled in teaching, working miracles, or hearing the prophetic voice of the Lord. Within the local churches that Paul established in the Gentile communities, the people were led by elders and assisted by deacons (Acts 14:23; Philippians 1:1; 1 Timothy 3:1; Titus 1:5), all holding fast the vision and strategies unfolded by the Holy Spirit.

The fivefold ministries mentioned in Ephesians 4 show that church planting and supervision (apostles), hearing from God (prophets), reaching the lost (evangelists), caring for the local people (pastors) and teaching the Scripture and practical living (teachers) were considered all-important, and all such leaders would be mature servants. Also, the fivefold ministry concept was not only leader-individuals, but functioning *principles of spiritual life* that kept balance in the church, like the great equalizers that hold steady the great ships at sea. (See Chapter 17)

Deacons joyfully served both leaders and people, but everyone was considered a helper. As ministries developed, their proficiency proliferated into other communities and churches, giving the church a mobile dimension.

Is this just an impossible dream? No, but such a program requires a membership that is Spirit-filled, dedication to Scriptural principles, sustainment by a strong prayer base and a unified leadership team.

Today's churches have drifted far from the original simplicity described, becoming organizations rather than the intended organisms. One of the main functions of apostles and the other fivefold ministers is to contend uppermost for this faith and purpose of Jesus.

Second Sign: Spiritual Reality

The Presence of Christ in the Person of the Holy Spirit is experienced. People have meaningful, vital religious encounter with God, an intense, gratifying experience and relationship with the blessing and guidance of the Holy Spirit.

An authentic church knows the true and living God – His Son Jesus – and the Holy Spirit -- in a real and dynamic way. Members of such a church certainly have an academic, intellectual knowledge of God, but, *just as important*, they know God in a personal, dynamic, spiritual relationship and reality. Such Christians have experienced new beginning through the reality of God. They are a family of believers where Jesus is Lord. The Holy Spirit unites such Christians into genuine community. God is real among the people, and prayer is answered.

The Pattern

> For by one Spirit we were all baptized into one body…and have all been made to drink into one Spirit (1 Corinthians 12:13).

The awesome awareness of the nearness and person of God is conceived in the dynamic, *threefold initiation of each believer* into the Body of Christ. "The Peter and Paul Pattern" as first presented by Peter in Acts 2:38, was still carried on by Paul twenty years later in Ephesus (Acts 19).

1) *Conversion:* spiritual birth, being "born again," being forgiven.
2) *Water Baptism:* personal dedication to God in public action, making full personal devotion to the ways of Christ.
3) *Baptism with the Holy Spirit:* empowerment with the Holy Spirit, being "filled" with the Holy Spirit and enabled to serve God in an empowered, anointed way.

The Circle of Fellowship

In Bible days, people became Christians both in the church gatherings and also outside the church, just as it is today. After conversion, regardless of when and where, the follower of Jesus must find a group of similarly minded Christians in the community with whom he/she may bond and serve; each new Christian must be caught up in reaching new people, drawing them into the circle of loving *koinonia* (fellowship), the main reason for a church's existence.

Corporate Worship

A major function of the congregational gathering is corporate prayer and meaningful worship. A felt-presence of God occurs in such a setting, the Holy Spirit moving among the people in personal, spiritual reality. Jesus foretold that this heart-felt, Spirit-inspired worship[2] would be notable in His Church.

> But the hour is coming, and now is when the true worshipers will worship the Father in spirit and truth; for the Father is seeking such to worship Him. God is Spirit, and those who worship Him must worship in spirit and truth (John 4:23-24).[3]

Paul confirmed the same concept:

> For we [Christians] are the true circumcision, who *worship God in spirit* and *by the Spirit of God*, and exult *and* glory *and* pride ourselves in Jesus Christ, and put no confidence *or* dependence [on what we are] in the flesh *and* on outward privileges *and* physical advantages and external appearances (Philippians 3:3, AMP).

The threefold categories of musical song in the early church is mentioned twice in Paul's writings: "psalms" (portions of Scripture), and "hymns" (humanly composed odes), and "spiritual songs" (spontaneous prophetic songs inspired by the Holy Spirit) (Ephesians 5:19; Colossians 3:16). Musical expression finds many expressions in the churches throughout the world, ranging from the simple beating of sticks and drums (that I have observed in Africa) to the use of the most modern electronic devices in advanced cultures.

The main thing is that people meet with God and experience the great flow of His grace and blessing.

Corporate Prayer

Congregational prayer *in the Spirit* is the power source, like the furnace room of a building. The early churches did not focus wearily on faithless prayer requests presented by sleepy clergy. New Testament prayer times were powerfully characterized by faith, fervency, passion, unity and empowerment.

This charismatic dimension of prayer and worship maintains life in the local church, throughout every department, young and old. An atmosphere of expectant faith is created which allows God to do astounding things.

> Jude 20: But you, beloved, building yourselves up on your most holy faith, *praying in the Holy Spirit.*
>
> Ephesians 6:18: [P]raying always with all prayer and supplication *in the Spirit....*
>
> Colossians 4:2: Continue earnestly in prayer, being vigilant in it with thanksgiving.

The one description of God's house that must not be lost is "A House of Prayer for All Nations" (Isaiah 56:7). The commercial confusion of Herod's Temple infuriated Jesus, and gives us insight on the importance of real space being given in our churches for prayer. Not just issuing books on prayer, talking about prayer, holding conferences on prayer – NO! Having prayer scheduled, led and performed in a place of prayer *with the obvious participation of the church leaders and every age group!* Wow! When you are part of a church that has prayer scheduled, especially before and after services, you will find yourself lifted to a new level of apostolic living. I don't mean for two minutes, but for at least 30 minutes: powerful prayer, sincere prayer, people kneeling, people standing, people walking, voices raised in intercession and shouts of jubilation, lifting hands in holy confidence, praying for one another and the nations! Once you experience this, you will discover the power-source of the early church.

Third Sign: God's Message

The full Bible is believed and presented with thoughtful and meaningful application, thereby enabling the people to live with hope and faith in the secular community. Prophetic ministry brings present application of the biblical message.

In addition to the experiential dimension of Christianity -- maintaining life through relationship, Spiritual worship and prayer -- an ongoing intellectual bonding to the great truths stated in the Scripture must take place. An active "apostolic church" is absolutely, totally devoted to the teachings of Christ and His original apostles. This is bed-rock doctrine: *an apostolic church does not forget or neglect the Scripture!*

An apostolic church believes the Scripture to be God's message to humankind. It would not be unusual for such churches to joyfully, and without embarrassment, lift their Bibles and loudly declare their dedication to God and His Word. Why? Because,

> All Scripture is given by inspiration of God, and is profitable for doctrine, for reproof, for correction, for instruction in righteousness, that the man of God may be complete, thoroughly equipped for every good work (2 Timothy 3:16).

The full Bible is presented and believed. The great truths are sung in worship, proclaimed passionately from the pulpit, taught in classes and studied personally. These truths are explained in context, and realistic application is made for today's generation. The families honor the Word of God as *sacred, workable* for children, youth and adults. People memorize passages of Scripture, devouring it like food. As Jesus said, quoting Deuteronomy 8:3:

> "It is written, 'Man shall not live by bread alone, but by every word that proceeds from the mouth of God'" (Matthew 4:4).

The people rejoice in the abounding grace of God, also committing to human responsibility. The Bible provides *a blueprint for living* that causes the church members to prosper and be in health. They contend for the faith! As Jude wrote to the ancient Christians:

> "Contend earnestly for the faith which was once for all delivered to the saints" (v. 3).

And as Paul said, "continue in the faith, grounded and steadfast…not moved away from the hope of the gospel" (Colossians 1:23).

Sometimes important things slip quietly from memory. Believers can easily neglect the practice and experience of their belief and mission statement, even their purpose for existence. Blissfully focusing on a glorious tradition and past experience, a church-goer can lose the present meaning and experience of Christianity. God's Word proclaimed by apostolic leaders keeps us on track!

Fourth Sign: Charismatic Community

> *Each member is an activated, joyful, gifted participant in the organism of Spiritual body life, participating in inspirational worship, Holy Spirit activity and community outreach. Ministries evolve and develop within the local church from this inward focus.*

Apostolic churches are in actuality apostolic people -- zealous, Spirit-filled people wanting to reach their world, wanting to associate with like-minded people. They wish to see the Church (local and world-wide) walk according to biblical standards. They are the sustaining infrastructure of true churches, contending for kingdom extension that supersedes vocational ambition or personal "creature comforts." Such Christians respond to world-changing, faith-preaching leaders. They like Bible Christianity and the whole program of Jesus!

Members of One Body

All the members of a local, apostolic church do not have the same ministry. All will, however, share a mutual faith in Jesus and walk in the Spirit. They will be born of the Spirit, baptized in water and filled with the Holy Spirit. Such spiritual vitality certainly produces emotional zeal, but also adds a balanced intellectual stability, good wisdom and a love of Scripture.

People mature in such an atmosphere, discovering spiritual giftings and God's will for their lives. They blend into a spiritual family in a given community, becoming part of a charismatic team determined to win the lost and extend the kingdom of God principles into every possible place. May every reader find the satisfaction of participating in a church powerfully influenced by apostles, prophets and other anointed leaders.

Taking Up Your Cross

Gospel fervency need not mandate abject poverty, foolish fanaticism, lack of family commitment or leaving school prematurely. Real dedication means "taking up your cross" and following Jesus. Regardless of social status, ethnicity, physical limitations and educational background, the call is to follow Christ and fulfill His Great Commission. *Apostolic people maintain global momentum and world vision.* These people have vision and commission, with a fiery zeal fed and maintained by apostles and prophets.

Like every nuclear family, every apostolic congregation will have a unique personality. The leaders and type of apostle(s) that relate to a church will affect it, and so will the surrounding society. Every church devoted to restoring the apostolic, will find its place in God as they follow the leading of the Holy Spirit. They will be like a spiritual city within their secular city.

Fifth Sign: Great Commission Focus

> *The guiding priority of the church is to reach people everywhere with the "Good News" of Jesus Christ. This outward focus enables each local church to maintain the life and growth of Christ's Universal Church.*

Reg Layzell
Apostle of the Latter Rain
By Ernest Gentile

In 1948 a visitation of God took place at the Sharon Orphanage and Schools at North Battleford, Saskatchewan. The leadership at Sharon had visited the William Branham meetings where they saw a man moving in the Spirit, bringing words of knowledge and praying for the sick. Returning home they began to diligently fast and pray for similar visitation. The outpouring came, accompanied by prophecy and the laying on of hands, a renewed emphasis on spiritual gifts, world harvest, the unity of the Church, worship and the seeking of

---

God. News of the visitation spread quickly throughout both Canada and the United States. Pastor Reg Layzell heard of the events taking place, and went to see for himself. His visit to what was called by some "the Latter Rain" greatly impacted his life and ministry.

Layzell pastored the Glad Tidings Temple of Vancouver, B. C., Canada, a small church anxious for revival. The leaders from Sharon were invited to his church, where they functioned as a prophetic team, giving personal prophecy and impartation to many of the church believers. God moved in a wonderful way, and after the team left Layzell spent three months in intense prayer. The church grew wonderfully from that point. To share the message with more people, Glad Tidings sponsored an annual summer camp meeting at Crescent Beach, B. C., Canada.

My wife Joy and I first met Reg Layzell in 1950, he was a man of 46 and we were fledging pastors of 20. We arrived at the Glad Tidings Camp grounds to see for ourselves. We were not disappointed, just overwhelmed. The people gathered at the altars for an hour before the regular services started. The prayer was fervent, anointed and totally impressive to us. The worship services were thunderous with praise for sometimes more than an hour. I was astounded at the intensity and the spiritual flow. The people employed psalmic worship forms in a natural, free-flowing style. With upraised hands they praised the Lord audibly. Gifts of the Spirit functioned.

The local church services were like the camp meeting. Layzell's apostolic dynamic was his integrity, dedication and absolute commitment to the gospel. He stayed with the basics: salvation, baptism in the Holy Spirit accompanied by tongues, the undergirding of prayer, fervent worship and praise, world missions, spiritual gifts and total belief in the Bible. The church planted other churches and sent missionaries. What an example!

"Layzell should be remembered first as a true shepherd and one who had a zeal for the restoration of the apostolic church. He had a great passion for equipping and training young men and women for ministry and world missions. Sometimes referred to as the Apostle of Praise, the revelation of the sacrifice of praise and that God lives in the praises of His people were central to his message. He spent his entire ministry life advancing the Gospel of Jesus Christ, equipping believers, pioneering churches and preaching on restoration. Today thousands of people around the world and hundreds of churches can trace their spiritual lineage back to this man. Truly he was an apostle of the Latter Rain."[4]

The original Twelve, and every apostle since, take the Great Commission as marching orders (Matthew 28:18-20):

> All authority has been given to Me in heaven and on earth.
> Go therefore and make disciples of all the nations,
> Baptizing them in the name of the Father and of the Son and of the
> Holy Spirit,

Teaching them to observe all things that I have commanded you;
And lo, I am with you always, even to the end of the age. Amen.

Going Forth or Staying Home

The local church is called to be a missionary enterprise, dedicated to the life and growth of the global Church in its pursuit to make Jesus Lord in the hearts of people everywhere. The practical strategy is to plant, foster and care for local churches at home and abroad -- *this is the best method of reaching and preserving the harvest.* This is apostolic purpose and procedure.

Global vision is attained through dynamic apostolic leadership and preaching, prophetic inspiration, aggressive evangelism, team ministry, financial aid and appropriate networking with other groups – all under girded by dynamic prayer, spiritual gifts and inspiring worship. As Dayton and Fraser say,

> ... the church is inherently missionary. Having been liberated by the power of the Spirit, the church cannot help but make this same liberation available to all the people of the earth. It is "outward bound," centered on the triune God and motivated to share his love and compassion for all peoples in all ages. *Unless the missionary nature of the church is understood, the meaning and significance of the church is completely obscured* (emphasis added).[5]

Every apostolic church should equip and mobilize for people-conversions, numerical growth, church planting, spiritual maturity, penetration of the secular market place and global expansion. Anything less does not meet apostolic standards. Arise! Let the message about the Lord spread widely, having powerful effect: *"So the word of the Lord grew mightily and prevailed,"* Acts 19:20!

Converts and Congregations

After exhaustive research in tracing the lives and ministries of the original Twelve Apostles, William Steuart McBirnie concluded that all of the investigation pointed to one unassailable truth: "most of the Apostles took seriously the great commission of

Jesus...and went forth ...to *evangelize* the nations with the Christian gospel."

> They set an example for all subsequent Christians that is clear, unmistakable and unswerving. They challenged commoners and kings alike. They did not become salaried ecclesiastics but often worked with their hands to support themselves, so that by any and all means they might share the good news in Jesus. Most, like St. Paul, sought to preach Christ, "not building upon other men's foundations, but going to the regions beyond."

"Above all," McBirnie says, "they founded *congregations.*" Those apostolic churches *structured their evangelistic efforts to build the converts into existing congregations or newly formed churches* – a secret today's churches must re-learn. "The Apostles enjoined upon their converts the responsibility to *become* the church."[6] This is the heart of being a growing, community-impacting "apostolic church."

Every Local Church an Apostolic Team

Every Christian should be an active part of *the* apostolic team (composed of *all* the local church members) as well as some specialized team. Every church is meant to be an apostolic company, led and influenced by apostolic leaders. Each person will not be an apostle, but every believer-disciple of Jesus should be part of those sent out by the Lord Jesus: "As You sent [apostello] Me into the world, I also have sent [apostello] them into the world" (John 17:18).

Even if a person lives his/her whole life in one city, or if a person's secular community is a small one, that person and his/her church can still be apostolic. I know of small-town churches that are dedicated to world evangelism; their pastor and church teams still go forth to teach and reach the nations of the world. Even if you live in only one city all your life, you can fulfill John 17:18: "As You sent [*apostello*] Me into the world I also have sent [*apostello*] them into the world."

The lofty vision of apostolic churches is sustained and accelerated by the contribution of contemporary apostles. They bring a blazing message, church renewal, prophetic revelation, biblical insight, mature experience, unlimited faith, networking contacts, miraculous ministry -- mobilizing for action and vision casting that leaps beyond church walls. *Apostles produce apostolic people who in turn produce apostolic church-teams.* How exciting!

Staying Current

The basic theology of the Church is set in the sense that the canon of Scripture and the belief system is securely established. But, the meaning and application of those teachings must be currently alive in the people's hearts. We certainly do not want the ancient foundation to become merely a historical monument (*good, true tenets chiseled into the foundation stone for mere memorial*).

Rick Warren, one of today's well-known church leaders, puts this concept of the "old and the new" in understandable terms (emphasis added):

> In ministry some things must never change, while other things must be constantly changing. God's five purposes for his church are nonnegotiable. If a church fails at worship, fellowship, discipleship, ministry, and evangelism, it is no longer a church....On the other hand, the way or style in which we fulfill these eternal purposes must continually be adjusted and modified, because human culture is always changing....*The only way to stay relevant is to anchor your ministry to unchanging truths and eternal purposes while being willing to continually adapt how you communicate those truths and purposes.*[7]

Modern apostles are not to rewrite the Bible or build a different underpinning, yet they are master-builders in their own right (1 Corinthians 3:10). They are to insure that the foundation of today's churches is that same, original, rock-hard belief system, made applicable to contemporary societal and cultural changes by the power and prophetic word of the Holy Spirit. The foundation given by the early apostles is not cast away -- it is *freshly appropriated* for the present generation. Our beliefs and actions are squared with Christ the chief cornerstone. The Great Commission keeps us on course!

Usually we think of the church as an upward, ever-growing building. Consider, this unique viewpoint of Gordon Walker:

39

…it will be well to get a better visual picture of the kind of building we are working on. We should not view the church just as a great skyscraper twenty centuries *tall*. Rather, the Church also is seen as a barrack building twenty centuries *long*. It is extremely important that the apostolic foundations be laid in the church in each generation.

Therefore, it is not enough to say that all the foundations were laid in the first century. In fact, that mentality has gotten us into trouble! Too often foundations have not been laid in each successive generation, or even in each century. We must also be busy laying twentieth century foundations, and this is the responsibility and work of twentieth century apostles. Today's apostles must be careful to build in continuity with the work of those apostles in past generations.[8]

Sixth Sign: Caring Community

An apostolic church is characterized by a great concern for the welfare of people, finding needs within the church and secular community and meeting them. The church is driven by vision and values; finances and faith are proactive; he church is a people on a mission. Giving and generosity characterize this kind of people.

Every genuine church of Christ will manifest and maintain the great love and compassion of Christ. To read the teachings and descriptions of Christ in the Gospels is to come face-to-face with His amazing compassion for the lost, the hungry, the troubled, the infirm, the demonized and the dying.

And Jesus went about all the cities and villages, teaching in their synagogues, preaching the gospel of the kingdom, and healing every sickness and every disease among the people. *But when He saw the multitudes, He was moved with compassion for them, because they were weary and scattered, like sheep having no shepherd* [because their problems were so great and they didn't know where to go for help (Matthew 9:35-36, NLT, emphasis added).

By nature we tend to be concerned about those close to us: our family, our friends, our church associates. Jesus raised the bar. His followers are to love the unlovely, minister to those in need, and reach out to every painful situation that they may encounter -- even if those we help do not come to our church meetings! Regardless of race or culture, social status or physical condition, all are candidates to hear and receive the good news of Jesus.

A truly apostolic church will *evidence the heart of Jesus*. In a time when half the population of the Roman Empire were slaves, the message of Jesus and His apostles brought a whole new concept of love, acceptance and forbearance. At times when plague would hit a city – and the inhabitants would panic and make exodus – the Christians remained behind and cared for the sick and dying. Such compassion of Jesus has produced hospitals, orphanages, schools and food relief around the world. The Church is the light and salt of the earth.

Seventh Sign: Nonsectarian Mentality

> *While maintaining the local vision, there is nevertheless an appreciation for and cooperation with all dedicated Christians of good will to impact our community and world. A "cultic attitude" should not characterize an apostolic church.*

Our religious biases have split the church into many groups. May the Holy Spirit work in all of our hearts to be tolerant of all God's people. Differences will exist (doctrinal, theological, methodological, and so on), and people may have favorite leaders, but the Christ-centered unity of the people and their faith in God must not be impaired. Paul did his best to rid his churches of such divisions. Be tolerant, still maintaining your personal convictions, but be friends with God's friends.

A Closing Thought

I once visited the chapel at Oberlin College where the famous revivalist Charles E. Finney was president. I had my picture taken standing by his bust, and truthfully felt quite thrilled by it.

But, things have changed: the revival fervor and dedication to Christ and His Word is no longer a characteristic of that institution. Religious life needs more than a statue of remembrance. As E. M. Bounds, the great prayer warrior of 160 years ago said:

> The past has not exhausted the possibilities nor the demands for doing great things for God. The church that is dependent on its past history for its miracles of power and grace is a fallen church. . . ."[9]

The Next Chapter

This chapter has presented the picture of churches apostolic, a glorious vision we should keep ever before us. The picture is the reflection of the vision of Jesus and the early apostles. We can see such churches take place in our time, but we must return to the faith once delivered to the saints, to a powered-up ministry of the Holy Spirit and a dedication to see the Great Commission fulfilled in our time.

The next chapters will be giving background for apostolic Christianity. We need to reflect on the dynamic apostolic efforts that have preceded us, then we will be returning to discuss again what it means to have "apostolic churches."

Chapter 2 Endnotes

[1] Charles Haddon Spurgeon, "Gospel Missions," *Spurgeon's Sermons*, Vol. 1 (Grand Rapids: Baker Books, originally published 1883), p. 337

[2] Psalmic worship characterizes the Spirit-filled church. The secret of David is enjoyed, that is, that God is delighted in the heart-felt, enthusiastic worship of the people. Psalmic worship involves (as taught in the Psalms) the nine-fold involvement of our total being (Voice: speaking, singing, shouting; Hands: raising, clapping, playing instruments; Posture: standing, kneeling, dancing). For a complete explanation, see Ernest Gentile, *Worship God: Exploring the Dynamics of Psalmic Worship,* (Portland, OR: City Christian Publishing).

[3] As I mention in *Worship God!,* Chapter 3, trustworthy scholars advocate that "spirit" in these two verses should be capitalized, indicating that Jesus meant worship in the Holy Spirit.

[4] Jonas Clark, "Reg Layzell: Apostle of the Latter Rain," *The Voice* (April, 2007): 18-21. Some of Layzell's basic teachings were compiled by B. M. Gaglardi, *The Pastor's Pen* (Vancouver, B.C.: Mission, 1965).

[5] Edward R. Dayton and David A. Fraser, *Planning Strategies for World Evangelization* Grand Rapids: Eerdmans, 1980), p. 59.

[6] McBirnie, *The Search for the Twelve Apostles,* pp. 22-23.

[7] Dan Kimball, *The Emerging Church*, p. 7 of the Forward.

[8] Gordon Walker, *Twentieth Century Apostleship* (Mt. Hermon, CA: Conciliar Press), p. 8.

[9] E. M. Bounds, *Power Through Prayer*

Chapter 3
The Church Needs Apostles

In This Chapter

- *A shave and haircut opened Inland China to the gospel*
- *"Apostle" needs an upgrade*
- *"Ambassador in chains" can have two meanings*
- *Amazing Scriptures about Jesus The apostle*
- *Meet Sunday Adelaja, "The Unlikely Ambassador"*

He was understandably nervous.   His hair had been cut in the traditional manner all of his life, but what he himself now did was new, strange and certainly unlike the behavior of an English clergyman.[1]

He passed the razor over the front of his scalp … and the hair tumbled to the floor. Staring at his reflection, Hudson Taylor knew this performance would bring great results -- or sad repercussions.

Hope and expectancy filled his heart as he proceeded to dye the remaining hair black, attaching a temporary, braided queue on the back of his head. He stared at the new image: he was starting to look Chinese! The crowning touch was to don the loose, unaccustomed gown and satin shoes of the "Teacher" or man of the scholarly class.

The strong reaction by his fellow male, European missionaries was quick, insulting. Nearly all were upset, and none of the men were at all inclined to assume such bizarre makeup; however, the missionary woman soon to become his wife bubbled with enthusiasm and approval!

Out among the Chinese, the re-made missionary realized a new day had dawned. Everywhere he went, Hudson Taylor now received a gracious reception and sincere interest in his message and medical help; he was no longer treated as a foreigner, and formerly closed doors now opened to him.   In spite of strong criticism from other European missionaries, Hudson took the step that would have a profound influence on the evangelization of Inland China.

My first introduction to the amazing life story of James Hudson Taylor (1832-1905) came through a book called *Hudson Taylor's Spiritual Secret* written by his son and daughter-in-law (first published over 70 years ago). In the Introduction Professor Warneck said of Taylor, founder of the China Inland Mission:

> [H}e was a physician...full of the Holy Spirit and of faith, of entire surrender to God and His call, of great self-denial, heartfelt compassion, rare power in prayer, marvelous organizing faculty, energetic initiative, indefatigable perseverance, and of astonishing influence with men, and withal of childlike humility.[2]

Like Paul the apostle, Hudson adamantly believed God answers prayer, and He is utterly faithful to His Word. These two men knew, unlike some moderns who are so adequately provisioned, "the simple, profound secret of drawing for every need, temporal or spiritual, upon 'the fathomless wealth of Christ.'"[3]

Like Paul, Hudson faced mob violence, discrimination, confrontations with community leaders, spiritual resistance, sacrificial living, and the challenges of recruiting and training new workers. Paul wrote most of the New Testament; Hudson translated it into Chinese. Both Paul and Hudson recruited women to evangelize and teach, and both endeavored to reach those who had not yet heard the gospel. Unlike Paul, Hudson was married, three successive times, each time to a dedicated woman who worked diligently beside him to reach the Chinese; each, in turn, died and was buried in China.

Paul and Hudson defied unproductive, traditional approaches. Hudson adopted Paul's example of becoming "all things to all men, that I might by all means save some" (1 Corinthians 9:20-22); accordingly, he jettisoned his European appearance that appeared undignified, comical and untrustworthy to the Chinese.

Hudson Taylor lived a life of dedication, leadership and outreach to the lost, paralleling that of Paul the apostle. Asking for no funds, refusing debt and conducting himself like the Chinese, Hudson undergirded everything with prayer. He was innovative and indefatigable in reaching the lost, going where the message was not preached: to reach the inland river people, he lived and preached on the boats.

The efforts of that great man have since proliferated, reaching into the hundreds of thousands. He was an apostle, a man who simply believed God's Word: Paul reached the Roman Empire, Hudson reached Inland China.

> When Mr. Hudson Taylor laid down the leadership of the Mission in 1900, five years before his Home-call, the China Inland Mission numbered 750 missionaries. Today [1932] its membership is 1,285....Seven hundred Chinese workers were connected with the Mission, rich answer to Mr. Taylor's prayers, and the converts baptized from the commencement numbered thirteen thousand."[4]

Now, it is our turn at bat, time to win our confused world. Unreached tribes exist beside a world that has become quite sophisticated -- and people exist everywhere without the Savior. Today's Church needs intrepid apostles, leaders like Hudson Taylor, and apostolic churches with aggressive Spirit-filled people to impact every type of community, every nation and every sphere of influence.

In this chapter we seek a better definition of apostleship, leaving later chapters to discuss apostleship and apostolic churches in both biblical and modern times.

"Apostle" Is Supercharged

Originally, "apostle" was a secular Greek word *(apostolos)* with a simple meaning: "sent one," "messenger," "courier." Christianity, however, "picked a [this] secular term and made it into a specific office and title."[5]

Apostolos was supercharged by its link with Jesus and the dynamic leaders and sending program of the early Church, coming to designate the Church's most daring and responsible leadership position, epitomizing the true significance of Christianity's global mission.[6]

46

Typical Meaning

The average person associates "apostle" with Christ's commissioning of twelve disciples, or Paul establishing Christianity in an unbelieving culture. Sending a missionary is some times equated with sending an apostle. A typical definition would be: "a missionary 'sent' to an unreached culture to proclaim the 'Good News' of Jesus Christ and gather converts into local churches."

This sincere, well-worn statement certainly has merit -- but needs Holy Spirit upgrade, recapturing the deeper intentions of Paul when he invaded an idolatrous city to proclaim "the good news," or of Jesus sending the Twelve Apostles into the Jewish culture to bring the kingdom of God.

Rediscover the Mandate

"Apostle" appears 81 times in the New Testament (single and plural forms), with four-fifths of the biblical material coming from the writings of Paul and his associate Luke. These references portray the apostolate and churches of Bible days as a Spirit-empowered, mobilizing ministry, dead-set on fulfilling the Great Commission of Jesus.

Our premise: *Spirit-empowered apostolic Christianity is a Jesus mandate not only for ancient history but for today's society as well.* Societies have modernized and the international scene has changed drastically, but every nation and community still needs the power of the Spirit working through apostolic churches. Certainly we must update our style of relating to people needs, technological advances, and so on – but we dare not neglect our power source, the *dynamis* (power, potency, dynamite!) of the gospel of Jesus Christ working through His deputized servants.

Wherever the Good News of Jesus is proclaimed today with ambassadorial authority, wonderful, biblical results are occurring. We must contend for these things to happen ("I have to write insisting—begging! – that you fight with everything you have in you for this faith entrusted to us as a gift to guard and cherish," Jude 3, M), both in underdeveloped nations and advanced societies. The Great Commission accompanied by apostolic *dynamis* is intended for the *entire* Church age, accomplished today with apostles and apostolic churches wisely functioning in the power of the Holy Spirit.

Today's Church must rediscover the apostolic mandate; now is the time for rejuvenation, renewal and revival. Take down the sign: "business as usual." Today, we need wise apostles, associated fivefold ministries, apostolic Christians, cutting edge methodology, *and* Holy Spirit power – all reinforced by impacting prayer. Working together, the results will be magnificent:

- Church growth and church renewal
- Culture penetration and world harvest
- Completion of the Great Commission, and the
- Maturity of the Bride of Christ, His Church

Ambassadors of the King

Apostolos must convey again the wallop it packed in New Testament times. As the early Church did, let us today give high-status definition to this high-energy word: *ambassador, envoy, emissary, delegate or representative.*

A leading Greek scholar says:

"The word 'apostle' never means in the N.T. the act of sending, or the business involved, but is *always the designation of a man who is sent as ambassador, and indeed, an authorized ambassador*"(Karl Heinrich Rengstorf, emphasis added).[7]

Note the forceful effect when "*Apostolos means ambassador*" is fused with "*of the Kingdom of God*": "*Apostolos means ambassador of the Kingdom of God!*" Also, fuse the adjective *Apostolic* with *Christianity*: "*Apostolic Christianity!*"

Jesus had this in mind when He "sent" (*apostello,* verb form of *apostolos*[8]) the original Twelve as His authorized representatives. They brought a clear message, powerful and plainly understood: *the kingdom was near at hand* (i.e., within reach)*!* Jesus deputized these followers to *proclaim* His teachings, being *authenticated* by casting out unclean spirits, curing the sick and afflicted, and even raising the dead (Matthew 10:1-42; Mark 6:7-13; Luke 9:1-6). The ambassadors themselves were amazed (Luke 10:17ff)!

"Ambassador" Is an Appropriate Term

Ambassadors in the secular world are like "apostles" in the church world. A nation's ambassador is a diplomatic official of the highest rank, while an apostle is the Church's highest-ranking, leadership ministry (1 Corinthians 12:28; Ephesians 4:11). Ambassadors are sent to speak for and represent their governments; apostles are sent by God into dark places to bring His message of light, presenting the claims of the kingdom of Heaven to those spiritually blinded by Satan, planting God's flag on recaptured territory. Every Christian may not be an apostle, but every Christian needs to be part of an apostolic local or missionary team that is imbued with heaven's ambassadorial consciousness!

Herbert Lockyer, calls the apostles "the authorized representatives of Christ who commissioned them."[9] More than a messenger-boy singing "Happy Birthday," an apostle is commissioned with authority to make dynamic kingdom changes!

Jesus' prayed this remarkable insight: "As You sent [*apostello*] Me into the world, I also have sent [*apostello*] them into the world" (John 17:18). Those original apostles and their associates went forth with "credentials as potent and convincing as those the Lord Himself had possessed, perpetuating the work of the Master." This *ambassadorial consciousness* must be the driving force of our churches. The apostle speaks and acts boldly as God's authorized delegate and representative, boosting churches into apostolic mind-set, recruiting all members to do the business of God, and extending Christ's kingdom to all people. The glorious hope for these last days is the return of apostolic Christianity -- with functioning apostles and Spirit-filled apostolic Christians!

The early Christians broke cultural barriers, subdued demonic resistance, brought God's message of hope to hurting people everywhere. They acted as ambassadors plenipotentiary, having power to transact God's business.

> Therefore we are ambassadors for Christ, as though God were pleading through us: we implore you on Christ's behalf, be reconciled to God (2 Corinthians 5:20).

Ambassador to Trinidad

I have a friend in Trinidad whose life has been an amazing illustration of a Christian ambassador. Tony Kawalsingh is the director of Ministers Fellowship West Indies, where he has been a great blessing to the island, and in Suriname, Guyana. Down through the years Tony has had a true father's heart for the churches that have been planted in villages and towns that are hostile to Christians and the Church.

Now Tony oversees the younger people who are doing the pastoral work in those places and also others that have sought his spiritual oversight from other islands and South American countries.

It is not practical to share all of Tony's ministry, but suffice it to say that he has persevered through many difficult times and situations; for example, kidnapping his son, breaking into his home, beating him with a machete and threatening him to leave the country and never preach again.

Tony has always remained true to his calling and his concerns. Many in the islands consider him their spiritual father, a key characteristic of an apostle. His spiritual sons are active church planters in Guyana, Trinidad and Tobago, Caribbean, Toronto, New York—just to name a few places.

An "Ambassador in [Iron] Chains"

Not all governments or spiritual powers yielded easily to Jesus' people. Although many did accept the good news of Christ, religious factions, civil authorities, and even common people resisted the Gospel's advance. While secular ambassadors enjoyed diplomatic immunity, the apostles of Bible days were often objects of scorn, ridicule, persecution, beatings and imprisonment. Paul and Barnabas, speaking from first-hand experience, advised their churches that we enter the kingdom of God "through many tribulations" (Acts 14:22).

Paul described himself as: "an ambassador in chains..." (Ephesians 6:20). He proudly arrived at Rome's imperial court as a common prisoner,[10] acting like the ambassador of a heavenly kingdom, heralding heaven's claims to the seamy side of earth's greatest city.

Although himself chained, Paul loudly proclaimed "the Word of God is *not* chained" (2 Timothy 2:9, emphasis added). The message moved with living force, even while the messenger was incarcerated!

An ambassador can be snubbed or expelled, but not ordinarily imprisoned. Markus Barth says, "When a delegate is imprisoned his mission appears to be not only in jeopardy, but at an end." Instead, Paul's status and discomfort spread the gospel, assisting him as a servant and providing a model for those who believed in Christ.

While "in my chains," Paul converted Onesimus, a run-away slave (Philemon 10). Roman guards accepted Christ and testified to Paul's message (Philippians 1:13-14; 4:22). Jerome states (in *Philemon*) that St. Paul had converted many in Caesar's family: "being by the emperor cast into prison, he became more known to his family, and turned the house of Christ's persecutor into a church."

"Chain" (*alysis*) can also signify the golden ornaments worn around the neck and wrists by rich ladies and high-ranking men. Barth mentions:

> On festive occasions ambassadors wear such chains in order to reveal the riches, power, and dignity of the government they represent. Because Paul serves Christ crucified, he considers the painful, iron prison chains as most appropriate insignia for the representation of his Lord. [11]

Background of "Apostle"

Greek lexicons contrast the significance of *apostolos* in the New Testament with ancient Greek meaning. Christianity definitely *powered up* the word!

Ancient Greek Usage

Scholars agree: "The word *apostolos* rarely has in classical Greek anything like the meaning which it has in the N.T." [12] C.K. Barrett says, "The pre-Christian history of the Greek word 'apostle' (*apostolos*) does little or nothing to illustrate its Christian usage." [13] Commentaries list various early usages:

> • "a naval expedition, prob. also its commander" • "a ship ready for departure" • "sending out" • "bill of lading" (in pap. mostly) • "dispatch, letter" • "In isolated cases it means ambassador, delegate, messenger." [14] • "A group of colonists" • "a personal envoy" • "a dispatch given to a ship or for an export license." [15]

Jewish Usage

The closest Hebrew word to *apostolos* is *shaliah*. The Hebrew *shaliah* (*ambassador* in modern Hebrew) comes from the verb *shalach* (to send). My professor at Fuller Seminary, Ray S. Anderson, explained the post-first century meaning like this: "The *emphasis is on the sender*, rather than the one sent. The one sent was viewed as an extension of the personality of the sender. The *shaliach* received a specific commission in the nature of *a function, rather than an office, or a status*" (emphasis added).[16] This means, when the action was completed, the term "apostle" no longer applied.[17]

The Greek Old Testament

The Hebrew Scriptures were translated into Greek (the *Septuagint Version* or *LXX*) about 250 years before the New Testament books.

> The LXX translation of the Old Testament had already found its way into every city of the Roman Empire to which the Jews of the Dispersion had gone. It was virtually the only form of the Old Testament in the hands of Jewish believers outside Palestine, and it was certainly the only available form for Gentile converts to the Jewish or Christian faiths (Gleason Archer and Gregory Chirichigno).[18]

Paul frequently quotes from the LXX, and the Book of Hebrews quotes its many references exclusively from the Septuagint.[19]

Some 700 times in the *LXX apostello* and *exapostello* are used "to denote not the institutional appointment of someone to an office, but the authorization of him to fulfill a particular function or a task which is normally clearly defined" (Dietrich Muller).[20] We conclude the Greek Old Testament did not present the exact role that *apostolos* assumed in New Testament churches.

A Specific Ministry

Usually, "apostle" in New Testament times was elevated from "temporary messenger" or mere "courier" to a specific position or title in the Body of Christ. Although *apostolos* did at times refer to a person sent on *temporary*, specific apostolic mission, most of the time *apostolos* referred to an authoritative, delegated leader able to articulate, demonstrate and enforce the Gospel of God.

The following references show "apostle" referring to a bestowed, titled, ongoing, real, observable, functioning ministry (emphasis added):

- Acts 1:25: "to take part in *this ministry and apostleship* from which Judas by transgression fell…And he was *numbered with* the eleven apostles." (Acts 1:20, "Let another *take his office*.")

- Acts 14:14: "But when *the apostles* Barnabas and Paul heard this…."

- Romans 1:5: "*we have received grace and apostleship* for obedience to The faith among all nations."

- 1 Corinthians 4:9: "For I think that God has displayed us *the apostles* last…."

- 1 Corinthians 9:1-2: "Am I not *an apostle*? …. Are you not my work in the Lord? For you are *the seal of my apostleship* in the Lord."

- 1 Corinthians 12:17-28: "you are…members individually. And *God Has appointed these* in the church: first *apostles*…." V. 29, "are all apostles?"

- Galatians 2:8: "(for He who worked effectively in Peter for the *apostleship to the circumcised* also worked effectively in me *toward the Gentiles*)"
- Ephesians 4:11: "And *He Himself gave* some to be apostles…."

Paul defended his apostleship in 2 Corinthians 10 and 11. Declaring that fruitful ministry ("credentials") authenticated his gifting and office, he clearly established that an apostle could be more than someone sent on temporary assignment to deliver a message. Paul certainly went where he was sent, did the job assigned to do, but "messenger" was *power-jumped* into the office of apostle. E. F. Harrison gives logical, credible reason for the above Scriptures and Paul's defense:

> Paul would not have needed to defend his apostleship with such vehemence if he were only defending his right to proclaim the gospel.[21]

Jesus Christ, Chief Apostle

Hebrews 3:1 calls Jesus an apostle:

> ...consider the Apostle and High Priest of our confession, Christ Jesus, who was faithful to Him who appointed Him...."

Jesus, ambassador of the kingdom of heaven, brought God's message, authority, and power to mankind. "He is the supreme apostle from whom all other apostleship flows."[22] Jesus knew He carried more than a title.

Many verses declare that Jesus Christ – Son, Image and Logos of God -- was sent from/by God into this world. [23] Christ Jesus literally embodied apostleship, He was the original "sent one." He said: "...for I proceeded forth and came from God; nor have I come of Myself, but He sent me" (John 8:42).[24] John declared: "we have seen and testify that the Father has sent the Son as savior of the world" (1 John 4:14).

Jesus truly/fully represented the heavenly Father who commissioned Him, always remembering "a servant is not greater than his master; nor is he who is sent (Greek, *'an apostolos'*) greater than he who sent him" (John 13:16). In this humility, Jesus spoke as God would speak, and acted as God would act, bearing the full authority of His heavenly Father to do so.

Various References

Coming from the Father, Jesus proclaimed and demonstrated God's love and concern for mankind: the prototype emissary, the leader and example of all who would follow and be sent on God's mission. Matthew 15:24; Mark 9:37; Luke 4:18, 43; 9:48; 10:16; Acts 3:20, 26; 1 John 4:9,10,14.

As F. B. Meyer says, *sent*

> was one of the watchwords of Jesus; and, with the exception of the word Father, oftener on His lips than almost any other; occurring ... more than forty times [in John], it challenges our attention....Insofar, then, as we can understand the true meaning of the Father's mission of the Son, *we shall be able to understand also the Son's mission of that little band which included not the Apostles only, but ... the entire Church, of which we are part* (emphasis added).[25]

54

Jesus' declarations about being sent from God and returning to God confused and concerned the Twelve Apostles. Finally, making this lucid statement, Jesus said: "I came forth from the Father and have come into the world. Again, I leave the world and go to the Father," John 16:28. It was an epiphany! At that right moment light suddenly dawned -- an intuitive grasp of Jesus' meaning -- undoubtedly enabled by the Holy Spirit. They cried out: "Now we know what you're talking about!"

References from John

John did *not* call Jesus an apostle, but he did quote Jesus using the verb *apostello* ("the terminology of sending," Betz).[26] This verified that God "sent" or apostolized His Son to save the lost. Fifteen of John's 21 chapters declare that *God sent Jesus.*[27]

Consider the repeated use of "sent" in Jesus' prayer (John 17):

- "and Jesus Christ, whom You have *sent*" (v. 3)
- "and they have believed that You *sent* me" (v. 8)
- "as You have *sent* Me into the world" (v. 18a)
- "I have also *sent* them into the world" (v. 18b)
- "that the world may believe that You *sent* Me" (v. 21)
- "that the world may know that You *sent* Me" (v. 23)
- "these have known that You *sent* me" (v. 25)

John's Gospel, however, "studiously avoids the title of apostle" (Betz).[28] Why? Jesus understood the necessity of modeling the action/function *first,* rather than emphasizing an authoritative, religious title, so easily misconstrued or misused by ambitious disciples. Once the Church began to function, the title naturally assumed appropriate meaning.

The Unlikely Ambassador

A Nigerian immigrant moved to Kyiv, Ukraine, to pursue schooling, and has now raised up – in the past fifteen years -- the largest evangelical church in Europe (which incidentally has a 98% white congregation).[29] When a person visits services of the 25,000-member Embassy of God Church, you see people packed wall-to-wall in a huge auditorium. One well-known American pastor said, "I've never seen such a happy church. It's the greatest celebration I've ever seen of God's mercy and grace."

The name of the church certainly fits the ambassadorial ministry of Pastor Sunday Adelaja. He founded and oversees over 400 churches in over 30 countries; it is said that 1,000,000 people have confessed Jesus as Lord through his ministry. He is a journalist, international speaker, advisor to heads of states, and an advocate of national transformation. C. Peter Wagner says: "It would be difficult to point to a local church and its growing apostolic network of daughter churches that has had more influence on a nation than the Embassy of God has had on Ukraine."

Pastor Adelaja's success, like that of any modern apostle, can be traced to a conviction that the Bible is God's Word and that God will do what He says he will do. Combined with humility, dependence on God, and an astounding prayer base, this persuasion produces a fervent atmosphere that incites the church members to reach out to the community with signs and wonders. This church proclaims freedom from sin, pain, and poverty – good news to needy people.

John Bevere comments:
"I am in absolute awe of how God can send someone from a different continent, place him into an Eastern European nation and build the largest church in the continent; and then, for this man to build such a passion into these people is staggering and encouraging to all the world."

Charisma Magazine understandably calls Adelaja "The Unlikely Ambassador."[30]

Can There Be Apostles Today?

The thought of modern apostles can be mind-boggling, so if you doubt such apostles exist or can exist, please hear me out in this chapter and those that follow. Allow the Scriptures, the examples and the reasoning to speak.

By the way, the previous vignette does not diminish the labor of or esteem for lesser-known but equally dedicated ministers/missionaries throughout the world. The size, however, and effectiveness of this above-mentioned ministry does show-case the possibilities of what can take place in our day.

Don't Underestimate the Miraculous

Regardless of notoriety or ministry, a functioning apostle produces results: light invades dungeons -- people are delivered from evil powers, given a reason to live, set free and made joyful. In other words, as said earlier, "apostle" needs a power upgrade from mere messenger to ambassador. *The ministries of Paul and others would have made no impression as mere messengers.* They did more than knock on the door and sing "Happy Birthday."

The apostle of New Testament times was an ambassador who spoke and acted on behalf of God's wishes, anointed and directed by the Holy Spirit. The apostles, of course, were not replacing God, just doing as God instructed them, acting on His behalf. They followed in Jesus' footsteps, believing that the fulfillment of Isaiah 61 (Luke 4:18) was a world-wide mandate they had the authority to enforce; they carried out the "Great Commission" of Jesus.

Global Acceleration

Healings, miracles and manifestations of the Holy Spirit accelerate the dramatic, forward thrust of Christianity. Wherever it is -- Ukraine, Africa, China, Brazil, the United States, the islands of the sea – the powerful working of the Holy Spirit is always associated with apostles, apostolic churches and apostolic thinking. Today, we need this kind of faith to advance Christ and His Church *worldwide.* Read the New Testament through eyes of faith, expectant faith, believing that the teachings and actions of the early Church will work today.

The next chapter introduces Jesus' original Twelve Apostles: a story of how ordinary men became awesome world-changers. May their example grip all of our hearts.

Chapter 3 Endnotes

[1] Howard Taylor, *Hudson Taylor's Spiritual Secret* (Chicago: Moody Press, repub.1989), p. 67.
[2] Ibid, pp. vi-vii.
[3] Ibid, p. 14.
[4] Ibid, p. 230.
[5] Hans Dieter Betz, "Apostle," *The Anchor Bible Dictionary* on CD-ROM, Logos Library Version 2.Oc. 1995, 1996. Print ed: David Noel Freedman, ed., *Anchor Bible Dictionary,* 6 Volumes (NY: Doubleday, 1992).
[6] Archbishop Trench, in *Synonyms of the New Testament,* makes a statement that certainly applies to *apostolos:* "Greek words taken up into Christian use are glorified and transformed, seeming to have waited for this adoption of them, to come to their full rights, and to reveal all the depth and the riches of meaning which they contain," p. 156.
[7] Karl Heinrich Rengstorf, trans. by J. R. Coates in 1933, *Apostleship* (London: Adam and Charles Black, 1952) pp.25-26. This landmark article was originally put in manual form and later retranslated and edited by Geoffrey W. Bromiley for Kittel's *Theological Dictionary of the New Testament.* Bromiley's translation: "It [*apostolos*] always denotes a man who is sent, and sent with full authority" (Vol. I, p. 421).

Bill Scheidler makes this humorous comment in *Apostles: the Fathering Spirit* (Portland, OR: City Christian Publishing, 2001), pp. xii-xiii: "I had an interesting conversation recently with a pastor from Greece. He was talking about how English speakers tend to do a lot of damage to the Greek language when they preach....He went on to say, 'I don't know what the big deal is nowadays about the function of apostles. In Greece an apostle is simply a messenger. It is not uncommon to see an ad in the paper, 'Wanted: Apostle. Must have His own bicycle.'"
[8] See references in endnote #27. A good discussion of the noun and verb form is found in the one-volume abridgement by Geoffrey W. Bromiley of *Theological Dictionary of the New Testament,* Gerhard Kittel and Gerhard Friedrich, editors, "Apostle," K. H. Rengstorf (Grand Rapids: Eerdmans, 1986), pp. 67-75. "[The Twelve] become his authoritative representatives, but the very nature of their commission means that they are now also missionaries....The missionary aspect is something new compared to the Jewish *sali(a)h* institution. The new commission is also of a more lasting character, applying to the whole period between the ascension and the return," p. 72.
[9] Herbert Lockyer, *All the Apostles of the Bible* (Grand Rapids: Zondervan, 1972), p. 19.
[10] A. Skevington Wood: "'In chains' is actually 'in a chain' (*en halysei*); this may be intended to imply that he was handcuffed to one soldier in military custody (Acts 28:20; 2 Tim 1:16)." "Ephesians," *The Expositor's Bible Commentary*, Vol. 11, (Grand Rapids: Zondervan, 1978), p. 90,
[11] Marcus Barth, *Ephesians 4-6, The Anchor Bible,* Vol. 34A (Garden City, NY: Doubleday & Co., 1974), p. 782.
[12] Rengstorf, p. 1.
[13] C. K. Barrett, *The Epistle to the Romans* (NY: Harper & Row, 1957), p. 16. He goes on to say that *apostolos* does call to mind the Hebrew *shaliah* (from *shaluah,* "to send") which is common in post-biblical Hebrew for "an authorized representative or delegate,

legally empowered to act (within prescribed limits) on behalf of his principal." However, Barrett says it is not certain that first century, Greek-speaking Jews would use *apostolos* to represent this technical term, but possibly they did.

[14] William Arndt and F. Wilbur Gingrich, *A Greek-English Lexicon of the NT and Other Early Christian Literature* (Chicago: The University of Chicago Press, 1957), p. 99.

[15] M. H. Shepherd, "Apostle," George Arthur Buttrick, dict. ed., *The Interpreter's Dictionary of the Bible,* Vol. 4 (NY: Abingdon Press, 1962), pp. 170-172.

[16] Ray S. Anderson, Fuller Seminary class notes for Systematic Theology (Spring 1983). M. H. Shepherd adds: "...the *shaliah,* unlike the later Christian apostle, has no institutional status or missionary responsibility. His authority is precisely defined and given for a *limited term,* and the character of his commission is more juridical than religious in quality (emphasis added)" (p. 170).

[17] Hans Küng says: "In many respects the concept of apostle has been derived from the Hebrew *"schaliah"* (e.g. 1 Kg. 143:6, where the prophet [Ahija] appears as God's messenger). In the post-exilic period *schalliach* is a technical term for the envoys of Jewish authorities – the name does not appear, however, until the second century A.D.; in the case of such a man the fundamental rabbinical principle applies: that an authorized representative is the same as the person himself. The connection between the two ideas is a matter of controversy and the basic [semantic] problem of the origin of the apostolic idea which we find in the New Testament remains unsolved." *The Church,* p. 446.

[18] Gleason L. Archer and Gregory Chirichigno, *Old Testament Quotations in the New Testament* (Chicago: Moody Press, 1983), p. ix.

[19] "[W]hen the author [of Hebrews] quotes from the Old Testament he uses the Greek translation (the Septuagint) of the Hebrew text." Simon J. Kistemaker, *New Testament Commentary: Exposition of the Epistle to the Hebrews* (Grand Rapids: Baker Books, 1984), p. 5.

[20] Dietrich Müller, "Apostle," Colin Brown, ed., *The New International Dictionary of NT Theology,* Vol. 1 (Grand Rapids: Zondervan, 1975), p. 127.

[21] E. F. Harrison, "Apostle, Apostleship," *Evangelical Dictionary of the Bible, 2nd Edition* (Grand Rapids: Baker Academic, 2001), pp. 86-87.

[22] *The NIV Study Bible* (Grand Rapids: Zondervan Bible Publishers, 1985), p. 1861.

[23] Rengstorf says, "In John...the sending brings out the significance of the person of Christ and of what is done in him, namely, that the father speaks and acts by him."

[24] Content is so clear that *apostello* is not required.

[25] F. B. Meyer, *The Life of Love* (Old Tappan, NJ: Fleming H. Revell Company, 1987 reprint), p. 81.

[26] Betz, Ibid.

[27] *Apostello:* John 3:17, 34; 5:36, 38; 6:29, 57; 7:29; 8:42; 10:36; 11:42; 17:3, 8, 18, 21, 23, 25; 20:21. References using *pempto* (more general term): John 4:34; 5:23, 24, 30, 37; 6:38, 39, 44; 7:16, 18, 28, 33; 8:16, 18, 26, 29; 9:4; 12:44, 45, 49; 13:20; 14:24; 15:21; 16:5. Sometimes used interchangeably, yet the distinction is discernible on close examination.

[28] Betz, Ibid.

[29] Ken Walker, "European Church Fuses Faith, Politics," *Charisma* (November 2006): 22-23.

---

[30]Valerie G. Lowe, "The Unlikely Ambassador," *Charisma* (October 2007): 38-43. See www.GODEMBASSY.ORG.

Part II – The Apostolic Momentum

Chapter 4 – He Chose Twelve . . . Apostles

Chapter 5 – Paul, Apostle Extraordinary

Chapter 6 – Validation for Additional Apostles

Chapter 7 – Reasons for More Apostles

Chapter 4
He Chose Twelve . . . Apostles

In This Chapter

- *Why "Twelve" Apostles?*
- *What made the Twelve appealing to Jesus?*
- *Good reasons cancelled out other candidates*
- *Why was ministry time in Galilee so important?*

The setting sun retreated before the overspreading darkness: night had come to the Sea of Galilee and the town of Capernaum. Bright stars began appearing, filling the deep, deep blue of the evening sky with their scintillating light. On a small mountain nearby, Jesus and His followers camped out.

Although weary, Jesus concentrated on the preeminent reason for being there: *"He went out to the mountain to pray, and continued all night in prayer to God,"* Luke 6:12.

A non-stop year and a half of exciting, fruitful ministry in Judea, Galilee and beside the Jordan had now been completed; skyrocketing fame had made Jesus the most popular figure in Israel, some calling Him the Messiah. Common people were refreshed by His spirituality, awed by His healings, amazed by His miracles. "Jesus" was on every tongue. As Wilbur Smith said,

> His message, His demands, His statements concerning Himself, as being the Son of God, -- all these things were now well known throughout Palestine.[1]

The imprisonment of John the Baptist was like a prearranged signal, causing Jesus to move swiftly north to the Galilean area. News of His arrival swept like wildfire through the countryside, even beyond Israel's borders. The religious factions (usually quarreling) desperately joined forces to oppose and destroy the Nazarene's credibility: He must be stopped.

The Scribes and Pharisees were incensed by Jesus' words and actions. What nerve! How could He possibly forgive sins? The open disregard for Sabbath traditions was infuriating: disciples deliberately plucking grain, and Jesus defiantly healing a withered hand. How they hated Him (Luke 6:11)!

Jesus' actions did not violate the true essence of Mosaic Law, challenging rather the meaningless traditions. Finally, the crowning touch came, a brilliant act causing hatred to burst into livid rage: Jesus invited a Jewish tax collector, a vassal of Rome, to leave his station and follow Him. How could this be possible? Every Jew considered a tax collector a despicable extortioner, taxing his own people -- to pay for the Roman occupation!

Seeking to buffer Himself with friends, gain receptive audiences *and fulfill Scripture*, Jesus moved to the northern shores of the Sea of Galilee, making Capernaum His base of operations. Two years of ministry now remained for Messiah's earthly mission.[2]

Galilee was a beautiful, heart-shaped, fresh-water lake, almost thirteen miles long and about eight miles wide, surrounded by high mountains. Located in the Upper Jordan River valley, the region was considered a lush garden, abounding in water, fish, fertile soil and a hot climate. Above all, the area was home to some 200,000 people, mostly Gentiles, scattered throughout the valley and the many towns and villages along the shores of the lake.[3]

Jesus would now begin aggressive evangelization of the Galilean rural towns, thereby fulfilling the prophecy of Isaiah 9:1-2 that a great light would dawn in "Galilee of the Gentiles" dispelling the spiritual darkness:

> ...that it might be fulfilled which was spoken by Isaiah the prophet, saying: "The land of Zebulun and the land of Naphtali, the way of the sea, beyond the Jordan, Galilee of the Gentiles: *the people who sat in darkness saw a great light, and upon those who sat in the region and shadow of death Light has dawned*" (Matthew 4:14-16, emphasis added).

Decisions To Be Made

On the mountain, Jesus' burden intensified. The people, "weary and scattered, having no shepherd," weighed heavily upon His heart. On the morrow many would gather for His help, and He must lift and inspire the depressed and downtrodden. Also, He must publicly replace rabbinic traditions with kingdom principles. The miraculous would make all this possible!

An urgent decision pressed His mind: the appointment of twelve disciples as apostles (personal ambassadors) to aid in ministry and oversight, with their selection *being* God's choice. This group would come from the larger crowd of disciple/followers that had come with Him, many of whom were even now bedding down for the night. The logical choices would be the disciples who followed in close association for the past year (since His baptism).

Jesus had come to know who would be His inner circle. Prophetic intuition aided and confirmed the decisions. The Father's heart had become His own ("All that the Father gives Me will come to Me," John 6:37). Guided now by the Holy Spirit, Jesus prayed for His followers, as Jesus later told Peter:

> Simon, Simon, listen! Satan has asked permission to sift all of you like wheat, but I have prayed especially for you that your own faith may not utterly fail" (Luke 22:31-32, W).

All-Night Prayer

Jesus was no stranger to daily, early-morning prayer.

> Now in the morning, having risen a long while before daylight, He went out and departed to a solitary [deserted] place, and there he prayed (Mark 1:35).[4]

Jesus also knew the secret of continual prayer ("pray without ceasing," 1 Thessalonians 5:17). Prayer was a way of life for Jesus.

> Jesus prayed, not because he had nothing better to do, but because He had *so much to do*....Jesus' habit of prayer teaches us that the closer one

is to the Lord the more he will stay in communication with the Lord (Dick Stark).[5]

Places of Rendezvous

The Master had learned the necessity of *longer times* in God's presence, using secluded places away from people and crowds:

- a wilderness ("often…into the wilderness and prayed," Luke 5:16)

- a mountain top ("He departed to the mountain to pray," Mark 6:46)

- a secluded garden ("He knelt down and prayed," Luke 22:41)

Jesus realized,

> For prayer to work [He must] put distance between Himself and the issue at hand…. Jesus' most important work took place beyond the peering eyes of men. In the mountain He was removed from the crossroads of life … in a place where He could be inspired.[6]

Such praying required praying through the night, a necessity for handling such immense responsibility. This was such a night. In the Greek text one word is used: *dianuktereuo.*

> The word is significant. It speaks of enduring at a task through the night….toiling through the night, staying at a task all night (MacArthur).[7]

Inflow . . . Out flow

Jesus was dependent on the "flow" of the Spirit's presence.

> And Jesus immediately knowing in Himself that *power had gone out of Him*, turned around to the crowd and said, "Who touched My clothing?" (Mark 5:30, emphasis added).

> And the whole multitude sought to touch Him, *for power went out from Him* and healed them all (Luke 6:19, emphasis added).

Jesus knew that awesome power issues from those who wait on God.[8]

> So He Himself often withdrew into the wilderness and prayed. Now it happened on a certain day, as he was teaching, that there were Pharisees and teachers of the law sitting by, who had come out of every town of Galilee, Judea, and Jerusalem. *And the power of the Lord was present to heal them"* (Luke 5:16-17, emphasis added).

He Chose Twelve

At daybreak, Jesus appeared and roused the disciples on the lower mountain. As they gathered about, Jesus performed an ordination – meaningful, basic, sincere, without ostentation.

> [Jesus] called His disciples to Himself; and from them He chose twelve whom He also named apostles" (Luke 6:13).

With prophetic acuity, Jesus singled out the Twelve, and wide-eyed they stepped forward. The larger contingent of disciples circled closer, realizing those selected had been associated with Jesus from the beginning of His ministry, nearly all coming from the greater Capernaum area, some having been followers of John the Baptist.

A Band of Brothers

The first four were well known. All were local fishermen, two sets of brothers, with the latter being Jesus' own cousins: *Simon Peter (Cephas),* who became leader of the apostles, and *Andrew,* his brother; *James* and *John,* the sons of Zebedee (*John* later known as the beloved apostle, *James* the first apostle martyred).

Four others were summoned: *Philip,* a fisherman from Bethsaida, and his friend *Nathanael* (or *Bartholomew*) from Cana of Galilee; *Matthew (Levi),* tax collector, and *Thomas (Didymus,* which means "Twin") from Galilee.

The final four: *James* (son of Alphaeus or Clopas), *Judas (Lebbaeus,* or *Thaddaeus)* and *Simon* the Zealot from Galilee (who might have been three brothers);[9] *Judas Iscariot*, the only one of Judean origin, was the last.

The Ordination of Twelve

Wonderment rippled through the followers. The felt-presence of the Lord descended, so sacred and tangible. The Twelve dropped to their knees as the Carpenter's hands were laid upon them.[10] These would be His leaders, foundation stones aligned to Himself, the corner stone. Now, they were student-learners, participating in the word and power of the kingdom of God; later, they would be channels of God's "Good News" and the flow of God's power.

Epiphany – a sudden, electrifying perception -- gripped the crowd: Jesus chose twelve*, the number of Israel!* "Every Jew knew in a moment what that choice of twelve implied" (Wilbur Smith).[11] Jesus was making a stupendous personal claim: *He was the long-expected and promised Messiah!* "[The number twelve] significantly hinted that Jesus was the divine Messianic King of Israel, come to set up the kingdom…" (A.B. Bruce).[12] Be assured, "*Twelve"* caught the attention of Jesus' hostile enemies!

> Christ was in effect appointing new leadership for the new covenant. And the apostles represented the new leaders of the true Israel of God – consisting of people who believe the gospel and were following the faith of Abraham (cf. Romans 4:16). In other words, the twelve apostles symbolized judgment against the twelve tribes of Old Testament Israel (MacArthur).[13]

Pragmatic Reasons for the Twelve

The appointments were also practical: Jesus needed companionship and sympathy, help in ministry and assurance that His work would continue after He was gone. The Twelve would "be with Him and that He might send (*apostello*) them out to preach, and to have power to heal sicknesses and to cast out demons" (Mark 3:14-15).

The Sermon on the Mount

Anxious people of every description gathered early at the mountain. Jesus approached and greeted the eager crowd, followed by the apostles and awe-struck disciples. The sick and afflicted, groaning and crying, surged forward as though drawn by some invisible magnet. Healings began to happen as "power went out from Him and healed them all" (Luke 6:19). Two passages written by Matthew, an eye-witness, described other scenes of what was now occurring.

> His fame went throughout all Syria; and they brought to Him all sick people who were afflicted with various diseases and torments, and those who were demon-possessed, epileptics, and paralytics; and He healed them. And great multitudes followed Him – from Galilee, and from Decapolis, Jerusalem, Judea, and beyond the Jordan (Matthew 4:24-25).

> Then great multitudes came to Him having with them those who were lame, blind, mute, maimed, and many others; and they laid them down at Jesus' feet, and He healed them. So the multitude marveled when they saw the mute speaking, the maimed made whole, the lame walking, and the blind seeing; and they glorified the God of Israel (Matthew 15:29-31).

Finally, all needs met, Jesus seated Himself and began teaching His followers, aware that the greater crowd also hung on every word. Miracles do have a way of whetting a person's appetite and attention!

The text of Matthew 5-7, called "Sermon on the Mount," is usually considered the same as a shorter version in Luke 6, called "Sermon on the Plain."[14] Of five major discourses in Matthew, this sermon is the most familiar and instructive, unveiling the heart of Jesus concerning the kingdom of God. Conceived during early manhood and a year of intense ministry and reflection – birthed in the night of prayer on the mountain -- the message, like a majestic, immortal song, still lingers with beauty and authority today. The presentation has been colorfully described as: "Jesus seated on a mountain, enunciating a new Torah, a greater than Moses addressing a new Israel" (Geroge R. Beasley-Murray).[15]

The Distinction of the Twelve

These twelve men, under God, changed the course of human history.

• They hold a unique and irreplaceable position in the Church historically, doctrinally and eschatologically (Matthew 19:28; Ephesians 2:20; Revelation 21:14).

• Their authority is timeless and universal in matters of ethics and doctrine. They, along with Paul, defined and determined what is normative Christianity (Galatians 1:8-9; 1 Timothy 1:3; 6:3-4; 1 Corinthians 5:6; 1 Peter 2:18; 3:1).

• They are the only bridge between Christ and us. Nearly all we know about Christ is mediated through them.

• Their words and practices form the heart of Christian tradition.[16]

Type of People Jesus Chose

The Apostles eventually became men of highest quality, but those sterling characteristics were not visible just yet: for now, the twelve men *were outstanding because they were not outstanding!*

We know the occupations of half these men: five were fishermen and one was a tax collector – ordinarily not the best qualifications for church leaders and theologians.

Younger Men

They were younger men, eager to serve their new-found Messiah. W. Phillip Keller shares this intriguing insight:

> Amongst the very first to follow Jesus were some of the ardent young fellows who had previously followed John. These were not old decrepit men with gray beards and bent backs, so often depicted in paintings and pictures of Jesus' disciples. Rather, they were rough, tough young men at the powerful peak of early manhood, either in their late teens or early twenties. Of all Jesus' disciples, only Peter was married, and even he could not have been much more than twenty-three or twenty-four.[17]

Introducing, proclaiming and demonstrating the kingdom of God required resolve, stamina and minimal encumbrances, truly a young man's cause. Like an assault team, they would establish beachheads for the kingdom. Jesus Himself was a hearty thirty, toughened by manual labor, experienced in business negotiation, and accustomed to leadership of a large family enterprise.

Socially Unimposing

Social standing did not disqualify candidates. The disciples were actually unimposing and insignificant. A. B. Bruce, in *The Training of the Twelve*, describes them as:

> a band of poor illiterate Galilean provincials, utterly devoid of social consequence, not likely to be chosen by one having supreme regard to prudential considerations…. The truth is, that Jesus was obliged to be content with fishermen, and publicans, and quondam zealots, for apostles. They were the best that could be had."[18]

We must agree with Bruce that if a priest, rabbi, rich man, government official or scholar would have given himself unreservedly to the service of the kingdom, the Master would have bid him welcome.

Consider the reaction of the rich young ruler to Jesus' invitation: "he went away sorrowful"; or, the supercilious outcry of the religious leaders: "Have any of the rulers or the Pharisees believed in Him?"

Devotion Required

Jesus preferred devoted men with no advantages over non-devoted men who had everything. His mission required hearts on fire, followers willing to risk their lives to proclaim Jesus the Messiah and Savior of the world. "[A] band of followers bound to Him by hooks of steel" (J. W. Shepard).[19]

Reasons "capable" men were eliminated and the Twelve chosen:

1. Not callable (trustworthy and believing),
2. Not moldable (open in their thinking),
3. Not persevering (determined and endurable),
4. Not common (relatable to ordinary people).
5. Not available (willing to follow now)

Family Associations

Family ties were not a problem. Jesus possibly chose three sets of brothers: (Peter and Andrew), (James and John), (James, Thaddaeus, and Simon). Debatable but possible, Matthew and James were brothers, and were cousins of Jesus. Also, Jude Thaddeus was the son of James the Great, which would make him a nephew of John.[20]

Most, if not all, were well known in the Galilean community. Jesus probably knew at least half as boys and later as adults in the marketplace. Each was familiar with Jesus' person and ministry, each was netted and drawn to discipleship by the master fisherman Himself.

Candidates for Change

Worldly wise men would surely have made better selections. Who would choose *Peter* (impulsive, fickle, unreliable), *James* (intolerant, ambitious), *John* (judgmental, ambitious), *Andrew* (self-effacing, modest), *Philip* (passive, curious), *Nathanael* (devotional), *Matthew* (vassal of Rome, despised by the average Jew), *Thomas* (skeptical, pessimistic), *James* (unknown), *Thaddaeus* (unknown), *Simon* (fiercely political), or *Judas* (treacherous, greedy)? Jesus chose the Twelve because He had confidence in *His Father's selections* and the ultimate outcomes.

> As the apostolic company was increased, it included some remarkable contrasts. The inclusion of a man who collected taxes for the Roman overlords or for their vassal Herod Antipas gave occasion for unfavourable [sic] comment. The inclusion of a Zealot, one of those who sought to hasten the divine kingdom by violence and gave no quarter to the Romans or their creatures, is equally noteworthy (F. F. Bruce).[21]

Consider two examples of *change*. Thomas was and is critically called "the doubter," but in striking contrast numerous Christians in Babylon, Syria, India and other places call him "Thomas the believer," a bold evangelist and church planter. Stan Fleming comments:

> Tradition says that he arrived in Malabar in southern India in 52 AD. He converted Hindu families and kings in various places. Thousands came

to the Lord. Thomas planted many churches....Syrian churches also celebrate Thomas' arrival to their country in 52. It could be that Thomas went first to Syria, then northern India and then to Malabar. The modern Christian community of southern India looks back to Thomas as the founding apostle. He changed society in that part of the world.... The miracles and missions ascribed to the apostle are too numerous to name.[22]

Also consider Matthew, a despised tax collector, a man disillusioned with the religious system and ensnared in the pursuit of ill-acquiring wealth. Jesus' abrupt call to "follow" Him brought immediate, irreversible response: Matthew left the tollbooth never to return. This was a dream come true, the answer to his sinful, empty life! Sharing his joy, he invited a unique group of friends to a farewell feast to hear for themselves the teachings of the Man who was his new master.

Matthew became a great scholar of the Jewish people, finally martyred violently in a distant land. His gospel is a masterpiece of spiritual insights, historical research and Hebrew Scripture. Using 40 direct quotations and 45 allusions, references, or indirect quotes from the Hebrew Scriptures, He presented Jesus as the Messiah, as only an eye-witness and serious historical scholar could.

A "Closed College"

The Twelve was a select (fixed) group of young, Jewish men driven by a precise commission for a limited sphere and time. More or less disciples could have been selected for the apostolic company, but Jesus deliberately chose twelve for the obvious association with the twelve tribes of Israel and the Messiah.

Listing of the Original Twelve Apostles
Jesus said, "they will send some of you to your death" (Luke 21:16).

Name	Description	Manner of Death
Group A: Lifelong friends, "tied together by common denominators."[23]		
1. Peter/Simon	Man of rock; steadfast, determined, zealous, overeager, impulsive, bold, outspoken. Mobile ministry in Palestine, Syria, Asia Minor, Rome – perhaps Babylon.[24] "…he was a long time in Britain where he converted many nations to the faith."[25] [?] Wrote two NT books. Considered the lead apostle and spokesman of the Twelve.	In Rome crucified upside down (felt unworthy to die in same way as Christ). Some said he was forced to watch his wife's crucifixion.[26]
2. Andrew	Peter's brother, one of the first to be called (John 1:35-40); introduced Peter to Christ. Less contentious and more thoughtful than his brother. A rather quiet, inconspicuous man, eager to follow and introduce others. "…tradition holds that he evangelized Scythia (the region North of the Black sea."[27] Apparently preached throughout Cappadocia, & Bythynia, regions forbidden to Paul.[28]	Crucified, probably in Patras, Greece (near Athens); tied to a St. Andrew's Cross (X) after severe whipping. He hung for two days, yet exhorted passersby's to accept Christ.
3. James	Fisherman; eldest son of Zebedee, a prominent community figure. He and John were "sons of thunder," indicating the brothers were passionate, reckless, zealous & ambitious; part of Jesus' inner circle. Supposedly the Roman officer guarding him was converted during James' trial, & knelt beside James to accept beheading as a Christian.	First martyr: decapitated in Jerusalem by Herod, 42-44 AD.
4. John	Fisherman, brother of James; beloved disciple. A member of Jesus' inner circle. Only eyewitness at the Cross. Author of five New Testament books; a	Exiled to Patmos; died of natural causes c 100 AD.

	"super apostle," who became pastor of the church at Ephesus. Constant companion of Peter in Acts 1-12, but no recorded words.	
Group B		
5. Philip	Earnest inquirer, a seeking heart, an administrative personality. MacArthur refers to him as a practical, "facts and figures guy," a pragmatist and cynic.[29] Ministered in Asia Minor, possibly Scythia (S. Russia) and even France.[30] Many came to Christ under his preaching. Killed 8 years after James.	Died suspended by the neck from a tall pillar;[31] buried at Hierapolis in Phrygia. No reliable records, but most say death by stoning.
6. Nathanael/ Bartholomew	Great moral excellence; guileless Israelite. Sincere of heart; "a true believer, openly confessing his faith in Christ and quick to have faith."[32] Went to Iran, India;[33] went into Armenia with Thaddaeus. Ministered some with Thomas. A missionary to Asia (present-day Turkey).	Skinned alive and beheaded,[34] or crucified upside down or flayed to death in Armenia.[35] No reliable record.
7. Thomas	The melancholy, a doubter. Actually more of a pessimist than doubter, an outspoken skeptic who wanted proof. Credited with taking the gospel to Babylon (modern Iran, Afghanistan and Pakistan) and Northern & Southern India. "Today, at least six [religious] communities in India still claim the link to Thomas...."[36]	Believed to have been martyred at Mylapore, near Madras in India – impaled by a lance while praying in a cave[37]
8. Matthew	The publican, called Levi. A tax collector, but also a gifted writer and scholar; a witness to people of authority. "...ministered in Parthia as well as Thomas and Bartholomew, but took the gospel further into India according to the historian, Metaphrastes."[38] Possibly also ministered in Ethiopia. Author of Gospel of Matthew.	Martyred and believed to be buried at Hierapolis. Slain at Nabadar, Ethiopia, with a halberd (hatchet)[39] Early traditions say was burned at the stake.[40]
Group C		
9. James	Son of Alphaeus; possibly James the Less and possibly the brother of	Killed by a blow to the head with a pole,

	Matthew. "reported to have preached in Spain, Britain and Ireland"[41] and in Ethiopia, the old term for Arabia.[42]	dealt him by Simon the Fuller.[43]
10. Judas (3 names: Lebbaeus, Thaddeus, Judas of James)	Possibly son of James the Great, grandson of Zebedee and nephew of John the apostle.[44] Eusebius tells that he healed Abgar, king of Edessa (in the region of Turkey).[45] Ministered in Assyria, Mesopotamia, Armenia. "He is also partly responsible for the gospel reaching China in that first century."[46]	Martyred with a heavy club,[47] probably in Syria.
11. Simon	The Zealot, a political malcontent.[48] He had belonged to a violent "outlaw political party" which hated Roman rule, using sabotage and assassination. We assume that Simon was a "man of fierce loyalties, amazing passion, courage and zeal."[49] According to Greek records he ministered in Egypt, Cyrene and Africa. "He preached all throughout Mauritania and Libya, and eventually went to Britain."[50]	Crucified and buried in Britain; "Sawn to death in a time of terrible persecution."[51]
12. Judas Iscariot	Man of Kerioth (Judea); the traitor and betrayer. He was in charge of the disciples' money box, and stole money from it regularly (John 12:6).	Hanged himself.

Note: *Other apostles were martyred:* **Mark** *was dragged to pieces through the streets of Alexandria;* **Luke** *was hanged by the neck in Greece;* **Jude** *was shot to death with arrows;* **Paul** *was beheaded in Rome by Nero's decree;* **Barnabas** *was stoned;* **Matthias** *was first stoned and then beheaded.* **James** *the Lord's brother was cast from the Temple pinnacle; discovering he had survived the fall, they beat him to death with fuller's clubs.[52]*

Four Listings of the Twelve

The lists (Matthew 10:2-4; Mark 3:16-19; Luke 6:14-16; Acts 1:13) each contain the names of the same twelve men, three groups of four names, the same person mentioned first in each group, and Peter mentioned first in each list; the order of arrangement varies somewhat.

The best known are the first group (all fishermen!), the lesser known the second and the least known the third (except for Judas

Iscariot). Peter, as the prominent character and leader, stands in the number one position; Judas Iscariot, the betrayer, is mentioned last. Peter, Philip and James appear to have been group leaders. The first four – Peter, Andrew, James, John – were the first summoned to full-time discipleship (Matthew 4:18, 21).

Requirements for Selection

The Twelve met specific qualifications, shown by the appointment of Matthias, the replacement of Judas Iscariot. Matthias met those *same* qualifications as Peter and the rest of the Eleven, being personally acquainted with the ministry of Jesus from the baptism of John till the Ascension.[53] Trained by Christ, Matthias participated in His activities and witnessed Jesus' miraculous ministry, the Resurrection, and Ascension.

> Therefore, one of the men who have been with us continuously throughout the time the Lord Yeshua traveled around among us, from the time Yochanan was immersing people until the day Yeshua was taken up from us – one of these must become a witness with us to his resurrection (Acts 1:21-22, JNT).

> Hebrews 2:2-3 says our salvation "was confirmed to us by those who heard Him, God also bearing witness both with signs and wonders, with various miracles and gifts of the Holy Spirit…"

Matthias replaced Judas to meet a specific, immediate need for a specific time; henceforth, however, the Church stopped filling vacancies for the other Twelve Apostles that died off, as James' martyrdom illustrates. David Cannistraci says in tribute to the Twelve:

> [T]hey shall remain preeminent among the entire apostolic company, and will possess a special prominence in the Kingdom that other [later] New Testament apostles will not achieve (see Matthew 19:28; Rev. 21:14)."[54]

Special Training

During the forty days following the Resurrection, Jesus showed convincing evidence to the Twelve, giving instruction about the kingdom of God (Acts 1:2-3). He showed His heart when

He said, "You are the ones who have stayed with me throughout my trials" (Luke 22:28, JNT).

Two significant statements appear in Matthew 13:11, 16: "...it has been given to you [the Twelve] to know the mysteries of the kingdom of heaven, but to them it has not been given....But blessed are your eyes for they see, and your ears for they hear."

Paul did not mention the Twelve in his writings, feeling perhaps that their function was for founding the Church, reaching the Jews and initiating evangelism. He did not discount their importance, concentrating rather on his own area of responsibility, mainly the Aegean and Galatian sectors of the Roman Empire.

The original Twelve eventually died out, but the idea of apostleship and its essential importance lived on. Christ sent out the original Twelve, later the churches – apostolic in the same spirit -- raised up additional apostles, and sent them forth (Acts 13:2; 14:14; Romans 16:7; 2 Corinthians 8:23).

Apostles of the Lamb

The Twelve bear the distinctive title, "Apostles of the Lamb" (Revelation 21:14), bringing to mind John 1:29:

> "The next day John [the Baptist] saw Jesus coming toward him, and said, 'Behold! The Lamb of God who takes away the sin of the world!'"

This identification linked Jesus with the Cross and the redemption of lost humanity, joining also the Twelve apostles with the beginning of His ministry. These Twelve eyewitnesses became the leading spokesmen for Christ's death, Resurrection and founding of the Church.

Pillar Apostles

Paul singled out three – James, Peter and John – as "pillars" of the Jewish Christian Church (Galatians 2:9).

Peter and John were part of Jesus' inner circle (Matthew 17:1; 16:18; 26:37; Mark 13:3; John 13:22-24; 21:20). The third member of that original group was James who later became the first martyr (Acts 12:2). Later, Jesus' brother James,[55] without recorded fanfare, replaced the martyr James in Jerusalem (Acts 12:17; 15:13; 21:18).[56] The Church recognized this later James as a "pillar apostle."

"Pillars" is a term that describes strong "chief supports" (mainstays, towers of strength) of Christ's Church. Usually, apostles are associated with foundations (Ephesians 2:20 and 3:5), but here Paul uses a different metaphor to emphasize oversight and heavy responsibility.

For about twelve years the Twelve stayed mainly in the Syro-Palestine region, but then scattered and ministered throughout the world,[57] both to Jews and Gentiles. David Cartledge says,

> In a special way the original apostles opened the way for others to follow. It is likely that their ministries actually brought the gospel to many nations....more than is commonly realized. [58]

Prototypical Apostles

Jesus' grand objective was to disciple *all* nations (Matthew 28:19), *starting with* the small Jewish nation of Israel. Jesus and the Twelve contacted every Jewish city and town and village in the small nation of Israel.

> Now it came to pass, afterward, that He went through every city and village, preaching and bringing the glad tidings of the kingdom of God. And the twelve were with him (Luke 8:1).[59]

This pilot program of one nation provided a prophetic forecast of worldwide kingdom expansion to all nations (which of course would necessitate more apostles, including Gentiles). The Twelve were prominent while missionary and church activity was focused on the Jews, but later their names (but not their activities) fade from the biblical record as Christianity spread through the Gentile world.

Luke's intent in writing Acts was not to give biographical sketches of the original apostles, but rather to show the triumphant expansion of the gospel -- growing like the unstoppable kudzu vine -- throughout the world. Luke's continuing interest in Paul was almost entirely in terms of the Gentile mission.[60]

Later Apostles

Jesus continued to supply the Church with apostles (Ephesians 4:11), but obviously *they did not, could not, or need not meet the original, specialized requirements of the Twelve* essential for the founding of the Church in a Jewish community -- or the unique qualifications of Paul who opened the Gentile world to the gospel.

The peripatetic Paul whose apostolic journeys took him throughout much of the Roman Empire, will be discussed in the next chapter. More than any other, Paul has given the Church the meaning of Jesus' Great Commission and apostleship.

The churches he founded and the disciples he shepherded are a magnificent testimony for "the apostolic consciousness" in the early Church.

Chapter 4 Endnotes

[1] Wilbur M. Smith, *Peloubet's Select Notes on the International Sunday School Lessons, 1942* (Boston: W. A. Wilde Company, 1941), p. 49.

[2] Based on four Passovers: AD 27, AD 28, AD 29, and AD 30 (Crucifixion).

[3] *The New Open Bible Study Edition* (Nashville: Thomas Nelson, 1990), p. 1168.

[4] See *Awaken the Dawn!* by the author for the amazing concept of early morning prayer described in Isaiah 50:4-6.

[5] Dick Stark, "Prayer – A Basic Necessity," Faith Temple, church Sunday bulletin (4-26-09), Alexander City, AL, p. 2.

[6] Ibid.

[7] John MacArthur, *Twelve Ordinary Men* (Nashville, TN: Thomas Nelson, 2002), p. 15.

[8] An eight-to-ten hour prayer vigil, or an all-night time of prayer, or several days of fasting and prayer should not seem strange. Jesus considered such praying vital to spiritual life, and effective ministers still follow His example.

[9] Alfred Edersheim, "we must forego all hope of arriving at any certain conclusion." *The Life and Times of Jesus the Messiah,* Vol. 1 (Grand Rapids: Eerdmans, 1950), p. 522. p. 521.

[10] Not stated but assumed, because this procedure was common to the Jews and Church (Acts 6:6; 8:17; 1 Timothy 4:14; 2 Timothy 1:6; Hebrews 6:2).

[11] Smith, p. 51.

[12] A. B. Bruce, *The Training of the Twelve* (Grand Rapids: Kregel Publications, 1971 [reprint from the 4th revised ed., 1894]), pp. 6-7.

[13] MacArthur, p. 19.

[14] Matthew 5:1-7:29 and Luke 6:17-49 have a remarkable similarity: the same flow of thought, although Luke's account more abbreviated.

[15] George R. Beasley-Murray, *Jesus and the Last Days* (Peabody, MASS: Hendrickson Publishers, 1993), p. 386.

[16] Four points from a D.Min. class at Oral Roberts University in 2006.

[17] W. Phillip Keller, *Rabboni...Which Is To Say Master* (Old Tappan, NJ: Fleming H. Revell Company, 1977), p. 84.

[18] A. B. Bruce, p, 37.

[19] J. W. Shepard, *The Christ of the Gospels* (Grand Rapids: Eerdmans, 1939), p. 170.

[20] William Steuart McBirnie, *The Search for the Twelve Apostles* (Wheaton, IL: Tyndale House, 1978), p. 196. See chapters 10 and 11 for information about Matthew/James.

[21] F. F. Bruce, *The Spreading Flame, Vol. 1* (Grand Rapids: Eerdmans, 1973), p. 39.

[22] Stan Fleming, "Thomas: From Doubter to World Changer," *Gate Breaker News* (Vol. 2, Issue 1, Jan. 2008): 4.

[23] MacArthur, p. 31.

[24] McBirnie : "The tradition of the eastern churches is united that he [Peter] did indeed go to Babylon, from which he wrote his first epistle." p. 57.

[25] Quote from William Cave, *Antiquities Apostolicae*, p. 45, taken from David Cartledge, *The Apostolic Revolution: The Restoration of Apostles and Prophets in the Assemblies of God in Australia* (Chester Hill, NSW, Australia: Paraclete Institute, 2000), p. 256.

[26] Eusebius cites Clement. *Ecclesiastical History*, 3:1, 30.

[27] Scheidler, *Apostles,* p. 40.

[28] Acts 16:6-7. See McBirnie, pp. 800-86.

[29] MacArthur, p. 121.

[30] McBirnie, chapter 7.

[31] Lockyer, p. 262

[32] MacArthur, chapter 7.

[33] Cartledge, p. 257.

[34] David Cannistraci, *Apostles and the Emerging Apostolic Movement* (Ventura, CA: Regal, 1996), p. 110. McBirnie, p. 140.

[35] Lockyer, p. 250.

[36] "India's Apostle," *Christian History & Biography,* 85 (Summer 2005): p. 3.

[37] McBirnie, p. 168d. Also, Fleming, pp. 1 & 4.

[38] Cave, *Antiquities,* p. 189, as stated by Cartledge, p. 257.

[39] Lockyer, p. 262.

[40] MacArthur, p. 157.

[41] Cartledge, p. 256. Lockyer, p. 250.

[42] Lockyer, p. 250.

[43] Ibid, p. 261.

[44] McBirnie, p. 196.

[45] Eusebius, *Ecclesiastical History* 1.13.5.

[46] Scheidler, p. 41.

[47] Lockyer, p. 262.

[48] A. B. Bruce, pp. 34-35.

[49] MacArthur, p. 177.

[50] Cartledge, Ibid.

[51] Lockyer, p. 262.

[52] Ibid., p. 251.

[53] John 1:35-51 introduces first disciples; at least two were disciples of John the Baptist.

[54]Cannistraci, p. 58.

[55] Herman N. Ridderbos: "...it is not strange at all that James, the brother of the Lord, to whom Jesus appeared after his resurrection, should here be reckoned alongside of Peter among the apostles." *The Epistle of Paul to the Churches of Galatia (TNICNT)*, (Grand Rapids: Eerdmans, 1979 [1953]), p. 69.

[56] James, Jesus' brother, was raised in the same household with Jesus. Nearly thirty years of close association gave him a unique relationship, insight and experience.

[57] "A source of great antiquity [Acts of the Holy Apostle Thomas] says the apostles divided up the regions of the world to evangelize." Fleming, Ibid.

[58] Cartledge, p. 255.

[59] George M. Lamsa, expert on Palestine and the Aramaic language, says all the cities of Palestine [at that time] could be covered in a few months. *Gospel Light* (Philadelphia: A. J. Holman, 1936), pp. 79-81. These references seem to confirm Lamsa's thesis: Matthew 4:23, 25; 9:35; 11:1; Luke 8:1, 4; 9:6, 56; 10:1; 13:22.

[60] Concept explained by Gordon Fee and Douglas Stuart in *How to Read the Bible for All Its Worth* (Grand Rapids: Zondervan, 1993), Chapter 6.

Chapter 5
Paul, Apostle Extraordinary

In This Chapter

- *The prisoner of Rome, visited by an angel, shipwrecked!*
- *Did Roman citizenship help Paul?*
- *Terrible Terminator stopped dead in his tracks by Merciful Messiah*
- *Impressive portfolio: Paul's fourteen-point resume*

The storm raged, and the Alexandrian freighter tossed and rolled, fighting to stay afloat. The violent, unrelenting wind and rain pummeled the groaning merchant ship and the 276 persons aboard. The crew and passengers were in despair. An eyewitness described the scene: "all hope that we would be saved was finally given up."

The ship was headed for Italy, presumably with a cargo of wheat from Egypt, a major food supplier for the impoverished Roman populace. The ship also carried human cargo: prisoners of Rome under the sharp surveillance of Julius the centurion. Most of the prisoners were condemned to death and would end up in the Roman arena. His biggest concern was a certain Jew, who as a citizen of Rome, had by-passed the lower courts of Judea and appealed for an audience with Caesar to vindicate his innocence: he must deliver this prisoner.

In Myra, a city of Lycia, Julius had shifted his charges from a smaller, coastal vessel to the more substantial grain carrier that could better stand the rigor of inclement weather. The ship's captain and the Centurion each had a personal reason for wishing quick passage (one monetary, the other professional), so the danger of sailing so late in the season was disregarded.

The winds were becoming contrary, the gentle southwester (the prevailing wind of summer) was giving way to stronger winds, and the ship detoured southward, laboring along the southern flank of Crete seeking any possible refuge. Taking temporary shelter at the small island of Clauda, the sailors lashed stout ropes around the hull to keep the boat from breaking apart, a process known as frapping.

Fearing the inescapable suction of the Syrtis Sands (off the African coast), they struck sail and were driven out into the Adria Sea (central Mediterranean) before the relentless typhoon-strength storm. The tackle was thrown overboard to lighten the tempest-tossed ship. Finally, after two weeks of merciless mauling, they discovered from their soundings that land was near. Jettisoning the grain, releasing the anchors to the sea, and hoisting the mainsail to the wind, they made for shore. Suddenly, the ship jolted . . . she had struck a sandbar and stuck fast . . . now her stern was smashed apart by the pounding surf. All hands aboard, frightened and fearful, swam desperately for the shore, some clinging to parts of the broken ship.

Thankfully, in the dark fury of the previous night, an angel of the Lord brought a reassuring message to the Jewish prisoner known as Paul the Apostle: *"Do not be afraid, Paul; you must be brought before Caesar; and indeed God has granted you all those who sail with you."*

Yes, Paul and his exhausted friends did reach the beach at Malta, and later Julius escorted them on to Rome. Having been rushed through life-threatening conditions, Paul now must patiently wait several years for trial, a fortuitous situation for a zealous soul winner!

This astounding adventure (Acts 27) closes Luke's written record, capturing symbolically Paul's whole, adventurous, dedicated life: surrounded by violence, sustained by God's hand, and blessed with grace to help others.[1]

The Benchmark Apostle

Paul's life presents the greatest example of apostleship the world has ever known -- a true "benchmark" by which others may be measured or judged. And, we might add, the churches he founded could also be considered benchmarks for the churches of succeeding generations. One of the first apostles commissioned outside of the Twelve, Paul was possibly preceded only by James, the brother of Jesus (Acts 12:17). He was an "Ascension gift apostle" – that is, ordained by the Lord Jesus after His Ascension back to heaven.

Paul would not have qualified for the original Twelve since he had not been a disciple during Jesus' earthly ministry, and probably did not even know Him. Later, Paul did come to know what Jesus did and said, spending quality time in close fellowship with other disciples, especially Peter ("I went up to Jerusalem to see Peter, and remained with him fifteen days," Galatians 1:18).

Paul articulated the gospel as well as any of the Twelve. As an example, while preaching at Antioch of Pisidia, he reviewed Jesus' ministry in an apostolic manner (Acts 13:23-41). Notice his quotation from Psalm 16:10, used by Peter on the day of Pentecost: "You will not allow Your Holy One to see corruption," Acts 13:35.

Was Paul the Last Apostle?

Some contend that Paul was the last apostle[2] and there will be no more. This is like arguing that George Washington our first president was such a towering leader and person, no one could replace him. Our young nation urgently required a continuing presidency -- even if available candidates felt below Washington's stature. Other brilliant men of that day, such as Adams and Jefferson, responded and served succeeding generations well, although confessing inferiority to Washington.

Similarly, great apostles have served well since Paul, even while feeling inferior to him. Nowhere in Scripture are we told there would only be twelve apostles, only that The Twelve would be given special recognition. Paul opened the door for more apostles and the formation of "apostolic" local churches.

Many have called Paul the "Apostle Extraordinary," a well-earned title and above controversy. Colin Brown says: "the picture that Acts paints is not that Paul was not an apostle, but that he was an apostle extraordinary...."[3] His performance is so overpowering that we all gauge apostleship by his Olympic-type record. Rengstorf explains the interest focused on Paul's life and ministry:

Paul is the classical representative of the apostolate in the NT. He is the only apostle who is to some extent known to us in his apostolic position; the others leave us no direct information concerning the manner of their apostolate. The reason is to be found partly in his special position in relation to the other *apostoloi* and partly in the extraordinary range of his activity.[4]

Paul's Background

Although thoroughly Jewish, Paul was born in the "Free City" of Tarsus, the capital of Cilicia in southeast Asia Minor, a city made famous by Anthony's meeting with Cleopatra.[5] Automatic Roman citizenship was granted because his family lived in Tarsus ("I was born a citizen," Acts 22:28), and was possibly among the social elite.[6] W. M. Ramsay, noted authority of that time, says:

> According to the law of his country, he was first of all a Roman citizen. That character superseded all others before the law and in the general opinion of society; and place him amid the aristocracy of any provincial town. In the first century, when the citizenship was still jealously guarded, the civitas may be taken as a proof that his family was one of distinction and at least moderate wealth.... He was not merely a person born in Tarsus, owing to the accident of his family being there: he had a citizen's rights in Tarsus....It is probable, but not certain, that the family had been planted in Tarsus with full rights as part of a colony settled there by one of the Seleucid kings in order to strengthen their hold on the city.[7]

Named Saul and home-trained to be a strict Jew, Paul grew as a child in one of the most Hellenized cities of the Empire. Along with religious training, he (like other Jewish boys) learned a trade, in his case tent making and weaving. G. G. Findlay shares this interesting sidelight on Tarsus:

> Tarsus was a centre for the manufacture of *cilicium*, the coarse goats' hair fabric of the district, famed for its durability, of which shoes, mats, and coverings of all kinds were made; and the boy Saul was taught this local handicraft. An industry everywhere in demand, this craft supplied him in his wandering apostleship with a means of livelihood, laborious and irksome enough, but adequate for his scanty needs (1 Th 2:9, 2 Th 3:8-10, 1 Cor 9:6-18 etc.).[8]

Saul was sent or brought to Jerusalem in his youth by his parents (Acts 22:3; 26:4), possibly "to be immunized against the infection of the Hellenistic world..." (F. F. Bruce).[9] He received religious training from the famous Rabbi Gamaliel (Acts 5:34), becoming a dedicated Pharisee (Acts 26:5).

Departing from the mild policy of his mentor, Saul became a vehement leader in stamping out the heresy of Christianity. The young Pharisee quickly realized that Jewish legalism and Christian grace were on a collision course. This new sect simply could not co-exist within the Jewish community! The Christians affirmed Jesus as the predicted Messiah. "Totally impossible!" would be Saul's response.

Christians proclaimed a New Covenant inaugurated by Jesus' death on the Cross. Saul's reply would be: "Was it not written, 'Cursed is everyone who hangs on a tree' (Deuteronomy 21:21; Galatians 3:13), so how could he be the Messiah?" Irreconcilable differences with momentous consequences dictated the extermination of the Jesus-people! Thus, a monster was birthed.

Saul the Terminator

Saul's terrible persecution is generally minimalized. It began when Saul, "breathing threats and murder against the disciples," an expression picturing a war-horse sniffing the battle from afar, went to gain official endorsement from the high priest (Acts 9:1). Nine passages describe this tragic period.

> [I]t is only when we weigh the terrible significance of the expressions used, that we feel the load of remorse which must have lain upon him [Paul] and the taunts to which he was liable from malignant enemies" (Frank J. Goodman).[10]

The extreme expression, "he was ravaging" the church (Galatians 1:13), was the same terminology in the *LXX* and classical Greek used to describe the uprooting of a vineyard by wild boars. Paul, in his defense before King Agrippa, described himself as "exceedingly enraged" against the Christians (Acts 26:11).

How Paul "Ravaged" the Church	
Reference	Activity
1. Acts 7:58; 8:1	Involved in and consented to the death of Stephen, the first martyr.
2. Acts 8:3-4	Made havoc of the church, committed people to prison.
3. Acts 22:4-5	Bound, imprisoned and persecuted to death.
4. Acts 22:19	Imprisoned and beat people in every synagogue.
5. Acts 26:9-11	Shut people up in prison, put them to death with his approval, often punished and compelled people to blaspheme, took persecution to other strange cities.
6. 1 Corinthians 15:9	Persecuted the Church of God.
7. Galatians 1:13, 22-24	Persecuted beyond measure, wasted the church, destroyed the faith.
8. Philippians 3:6	Persecuted the church
9. 1 Timothy 1:3	Blasphemed, persecuted and violently arrogant.

Hastening to Damascus (150 miles northeast of Jerusalem) to round up run-away Christian Jews, Saul was tackled and converted by the resurrected Jesus. Dazzling light – brighter than the noonday Syrian sun -- struck the proud Pharisee, who fell helplessly to the ground. Jesus spoke: "Saul, Saul, why are you persecuting Me?" (Acts 9:4) ... "I am Jesus of Nazareth, whom you are persecuting" (Acts 22:8).

At that electrifying moment Saul realized the identity of both Jesus and "the Church": the Messiah was saying, "If you hurt one of My followers, you hurt Me!" Jesus and His people are *one body! Christ is head and Christians are the members of His one body.* This revelation became a guiding light for Paul.

Like a stunned child, blind Saul was hand-led into Damascus, spending three days in prayer and sightlessness. At long last, Ananias, a godly Jewish Christian, was divinely sent to Saul. Addressing the stricken man as "Brother Saul" (indicating Saul's conversion), Ananias laid his hands on him and prayed. Instantly healed of blindness, Saul saw the face of Ananias, *Jesus made tangible in the face of one of His followers!*

Saul was baptized in water and filled with the Holy Spirit. The humbled Pharisee was enfolded by his new family, the local body of believers ("Saul spent some days with the disciples at Damascus," Acts 9:19) -- the very people he had come to arrest!

"Immediately he preached the Christ in the synagogues, that He is the Son of God" (Acts 9:20), and began seeking God and searching the Scriptures (Galatians 1:11-17).

> The transformation of the most dangerous persecutor into the most successful promoter of Christianity is nothing less than a miracle of divine grace (Philip Schaff).[11]

Summary of Paul's Ministry

Paul was one of history's most influential and inspiring men. The following fourteen-point summary cannot do justice to his accomplishments.

Paul Was Commissioned by the Lord, Not the Twelve

Summoned by Jesus Himself,[12] Paul regarded his authority and status comparable to that of the Twelve.

> "in nothing was I behind the most eminent apostles..." 2 Corinthians 12:11.

He actually felt his service and ministry was greater than the Twelve.

> I am the least of the apostles...but by the grace of God I am what I am, and His grace toward me was not in vain; but I labored more abundantly than they all..." (1 Corinthians 15:9-10).

Paul argued fervently that his apostleship was not initiated by the Twelve or dependent on their approval.

> I did not confer with flesh and blood, nor did I go up to Jerusalem to those who were apostles before me..." (Galatians 1:16-17).

> Paul definitely claims that his apostleship was not something which had come to him from any man, or school, or group of church officers, or was something conceived in his own mind, but was a lofty privilege and distinction conferred upon him "through the will of God" (Wilbur Smith).[13]

While conversing with King Agrippa, Paul said he was divinely called to be "a minister and witness both of the things which you have seen and of the things which I will yet reveal to you" (Acts 26:16).

Paul Was Never Considered One of the Twelve

He claimed appointment *after* the Twelve, giving no indication he was or would be the only post-Twelve apostle called (Acts 26:16-18; 1 Corinthians 15:11; Galatians 1:1). In fact, according to his writings, Paul believe there would be more called (1 Corinthians 12:28; Ephesians 3:20; 4:11).

On occasion he felt less significant than the Twelve, remembering his "ravaging" of the Church. Paul did not replace Judas as the 12th apostle; this is not taught in the Bible.

Paul Was Given an Assignment

• God's primary commission for Paul was primarily to reach Gentiles, kings and Caesar, although he would also reach Israelites.

> [H]e is a chosen vessel of Mine to bear My name before Gentiles, kings, and the children of Israel. (Acts 9:15; 28:17).
>
> [F]or He who worked effectively in Peter for the apostleship to the circumcised also worked effectively in me toward the Gentiles, Galatians 2:7. [14]
>
> [An] apostle to the Gentiles" (Romans 11:13). Also, Acts 22:21; 23:11; 27:24; 28:2

Paul's first stop in heathen cities was a visit to the local synagogue (a procedure explained later), where he contacted both Jews and Gentile "God-fearers."

• No person, was off limits. Paul's commission included "all men" (Acts 22:15), everyone a candidate, "a minister and a witness" (Acts 26:16) to all.

Paul's Calling Confirmed by Miraculous Signs and Convincing Proofs

Highlight of the Jerusalem Council (Acts 15) was the ringing testimony of God's missionary-apostles, Barnabas and Paul; their mind-boggling account declared that signs and wonders opened the door to the heathen. Verse 12 in *The Message* graphically describes the scene:

> There was dead silence. No one said a word. With the room quiet, Barnabas and Paul reported matter-of-factly on the miracles and wonders God had done among the other nations through their ministry. The silence deepened; you could hear a pin drop.

Romans 15:19: "in mighty signs and wonders, by the power of the Spirit of God ... I have fully preached the gospel of Christ."[15] Paul broke the curses of witchcraft (Acts 13:8-11; 16:16-18), cast out evil spirits (Acts 19:12), and proclaimed the Good News to half the Roman Empire.

> For our gospel did not come to you in word only, but also in power, and in the Holy Spirit and in much assurance, as you know what kind of men we were among you for your sake (1 Thessalonians 1:5).

Paul Was Driven by an Aching Remorse
He regretted his persecution, tormenting and hounding of Christians (p. 85).

Paul Suffered Much
Paul was "an ambassador in chains," often in prison (2 Timothy 1:8; 2:9), enduring much suffering (Acts 9:16; 2 Corinthians 11; 12; 2 Timothy 3:11). He endured such oppression because of his remorse for the persecution he inflicted upon the people of God. He considered his longsuffering to be "a pattern" for other Christians (1 Timothy 1:16).

The Physical Sufferings of Paul	
Activity	**References**
Plotted against	Acts 9:23, 29; 20:3; 21:30; 23:10, 12; 25:3
Run out of town numerous times	Acts 10:25, 30; 13:50; 14:6,19; 16:39; 17:10, 14; 20:1
Scourged, beaten, stoned and left for dead	Acts 14:19-20
Subjected to Satanic pressure	1 Thessalonians 2:18

Beaten & jailed at Philippi	Acts 16:19-24
Ridiculed	Acts 19:16-18; 26:24
Falsely accused	Acts 21:21, 28; 24:5-9
Subjected to violent storms at sea	Acts 27:14-20; 2 Corinthians 11:25
Bitten by a deadly serpent	Acts 28:3, 4
Forsaken by all	2 Timothy 4:10, 16
Imprisoned often	2 Corinthians 6:4, 5; 11:23-27; Colossians 4:10
Chained	Acts 12:7; 16:26-27; 26:29; 28:20; Ephesians 3:1-13; 4:1; 6:20; Philippians 1:7, 13, 16; Colossians 4:18; 2 Timothy 2:9
Constantly in danger	2 Corinthians 4:8-11; 11:26

Paul also bore rejection by church people (2 Timothy 4:9-18), religious leaders (Acts 23, 24), and Roman authorities (Acts 25). His biggest concern, however, was the spiritual care of the churches: "My little children, for whom I labor in birth again until Christ is formed in you" (Galatians 4:19). Paul told the Ephesian elders, "…remember that for three years I did not cease to warn everyone night and day with tears" (Acts 20:31).

Paul Was Born a Roman Citizen

Being a Roman citizen, Paul was "entitled to all the rights and privileges which Roman law provided" (F. F. Bruce).[16]

This included not being bound and imprisoned without trial, a privilege Paul only claimed when it served his objectives, as at Philippi:

> 'They have beaten us openly, uncondemned Romans, and have thrown us into prison. And now do they put us out secretly? No indeed! Let them come themselves and get us out.' And the officers told these words to the magistrates, and they were afraid when they heard that they were Romans (Acts 17:37-38).

At another time Claudius Lysias, Commander of the Jerusalem Garrison, snatched Paul from the clutches of a rioting mob of Jewish agitators. Paul *twice* told the Commander that he was a Roman (Acts 21:39 and 22:25-28), but during the riot either Claudius forgot or did not believe him. Finally, he had Paul transported under heavy guard to the Roman Garrison at Caesarea.

Claudius' letter to Felix, the governor, stated: "I rescued him, having learned that he was a Roman" (Acts 23:27).

Governor Festus, appointed two years later, quickly discovered he had inherited no ordinary prisoner. The burning hatred of the Jewish leaders who came to present indictment was obvious. Realizing his life was in jeopardy and knowing he must reach Rome ("the Lord ... said ....'you must also bear witness at Rome,'" Acts 23:11), Paul defiantly claimed the highest benefit of Roman citizenship: he shouted, *"I appeal to Caesar!"* To which Festus, with relief, retorted: "To Caesar you shall go!" (Acts 25:11-12).

Paul Was A Pharisee

Paul was a Pharisee and the son of a Pharisee (Acts 23:6), trained by Rabbi Gamaliel ("according to the strictness of our fathers' law," Acts 22:3; also 26:4).

> If anyone else thinks he may have confidence in the flesh, I more so: circumcised the eighth day...a Hebrew of the Hebrews; concerning the law, a Pharisee...concerning the righteousness which is in the law, blameless" (Philippians 3:4-5).

Before conversion, Paul led the lifestyle of a zealous, Pharisee (Acts 26:5; 2 Corinthians 11:22). He also lived a celibate life (1 Corinthians 7:7-8; 9:5).

> We may safely say that if Saul had been less of a Jew Paul the apostle would have been less bold and independent. His work would have been more superficial and his mind less unfettered. God did not choose a heathen to be the apostle of the heathen; for he might have been ensnared by the traditions of Judaism, by its priestly hierarchy and the splendors of its worship, as indeed it happened with the Church of the second century. On the contrary, God chose a Pharisee. *But this Pharisee had the most complete experience of the emptiness of external ceremonies and the crushing yoke of the law. There was no fear that he would ever look back, that he would be tempted to set up again what the grace of God had just overthrown, Gal 2:18. Judaism was wholly vanquished in his soul, for it was wholly displaced* (Sabatier; emphasis added).[17]

Paul Was Compelled to Write

Obsessed with propagating his message, Paul authored thirteen New Testament epistles and perhaps Hebrews. Letter writing was a vital communication tool -- clarifying, recalling, reinforcing and even commanding. The written words carried authority in his physical absence. Paul "viewed his letters as charged with apostolic 'power'" and "took his letters to be an extension of his person" (Martin). [18]

> [I]f anyone does not obey our word in this epistle, note that person and do not keep company with him…(2 Thessalonians 3:14).

Paul understood divine mysteries (Ephesians 3:9; 5:32; Colossians 1:26-27; 1 Timothy 1:16), saw revelations (2 Corinthians 12; Galatians 1:12; 2:2) and with concern observed the weaknesses and strengths of the local churches. Limited by physical contact, Paul launched missives and missionaries like flaming missiles to the scattered churches to answer their questions and establish their faith. Paul understood the enduring, impacting power of the printed page.

Peter commented, "…as also our beloved brother Paul, according to the wisdom given to him, has written to you, as also in all his epistles…" (2 Peter 3:15-16). Without these writings, the Church would be a house without bread.

Paul Was an Architect

Paul had a consuming passion for the building and function of local churches, much like a secular architect who plans buildings in detail, exercising careful supervision over their construction. The Greek word *architekton* (from which we get architect) is actually used in 1 Corinthians 3:10:

> As a skilled architect, in accordance with God's unmerited favor given to me, I laid a foundation, and now another is building upon it. But every builder must be careful how he builds upon it; for no one can lay any other foundation than the one that is laid, that is, Jesus Christ Himself (Williams Translation).

> *Note: Architekton* is also translated, "wise master builder" (NAS, NKJ) and "expert builder" (NIV, NLT, NCV, CEV).

The missionary journeys of this itinerant apostle opened the Gentile world to the gospel of grace. Many heathen were converted and gathered into local churches where they received teaching about beliefs and behavior. Paul shared his practical insights by epistles and in person. Our knowledge about spiritual gifts, the Second Coming, church structure, etc., would be sadly lacking without his instruction. One great accomplishment was that he exalted the status of women and opened the door for them to minister.[19]

Paul Was an Example of Industriousness

Paul sometimes worked to support himself, endeavoring to keep from being a burden to others (Acts 18:3; 20:34; 1 Corinthians 4:12; 1 Thessalonians 2:9; 2 Thessalonians 3:8). He believed "if you don't work, you don't eat." He modeled this principle before the churches, "in order that it might be clear to everyone that he was not to be classified with traveling philosophers whose aims and interests were often selfish" (Hendriksen and Kistemaker).[20]

Paul Was a Person of Frequent Prayer

The bottom-line secret of Paul's life and ministry was dynamic prayer ("continuing steadfastly in prayer," Romans 12:12). He walked and talked with the Lord, obedient to heaven's wishes, learning the marvelous secret of boldly coming to the throne of grace. He waited on God, depended on God, was directed by God and expected God to perform His promises and bless His servants. Prayer and communion was an on-going, ever-present experience – and included much thanksgiving (Philippians 4:6). He learned not only to bring his personal requests, but also to pray in the Spirit:

> Praying always with all prayer and supplication in the Spirit, being watchful to this end with all perseverance and supplication for all the saints... (Ephesians 6:28).[21]

Paul Had a Great Concern for the Poor

Paul brilliantly achieved a crowning act of organization that would benefit the poor and needy -- and also bring a closer bond between the Jewish church of Jerusalem and his beloved Gentile churches in four Roman provinces (Galatia, Asia, Macedonia and Achaia). To relieve famine conditions in Jerusalem, Paul used his influence to raise funds from his Gentile churches to alleviate the Jewish suffering.

God Himself initiated this tradition of care in the Pauline churches when he sent the prophet Agabus to the neophyte Antioch church where Barnabas and Saul (Paul) were teaching. A remarkable prediction of famine in Jerusalem was given and immediately accepted as a divine directive by all (because of the prophet's integrity, track record and witness of the Spirit).

> During this time some prophets came down from Jerusalem to Antioch. One of them, named Agabus, stood up and through the Spirit predicted that a severe famine would spread over the entire Roman world. (This happened during the reign of Claudius.) 'The disciples, as each one was able, decided to provide help for the believers living in Judea. This they did, sending their gift to the elders by Barnabas and Saul (Acts 11:27-29, NIV).

This project, then and at later times, became a strong concern to Paul and his associates, and was considered a vital part of "a true ministry" (Acts 21:29; 12:25; 20:24; 21:19). The apostles acted as administrators, no small task in itself, but they also gathered collections, carried money and made the hazardous journey to Jerusalem. We can assume they did more than hand out money to starving people or dump sacks of coins in the elders' laps; they probably arranged for and acquired food and then distributed it, staying in Jerusalem through the time of need, acting as providers and distributors – seizing the opportunity to encourage and comfort the distressed, demonstrating that Jews and Gentiles together made up the one body of Christ. "Noble work nobly done." [22] Romans 15:25-28; 2 Corinthians 8 and 9; Galatians 2:10.

Paul Wrote His Own Epitaph

Grave markings and tomb inscriptions often indicate the greatness of a person; however, when the Romans disposed of Paul's decapitated body, they probably recorded nothing. If a grave marking had been prepared by his beloved Timothy, the epitaph would probably read like 2 Timothy 4:7:

> *"Paul, the Apostle, He fought the good fight, He finished the race, He kept the faith"*

These three grand thoughts, amply enlarged in Paul's writings, clearly declared an active, Spirit-filled life. Determined to win souls to Christ and wrest them from the control of satanic power, Paul knew the ministry was a continual struggle with darkness that would finally be won.

Track coaches say, "Regardless, finish the race!" This Paul did, he lived for Christ and kept the faith of the gospel to the very end (1 Corinthians 9:24; Acts 20:24).

Paul's Threefold Commission

His ministry contained three assignments: "I was appointed a *preacher*, an *apostle*, and a *teacher* of the Gentiles" (2 Timothy 1:11 and 1 Timothy 2:7). "Appointed" = "placed" or "set" into ministry (1 Corinthians 12:28). "He had not *forced* his way to the front, but had been *called* to office [and set in] by no one less than God Himself (Hendriksen)"[23]

A Preacher

"Preacher" translates the Greek term *keryx*:

> A *herald, a messenger* vested with public authority, who conveyed the official messages of kings, magistrates, princes, military commanders, or who gave a public summons or demand…(Thayer).[24]

A "herald" was like the loudspeaker system at public events, as at athletic games where competitors' names and countries were called out. Wuest suggests the imperious meaning:

[W]as used of the imperial herald, spokesman of Caesar Augustus, who when entering a town as a representative of the Emperor would make a public proclamation of the Emperor's message with such formality, gravity, and authority as must be heeded and obeyed.[25]

Paul's motto was to "preach the word" (2 Timothy 4:2). This means proclaim the Gospel of Jesus Christ like "a king's herald," forgetting personal opinions or ideas of others. "Preach" did not mean the delivery of some inconsequential moral or religious discourse; in fact, just the opposite was true.

The word employed in the original means *proclaim* (cf. Matt. 10:27); literally, herald, make known officially and publicly a matter of great significance....According to Scripture … 'heralding' or 'preaching' is generally the divinely authorized proclamation of the message of God to men. It is the exercise of ambassadorship (Hendriksen).[26]

Aggressive ministry snatched converts from and opened conflict with: the Jewish community, Hebrew theologians, Roman authorities, idol makers, craftsmen in the marketplace, Greek philosophers at the Acropolis, pagan crowds and the followers of false religions. Slaves and freemen, male and female, Romans and Greeks, rich and poor – *every person was a candidate for the heavenly Kingdom and the Church of Jesus Christ.* The brief stay in Athens illustrates Paul's busyness.

He reasoned in the synagogue with the Jews and with the Gentile worshipers, and in the market-place daily with those who happened to be there (Acts 17:17).

He topped it all off by challenging Epicurean and Stoic philosophers in the Areopagus!

Paul declared Jesus as Lord, did "the work of an evangelist" (2 Timothy 4:5), and zealously trumpeted the Good News -- especially when pioneering virgin territory where no Christian witness existed (Romans 15:20). Healings and miracles confirmed his announcement of the kingdom of God. Churches were planted in every possible community so that not one person would miss the good news of Jesus Christ.

This astounding summary is given in Romans 15:18-19 (emphasis added):

> For I will not dare to speak of any of those things which Christ has not accomplished through me, in word and deed, to make the Gentiles obedient – in mighty signs and wonders, by the power of the Spirit of God, *so that from Jerusalem and round about to Illyricum I have fully preached the gospel of Christ.*

Illyricum was a Roman province on the east side of the Adriatic Sea, later called Yugoslavia. The distance from Jerusalem to Illyricum was a span of more than 1,400 miles, a daunting challenge when transportation was slow, travel dangerous, and much of the distance negotiated by walking. Some calculate that Paul's three missionary tours occupied about ten years and the distance covered was about 8,100 miles. He preached everywhere!

> Ephesians 3:8 – "To me...this grace was given, that I should preach among the Gentiles the unsearchable riches of Christ, and to make all people see what is the fellowship of the mystery...." Also, Acts 9:20; 1 Corinthians 1:17; Galatians 1:15; Colossians 1:28.

An Apostle

An ambassador and strategist, Paul planted churches in Roman colonies, joyfully welcoming Jews and Gentiles alike (Romans 10:12; Galatians 3:28; Colossians 3:11). He worked, preached and prayed until cultures were penetrated and demonic forces driven back. F. F. Bruce commented:

> No one could read the Acts without realizing that Paul was a genuine apostle of Christ, independently commissioned by Him, and proving by the "signs of an apostle" which accompanied his ministry the truth of his claim that he came in no way behind "the very chiefest apostles" (II Cor. 12:11).[27]

Paul's Strategy. Going first to the Jewish communities in Roman cities was a practical way to reach those most receptive to God's Word ("to the Jew first and also the Greeks," Romans 1:16; 2:9-10). Some Jews responded, but the Gentile God-fearers (the piously disposed men and women of Greek culture) who frequented the Hellenistic synagogues in search of true religion, proved to be the most responsive to his message (as in Iconium, Acts 14:1).

> ...they went together to the synagogue of the Jews, and so spoke that a great multitude both of the Jews and of the Greeks believed....they stayed there a long time, speaking boldly in the Lord, who was bearing witness to the word of His grace, granting signs and wonders to be done by their hands.

Devout Gentiles who feared the God of Israel were disenchanted with Greek paganism and immorality and were attracted to the ethical monotheism of Judaism; nevertheless, the challenge to convert totally was formidable, particularly since circumcision and other obligations were required.

The gospel -- "good news"! -- was like a breath of fresh air in a closed attic. Paul proclaimed a Scriptural, grace-filled message without food restrictions, holy days, and so on; above all, His message was accompanied by a transforming presence of the Holy Spirit (1 Thessalonians 1:5).

After planting a church in a strategic center, Paul would press on to another field. His objective was to open virgin territory and not infringe on someone else's sphere of authority ("to preach the gospel in the regions beyond you, and not to boast in another man's sphere of accomplishment," 2 Corinthians 10:16). Leslie Allen comments:

> Paul had evangelized half the Roman world by his method of visiting the main centres and leaving converts to preach the gospel in the surrounding regions. There were areas he had not visited but this was because they were already covered by other pioneer missionaries."[28]

A Man of Action. Although a theologian, author and man of letters, Paul made his mark on world history as *a man of action* (attribute of a true apostle). Converted about 34 A.D., he spent the next thirty years or so invading the pagan world from Syria to Italy and possibly Spain.[29] Roland Allen, in his ground-breaking book on missions, describes one period of Paul's apostolic ministry (47 and 57 A.D.):

> In little more than ten years St. Paul established the Church in four provinces of the Empire, Galatia, Macedonia, Achaia and Asia. Before A.D. 47 there were no Churches in these provinces; in A.D. 57 St. Paul could speak as if the work there was done, and could plan extensive tours into the far West without anxiety lest the Churches which he had founded might perish in his absence for want of his guidance and support.[30]

Letters of encouragement and instruction were dispatched to scattered disciples.[31] Younger associates were sent to support, help and hold accountable. Paul's authority, not based on denominational or ecclesiastical structure, flowed from a generous father's heart, appealing and compelling.

> 2 Corinthians 12:12 – "Truly the signs of an apostle were accomplished among you with all perseverance, in signs and wonders and mighty deeds." 1 Corinthians 4:9; Titus 1:1.

A Teacher

Paul's interpretation of the Scriptures was given with such joyful enthusiasm and authority that Jews and God-fearing Gentiles alike flocked to become disciples: a master theologian, Paul explained divine truths in brilliant, understandable, applicable ways (Acts 19:9; 2 Timothy 2:2). Epistles, rich with theological nuggets and practical Christian teaching, circulated throughout the churches (2 Peter 3:15-16).

> Acts 18:11 – "And he [Paul] continued there [Corinth] a year and six months, teaching the word of God among them." Also, Acts 15:35; 1 Corinthians 4:17.

One commentary makes this effusive statement:

> Next to the Master Teacher Himself, the apostle Paul is probably the most eloquent and persuasive teacher in the Bible. Many of the doctrines he expounded are considered the hallmarks of the Christian faith."[32]

Apostleship did not die with Paul.

The next two chapters will introduce other apostles mentioned in the New Testament, convincing evidence that the ascended Jesus continued calling others to be His ambassadors. Paul was the forerunner, and now the world is filled with members of the Church, the body of Christ.

Chapter 5 Endnotes

[1] Shipwrecked three times, adrift at sea for a night and a day, and experienced the perils of the sea (2 Corinthians 11:25-26).

[2] To take "last of all" absolutely (1 Corinthians 15:8), we must conclude that the Christian apostolate is finished, but Ephesians 4:11 refutes this.

[3] Colin Brown, *The New International Dictionary of New Testament Theology,* Vol. 1, p. 136.
Also, F. F. Bruce says that Paul "outstripped all others as a pioneer missionary and planter of churches, and nothing can detract from his achievement as the Gentiles' apostle *par excellence." Paul: Apostle of the Heart Set Free* (Grand Rapids: Eerdmans, 1991 reprint), p. 18.

[4] Karl Heinrich Rengstorf, "Apostello," Geoffrey W. Bromiley, tr. and ed., Gerhard Kittel, ed., *Theological Dictionary of the New Testament,* Vol. 1 (Grand Rapids, Eerdmans, 1976 [1964], p. 437.

[5] "[T]he Romans consolidated their empire by granting Roman citizenship to certain non-Romans. Paul's parents must have enjoyed this right before him, and he automatically became a Roman citizen at birth." *The New Open Bible,* p. 1309. In 42 B. C. the Roman general Mark Anthony granted Tarsus liberty, thereby making it a free, self-governing city not required to pay tribute to Rome.

[6] F.F. Bruce, Chapters 3 and 4. Paul's name on the roll of citizens of Tarsus would indicate a family of well-to-do citizens, with his father being a citizen before him – possibly because of some special kindness or benevolence.

[7] W. M. Ramsay, *St. Paul the Traveller and the Roman Citizen* (London: Hodder and Stoughton, 1907, tenth ed.), p. 31.

[8] G. G. Findlay, "Paul the Apostle," James Hastings, ed., *A Dictionary of the Bible,* Vol. III, (NY: Charles Scribner's Sons, 1902), p. 699.

[9] Bruce, p. 126.

[10] Frank J. Goodwin, *A Harmony of the Life of St. Paul* (Grand Rapids: Baker Book House, 1953), pp. 18-19.

[11] Philip Schaff, *History of the Christian Church, Volume 1*, p. 206.

[12] Acts 9:15; 22:15; 26:15-18; Romans 1:1; 11:13; 15:15-20; 1 Corinthians 1:1; 9:1-2; Galatians 1:1,15-17; Ephesians 3:7; 1 Timothy 1:12; 2:7.

[13] Wilbur Smith, *Peloubet's Select Notes on the International Sunday School Lessons, 1939* (Boston: W. A. Wilde Company, p. 200).

---

[14] Acts 9:15-16; 13:2; 22:21; 23:11; 26:17-18; 27:24; Romans 1:5; 11:13; Galatians 1:16; 2:8; Ephesians 3:8; Philippians 2:7; Colossians 1:25; 1 Timothy 1:7; 2 Timothy 1:11; 4:17. Note that Peter also reached Gentiles: 1 Peter 1:2; 2 Peter 2:2; Galatians 2:11.

[15] Acts 14:27; 15:3, 4, 12; 19:11; 2 Corinthians 12:12.

[16] F. F. Bruce, p. 38. Acts 21:39; 22:25-29; 23:27, 34; 25:10ff; 26:32.

[17] Sabatier, *The Apostle Paul*, pp. 69-70. Quoted in Goodwin, *Harmony,* p. 16.

[18] Ralph P. Martin, *New Testament Foundations: A Guide for Christian Students,* Volume 2 (Grand Rapids: Eerdmans, 1978), p. 247.

[19] See Chapter 18 and Appendix B.

[20] William Hendriksen and Simon J. Kistemaker, *New Testament Commentary: Thessalonians, the Pastorals and Hebrews* (Grand Rapids: Baker Books, 1995), p. 7.

[21] Acts 9:11; 14:23; 16:16, 25; 20:36; 21:5; 22:17; Romans 1:9-10; 8:26; 10:1; 12:12; 15:30; 1 Corinthians 1:2, 4; 7:5; 14:14; 2 Corinthians 1:11; 12:8; 13:9; Galatians 4:19; Ephesians 1:16-19; 5:20; 6:18; Philippians 1:3-4, 9; 4:6; Colossians 1:3, 9; 4:2-3; 1 Thessalonians 1:2; 3:9; 5:17; 2 Thessalonians 1:3, 11; 2:13; 3:1; 1 Timothy 1:12; 2:1-2, 8; 4:4-5; 2 Timothy 1:3; Philemon 4.

[22] See Ramsay's discussion, p. 51.

[23] William Hendriksen, "1 Timothy," *New Testament Commentary, Exposition of Thessalonians, the Pastorals, and Hebrews*, p.100.

[24] J. H. Thayer, *A Greek-English Lexicon of the NT* (NY: American Book, 1886), p. 346.

[25] Kenneth S. Wuest, *The New Testament: An Expanded Translation* (Grand Rapids: Eerdmans, 2002 reprint), p. ix.

[26] Hendriksen and Kistemaker, *Thessalonians*, p. 309. A footnote mentions: "In Paul *the verb* "to herald" (*kerusso*) occurs in the following passages: Rom. 2:21; 10:8, 14, 15; I Cor. 1:23; 9:27; 15:11, 12; II Cor. 1:19; 4:5; 11:4; Gal. 2:2; 5:11; Phil. 1:15; Col. 1:23; I Thess. 2:9; I Tim. 3:16; II Tim. 4:2. p. 309."

[27] F. F. Bruce, "The Acts of the Apostles," *Exploring New Testament Backgrounds,* (Washington, D.C.: *Christianity Today*), p. 15.

[28] Leslie C. Allen, "Romans, " F.F. Bruce, ed., *The International Bible Commentary* (rev. ed), (Grand Rapids: Zondervan, 1986), p. 1343.

[29] "Early church tradition holds that Paul did go to Spain. Before the end of the first century, Clement of Rome said that Paul 'reached the limits of the West' (1 Clement 5:7)." *The New Open Bible,* p. 1423.

[30] Roland Allen, *Missionary Methods: St. Paul's or Ours?* (Grand Rapids: Eerdmans, 1962), pp. 3, 13.

[31] A technique possibly learned from Rabbi Gamaliel who sent epistles to far-flung disciples by messengers.

[32] "Paul's Major Teachings," *The New Open Bible*, p. 1338.

Chapter 6
Validation for Additional Apostles

In This Chapter

- *Some scholarly support for our thesis*
- *What! A possible 25 more apostles?*
- *Three primary "proof texts" fused to seven compelling reasons*
- *Who's the foundation – Jesus, the apostles and prophets, or both?*

Most of what we know about biblical apostles comes from the writings of Paul and Luke and is based on Paul's life as an itinerant, missionary church-planter. This information is not meant to be an *exact* blueprint for every other apostle. Basics remain, assignments or "spheres" of influence differ.

One clear example: Peter and Paul, the leading apostles, each had an influential ministry. Peter, however, was primarily an apostle to the Jews, visiting their communities and synagogues, keeping their traditions, staying close with the Jerusalem church and elders. In contrast, Paul's burning vision was to reach both Jews and Gentiles in the heathen population centers, places were the gospel had not been preached; he was not hesitant to plant churches, and even pull people out of the synagogues to do it. Both men brought the message of Christ with apostolic signs and wonders of the Holy Spirit.

A Wider Circle

The Twelve and Paul were apostles *par excellence*, and any others would be inferior in some sense of greatness, magnitude or influence. Notwithstanding, more and more church leaders believe that apostles other than the Twelve and Paul existed in Bible days – and can exist in our day.

Ten Supportive Comments

In [Ephesians] 4:11 it is assumed that the church at all times needs the witness of "apostles" and "prophets." The author of this epistle did not anticipate that the inspired and enthusiastic ministry was to be absorbed by, and "disappear" into, offices and officers bare of the Holy Spirit and resentful of any reference to spiritual things. *Eph. 4 does not contain the faintest hint that the charismatic character of all church ministries was restricted to a certain period of church history and was later to die out* (emphasis added).[1]

Markus Barth, professor of New Testament,
University of Basel, Switzerland

[T]he circle of apostles was closed so far as human appointment was concerned. However, the Holy Spirit could [and later did] raise up new apostles, whose apostolic function was recognized by the churches as resting on their charismatic (i.e., Spirit-imparted) gifts and not on human authorization.[2]

George Ladd, professor of New Testament,
Exegesis and Theology at Fuller Theological Seminary

[T]he New Testament nowhere suggests that the apostolic ministry was intended only for first-century Christians.[3]

Arnold Bittlinger, German charismatic theologian

It is clear that there were more apostles than the twelve apostles of the Lamb. These are referred to as secondary apostles by some theologians because they are designated in Scripture as apostles, but do not have the unique prominence in the Kingdom that the original twelve had. These apostles include some of the greatest world changers in history, and this kind of apostle continues on today as the normative kind. . . . . All of these were sent by God as valid apostolic ministers and members of the apostolic company of the New Testament.[4]

David Cannistraci, pastor and apostolic leader

The office of 'apostle' ... even in New Testament times was not coterminous with the twelve apostles, nor has it actually ever been so down through the centuries. (*He suggests these other biblical examples: Barnabas, James, Andronicus and Junias.*)[5]

J. Rodman Williams, professor of Theology at Regent University

He [Christ] is building his church still. To that end his ascension gifts of ministry have no more ceased than his ascension gift of the Holy Spirit. Today's church needs both.[6]

Philip Greenslade, charismatic minister in the UK

We were taught that the original 12 apostles had a singular, one-of-a-kind mission that was completed by the time of their deaths, and that was that – the end of the brief life of apostles on earth…. A growing number of Christian leaders now recognize, acknowledge and affirm both the gift and the office of apostle in today's churches. The apostles have surfaced![7]

C. Peter Wagner, chancellor of the Wagner Leadership Institute

Nothing is said of the *time* when these gifts were given. But as they are the gifts of the exalted Christ, it is plain that the *apostolous* are not to be restricted to the original Twelve, but are to be taken in the wider sense, including not only Paul, but Barnabas, probably James, Silvanus, perhaps also Andronicus and Junias.[8]

S.D.F. Salmond, "Ephesians," *The Expositor's Greek Testament*

[T]he Apostles were not designed to be an order ceasing with the first twelve Jewish Apostles….beside Paul, who was not one of the twelve, there were at least twelve other mentioned in the Scriptures. [9]

Musgrave Reade, teacher-theologian of the Apostolic Faith Church at the 1913 Bournemouth Convention in Wales

[A] special messenger, a delegate, one commissioned for a particular task or role, one who is sent forth with a message. In the New Testament the word denotes both the original twelve disciples and predominant leaders outside the Twelve.[10]

Hayford's Bible Handbook

Listing of Other Biblical Apostles

The chart below may be a surprise, listing eighteen "Other Apostles" and an additional six "Other Possible Apostles," all in addition to the Twelve and Paul. This chapter and the one following provide the Bible references and the reasoning for this list. All these people would certainly be classified as "apostolic" in doctrine and practice, but were there really other actual apostles mentioned in the New Testament? Judge for yourself, not letting prejudice override compelling evidence. My count of thirty-seven may be too many, but it will be close.[11] If you feel some of these people were *not* apostles, I am sure you would agree that they were apostolic: either way, my objective of promoting apostolic ministry in the churches is fulfilled – and I hope more are forthcoming!

Other Apostles		
Name	**Description**	**References**
1. & 2. Andronicus and Junia	Notable Apostles	*Romans 16:7*
3. Apollos	The Eloquent	Acts 18:24-28; 1 Corinthians 1:12; 3:4, 6, 9, 22; 4:6-9; 16:12; Titus 3:13
4. Barnabas	The Encourager	Acts 4:36-37; 9:27; 11:22-26, 30; 12:25; 13:2; 14:4, 14; 1 Corinthians 9:5-6
5. Epaphroditus	The Consoler	Philippians 2:25-29; 4:18
6. Erastus	The Minister	Acts 19:21-22; 2 Timothy 4:20; Romans 16:23
7. James	The Devoted Brother of Jesus	Acts 1:14; 12:17; 21:18; 1 Corinthians 9:5; 15:7; Galatians 1:19; James 1:1
8. Jude	Author (Brother of Jesus)	1 Corinthians 9:5; Jude 1
9. Judas	Associate of Silas	Acts 15:22, 27, 32; 1 Thessalonians 2:6
10. Luke	Author of Luke and Acts	Colossians 4:14; 2 Timothy 4:11: Philemon 24
11. Mark (aka, "John")	Author of Mark and Cousin of Barnabas	Acts 12:25; 15:37-38; Colossians 4:10; 2 Timothy 4:11; Philemon 24; 1 Peter 5:13
12. Matthias	Replacement of Judas	Acts 1:26
13. Silas/Silvanus	Our Faithful Brother; A Prophet & Writer	Acts 15:22, 27, 32; 1 Thessalonians 1:1; 2:6; 2 Thessalonians 1;1; 1 Peter 5:12
14. Timothy	The Faithful	Acts 19:22; 20:4; 1 Corinthians 4:17; 16:10; 1 Thessalonians 1:1; 2:6; 3:2, 6; Philippians 1:1; 2:10, 19-23; Colossians 1:1; Philemon 1; Hebrews 13:23
15. Titus	The Diligent, Trusted Companion	2 Corinthians 2:13; 7:6; 13-14; 8:6, 23; Galatians 2:1; 2 Timothy 4:10; Titus 1:4-5 (13 references in Pauline Epistles)
16. Tychicus	The Companion	Acts 20:4; Ephesians 6:21-22; Colossians 4:7-8; 2 Timothy 4:12; Titus 3:12
17. & 18. Unnamed	Fellow Servants	2 Corinthians 8:23

Other Possible Apostles		
19. Epaphras	Founder of Church at Colosse	Colossians 1:7; 4:12; Philemon 23
20. Lydia	Leader in Philippi[12]	Acts 16:14-15
21. & 22. Priscilla and Acquila	Fellow Workers	Acts 18:2, 18, 26; Romans 16:3-5; 1 Corinthians 16:19; 2 Timothy 4:19
23. & 24. Joses and Simon	Brothers of Jesus	1 Corinthians 9:5-6

Validation for Continuing Apostles

Seven compelling reasons are presented in this chapter and the next:

1. The Bible Affirms Continuance
2. Paul and James Are Key Proofs
3. Only Apostles Wrote Scripture
4. Examples Confirm Continuance
5. The Testing of Apostles Continued
6. Living Apostles Trump Dead Tradition.
7. The Great Commission Is Apostolic

Reason 1. The Bible Affirms Continuance

The subject of continuing apostleship is handled easily in the New Testament -- no Scripture to the contrary! – and, three cast-iron proof texts cinch the validity of our thesis: 1 Corinthians 12:28, Ephesians 2:20 and 4:11.

First Text: 1 Corinthians 12:28

> And God has appointed these in the church; first apostles, second prophets, third teachers, after that miracles, then gifts of healings ….

Spiritual gifts and ministries are listed in eight places,[13] but this text uses numerical sequence. In either English or Greek the use of "first" indicates order, position, sequence or importance. This reference does not imply that an apostle is greater than someone with another ministry or gift, instead indicating primary importance for maintaining health in the local churches. Apostles and prophets are foundational for the function of all church members, just as a father and mother form the infrastructure for a family, or a manager is responsible for directing his sales force, or a general commands his army. Paul's statement to Corinth was true then and applies now: nothing in the New Testament indicates that apostleship would cease. Also, "first" refers to the apostle's role in founding churches and being an on-going influence in the life of those churches.

This question is sometimes asked: "Does 1 Corinthians 12:28 mean that every local church should or must have an apostle in it?" Every church may not have a titled apostle functioning in it, but every church that does have a functioning apostle or a leadership who comes under the strong influence of one will function much more effectively.

"Church" in 1 Corinthians usually refers to the local church, and this text seems to do so. In contrast, Ephesians uses "church" nine times, referring always to the universal Church. Every Christian church should be apostolic (having active apostolic people as members) even if there is no recognized apostle in residence.

The "movers and shakers" in local churches or organizations will generally be apostles, although they themselves or the people they serve may not understand, acknowledge or use the title. Churches impacting their communities are usually led by pastor-apostles.[14]

Second Text: Ephesians 2:19-22

> ...you are no longer strangers and foreigners, but fellow citizens with the saints and members of the household of God, *having been built on the foundation of the apostles and prophets, Jesus Christ Himself being the chief cornerstone*, in whom the whole building, being joined together grows into a holy temple in the Lord, in whom you also are being built together for a habitation of God in the Spirit (emphasis added).

The above Scripture can be confusing if you have sung for years that "The Church's one foundation is Jesus Christ her Lord." Actually, several metaphors about church foundations are mentioned in the New Testament, each analogy having a special emphasis. But, mixing metaphors can be confusing. The foundations presented below, each make a special point.

Foundation Metaphors		
"Foundation": the lowest part of a building, and on which it rests		
References	Christ's Position	Church's Position
Mathew 7:25; Luke 6:48; Hebrews 6:1,2	A rock (the teachings of Christ), is a solid foundation	A house built upon the Rock
Matthew 16:18	Revelation of Christ is a Great Rock	The Church built upon the Rock
1 Corinthians 3:9-11; 2 Timothy 2:19	Christ is the foundation	Local church is God's building; apostle is foundation-layer
Ephesians 2:20	Christ is the chief cornerstone, inter-locking with the apostles and prophets	Household of God/whole building/holy temple/habitation of God
Mark 12:10; Luke 20:17; Acts 4:11; Romans 9:33 1 Peter 2:6-8 (Psalm 118:22; Isaiah 8:23; 28:16)	A living stone, a chief cornerstone; a stone of stumbling and a rock of offense; a rejected stone	The Church, a spiritual house, with all members as living stones
1 Timothy 3:15	------------	House of God/Pillar and Foundation of the truth
Hebrews 11:10; Revelation 21:9,10,14	God the builder and maker of the city with foundations	The city = the Church; apostles' names in the wall foundations

Before discussing Ephesians 2:20 (with its reference to Christ as a cornerstone and apostles and prophets as foundation), consider Christ the rock and foundation.

Christ the Rock. Jesus' statement to Peter in Matthew 16:13-18 means simply that Christ Himself is *the* foundation, not Peter.[15] Jesus acknowledged Peter's revelation of Jesus being *the massive rock-like under-girding* of the Church. Peter himself, in contrast, was *merely a fragment* of rock, but still a vital part of the Church. The sensitive, expanded translation of Greek scholar Kenneth S. Wuest gives this confirmation:

> You are Rock [*petros,* masculine in gender, a detached but large fragment of rock], and upon this massive rock [*petra, feminine in gender, a rocky peak, a massive rock,* cannot refer back to masculine *petros*] I will build My Church.[16]

Jesus repeated the concept when concluding the Sermon on the Mount:

> Therefore whoever hears these sayings of Mine, and does them, I will liken him to a wise man who built his house on the rock [again *petra,* as above]: and the rain descended, the floods came, and the winds blew and beat on that house; and it did not fall, for it was founded on the rock (Matthew 7:24-25).

The *teaching* of Jesus and the apostles makes up the Church's foundation, and does not need additions, just up-to-date application. This original teaching came first through Christ, then by revelation from the apostles. This foundation is the essence of who and what Christ is, and it remains the only Rock of our salvation.

Christ the Foundation. "For no other foundation can anyone lay than that which is laid, which is Jesus Christ" (1 Corinthians 3:11). Both newer and older churches, must be diligent in maintaining the eternal, unchanging foundation of the living Jesus Christ.

The foundation of the church at Corinth was not Paul, but he was the foundation layer (1 Corinthians 3:10, emphasis added):

> According to the grace of God which was given to me, as a wise master builder [Greek, *architectos*] I *have laid the foundation,* and another builds on it.

Paul took the truths of Jesus Christ and, empowered by the Holy Spirit, made those truths understandable, real and workable for the people. Such a foundation must be more than a written statement of faith *about* Christ or mere acceptance of a belief system. Tenets are important, but Paul knew that people must also experience the Spirit and person of Christ in life-changing reality.

Modern apostles, like those of Bible days, are to establish and reaffirm that one and only foundation of Christ in the current generation; apostles are the foundation layers, protectors and advocates of Jesus Christ Himself.

Apostles, Prophets and Christ. The household of God (the Church) is like a building of tightly-knit, well-fitting stones, each Christian being a "living," Spirit-filled stone built up from a "living" solid foundation. Peter's building metaphor calls the church "a spiritual house" and makes Jesus Christ "a living stone" and "the chief cornerstone."

> Coming to Him as to *a living stone,* rejected by men, but chosen by God and precious, you also, as *living stones,* are being built up a spiritual house....Behold I lay in Zion *a chief cornerstone,* elect, precious...(1 Peter 2:4-7, emphasis added).

The Chief Cornerstone

Ephesians 2:20 makes Jesus Christ the chief cornerstone. This unique, essential stone was *created perfect and set precisely.* The apostles and prophets were then set in place as interlocking foundation stones to complete the foundation, positioned in perfect symmetry, squared exactly (in close association and calling) with Jesus Christ the chief cornerstone.[17] The Church, composed of all its members, is built solidly on this foundation and grows to become "the whole building," "a holy temple of the Lord," "a habitation of God in the Spirit" (Ephesians 2:21-22).

Jesus the cornerstone is a "living stone" and all believers in the structure are "living stones" as well (1 Peter 2:4-5). Peter's phrase appears paradoxical because literal stones are lifeless. Kristemaker's clarification is good:

> when Peter qualifies the word *stone* with the descriptive adjective *living,* he is no longer speaking of a stone but of a person."[18]

Jesus is the perfect cornerstone for God's building -- the key stone for the placement of all others. The apostles and prophets who adopted those teachings found their ministries perfectly aligned and symmetrically set in place, bonded together with Him so that all the other member-stones in the Church building are also in exact alignment.

Maintaining the Foundation

Every generation needs fresh, personalized, updated, Spirit-inspired, relevant application of Christ and His teachings. This is best accomplished by *contemporary* fivefold ministry (Ephesians 4:11). The original foundation *is to be maintained* intact by an ongoing apostolate that contends "earnestly for the faith which was *once for all* delivered to the saints" (Jude 3, emphasis added). Societal changes (like language, culture, technology) must not dull the clear perception of Christ our Rock – and neither must apathy, luke-warmness or irrelevant tradition rob us of spiritual liveliness.

Each generation needs the faith clearly reaffirmed, understood and experienced. Peter's inspired statement must be made alive to every generation: *"You are the Christ, the Son of the living God"* (Matthew 16:16). As the rock followed Israel, the Rock of Christ follows His Church through the present age (1 Corinthians 10:4). *The foundation is eternal, but periodic affirmation keeps the truth relevant.* A new church plant needs the foundation of Christ laid for that group of new believers, hopefully the same foundation Paul laid for the Corinthians: Christ! Thus, apostolic foundation-laying and affirming should always be in progress!

Third Text: Ephesians 4:10-13

> He who descended is also the One who ascended far above all the heavens, that He might fill all things.) And *He himself gave some to be apostles,* some prophets, some evangelists, and some pastors and teachers, for the equipping of the saints for the work of ministry, for the edifying of the body of Christ, *till we all come* to the unity of the faith and the knowledge of the Son of God, to a perfect man, to the measure of the stature of the fullness of Christ (emphasis added).

Paul clearly states (and what else could he mean?) that apostleship was meant to continue in the Church past the time of the original Twelve; the ongoing Church was not meant to exist without the influence of the original Twelve, application being made by contemporary apostles!

> Does not the very fact of the Apostles and prophets as members in the Body – the Church – prove that they were designed to continue with the Church? Can you conceive of God calling this wonderful Body, as the similitude of the natural body? Does God take away any members of your body, and say now you have grown up you do not need them, they cease to be part of your body? …. Then the Church was designed to have Apostles and Prophets….They all were to remain in the Church until the Church age was finished (Reade).[19]

The final objective -- the ultimate intention, "perfection" or maturity -- must be reached, and *then* apostles will have fulfilled their earthly calling. After Paul says that the five leadership/governmental ministries are "for the equipping of the saints for the work of ministry, for the edifying of the body of Christ," he adds, "*till* we all come to the unity of faith… " (Ephesians 4:12-16). Since the Church has not yet arrived at this predicted maturity, it is apparent that apostles (and the other four offices) are needed to function *until* it actually does come to pass.

Two Types of Apostles

When Jesus Christ ascended to the Father, He *continued* to appoint apostles in the Church. This explains why some or all on the chart could be apostles, yet not part of the Twelve. John Alley says:

> The twelve were not appointed in His ascension – they were appointed from amongst His disciples some three years before. When Christ ascended, He began to appoint *more* apostles…the fivefold ministry to represent His headship to the body…to equip the saints for the ministry and to build up the body of Christ."[20]

A good way to identify these two groups is suggested by Philip Greenslade: "apostles of the Resurrection" and "apostles of the Ascension." The first group is the original Twelve (with Mathias replacing Judas) who was recommissioned by the Risen Christ. These are the ones who received the inbreathing of resurrection life from Jesus, proof of His being alive, special kingdom teaching, the Great Commission and the outpouring of the Spirit at Pentecost.

The testimony of this exclusive group of men forms the definitive standard of teaching and doctrine for us....All subsequent apostolic ministry must submit to and accurately reflect this normative apostolic testimony.[21]

The second group are apostles commissioned by Jesus *after* He ascended to the Father, being foundation layers of new fields and succeeding generations.

To accept evangelists, pastors and teachers -- while rejecting apostles and prophets – is Scripturally impossible. The three key texts show that all five of the governmental leadership were *intended to be* in the Church as long as the Church lasted! No reasonable answer exists for: "Why would Christ continue ordaining *only* evangelists, pastors and teachers?" Ron Myer, like many of us, says:

I cannot deny the operation of the fivefold gifts [which includes apostles] in the church today. I have seen them working firsthand. They are not lost. They did not disappear after the first century. These gifts have a vital role and purpose in the New Testament church just as they did in the book of Acts and the first three centuries of church history.[22]

Where, Then, Are the Apostles?

The answer is simple, practical and apparent. The gifts of the Spirit, charismatic worship services, fervent prayer, aggressive evangelism and the leadership of apostles and prophets are not *automatically inherited* by each new generation of the Church or churches. The belief in such things is easily passed on, like oral traditions, but allowed to go unpracticed. *Our biblical and spiritual inheritance stays alive by the Spirit.*

Hold fast the pattern of sound words which you have heard from me, in faith and love which are in Christ Jesus. *That good thing which was committed to you* keep by the Holy Spirit who dwells in us (2 Timothy 1:13-14, emphasis added).

A church easily retains form and tradition. Systems *theologically* entrenched in our message, our methods and our music make good tradition -- but are dead in the water without the dynamic of the Holy Spirit. As an example, hands can be laid mechanically on people for blessing, ordination and confirmation, but the power of God may be missing ("empty hands on empty heads"). Also, hymns of adoration and blessing should be sung by people heart-involved and Spirit-inspired.

Spiritually essential things are hardest to maintain, because they are only alive when the people pray, worship in the Spirit and serve the Lord empowered by the Holy Spirit. We may believe that apostles and miracles of the past *did* happen once upon a time; however, we must faithfully contend for apostolic continuance today:

> [C]ontinue in the faith, grounded and steadfast, and are [be] not moved away from the hope of the gospel which you heard... (Colossians 1:23).

> [S]tand fast in one spirit, with one mind striving together for the faith of the gospel (Philippians 1:27).

We need apostles today. Already, an army of humble, Paul-like, servant-apostles labor without fanfare to establish churches in underdeveloped nations of the world. In contrast, better-known apostles oversee global ministries of major influence. What a variety exists! Some serve with title, some go untitled; some are denominational, some independent; some have major influence, some very little. Regardless of notoriety or placement, apostles work and serve to reach the world in our generation. Hopefully, a global unity of the leadership of Christ's Church will occur within our time.

Reason 2. Paul and James Are Key Proofs

Paul and James were *bona fide* apostles who were not of the Twelve, being appointed after Jesus' Ascension. Both wrote books of the New Testament. By the time of the Jerusalem Council (Acts 15, circa 50 A.D.), both James and Paul had achieved significant status, with James being the undisputed leader of the church at Jerusalem. Significantly, both were personally visited by the resurrected Jesus (1 Corinthians 15; Acts 9), both came slowly to the acceptance of Jesus as the Christ, but they came along very different paths.

Paul

> Romans 1:13 – "an apostle to the Gentiles." 1 Corinthians 1:1 – "called to be an apostle...."

Paul was directly commissioned by the ascended, glorified Christ; in fact, he goes to great lengths to make the Corinthian Church know that his ordination was directly from God and did not stand on the approval of the Twelve.

Consider Paul as a proto-type gift-apostle of those Jesus would appoint after ascending to heaven. Paul was a bridge between the Twelve, an innovative trail-blazer for additional apostles. Future apostles might not have such a spectacular conversion (as, for example Barnabas, James and Timothy), but their call and dedication would be above question.

Judas Iscariot the traitor was not replaced by Paul, no Scripture indicates this; Paul could not meet the requirements to be one of the Twelve. Matthias' appointment was the fulfillment of Psalm 109:8 (quoted in Acts 1:20): "Let his days be few, and let another take his office [apostleship]." The post-ascension apostles, like Paul and James, were the fulfillment of Psalm 68:18 (Ephesians 4:8): "When He ascended on high, He led captivity captive, and gave gifts to men."[23]

James

> Galatians 1:19 – "...I saw none of the other apostles except James the Lord's brother."
> Galatians 2:9 – "James, Cephas [Peter], and John who seemed to be pillars...."

The Church recognized James because of his godly life style, prayer discipline, proven ministry, wisdom, prophetic insight and dedication to his Jewish heritage. Being a brother to Jesus did not qualify him for membership in the Twelve, nor did it mean his automatic apostleship.

During Jesus' earthly ministry, James was "reserved if not hostile."[24]

> "For even His brothers did not believe in Him," John 7:5, 10.

"His own people…said, 'He is out of His mind,'" Mark 3:21.

Some 15 or so years with Jesus as the head of the family must have had an awesome effect on James, later causing deep regret for his reluctance to accept Jesus as Savior and Lord.

Jesus privately appeared to James after His resurrection ("After that He was seen by James, then by all the apostles,"1 Corinthians 15:7). Von Campenhausen suggests that this appearance of the risen Christ

> may therefore in his case – as was to happen later in that of Paul – have acquired the simultaneous significance of a conversion. This event also immediately established his position and authority.[25]

James was a believing disciple along with 119 others on that glorious day of Pentecost when the Holy Spirit was outpoured (Acts 1:14). He had already seen the resurrected Jesus, but now he experienced a tongue of heavenly fire lighting upon him, causing him to speak forth miraculously in an unlearned Gentile tongue.

James was recognized an apostle *after* Pentecost and confirmed by the Church (Galatians 1:19; 1 Corinthians 9:5). When Paul wrote in Galatians 2:9 that James, Cephas (Peter) and John (listed in that order) were "reputed to be pillars," he is saying that they were "personalities who 'carried' the church, and on whom its structure rested" (Von Campenhausen).[26] "Paul designates him [James] an apostle as a matter of course" (F. F. Bruce).[27]

At the Jerusalem Council, James' authority seemed to overshadow all the apostles except Peter and Paul, and he was the one to announce to the waiting conference the prophetic direction of the Holy Spirit ("And after they had become silent, James answered….Therefore I judge…" Acts 15:13-21). The epochal gathering of apostles, elders and church in Jerusalem (Acts 15) will be discussed in Chapter 8: there it will become apparent why James was an apostle and why more apostles would be essential.

David Carteledge makes the significant point that James' selection "is strong proof of the extension of the apostolic ranks as a matter of course."[28]

The five remaining reasons for a continuing apostolate follow in the next chapter.

Chapter 6 Endnotes

[1] Markus Barth, *Ephesians 4-6, Anchor Bible,* Vol. 34A, p. 437.

[2] George Ladd, *A Theology of the New Testament* (Grand Rapids: Eerdmans, 1974), p. 257.

[3] Arnold Bittlinger, *Gifts and Ministries* (Grand Rapids: Eerdmans, 1974), p. 77.

[4] Cannistraci, *Apostles,* p. 58-59.

[5] J. Rodman Williams, *Renewal Theology: Systematic Theology from a Charismatic Perspective, Vol. 2* (Grand Rapids: Zondervan, 1990), p. 25.

[6] Philip Greenslade, *Leadership, Greatness and Servanthood* (Minneapolis, MN: Bethany House Publishers, 1984), pp. 139-140.

[7] Wagner, *Apostles Today,* pp. 6-7.

[8] S. D. F. Salmond, "The Epistle to the Ephesians," W. Robertson Nicoll, ed., *The Expositor's Greek Testament* (Grand Rapids, MI: Eerdmans, 1951), p. 329.

[9] Quoted by James E. Worsfold, *The Origins of the Apostolic Church of Great Britain.* Thorndon, Wellington, New Zealand: The Julian Literature Trust, 1991, p. 81.

[10] Jack Hayford, gen. ed., *Hayford's Bible Handbook* (Nashville, TN: Thomas Nelson Publishers, 1995), p 546.

[11] Selected because of the use of either the noun or verb form of *apostolos* or obvious apostolic activity. Different opinions exist.

Doug Beacham: "the evidence is not as clear" (for some in this author's list). "...my reading of the various texts indicates that at best these can be inferred to be apostles: Erastus...Tychicus...Titus is uncertain...Part of my rationale in not naming all these companions of Paul as apostles is that it is possible they were sent (*apostello*) with him but with other primary equipping gifts...." *Rediscovering the Role of Apostles and Prophets* (Franklin Springs, GA: LifeSprings Resources, rev. 2004), p. 150, n. 17.

David Cannistraci: "If the twelve apostles are added to this [his] list, a total of 32 apostles would be mentioned in the New Testament," p. 59.

Wayne Grudem: "There seem to have been a least fifteen [including the Twelve], and perhaps sixteen or even a few more who are not recorded in the New Testament. Yet it seems quite certain [?!] that there were none appointed after Paul." *Systematic Theology: An Introduction to Biblical Doctrine* (Grand Rapids: Zondervan, 1994).

J. L. Meredith gives eight in his *Book of Bible Lists:* Matthias, Barnabas, Paul, Androniocus, Junia, James, Silvanus and Timothy. (Minneapolis, MN: Bethany House Publishers, 1980), p. 149.

[12] Wagner: "Luke...Lydia, provided a biblical prototype of a workplace apostle." p. 113.

[13] 1 Corinthians 12:28; 29-30; 8-10; 13:1-3; 14:26; Romans 12:6-8; Ephesians 4:11;1 Peter 4:10-11. Some twenty "gifts" altogether suggest that neither Paul or Peter intended a single exhaustive list; the emphasis was on the operational unity in the church.

[14] "A pastor can build a church to 200, a leader can take a church over 200, but it requires a congregational apostle to move the church past 700 to 800 and have it continue to grow vigorously." Wagner, p. 95.

[15] Rev. 21:14 says: "Now the wall of the city had twelve foundations, and on them were the names of the twelve apostles of the Lamb." That same wall in 21:12 is described having twelve gates "and names written on them, which are the names of the twelve tribes of the children of Israel." The inscribed names mean that their lives and ministries are honored and memorialized by the inscriptions because of their faithful contribution.

[16] Kenneth S. Wuest, *The New Testament: An Expanded Translation*, p. 42.

[17] Salmond says, p. 299: "…the foundation of the apostles and prophets uses one 'the' [in the Greek] for the two ministries, indicating that they both belong to the same class." Commentators do not always agree on the intent of "of."
"The *gen*[itive, *of*] is variously understood as:
  (1) the gen. of *apposition* = the foundation which *is* or *consists in* the Apostles;
  (2) the gen. of *originating cause* = the foundation *laid by* them;
  (3) the *possess*. gen. = 'the Apostles' foundation' – in the sense of that on which they built … or that on which they also were built."

The following two authors illustrate different meanings of the genitive:

Eddie L. Hyatt: "This is popularly understood to mean that individual apostles and prophets are the foundation of the Church. In the Greek…the genitive case…shows possession. It is like saying 'the car of John Doe.' Although the car and John Doe are related, it does not follow that the car is John Doe or that John Doe is the car. In the same way, it does not follow that the foundation is identical with the apostles and prophets or that the apostles and prophets are identical with the foundation. Paul is actually referring to the foundation that is laid by the apostles and prophets…." From *Thinking Biblically About Apostolic Ministry*. p. 1, www.revivalandreformation.org.

C. Peter Wagner: "Jesus founded the Church, but at His ascension He delegated the operational nuts and bolts for its future growth to apostles and prophets. He remains as the cornerstone. The cornerstone is not the foundation, per se, but it is the unit that holds the foundation together. The foundation is apostles and prophets." *Dominion:How Kingdom Action Can Change the World* (Grand Rapids: Chosen Books, 2008), p. 28.

[18] Simon J. Kistemaker, *New Testament Commentary: Peter and Jude* (Grand Rapids: Baker Book House, 1987), p. 85.

[19] Statement by Musgrave Reade to the 1913 Bournemouth Convention in Wales, as quoted by Worsfold, *Origins,* p. 83.

[20] John Kingsley Alley, *The Apostolic Revelation: The Reformation of the Church* (Surprise, AZ: Selah Publishing Group, LLC [US Publishers], 2002), p. 39.

[21] Greenslade, p. 139.

[22] Ron Myer, *Fivefold Ministry Made Practical* (Lititz, PA: House to House, 2006), p. 26.

[23] F. F. Bruce explains in *Paul: Apostle,* pp. 436-438. Paul's interpretation in Eph. 4 is not in terms of the historical setting of Psa. 68. "What is most striking is that, instead of the Massoretic and Septuagint reading, '*received* gifts among men', a reading is here chosen which agrees with the Aramaic Targum and the Syriac version: '*gave* gifts to men'….in Ephesians it is interpreted of Christ's ascent on high and his bestowal thence upon his church of the ministers or ministries necessary for its growth to maturity."

[24] F.F. Bruce, *New Testament History* (Garden City, NY: Anchor Books, 1972 ed), p.211.
[25] Hans von Campenhausen, *Ecclesiastical Authority and Spiritual Power in the Church of the First Three Centuries* (Peabody, MASS: Hendrickson Publishers, 1997), p. 20.
[26] Ibid, p. 19.
[27] Bruce, Ibid.
[28] Cartelege, p. 250.

Chapter 7
Reasons for More Apostles

In This Chapter

- *Five more reasons validate our claim*
- *Were the authors of Luke, Acts, Mark and Jude apostles?*
- *Why "test" visiting apostles?*
- *How do "Living apostles trump dead tradition"?*

In the previous chapter we covered two of seven reasons for believing in the continuance of apostles. This chapter will present the remaining five.

Restated, the seven are:

1. The Bible Affirms Continuance
2. Paul and James Are Key Proofs
3. Only Apostles Wrote Scripture
4. Examples Confirm Continuance
5. The Testing of Apostles Continued
6. Living Apostles Trump Dead Tradition.
7. The Great Commission Is Apostolic

Reason 3. Only Apostles Wrote Scripture

It is commonly said that "the apostles wrote the New Testament."

Of the eight inspired authors -- Matthew, Mark, Luke, John, Paul, Peter, James and Jude -- only *four of the eight* are specifically called apostles (Matthew, John, Paul and Peter), and only *three of the four* (Matthew, John and Peter) belonged to the original Twelve. What about Mark, Luke, James and Jude? Were they apostles? As already explained, James certainly qualifies.

A Function of Apostles

Jonas Clark makes a significant point: the writers of the New Testament were used of God "to lay the doctrinal foundation of the early church." Clark rightfully concludes, I believe, that this inspired writing was a function of apostles.[1] Paul seems to concur:

> "having been built on the foundation of apostles and prophets" (Ephesians 2:20)
> "now been revealed by the Spirit to His holy apostles and prophets" (Ephesians 3:5).

This activity alone should qualify Luke, Mark, James and Jude as apostles. Paul spoke of himself and his fellow-apostles as "stewards of the mysteries of God," or, in modern terminology, "look at Apollos and me as mere servants … put in charge of explaining God's secrets" (NLT, 1 Corinthians 4:1). They proclaimed the arrival of what was "promised beforehand … in the holy Scriptures" (Romans 1:2).

Today we need apostles, not to write more Bible, but to continue the work the early apostles began of starting, establishing and grounding churches in Christ, the power of the Holy Spirit, and the great teachings of the New Testament *already given* us.

Modern apostles are to interpret and apply the *Bible principles previously given* to new generations of people. Today's ministers certainly write helpful material, but they are *not* called to write "inscripturated"[2] portions to be accepted on a par with the Bible. The Bible is complete (Revelation 22:18-19).

Luke, Mark and Jude

Not specifically identified as apostles, these three zealous men functioned actively in apostolic work, journeys, and writing books of the New Testament, probably beginning as apostolic assistants.

Luke. Luke's insightful account of Holy Spirit activity and his significant role in the triumphant spread of Christianity would seem to qualify him as an apostle. This physician-historian wrote Acts as a vigorous *associate* and companion on apostolic mission trips (using "we" or "us").[3] Luke was the only Gentile contributor to the New Testament and "a fellow laborer" of Paul (Philemon 24). He encouraged Paul during his imprisonment (2 Timothy 4:11).

Wagner says Luke was

> the prototype of a workplace apostle .... Perhaps the greatest apostolic credential that Luke had was being inspired by the Holy Spirit to write 25% of the New Testament...the same percentage...as Paul.[4]

Mark. The early Church believed Mark to be the author of the Gospel of Mark, a document of great importance in the Apostolic Age. The long-time assumption that Mark's gospel, based on the recollections of the Apostle Peter, was set down in writing shortly before Peter's death in Rome (circ 68 AD), has been successfully challenged by 19 tiny scraps of papyrus, found in 1947 among the Dead Sea Scrolls. Scientific methods indicate the possibility that "Mark's gospel may well have been in circulation within about a dozen years of the time of Jesus' death."[5]

Involved with Peter, Paul and Barnabas in apostolic work and journeys (Acts 12:25; 13:5, 13; 2 Timothy 4:11; 1 Peter 5:13), Mark started poorly, abruptly resigning from his first missionary assignment, thereby irritating Paul greatly (Acts 16:38). Cousin Barnabas (Colossians 4:10) then took him on an apostolic journey to Cyprus. Finally, after some years, Mark did finish strongly -- commended by both Paul and Peter for his profitable help. Paul commented that Mark was with him during his first Roman imprisonment (Colossians 4:10; Philemon 24).

Mark is usually given bad press for his opening failure with Paul. However, between that time and his being with Paul in Rome, there is credible possibility of real apostolic ministry. McBirnie, in *The Search of the Twelve Apostles,* devotes some eight pages to Mark's activities, quoting heavily from "Origins of Coptic Christianity," a chapter by Aziz S. Atiya.[6] Atiya tells of the detailed and strong traditions among the Coptic Churches regarding St. Mark, especially his ministry and martyrdom in Alexandria, Egypt.

Jude. Jude, the brother of Jesus and James, was present at Pentecost. His one recorded epistle, the Book of Jude, was short but impressive, a fiery exhortation to fight the encroachment of false teachers. Jude labored with other apostles, quoting for instance the fulfillment of Peter's words (2 Peter 2:1, 2; 3:3; Jude 4, 11, 12, 17, 18). Paul indicates Jude and James were *married apostles*: "Do we have no right to take along a believing wife, as do also the *other* apostles, the brothers of the Lord, and Cephas?" (1 Corinthians 9:5, emphasis added).

Reason 4. Bible Examples Confirm Continuance
So far, we have discussed six probable apostles *appointed after Jesus' ascension*: James, Jude, Luke, Mark, Matthias and Paul. Consider sixteen more.

Barnabas, the Encourager
Barnabas labored with Paul on his first missionary trip, and Luke twice records him as an apostle:

> Acts 14:4, 14 – "But the multitude of the city was divided: part sided with the Jews, and part with the apostles....But when the apostles Barnabas and Paul heard this...."

Barnabas was involved with the Jerusalem Church from the beginning. Luke describes him as a Levite from Cyprus who sold property and gave the proceeds to the Church (Acts 4:36). The Twelve nicknamed him "The Son of Encouragement." When the news of revival in Antioch reached Jerusalem, the apostles sent Barnabas to investigate (Acts 11:22-30), possibly because he was a Cypriot Jew having similar background as the founders of the Antioch church. "[H]e was a good man, full of the Holy Spirit and of faith" (Acts 11:24).
Excited by what he discovered in Antioch, Barnabas realized Antioch needed Saul's dynamic enthusiasm. He fetched Saul to Antioch, and the two became an influential team teaching many people, finally being sent forth as an apostolic team (Acts 13:1-4).

Judas and Silas [Silvanus], *Faithful Servants*

> Acts 15:27 – "We have therefore sent [from *apostello*] Judas and Silas, who will also report the same things by word of mouth." Acts 15:32 – "Now Judas and Silas, themselves being prophets also...."   1

Thessalonians 1:1; 2:6 – "Paul, Silvanus, and Timothy…we might have made demands as apostles of Christ…."

The Jerusalem elders enthusiastically endorsed two outstanding, proven men to carry and authenticate the letter to the Gentile converts. These messengers were also prophets and capable preachers (Acts 15:12). Judas, called Barsabas, was possibly the same man or brother of the man who narrowly missed being appointed to the Twelve Apostles (Acts 1:23).

Paul selected Silas to replace Barnabas for his 2nd Missionary Journey (see chapter 9). Silas' close association with the Jerusalem church must have impressed the Gentile converts. Also, being a close friend of Peter, Silas (Silvanus) was the scribe who participated in the preparation of 1 Peter (5:12).

Apollos the Eloquent

1 Corinthians 3:5 - "Who then is Paul, and who is Apollos, but ministers through whom you believed … I planted, Apollos watered, but God gave the increase."

Paul strongly acknowledged that Apollos, the golden-voiced preacher from Alexandria, was an apostle in four ways:

First, Paul includes Apollos with himself in apostleship ("… I have transferred to myself and Apollos….For I think that God has displayed *us the apostles* last…." 1 Corinthians 4:6-9, emphasis added).

Second, Paul also names Apollos along with himself and Cephas (Peter) in speaking of "servants of Christ and stewards of the mysteries of God," 1 Corinthians 4:1.[7]

Third, Paul then speaks of the three apostles, using "us" four times and "we" eleven times in 1 Corinthians 4:1-13.

Fourth, Paul criticized four splinter groups in the church, each having a favorite apostle: "What I mean is this: one of you says, 'I follow Paul'; another, 'I follow Apollos'; another, 'I follow Cephas [that is, Peter]'; still another, 'I follow Christ [the ultimate Apostle],'" 1 Corinthians 1:12, NIV).

Paul wants the church to know that all three are God's "fellow workers" or "partners" (1 Corinthians 3:9); certainly he seems to mean apostles. 3:21 adds: "So don't take pride in following a particular leader. Everything belongs to you: Paul and Apollos and Peter (NLT)."

Timothy and Titus

These younger associates toiled tirelessly with Paul, carrying on and expanding his apostolic work. Apparently both were converted by Paul and are called "sons," "partners" and "fellow workers." Paul said to "submit to such," that is accept their apostolic leadership (1 Corinthians 16:16). Their duties:

- Establish and strengthen churches
- Develop qualified leaders
- Teach and preach God's Word
- Combat false doctrine
- Encourage Christian conduct
- Speak in behalf of Paul

1st and 2nd Timothy and Titus were Paul's personal letters to these young adjutants (the last that he wrote). Usually called "The Pastoral Epistles," but more preferably called "Apostolic Epistles," they were written with deep conviction from a jail cell.

These men were not messenger boys, reading letters and patronizing customers. They were persuasive *ambassadors,* authorized to speak and act for Paul and the gospel he preached. Subordinates, yes, but each entitled to wear an apostolic mantle to represent both God and Paul.

Timothy. His name appears 25 times in the New Testament. Totally aware of Paul's way of life and his teachings (1 Corinthians 4:17), Timothy was:

- a faithful worker (1 Corinthians 16:10)
- a fellow laborer
- a minister of God (1 Thessalonians 3:2)
- a servant (Philippians 1:1)
- Paul's beloved and faithful (spiritual) son (1 Corinthians 4:17; Philippians 2:2-23)
- a man of proven character with genuine regard for the churches

Timothy's Connection with Paul [8]		
Date AD	*Location and Activity*	*References*
45	Converted by Paul at Lystra	Ac. 14:6
51	Recruited and circumcised by Paul; Accompanied Paul to Troas, Philippi and Berea Sent from Berea to Thessalonica	Ac. 16:1 Ac. 16:8, 11-12 Ac. 17:14; 1 Thess. 3:2
52 Winter	With Silas, joined Paul at Corinth With Paul	Ac. 18:5; 1 Thess. 3:6 1 Thess. 1:1; 2 Thess. 1:1
57 Spring Winter	With Paul at Ephesus Sent from Ephesus into Macedonia and to Corinth Joined Paul in Macedonia	Ac. 19:22: 1 Cor. 4:17; 16:10 2 Cor. 1:1
58 Beginning Spring	Both then proceeded to Corinth Journeyed with Paul from Corinth to Asia	Rom. 16:21 Ac. 20:4
62 or 63	With Paul in Rome	Phil. 1:1; Col. 1:1; Phile. 1
63 to 66	Uncertain	
66 or 67	Left in charge of church at Ephesus	1 Timothy
67 or 68	Sets out to join Paul at Rome	2 Timothy
Afterwards	Uncertain	

Timothy was a co-author of 1 Thessalonians: "Paul, Silvanus [Silas] and Timothy, to the church of the Thessalonians…" (1:1). This statement is more than a gracious gesture. The frequent use of "we" (41 times), "us" (22 times) and "our" (20 times) throughout the epistle indicates close collaboration. Five times Paul inserts "I," but it is obvious to the reader that Timothy and Silas are joint-authors participating with Paul -- thereby identified and affirmed as *apostles*: "we might have made demands as *apostles* of Christ," 2:6, emphasis added.

Paul used Timothy as *an extension of his own ministry*. The verb form of *apostolos* in the following quote suggests Timothy was an apostle.

> So he [Paul] *sent* into Macedonia two of those who ministered to him, Timothy and Erastus, but he himself stayed in Asia for a time (Acts 19:22, emphasis added).

Timothy was Paul's ambassador to the church at Corinth (1 Corinthians 4:17), also linked with Paul in the greeting of 2 Corinthians. Timothy went to and fro between Paul and Thessalonica (1 Thessalonians 3:2, 6), and he must have been in Rome with Paul (Philippians 1:1; 2:10; Colossians 1:1; Philemon 1). Also, Timothy was imprisoned (Hebrews 13:23). He could be trusted to arbitrate difficult situations; when necessary, he was an apostle with authority backed by Paul himself, and, of course, the Holy Spirit! Toward the end, Paul said, " I'm passing this work on to you, my son Timothy. The prophetic word that was directed to you prepared us" (1 Tim 1:18, M).

Titus. Fourteen years after his conversion, Paul took Barnabas with him to talk with the elders at Jerusalem, also bringing Titus, a rather new convert at the time and a young adjutant in training. The young man showed first-hand what Paul's gospel could accomplish in a raw heathen; Titus was an uncircumcised Greek who loved and served Jesus Christ with all his heart (Galatians 2:1).

Although his name occurs thirteen times in the New Testament, Titus is not mentioned in the Acts of the Apostles, possibly, as some contend, because he was Luke's brother.[9] Paul speaks affectionately of Titus as "my true son in our common faith" (Titus 1:4), "my brother" (2 Corinthians 2:13), "my partner and fellow worker" (2 Corinthians 8:23).

Titus was sent to Corinth on Paul's behalf, and did a stellar job of working with a challenging situation, returning with a joyful, good report (2 Corinthians 7:13-15). Significantly, Paul called Titus a messenger [*apostolos*] of the churches (2 Corinthians 8:23), commending his exemplary life and manner of walking in the same spirit and same steps as his mentor.

The book of Titus defines his apostolic work. Left on Crete (to "complete what I [Paul] left half-done," Titus 1:5, M), Titus set things in order, appointed elders, challenged insubordinates, spoke sound doctrine, exhorted and exercised discipline; he affirmed constantly the Gospel of God, rebuking and encouraging with an apostle's authority.

Later, as the aging Paul was finishing his life-work, Titus went to Dalmatia as a mature man and apostle (2 Timothy 4:10).

> Dalmatia was a district in the southern part of Illyricum, a somewhat vaguely defined area of coast and mountain hinterland that lay E of the Adriatic Sea confronting Italy.[10]

There, among a warlike people who created military problems for the Romans, Titus once again continued the work of his mentor (Romans 15:19).

Two Apostolic Couples

A husband-wife team can be a powerful force for God.

Andronicus and Junia. Paul makes this impressive statement:

> Greet Andronicus and Junia, my kinsmen and my fellow prisoners, who are of note among the apostles, who also were in Christ before me (Romans 16:7).

In Romans 16 Paul greets twenty-six persons by name (in a church he has never visited), having met these people during his missionary journeys. The above greeting introduces a married couple who faithfully shared their testimony for some twenty-five years, longer than Paul had been a Christian. They were considered *notable apostles.* Don Williams says:

> The unresolved issue is whether Junias in Greek is a masculine contraction of Junianus or the femine Junia. The spelling in the original language is the same for either possibility. Furthermore, the phrase "they are men of note" literally reads "they are of note." "Men" is absent in the Greek, and is inserted by the translators. Thus Paul could be referring to a woman here, quite probably a husband-wife team.[11]

Some commentators resist accepting Junias as Junia, a conclusion seemingly based on the assumption that a woman could not be an apostle. In contrast the Early Church Father Chrysostom did not share that prejudice:

> And indeed to be Apostles at all is a great thing. But to be even amongst these of note, just consider what a great encomium this is! But they were

of note owing to their works, to their achievements. Oh! How great is the devotion of this woman that she should be even counted worthy of the appellation of apostle![12]

Priscilla and Aquila. This second husband–and-wife team is mentioned six times in the New Testament, and four of those times Priscilla's name precedes that of Aquila (Acts 18:1-3, 18, 19, 26; Romans 16:3-5; 1 Corinthians 16:19; 2 Timothy 4:19), suggesting superior ability, dominant personality or more prominent ministry.

They were tentmakers who had been expelled with their fellow Jews from Rome because of the edict of Claudius (circa 49/50 A.D.). Moving to Corinth, they became fast friends and devoted workers with Paul (Acts 18:1-3). Also, moving their business to Ephesus, they helped plant a church in that major city. While Paul finished a missionary journey, the couple stayed in Ephesus (Acts 18:19), laying the groundwork in Synagogue and marketplace for the great church that later developed (Acts 18-19). Their cordial home was a meeting place for Ephesian believers (1 Corinthians 16:19), and they were influential in tutoring Apollos (Acts 18:26), later called an apostle. Aquila and Priscilla returned to Rome and held believers' meetings in their home. Paul expressed his deep respect in Romans 16:3-4 (emphasis added):

> Greet Priscilla and Aquila, my fellow workers in Christ Jesus, who risked their own necks for my life, to whom not only I give thanks, but also all the churches of the Gentiles.

Although the wording is not used, all signs indicate their being associate apostles ("fellow workers") with Paul in establishing house churches, impacting the Jewish community and penetrating the marketplace culture through their business. Some today might call them "marketplace apostles."

Tychicus the Companion

Tychicus was a member of Paul's missionary team (Acts 20:4), a "beloved brother and faithful minister in the Lord" (Ephesians 6:21) and "fellow servant" (Colossians 4:7). Paul sent (*apostello*) him to encourage, strengthen and bring news to

Ephesus (2 Timothy 4:12), Colosse (Colossians 4:8) and other places (Titus 3:12).

Epaphroditus the Consoler

Philippians 2:25, 29 – "...I ...send Epaphroditus, my brother, fellow worker, and fellow soldier, but your messenger [*apostolos*]....hold such men in esteem." He brought needed provisions to Paul in prison, Philippians 4:18.

Erastus the Minister

Acts 19:22 – "So he sent [*apostello*] into Macedonia two of those who ministered to him, Timothy and Erastus...." Also, 2 Timothy 4:20; Romans 16:23.

Epaphras

A true servant of Christ, associate of Paul, and probably the founder of the church at Colosse (Colossians 1:7; 4:12; Philemon 23). He was a man of prayer who had great zeal for the Christians in the Lycus Valley (Colosse, Hierapolis, and Laodicea).

Two Unnamed Apostles

"Or if our brethren are inquired about, they are messengers (plural of *apostolos*) of the churches...(2 Corinthians 8:23).

Reason 5. The Testing of Apostles Continued

The early churches tested all claims to apostleship and spiritual authority. This practice was standard procedure, and should be today. Jesus clearly stated that a tree is identified by its fruit (Matthew 7:15-20), and Paul urges us to judge ourselves ("For if we would judge ourselves, we would not be judged,"1 Corinthians 11:31). We are, in fact, to judge all things spiritual ("Test all things; hold fast what is good," 1 Thessalonians 5:21).

Testing was an ongoing "fruit examining" practice in the New Testament churches; they were to *continue evaluating* ministerial credentials. This principle refers particularly to the testing of *newly arriving* ministries in a local church -- other than those *already* know to be authentic.

The church at Ephesus was commended because "you have tested those who say they are apostles and are not, and have found them liars" (Revelation 2:2); apparently they remembered Paul's admonitions that "savage wolves will come in among you [the church at Ephesus], not sparing the flock" (Acts 20:29). Paul himself passed the prescribed criteria: "we have been thoroughly manifested among you in all things" (2 Corinthians 11:6).

Who Were Tested?

Paul boldly denounced false apostles: "For such are false apostles, deceitful workers, transforming themselves into apostles of Christ," 2 Corinthians 11:13). Each local church was to evaluate apostles *not known* who show up *uninvited* on the local church scene expecting to minister.

This policy confirms that *the early churches did not limit apostleship to just the Twelve and Paul.* Rather, the churches expected a continuation of apostolic ministry, knowing that all claims to such apostleship *must* be evaluated, an activity to be practiced in our day as well.

Method of Testing

To test means to make proof or trial of, put to the proof, just as the religious leaders tested Jesus.

> Matthew 16:1: "The Pharisees and Sadducees came and testing Him, asked…."
> Matthew 22:35: "Then one of them, a lawyer, asked Him a question, testing him…."

Testing, rendering an unbiased recommendation, is administered by questions and confirmed by observation.[13]

The ancient caravan trader with his hand-held scales illustrates the method and importance of "testing." Traveling from city-to-city and country-to-country, these nomadic venders exchanged their wares for the goods and currency of the community in which they worked. Naturally, a great diversity of metal coins existed. In those days inscriptions on the coins were secondary to the value of the metal. A coin might look like gold or silver, but the wise trader knew better than to trust his eyesight or touch. The miniature scale told him immediately if a coin was what it appeared to be: the weight checked out accurately.

A local church tests a visiting minister (apostle, prophet, teacher) by soundness of doctrine taught, moral character displayed, behavior observed, spiritual life imparted and track record proven. The admonitions of Paul (2 Thessalonians 3:6-15), Peter (2 Peter 2:1-3, 10-22) and Jude (3-4, 17-19) would certainly apply to this kind of testing. Paul felt strongly about this: "Now I urge you, brethren, note those who cause divisions and offenses, contrary to the doctrine which you learned, and avoid them," Romans 16:17.

Eight Signs of a False Apostle

2 Corinthians 11:5-20 describes the false apostle in eight ways:

1. Burdensome (irritating presence), v. 9
2. Deceitful (impure motives), v. 13
3. Charlatans (fakes), vss. 13-15
4. Bondage bringers, v. 20
5. Devourers of the people (taking advantage of), v. 20
6. Thieves (who steal authority, finances, property), v. 20
7. Arrogant (Self-exalting, proud), vss. 12, 20
8. Insulting (dignity and authority), v. 20

Reason 6. Living Apostles Trump Dead Tradition

In 2005 my wife Joy and I visited the Cathedral of St. Paul of Rome. We were greeted near the entrance by a large, magnificent statue of a militant Paul standing on a pedestal in front of the entrance. Tightly clutched by his left hand were the Scriptures, a great sword in his right hand (representing the Word of God) pressed upon his chest. A truly awe-inspiring figure![14]

Inside the Cathedral we were immediately struck by the amazing array of portraits that circled the ceiling of the great sanctuary. Starting with Peter, an unbroken series of Roman Catholic popes presented an impressive visual display to reinforce the belief that that church can trace its apostolic ancestry to St. Peter himself. Amazing when you think about it, Paul's picture was not included in the line-up (he would not qualify), although the building bears his name.

The claim is that the authorized apostolic mission of Christ has been handed down in the Roman Catholic Church generation to generation, thereby vindicating that church's present activity as operating directly under the commission of Christ and His deceased apostles. Hans Küng, Roman Catholic theologian, says "The apostles are dead; there are no new apostles. But the *apostolic mission* remains."[15]

This statement is only two-thirds true: "The apostles are dead .... the apostolic mission remains." This attitude that "there are no new apostles" has enfeebled the Church. How can there be a *present* apostolic mission without *living, present-day* apostles and prophets? Tradition alone does not make a mission or confirm apostolic authority. Placing empty hands on empty heads does not bequeath the Holy Spirit, claiming tradition as the church dynamic is not sufficient.

In my book *Your Sons & Daughters Shall Prophesy* I made this comment while discussing "When Bishops Replace Prophets" (emphasis added):

> To keep connection with her founders without "endangering" the Church by depending on unpredictable prophetic manifestation, *the leadership decided to let the office inherit the apostolic authority, even if the man occupying the office lacked the power of the Spirit.* Thus was the authority passed from one generation to another. Called "apostolic succession," it merely represented *the passing on of a religious family business rather than the fresh impartation and call of the Holy Spirit.* This sealed the demise of the ecstatic prophet. It was the time of the sophistication of the Church and the domestication of the Spirit.[16]

The doctrine of "Apostolic Succession" did *not* exist in the New Testament Church. It was "a theory of ministry in the church that arose after A.D. 170-200."[17] The basic thought is that certain religious leaders (popes and bishops) represent a direct, uninterrupted line of spiritual descent from the apostles chosen by Christ. The authority of the Twelve Apostles has been passed down through the ages by the sacrament of laying on of hands, starting with Peter. The mission of the early Church supposedly has by this means been extended to today's successors in an unbroken line of tradition.

Actually Apostolic Succession and ordination operate dynamically by the Holy Spirit. The body of Christ, the true Church, is made up of joined-together, living stones; these people follow the witness, the faith and the confession of the early apostles in the full sense of the word. They follow in the footsteps Christ, the Twelve Apostles and Paul -- and believe for and participate in a fresh, recurring, *ongoing event* in living history. The New Testament does not claim to have replaced the Twelve Apostles, but rather it shows a pattern of *perpetuating* the apostolate with contemporary ministers filled with the Holy Spirit, proclaiming the Gospel as it was done in the beginning.

Living apostles trump dead traditions. Constant vigilance is needed to keep apostolic Christianity alive and well. Jude said "to contend earnestly for the faith which was once for all delivered to the saints" (Jude 3). Let us not allow active faith to slip into inactive tradition. Biblical Christianity has living faith, set on fire by the Holy Spirit: "for the letter kills, but the Spirit gives life" (2 Corinthians 3:6).

The essence and dynamic of Jesus' teaching was in the experience and application of the message. We have seen, as modern people, how weariness, tradition and so on, have contributed to the erosion of vital Christianity, leaving but a shell. Since some have not seen or experienced the reality of New Testament living, the Bible has become the account of a bygone era, accompanied by a pathetic slogan: "The day of miracles is past."

This deterioration need not cancel vital Christianity. Churches can be "on fire," contemporary apostles and miraculous gifts can happen even in our modern society. Faith and belief are possible: it is doable, it is our heritage! "The kingdom of heaven has been forcefully advancing," Jesus said, adding quickly, "and forceful men lay hold of it" (Matthew 11:12, NIV).

Reason 7. The Great Commission Is Apostolic

Since the early apostles and prophets laid the original foundation of the Church, we moderns do not usually think about the need for a new foundation.

At first, this seems reasonable. After all, the Church was successfully launched, miracles confirmed the ministry of those early apostles, a canon of Scripture was established and the early missionaries planted the Church all over the known world. A wonderful beginning and foundation!

"But this is all past history," some say, "there is no need to duplicate what they did." It is true, the Twelve laid the foundation, and nothing else need be added. We are told, "The miraculous and apostolic have ceased because they fulfilled their purposes, and we must be content with the inspired canon of New Testament Scripture left for us." Supposedly the conclusion is:

> The real successor to the apostolate is the NT itself, since it continues their ministry within the church of God."[18]

The apostles' writings may replace the apostles, but this does not automatically restore their powerful Spirit-impartation into the Church's life and mission!

Meanwhile, the human race has proliferated around the earth, and many modern and ancient peoples and cultures still wait for the saving message of Christ. The churches must maintain their apostolic zeal or these unsaved peoples will never experience the good news of Jesus.

The end of the age seems a poor time to abandon miracles and the leadership that Christ ordained!

Our closed-minded approach in a time of global crisis needs immediate attention. The world is too big, the churches accelerate too fast, cultural/societal problems are too challenging! The Church of Jesus Christ needs apostles, prophets and rank-and-file Christians with faith, wisdom and miracle-power now more than ever before. We must reach the nations, and this cannot be done effectively without the unique leadership and miraculous ministry of *contemporary* apostles and churches. The Bible nowhere hints that miracles, spiritual gifts, apostles and spiritual churches should cease; they will continue to the end *if we exercise faith for their continuance.*

Part III. "A New Kind of Apostles" is next. You will get the inside story of how a major tragedy was averted because apostles followed the guidance of the Holy Spirit. They challenged the status quo of that day, making the Church into the mighty missionary force that Jesus intended.

Chapter 7 Endnotes

[1] Jonas Clark, *Advanced Apostolic Studies* (Hallandale Beach, FL: Spirit of Life Publishing, 2002), Lesson 1, p. 3. John MacArthur says, "every NT book was written either by an apostle or under his auspices (cf. John 14:26)" (*MacArthur Study Bible, p. 1691).*

[2] "Inscripturated" is not in all dictionaries; used by evangelical theologians to describe inspired (God-breathed) Scripture (2 Timothy 3:16; 2 Peter 1:21).

[3] Acts 16:10-17; 20:5-21:18; 27:1-28:16.

[4] Wagner, *Apostles Today,* p. 114.

[5] McBirnie, p. 251.

[6] Aziz Atiya, *A History of Eastern Christianity* (London: Methuen & Co, Ltd., 1968), pp. 25-28.

[7] 1 Cor. 3:22, Apollos is sandwiched between Paul and Peter, seemingly making Apollos on a par with the other two apostles: Paul – Apollos – Peter.

[8] Timothy helped Paul in the writing of five epistles: Philippians, Colossians, 1st and 2nd Thessalonians and Philemon. The chart is based on chart in *A Harmony of the Life of St. Paul* by Frank J. Goodwin, p. 64.

[9] McBirnie, p. 269.

[10] E. M. Blaiklock, "Dalmatia," *Zondervan Pictorial Encyclopedia of the Bible,* Volume 2 (Grand Rapids: Zondervan, 1975), pp. 6, 7.

[11] Don Williams, *The Apostle Paul and Women in the Church* (Van Nuys, CA 91409: BIM Publishing Co., 1977), p. 44.

[12] Cited in William Sandy and Arthur Headian, *The Epistle to the Romans* (Edinburgh: T. & T. Clark, 1902), p. 423.

[13] Compare 1 Corinthians 14:29; 1 Thessalonians 5:21; 1 John 4:1.

[14] Picture shown in *The Zondervan Pictorial Encyclopedia of the Bible,* p. 656.

[15] Küng, *The Church,* p. 456.

---

[16] Ernest B. Gentile, *Your Sons & Daughters Shall Prophesy* (Grand Rapids: Chosen Books, 1999), p. 258.

[17] R. E. Higginson, "Apostolic Succession," Walter A. Elwell, ed., *Evangelical Dictionary of Theology,* Second Edition (Grand Rapids: Baker Academic, 2001), p. 89.

[18] Higginson, Ibid.

Part III – A New Kind of Apostles and People of God

Chapter 8 – Four Apostles Save the Gentile Mission

Chapter 9 – An Open Door for the Gentiles

Chapter 10 – The Macedonian Crusade

Chapter 11 – The Word to All Asia

Chapter 8
Four Apostles
Save the Gentile Mission

In This Chapter

- *Three great events launched the Church*
- *What and why was the "Council at Jerusalem"?*
- *The bottom line of the Pharisees' opposition*
- *Peter's great story, told three times in Acts!*
- *Irrefutable evidences that God had invaded history again*

Three events – dramatically fulfilling Hebrew Scripture -- were possibly the most significant happenings in the total life of the Church, *even to this present time in history*. They are still our foundation . . . and, marching orders.

First, was Jesus' dramatic announcement in the Nazareth synagogue that Isaiah 61 was *at that moment* fulfilled: "You've just heard Scripture make history. It came true just now in this place" (Luke 4:21, M). He introduced the good news of the kingdom of God, and then proceeded throughout Galilee, accompanied by signs and wonders, salvation, deliverance and transformation.

Second, was the birth of the Church on Pentecost (Acts 2): the Holy Spirit made grand entrance with blazing fire, howling wind and Gentile tongues – all of which Peter documented with a Scripture: "This is what the prophet Joel announced would happen" (Acts 2:16, M). Prophecy – God speaking to and through His people -- had returned, but not just for the prophets, but for all God's children!

The third event, the focus of this chapter, was the Council at Jerusalem recorded in Acts 15 (49 A.D.): guided by the Holy Spirit, four intrepid apostles averted a terrible tragedy, the ending of Jesus' mission to the heathen nations. Using "just as it is written" for authentication, James showed how Amos 9:11-12 was now fulfilled by racial outsiders – the Gentiles -- joining the people of God.

Peter and three post-Ascension apostles (James, Barnabas and Paul) presented their case, overcoming the strident cries of Pharisees to require Gentile converts to be circumcised and keep the law. Had legalism prevailed, William Barclay says, "Christianity would have become nothing other than a sect of Judaism."[1]

The joyful Council unlocked and flung wide the gates of God's kingdom to all who would believe; endorsed by the apostles and elders in Jerusalem, this open-minded, heart-warming policy ensured all believing Gentiles a sincere welcome into the people of God. Christianity, in good conscience, would now continue the evangelization of Gentile communities. The announcement – "whosoever will, may come!" -- like the tolling of a massive bell, sent the resounding call to everyone everywhere to join God's family.

The Importance of Acts 15

The Council of Jerusalem was no brief encounter. Although we do not know the length of the conference, we assume, as Kistemaker suggests, the leaders "met for many days to discuss the matter at hand."[2] The outcome was truly significant.

- "one of the most important chapters in the history of the Church" (Conner).[3]
- "forms the centre of Acts both structurally and theologically" (Marshall).[4]
- "a watershed….of epochal significance for the future of Christianity" (Dunn).[5]
- "an event to which Luke attaches the highest importance" (F.F. Bruce).[6]
- "the leaders were fully aware of the transcendent significance" (Wagner).[7]
- "This chapter is one of the most significant in the Bible" (Beacham).[8]
- "the charter of freedom for the Gentiles" (Barclay).[9]

Background to the Council

Wholesale entry of Gentiles into the churches of Antioch, Cyprus and Galatia enraged the Jerusalem Pharisees: *they charged like a run of angry bulls.*

The Issue at Hand

The Pharisees demand was clear and emphatic: "It is necessary to circumcise them [the Gentiles], and to command them to keep the law of Moses" (Acts 15:5).

Jewish Christians had not previously considered circumcision and the law to be *un*essential; after all, becoming a part of God's people could not overlook Abraham and Moses! Paul and Barnabas, on the other hand, had not included circumcision and the legalistic teachings of Rabbinical Judaism in their convert requirements. This new idea of revoking the long-standing requirements for converted pagans (i.e., proselytes) was quite unnerving to Jewish Christians: this bone of contention could and would split the Church!

Unauthorized legalists strong-armed their doctrine among the converts, causing another pet peeve to surface, socializing with Gentiles, eating at table with them. Making fierce protest, Paul and Barnabas resisted these radical demands.

Tensions mounting, matters at a deadlock, the pressure cooker was about to explode! Quickly the Antioch leaders deputized Barnabas, Paul and "certain others" to bring this question to the apostles and elders at Jerusalem. The decision was not forced by the Judaizers or summoned by James or the Twelve apostles; the Antioch church leadership made the decision, and Paul and Barnabas gladly cooperated.[10]

Why Jerusalem?

Jerusalem was not the "Headquarters of the Church," rather the location of the mother church, its elders, and the Twelve Apostles. The Council convened to *settle a doctrinal matter,* actually a local church problem with far-reaching consequences for all Gentile believers: Antioch was a test case. Conner says:

[T]he matter had to be dealt with there [in Jerusalem] because these teachers came from the Jerusalem Church. The principle of truth is that all problems should be dealt with in the local church where they originated....Seeing the 'problem' had come from Judea and from the church at Jerusalem, the apostles [Paul and Barnabas] agreed to go back to the 'home church' from whence these legalistic teachers had come and have the matter dealt with there.[11]

The delegation's trip to Jerusalem occurred between Paul's first and second missionary journeys, "a necessary pause" to settle an important difficulty.[12] The decision would determine if apostolic approval would be given to the Judaizers. This following statement by Morgan (referencing Farrar) gives special insight:

This has sometimes been called the story of the first council of the Christian Church. To that description of the gathering in Jerusalem Farrar in his "Life and Work of St. Paul" objected, for excellent reasons. He showed that the council in Jerusalem *was not a convention of delegates, but a meeting of the Church at Jerusalem*, to receive a deputation from the Church at Antioch, and to consider a subject of grave importance in the matter of missionary enterprise. *He pointed out moreover, that this gathering in Jerusalem was for purposes of consultation, and not for final and dogmatic decision....* Almost all councils subsequent to the first have attempted to fix some habit of ritual, or to give final form to the expression of some great truth. Neither of these things was attempted in the gathering in Jerusalem. *The true function of a council as herein revealed, is that of considering an immediate subject, and finding an immediate application of principles....such consideration and such finding must necessarily have a most important bearing on future development.[13]*

What Was the "Council" Like?

This council was unlike those described in religious encyclopedias, unlike modern conventions with thousands of voting delegates: not political and not convened for public opinion, the gathering would not warrant a news conference.

These leaders were not erudite minds, pompous male clerics robed in fine vestments, wearing bishop's hats, meeting in a Gothic cathedral. The Twelve apostles were commoners, having no advanced degrees, living humbly by faith, adopting Jesus' life style.

The contemptuous religious leaders considered them "ordinary men who had no special training" (Acts 4:13, NLT).

The tongues of fire that fell at Pentecost still blazed in their hearts. These Spirit-baptized Jews had spoken miraculously in Gentile languages and now realized that the miracle was both a confirming sign *and* a call to the nations. The Church and its leaders could no longer be content with the Christian Jew status quo.

How Would They Decide?

They gave themselves to prayer, serious discussion and openness to the Holy Spirit. Little is recorded about spiritual activity at the Council, but rest assured the subject was a matter of major, prayerful concern by the whole church body; all remained sensitive to prophetic confirmation. Finally, a unified church declared, "For it seemed good to the Holy Spirit, and to us..." (Acts 15:28).

The Objective of the Legalists

Modern Christians find the Jewish attitude difficult to comprehend. Simply put, the legalists felt the Greek converts were starting their lives in *the middle of a process*, eliminating the fundamentals: like starting school in the ninth grade without knowing the A-B-Cs or multiplication table. Accepting Christ was good, but the convert must also accept and experience everything that preceded Jesus Messiah--as though making up missing grades. This meant accept *and participate in* the Abrahamic and Mosaic Covenants (be circumcised, and keep the ceremonial laws). The legalists could not fathom that God had invaded history again, rendering their traditions outdated, like emaciated wineskins unable to hold new wine.

What Would the Ramifications Be?

Jesus predicted Jerusalem's destruction (Luke 21:20-14), but the apostles' immediate concerns preempted worry about the future demise of city and local church. *The apostles did not know that the Romans would level Jerusalem and scatter the Christians in about 20 years.* F. F. Bruce says in *The Spreading Flame:*

> The situation which gave rise to the whole controversy was a temporary one. It was no longer urgent after A. D. 70 [when Jerusalem was destroyed]. And after A. D. 135 the church of Jerusalem itself was a Gentile church.[14]

The apostles, by divine guidance, saved the Church. Before Roman legions marched on Jerusalem, the Church opened the door of welcome that allowed the gospel of grace to go world-wide, producing one great, global, people of God, both Jew and Gentile. Within the intervening 20 years, the unfettered Paul, his associate apostles, and the original Twelve planted churches throughout the nations, declaring the New Covenant as a "law-free," "grace-filled," God-established gospel.[15]

How the Pharisees Presented Their Argument

One attitude resonated in every Jewish breast: salvation without circumcision and the Jewish legal system was *unthinkable*, therefore *undoable.* "[T]hey saw themselves as the chosen people . . . the special possession of God . . . also that God was the special possession of the Jews" (Barclay).[16]

The Case for Circumcision

1. Circumcision was the seal of the Abrahamic Covenant (Genesis 17; Romans 4:11; Acts 7:8), the sign of covenant relationship and the covenant seed. All promises and privileges depended on circumcision.
2. Circumcision was confirmed by the Law of Moses. Exodus 12:43-50; Joshua 5:1-10.
3. Without the circumcision of his sons, Moses faced divine retribution. Exodus 4:24-26.
4. Only the circumcised could partake of the Passover (Exodus 12:48).
5. Every Jewish mind automatically would ask: "What evidence exists that the law, which represents the will of God for His covenant people, has been repealed?"
6. "The link between 'Jew', 'Judaism' and circumcision was axiomatic; *an uncircumcised Jew was virtually a contradiction in terms*...no Gentile could surely think to have a share in that inheritance without first being circumcised" (Dunn, emphasis added).[17]

The Original Purpose for Circumcision

God originally used circumcision to cure the self-righteousness of His people. Circumcision was to cut away -- separate -- His people unto God, making them dependent on God. The visible sign or symbol constantly reminded them to retain the government of God in their lives.

Jewish legalism nullified this original intent, transforming circumcision into an expression of independence and self-righteousness. Israel's religion of the Spirit became subservient to a system of observing a physical ritual.

The Jewish Status Quo

Although the Pharisees and Judean Jews were quite punctilious about keeping laws and traditions, the folks from Galilee like Peter, James and John were from the working class, not disposed to keep the stringent Rabbinical requirements. The Twelve Apostles (except Judas Iscariot) were from Galilee, and *they all had been exposed to the unrelenting, vehement antagonism that the Pharisees hurled like stones against Jesus.*[18] They certainly knew Jesus' hostility toward hollow religion.

The following chart gives a brief summary of things that the legalists wished to require of the new converts.

Elements of the "Yoke of Bondage"		
(Gal 5:1; Acts 15:10, 24), also called "the Works of the Law" (2:16). "[T]he whole Levitical and ceremonial law, every last part of it, was abrogated for all Christians" (Lenski).[19]		
Twelve Elements	Examples	References
1. Circumcision	• Titus not required to be circumcised • Concern of Jewish Apostles • Apostles "gave no such commandment"	Gal 2:3; 5:2,6; 6:12-15; 1 Cor 7:10; Acts 21:21 Acts 15:24
2. Table Fellowship – Eat only with Jews	• Jesus ate with sinners (Matthew 9:11) • Peter in Antioch • Peter in Caesarea • Peter with Jerusalem Elders	Mt 9:11 Gal 2:11-14 Acts 10:28 Acts 11:2-3 1 Tim 5:3
3. Kosher Foods	• Abstain from certain foods	1 Tim 4:3 ;

		• Let no one judge you in food or drink • Peter's vision	Heb13:9; 10:10; Col 2:16 Acts 10
4.	Religious Holidays	• "regarding a festival or a new moon or Sabbaths" • "You observe days and months and seasons & years. I am afraid for you, lest I have labored in vain" • "Keeping the day" or not keeping • Lawful to do good on Sabbath	Col 2:16 Gal 4:10-11 Rom 14:5-6 Matt 12:12
5.	Regulations	• "Do not touch, do not taste, do not handle" • Wash hands certain way	Col 2:20-23 Mark 7:3-4, 8
6.	Disputations	• "foolish & arrogant disputes" • "words to no profit"	2 Tim 2:23 2 Tim 1;14
7.	Heeding Unprofitable Discussions	• "Giving heed to fables and endless genealogies"	1 Tim 4:3
8.	Hypocrisy	• Jesus' scathing rebuke Matt 23:3-16	1 Tim 4:3
9.	Temple Rituals	• Paul's trouble while in the Temple and the Apostles' attitude about it	Acts 21:24-25
10.	Synagogue Attendance	• No prayer & worship in Jesus' name and no New Covenant teaching or prayer/deliverance for the needy	
11.	No world vision	• In contrast, the Christians were to pray for all men to be saved	1 Tim 2:2
12.	The Great Contrast	• Works of the Law vs. Faith in Jesus Christ and fulfilling the 10 Commandments	Gal 2:16

Apostles and elders did not circumvent the Ten Commandments, and Jesus did not destroy but fulfill: the new emphasis was heart-meaning, God-intent and faith in God (all of which were found in the Torah). Some things were eliminated: how to wash your hands, your pots and pans, or your couch, things of that nature. The Ten Commandments remained, presented throughout the New Testament as Jesus meant them to be. Paul later gave this perceptive advice: "But we know that the law is good if one uses it lawfully."[20]

Three Separate Meetings

The order of events at the Council is not specified, nor is it clear that this is the same meeting that Paul mentioned in Galatians 2:1.[21]

The Council probably had three phases or separate meetings:

1. A general meeting that welcomed the delegates and they report (4-5).
2. A separate meeting of the Apostles and elders with Paul and Barnabas (6-11).
3. A full church assembly heard the missionaries and James, and the four requirements were formulated and approved (Kistemaker).[22]

The Opening Scenes

The Antioch delegation was greeted with keen excitement and great enthusiasm! Barnabas and Paul gladly shared some of their exciting adventures in the Gentile world,[23] the crowd holding rapt attention and whetted expectation.

A secluded meeting for the leaders was a necessity, not specifically recorded in Acts, but referenced, we believe, by Paul in Galatians 2:1-10.

> Then after fourteen years I went up again to Jerusalem with Barnabas, and also took Titus with me. And I went up by revelation, and communicated to them that gospel which I preach among the Gentiles, but privately to those who were of reputation, lest by any means I might run, or had run, in vain.

This private meeting had a special purpose: "to consider this matter" ["subject," *logos*, Acts 15:6]; i.e., have appropriate *deliberation,* allowing each apostle time to express his point of view. Undoubtedly, Jesus' vehement opinion about Pharisaism would be reviewed. Luke's account in Acts was sketchy, while Paul's account, showing deep emotion, noted that he went to Jerusalem "by revelation," that is, directed by the Holy Spirit.[24]

Titus was introduced to the Jerusalem leaders: an uncircumcised Greek, an impressive young man who truly loved and served Jesus Christ. His transparent genuineness and excitement must have reminded the Twelve of their own early enthusiasm. Their swift conclusion: "No circumcision needed!"

> Gal 2:3 shows that Titus accompanied Paul...as Paul's companion and not as one of the delegates.... It seems that he purposely took uncircumcised Titus along as a sample of a Gentile convert and as a direct challenge to the Judaizers, and no apostle even suggested that Paul should have him circumcised if only to placate the Judaizers (Lenski).[25]

The general conference followed, the Pharisees boisterous, confrontational and argumentative. As the apostles spoke and the meetings continued, the blatant opposition faded away, like night before day. The legalists were flabbergasted when they discovered that Peter *and James* did not side with them! We are not told how and when, but the tide turned and opposing voices grew silent.

The Membership Gathered

Peter told again how God had sent him to Cornelius' home and how the Gentiles received the Holy Spirit *just as the Jews did* on the day of Pentecost. This astounding story had been much discussed among the Jewish believers, especially the apostles and elders. Significantly, Luke gave the story three-time coverage (Acts 10, 11, 15).

Peter's humble fisherman approach carried more weight than trying to argue like a scholar or theologian. Wisely, he just told what God did! Without doubt the apostles and elders had already reached consensus, so an emboldened Peter enthusiastically told the good story yet again. The bottom line: "God had manifested His saving Grace without the rite of Circumcision" (Conner).[26]

Soaring eloquently, Peter declared convictions buried in many hearts, labeling the law "a yoke" the Jews could not bear, asking "So why put it on the converted Gentiles?"[27] Proud of his

Jewish heritage, Peter still chafed under the heavy traditions imposed by the rabbis -- he spoke for every common man.

The metaphor of carrying and pulling heavy loads with yokes, was clearly understood. Jesus' words quickly come to mind: "they bind heavy burdens, hard to bear, and lay them on men's shoulders; but they themselves will not move them with one of their fingers" (Matthew 23:4). All would also remember how Jesus (Matthew 11:29) referred to His yoke as "easy" (well-fitting) and His burden "light" (easily managed). Peter's forceful, heart-felt, Spirit-anointed message was possibly his finest moment.

Report on the Gentile Mission

Barnabas and Paul told of the "many wonders and signs God had worked through them among the Gentiles." The account by the grizzled apostle and his beloved companion caused awesome silence: one could hear a pin drop! Void of religious argument, their story was a simple one -- God had worked through them, the miracles were real.

Barnabas, being senior, spoke first, enabling him to present both what God had done and how remarkably the Lord had used his servant Paul. Their account would include activities in Antioch, Cyprus and southern Galatia. Their story-telling held the crowd spellbound (Acts 14:3). The triumphant confrontation with Bar-Jesus the sorcerer must have brought spontaneous applause (Acts 13:6-13), also the amazing healing of the lame man in Lystra (Acts 14:6-18). Finally, Paul stoned to death and ... raised from the dead (Acts 14:19, 20)!

An unpretentious Paul stood before the assembly, clothed simply, tired in appearance, face scared from stoning, graying hair - but passionate for Jesus and souls. Could this possibly be that maniacal Pharisee, the high priest's executioner? Some had suffered at this man's hands, but now their hearts were melted. God's grace made all eyes moist while voices rose in praise.

The Epochal Statement of James

Finally, the Church came to *the last court of appeal, the Word of God.* Using Amos 9:11, 12 (having the tenor of all the prophets[28]) and anointed by the Holy Spirit, James showed conclusively that the Gentile converts were part of God's unfolding plan for *all mankind*. James unreservedly affirmed the testimonies of Paul, Barnabas and Peter, cinching the argument that everything was in perfect accord with Amos' prophecy and God's intentions. The Spirit's bestowal on Jews and Gentile alike pointed, like a huge, flashing sign to *immediate change*.

This is the third *epochal interpretation of God's Word* introducing the new era ("Epochal": of or relating to an epoch; unique, highly significant; unparalleled):

> *First*.........**Jesus quoted Isaiah 61:1-2** to confirm His ministry of signs and wonders, and the immediate introduction of the Kingdom of God.

> *Second*.......**Peter quoted Joel 2:28-29** to explain the Pentecostal outpouring of the Spirit, explaining that prophecy had returned – not just to the prophets, but to all God's people.

> *Third*.......**James quoted Amos 9:11-12**, to authenticate the conversion of Gentiles and their acceptance into the people of God (without legal restrictions).

The Quotation of Amos 9:11-12 in Acts 15:16-17

As a teen-aged convert, I puzzled over these two texts. Shouldn't the words be the same? I now realize, of course, that some New Testament quotations do not agree with Old Testament sources because different versions are quoted and linguistic problems sometimes exist. Luke, Paul and other writers quoted from the Hebrew Scriptures and sometimes from the more easily understood *LXX*, the Septuagint Greek translation of the Hebrew Scriptures: it was like hearing a modern preacher quote from a recent version which gives contemporary flavor.

Written about 250 years before the New Testament books, the *LXX* was the most available and readable edition of the Scriptures in the Greco-Roman world. Luke and James knew the Greek text, in this case actually *the best version to present the true intent* of this prophecy.

> Acts 15:16-17 in the New King James Version:
>
> After this I will return
> And will rebuild the tabernacle of David which has fallen down.
> I will rebuild its ruins
> And I will set it up,
> So that the rest of mankind may seek the LORD.
> Even all the Gentiles who are called by My name,
> Says the LORD who does all these things.
>
> F. F. Bruce sums it up like this:
>
> The Septuagint version, partly by following variant Hebrew readings, universalizes and spiritualizes this oracle so that *it becomes a promise of the day when all mankind will seek the true God and be called by his name* (emphasis added).[29]

James announced that God was bringing converted Gentiles into a renewed Israel, and *both factions would now be considered one people:* awesome announcement! The Spirit-filled Jews made up renewed Israel, the converted Gentiles were the remnant of mankind: together they made up the people called by His name.

> What is clearly intended is an understanding of a people of God in which Jew and Gentile are one, a restored Israel into which Gentiles called by God in their own right, and not as petitioning proselytes, are integrated (not assimilated) (Dunn).[30]

The Jerusalem church, the apostles and elders now realized that God Himself had brought change and enlargement to His people. Also, God clearly indicated that He would use apostles like Paul and Barnabas in accomplishing His ongoing mission.

Three Arguments Refute the Pharisees

Every Jew wanted this bottom-line question answered:

"What evidence exists that the Covenant of Circumcision (through Abraham) and the Covenant of Law (through Moses) have been repealed?"

The Council met the challenge head on, showing three undeniable, divine evidences that affirmed *an intervention of God in history and an updated covenant:*

1) Signs and wonders, begun by Jesus and continued by the Church
2) The Spirit's witness, outpoured at Pentecost and now on the Gentiles
3) Conversions in the Gentile world, responding to Amos' Prophecy

A change point had come, as dramatic and dynamic as Abraham's circumcision and Moses' receiving the Law. Circumcision and Law were not thrown aside, rather given an upgrade, a promotion, elevated to the objectives that God always had in mind! Nothing was lost, God's people could now move to a higher plain where true spirituality and not mere outward observance is primary.

1. Signs and Wonders

"Then all the multitude kept [dead] silence and listened to Barnabas and Paul declaring how many miracles and wonders God had worked through them among the Gentiles" (Acts 15:12). These supernatural evidences confirmed that the message of God's kingdom delivered by Christ's apostle-ambassadors was truly authentic. Pagan fascination with foolish idols was broken by the revelation of Jesus Savior of the whole world, undeniable evidence!

The signs and wonders experienced by the missionary-apostles, as well as the miraculous experienced in the Judean churches, were the ongoing demonstration of the kingdom of God (Isaiah 61) introduced by Jesus Himself. What Jesus had done in the nation of Israel was being duplicated in the nations!

2. The Spirit's Witness

Jesus taught that the Holy Spirit in a believer would gush forth like rivers of living water (John 7:38-39). This prediction found glorious fulfillment on the Day of Pentecost when the Spirit of God was outpoured upon 120 of Jesus' disciples (including the Twelve, James, Jude, Mary and others). Immediate evidence occurred, the disciples bursting forth supernaturally in *Gentile* tongues, glorifying God in an area of Herod's Temple where no Gentile languages were allowed![31]

Later, this same manifestation took place in the house of Cornelius the Roman centurion, dumbfounding Peter and six of his Jewish friends. As had happened with the Jews, Gentiles were filled with the Holy Spirit and spoke miraculously in *languages not learned.* Peter's response, and that of all the elders when later told, was that God had accepted the Gentiles because of their faith in Christ, *without circumcision!* "Then God has also granted to the Gentiles repentance to life" (Acts 11:18). The Spirit's evidence of speaking in tongues was incontrovertible proof!

Charismatic gifts were functioning in the church at Antioch. Paul and Barnabas were accustomed to the miracle of prophecy and speaking in tongues among the Gentile converts. This was *a continuing pattern,* "standard operating procedure," established for new Christians: salvation by faith, baptism in water, baptism with the Spirit accompanied by the evidence of speaking in an unlearned tongue (Acts 2:38; 19:6).[32] If the Twelve asked Paul and Barnabas whether or not the sign of tongues at Caesarea was repeated in other Gentile gatherings, Paul's affirmative answer would certainly reinforce this conclusion.

The miracle of tongues not only confirmed the Spirit's presence at Jerusalem and Caesarea, but also bound together all believers, Jews and Gentiles, with a "uniform evidence that authenticates the experience of all believers everywhere and in every generation."[33] The voice of God – the prophetic, silenced too long – had now returned!

3. The Prophetic Word

Finally, James presented the prophecy of Amos as authentication of the surge of faith in the Gentile communities. God already had a faithful remnant of Israel going His way (the Jewish converts); God was now reaping a believing remnant from the rest of mankind. The merging groups became one people of God called by His name. *A new change point in history occurred.* God Himself initiated this response taking place among the Gentiles, and the believing Jews should rejoice in it! Like the first and second evidences, the third evidence also fulfills the Scripture.

David's Tabernacle

Amos foretold that the gathering Jews and Gentiles fulfilled the reestablishing of *the Tabernacle of David*, not the Tabernacle of Moses. This oracle did not refer to reinstituting the kingdom of David on a natural throne; this text affirms the New Covenant instituted by Jesus the son of David! The early Church believed that Jesus the resurrected Messiah was *now* on the Davidic throne.[34] Jesus said, "I am the root and offspring of David," or "the source of David and the heir to his throne" (Revelation 22:16, NLT).

Are you aware that the Tabernacle of Moses (Gibeon) and the Tabernacle of David (Mt. Zion) existed for a period at the same time, but in different locations?[35] Frustrated with ceremonial ritualism, David introduced (by Spirit inspiration) expressive, psalmic, heart-worship in a special tent or tabernacle pitched on Mt. Zion. Utilizing the nine expressions of worship mentioned in the book of Psalms,[36] this new priestly worship was maintained 24-7. Priests and sacrifices still functioned at Gibeon, but David's order of worship on Mt. Zion specialized in sacrifices of praise and joy.

Returning the ark with great exuberance (2 Samuel 6; 1 Chronicles 15 and 16), David placed it in the new Tabernacle of David at Zion: God was introducing a new approach to Himself. James made clear from Amos 9 that the Pharisees' talk of Moses was antiquated! Moses was replaced by David's greater Son, Jesus the Messiah and Davidic king, now enthroned in the household of God where Jews and Gentiles worship in Spirit and in Truth -- the one people of God.

The Letter to the Gentiles

The Council drafted a letter "to the brethren who are of the Gentiles in Antioch, Syria, and Cilicia," informing them that all people are saved by grace and faith in Christ, keeping the legalistic laws would not be necessary.

The Gentiles were asked, however, to refrain from immorality (fornication), idolatry (including meat offered to idols) and eating things strangled or blood.[37] Such actions characterized raw heathenism, and were abominable to God and the Jews; the restrictions were accepted by Antioch as reasonable and perfectly in order.

> Its first lesson is that the Christian man and the Christian Church is free from the bondage of Hebraism….The second lesson….There must be, on the part of all Christian souls, abstention from the haunts and the habits of idolatry (Morgan).[38]

A mighty quaternion delivered the Council's letter: Paul and Barnabas, apostles to the Gentiles, and Judas (Barsabas) and Silas (Silvanus), "leaders among the brothers" (Gk.). Judas & Silas exhorted, strengthened and edified the church, adding the final touch to a marvelous episode superintended by the Holy Spirit.

Apostolic Confirmation

James, Peter and John clearly saw the grace of God on Paul and Barnabas, and gave them "the right hand of fellowship" (Galatians 2:9). This action was not only a token of fellowship and approval, but the recognition of the apostolic office *already possessed: now proven*. God had opened the door to the Gentile heathen and birthed a new awareness: other apostles existed and were being commissioned by Christ Himself, the head of the whole Church.

Chapter 8 Endnotes

[1] William Barclay, *The New Daily Study Bible: The Acts of the Apostles* (Louisville, KT: Westminster John Knox Press, 2003 third ed.), p. 132.

[2] Simon J. Kistemaker, *New Testament Commentary: Acts* (Grand Rapids: Baker, 1990), p. 543.

[3] Kevin J. Conner, *The Book of Acts* (Portland, OR: City Christian Publishing, 1973), p. 93.

[4] I. Howard Marshall, *Acts* (Tyndale New Testament Commentaries)(Grand Rapids: Eerdmans, 1988, 2nd ed.), p. 242.

[5] James D. G. Dunn, *The Acts of the Apostles* (Valley Forge: PN: Trinity Press International, 1996), pp. 195, 198.

[6] F. F. Bruce, *The Book of the Acts Revised* (The New International Commentary on the New Testament) (Grand Rapids: Eerdmans, 1988), p. 282.

[7] C. Peter Wagner, *Acts of the Holy Spirit* (Ventura, CA: Regal, 2000), p. 354.

[8] Beacham, *Rediscovering the Role,* p. 136.

[9] Barclay, p. 131.

[10] Kistemaker feels that the "immediate context (v. 3) confirms that the Antiochean church, not the Judaizers, dispatched the missionaries to Jerusalem" (p. 539), in spite of the expanded verses 1 and 2 in the Western manuscripts of the Greek text. This is most logical.

[11] Conner, p. 93.

[12] G. Campbell Morgan, *The Acts of the Apostles* (Fleming H. Revell, 1924), p. 364.

[13] Ibid., p. 356.

[14] F. F. Bruce, *The Spreading Flame*, p. 110.

[15] It is a sad fact that a decade after the Council when Paul returned to Jerusalem from his third missionary journey, legalists in the Church still numbered in the thousands (Acts 21:20-21).

[16] Barclay, pp. 130-131.

[17] Dunn points out that in the Maccabean defense of Jerusalem, the reassertion of circumcision as indispensable for all Jews was made, p. 198.

[18] Jesus considered them a "brood of vipers." Matthew 3:7; 5:17, 19-20; 7:23; 9:11, 14; 12:2, 8-9, 12; 15:4, 6, 9, 14, 20; 16:4, 16;19:3, 7; 22:15, 17, 36; 23:3, 13-16, 23-28, 31, 33.

[19] Lenski, R. C. H., *The Interpretation of the Acts of the Apostles* (Minneapolis, MINN: Augsburg Publishing House, 1961), p. 627.

[20] Matthew 5:17; 6:3, 8, 13; 1 Timothy 8:1.

[21] Johannes Münck says there are "important deviations" in Luke's and Paul's accounts; "Luke cannot have been right in every detail." *The Acts of the Apostles (The Anchor Bible)* (Garden City, NY: Doubleday & Co., Inc., 1967), p. LXVII. Both Marshall and Kistemaker give convincing solutions to the so-called deviations.

[22] Kistemaker, Ibid.

[23] Barnabas (mentioned first because older and one of the founders of the church) was favorably known. Outside of Jerusalem, Paul is mentioned first.

---

[24] F. F. Bruce concedes that "The great majority [of scholars] hold that Luke and Paul report the same occasion," but he also feels "there are strong reasons to question the identity of these two visits." *Paul,* p. 283.

[25] Lenski, pp. 595, 601.

[26] Conner, p. 93. Now, under the New Covenant "circumcision of heart" is as strong a covenant mandate – for both Jew and Gentile converts – as physical circumcision had been for the Jews under the Old Covenant. Physical circumcision is no longer a requirement, but the spiritual work of the Holy Spirit in our hearts is a necessity. Paul was uncompromising on this.

[27] "Yoke" is an apt description, picturing the binding apparatus that subdued and harnessed a domesticated animal. Matthew 23:4; Luke 11:46. "Yoke" in Acts 15:10 pictures the ceremonial part of the Jewish law and the regulations taught by the rabbis as an unbearable, unreasonable obligation. The Rabbinical 613 commandments would tend to make a person focus on external observance more than on God.

[28] Psalm 2:8; 113:3; Isaiah 11:10; 52:10; 56:7; 60:3; Jeremiah 16:19; Micah 4:1-2; Malachai 1:11. These and other Scriptures were the theological substructure for "Go therefore and make disciples of *all the nations*" (Matthew 28:19, emphasis added).

[29] F. F. Bruce, *New Testament History,* p. 286. Footnote 11: "The LXX version universalizes the scope of the prophecy by vocalizing *edom* (Edom) as *adam* (mankind) and spiritualizes it by reading *yidresu* ('that the remnant of mankind may seek Yahweh') in place of *yiresu* ('that they may *possess* the remnant of Edom).

[30] Dunn, p. 204.

[31] For a full discussion see: Ernest B. Gentile, *The Glorious Disturbance* (Grand Rapids, MI: Chosen Books, 2004), Chapter 4.

[32] Ibid., Chapter 6.

[33] Ibid., p. 115.

[34] Isaiah 9:6-7; Psalm 68:18; Mark 16:19; Luke 1:32-33; Acts 2:30-33; Romans 15:12; Hebrews 1:3; 4:14-16; 8:1; 9:24; 12:2; Revelation 5:5-6.

[35] 1 Chronicles 16:37-43; 2 Chronicles 1:1-13.

[36] Ernest B. Gentile, *Worship God!* (Portland, OR: City Christian Publishing, 1994). Davidic or Psalmic worship involves the whole person: using the voice (speaking, singing, shouting), the hands (raising, clapping, playing instruments), and posture (standing, kneeling, dancing). Add to this the inspiration of the Holy Spirit!

[37] Actually, the apostles ruled exactly according to the law of their day. The *Encyclopedia Judaica* (Vol. 12, Col. 1189) states: "The seven Noachide laws as traditionally enumerated are: the prohibition of idolatry, blasphemy, blood-shed, sexual sins, theft, and eating from a living animal, as well as the injunction to establish a legal system." This interesting comment is added, "Jews are obligated to observe the whole Torah, while every non-Jew is a 'son of the covenant of Noah.' Maimonides equates the 'righteous man of the (gentile) nations who has a share in the world to come even without becoming a Jew with a gentile who keeps these laws. Such a man is entitled to full material support from the Jewish community and to the highest earthly honors." Also see Lenski's thoughtful discussion, *Acts,* pp. 612-618.

[38] Morgan, p. 365.

Chapter 9
An Open Door to the Gentiles

In This Chapter

- *Challenging the Jewish "status quo"*
- *Oh! The wonderful, lavish grace of Jesus!*
- *Let's rethink the traditional four qualifications of an apostle*
- *Has the Body lost an important member?*

The ambitious goal of Jesus and Paul to reach the Gentile world will require more apostles than the Jewish Twelve and Paul. In addition, every Christian local church must upgrade to become apostolic in nature.

The Status Quo

Paul's ministry to the outside world was a radical departure from the "status quo" (the existing state of affairs) of the Jewish Christian community. He brought a new kind of apostleship, a refreshingly new understanding of God's Grace, Christ's Church and Holy Scripture. This approach proved to be understandable and dynamically workable among all people. As already explained, the Twelve Apostles stamped their approval on Paul's efforts, so he launched forth into his second missionary journey with renewed vigor and high expectation, taking Silas with him.

The Open Door

The early Judean Christian Church was clutched in the iron grip of Hebrew tradition -- elders, apostles, behavior, food, culture, language – all headquartered in *Jewish* Jerusalem. Christianity could never have broken out of that confinement and affected the world without the resolute leadership of Paul the apostle. His bravery, fortitude, endurance, and particularly his experience of the abounding grace of God, enabled Christianity to break forth to all nations. The "doorway" or "gateway" opened by the Council at Jerusalem provided unrestricted passage into the kingdom of God. Now, all nations must be invited to respond!

This concept of "open door" became one of Paul's favorite metaphors: opportunity, clear passage, no obstructions, manageable hindrances.

> Acts 11:18 – "[God] had opened the door of faith to the Gentiles"
> 1 Corinthians 16:9 – "a great and effective door has opened to me"
> 2 Corinthians 2:12 – "a door was opened to me by the Lord"
> Colossians 4:3 – "praying ... that God would open a door for the word"

Response of the Twelve

Paul's break with useless ritual in reaching new converts struck a resonate chord in every apostle. Remember Paul's words to the people of Antioch of Pisidia? "Everyone who believes in him [the Lord Jesus Christ] is freed from all guilt and declared right with God – something the Jewish law could never do" (Acts 13:39, NLT). The Galilean Twelve must have had a new birth of freedom

---

A Sampling of Paul's Good News for Gentiles
From the New Living Translation (Emphasis added)

Romans 3:29-30:
After all, God is not the God of the Jews only, is he? Isn't he also the God of the Gentiles? Of course he is. *There is only one God, and there is only one way of being accepted by him. He makes people right with himself only by faith, whether they are Jews or Gentiles.*

Ephesians 2:14 –22:
For Christ himself has made peace between us Jews and you Gentiles by making us all one people.... BY HIS DEATH HE ENDED THE WHOLE SYSTEM OF JEWISH LAW THAT EXCLUDED THE GENTILES. His purpose was to make peace between Jews and Gentiles by *creating in himself one new person from the two groups. Together as one body, Christ reconciled both groups to God* by means of his death, and our hostility toward each other was put to death. 17 He has broughtthis Good News of peace to you Gentiles who were far away from him, and to us Jews who were near. 18 Now all of us, both Jews and Gentiles,

may come to the Father through the same Holy Spirit because of what Christ has done for us. 19 *So now you Gentiles are no longer strangers and foreigners. You are citizens along with all of God's holy people. You are members of God's family.* 20 We are his house, built on the foundation of the apostles and prophets. And the cornerstone is Christ Jesus himself. 21 We who believe are carefully joined together, becoming a holy temple for the Lord. 22 Through him you Gentiles are also joined together as part of this dwelling where God lives by his Spirit.

Ephesians 3:6:
And this is the secret plan: *The Gentiles have an equal share with the Jews in all the riches inherited by God's children.* Both groups have believed the Good News, and both are part of the same body and enjoy together the promise of blessings through Christ Jesus.

Ephesians 6:19:
And pray for me, too. Ask God to give me the right words as I boldly explain God's secret plan that *the Good News is for the Gentiles too.*

Philippians 3:2:
Watch out for those dogs, those wicked men and their evil deeds, those mutilators who say you must be circumcised to be saved. *For we who worship God in the Spirit are the only ones who are truly circumcised.*

Colossians 1:27:
For it has pleased God to tell his people that *the riches and glory of Christ are for you Gentiles, too.*

Colossians 2:11:
When you came to Christ, you were "circumcised," but not by a physical procedure. It was a spiritual procedure – the cutting away of your sinful nature.

Colossians 2:16-17:
So don't let anyone condemn you for what you eat or drink, or for not celebrating certain holy days or new-moon ceremonies or Sabbaths. For *these rules were only shadows of the real thing, Christ himself.*

Colossians 3:11:
In this new life, it doesn't matter if you are a Jew or a Gentile, circumcised or uncircumcised, barbaric, uncivilized, slave, or free. Christ is all that matters, and he lives in all of us.

after the Jerusalem summit meeting. Their unanimous decision at the Council was that tradition and ceremony was an unbearable yoke for the converted Gentile. Jesus previously opened their understanding; Paul now showed them what must be done.

The Twelve began to go forth, emulating Paul's aggressive attitude. Our chart in chapter 4 tells of their final exploits and martyrdoms. There is disagreement among historical scholars about where and when the Twelve went and what they did, and we certainly can appreciate hesitancy to declare facts based on tradition.

One thing is certain, the Twelve did not spend the rest of their lives sitting on their hands in Jerusalem! Traditions tell us they were thrown forth, scattered like seed to the nations: Africa, Spain, Britain, Europe, Iran, India, the eastern countries, and so on. It goes without saying: *These Galileans were not about to risk their lives and undergo unbelievable privations just to bring pagan converts under the yoke of the Jewish system.* They willingly brought "good news" to all people, joyfully becoming martyrs in the process. The Amos prophecy rang in their hearts as they sought to bring all mankind into the New Covenant provided by Jesus the Messiah, the Davidic king on the throne of the kingdom of God.

Was Paul's Apostleship Genuine?

Who today would challenge Paul's apostleship? This, however, was not the case during his lifetime. Certain "unauthorized" teachers from Jerusalem vigorously tried to undermine Paul's authority in some of the churches he established. These self-proclaimed experts from the Jerusalem community did not have the will, ability or spiritual dynamic to plant Christian congregations in heathen cities, confronting Satanic control, setting captives free. They were adept and unconscionable, however, at sheep-stealing from Paul's congregations.

A noticeable example was Corinth where Judaizers confused the church members, insisting that Paul neglected Jewish traditions that the Mother Church cherished and observed. They impugned his ministry and character without batting an eye.

The false teachers or apostles were happy with the conversion of pagan sinners, but the real proof of the Gentiles' sincerity, *they felt,* would be coming under the mantle of Judaism's legal system (their authority): circumcision, holy days, kosher foods, Jewish traditions and laws, purification, sacrifice, and so on. Actually, Paul was carefully observing all that the elders and apostles in Jerusalem had included in their letter to the converted Gentiles (Acts 15); he wanted good standing with the original Twelve Apostles, desiring to do what was best.

Some Christian Jews, unwavering in their loyalty to Judaism, were hesitant to promote or participate in proselytizing Gentiles, grieved that "Paul was offering Gentiles equal privileges with Jews, without requiring them to submit to the obligations of the Law" (F. F. Bruce).[1]

When Jewish zealots invaded Greece in his absence, Paul found it necessary to write two epistles to the church at Corinth. Both letters stoutly defended his integrity and apostleship, giving modern readers some idea of the struggles he faced and what he considered apostleship to be.[2]

Paul's Grand Statement in 1 Corinthians 15:9-10

*"For I am the least of the apostles and do not even deserve to be called an apostle, because I persecuted the church of God. But by **the grace of God** I am what I am, and **his grace** to me was not without effect. No, I worked harder than all of them – yet not I, but **the grace of God** that was with me."*

Wonderful Grace of Jesus

Using "grace" three times in this text, Paul made clear that grace is more than a static attribute of God's nature or just a divine trait that somehow permits us to be saved. Lavish grace is *a pro-active force of the Spirit* in our total life!

[T]he doctrine of grace pertains to God's activity rather than to his nature....grace is to be understood in terms of *a dynamic expression of the divine personality*...the dimension of *divine activity* that enables God to confront human indifference and rebellion with an inexhaustible capacity to forgive and to bless. God is gracious in action (Bilezikian, emphasis added).[3]

The wonderful grace of Jesus saved Paul, continued working with and in him, and made him what he became. *Grace was ongoing and continuous!*

The Greek word for grace is *charis* (156 occurrences), deriving from *chairo*, the verb for rejoice. Let's expand the traditional meaning to: "divine favor completely undeserved by man, making him joyful." Like an amazing whale, "Grace" breaches majestically 130 times from the pages of the New Testament (as, 17 times in Romans, 11 in 2 Corinthians).

Grace is forcefully associated with both personal salvation and empowered Christian living, as in these sample references:

> Romans 3:23-24: "for all have sinned and fall short of the glory of God, being justified freely by His grace through the redemption that is in Christ Jesus."

> 2 Thessalonians 1:12: "that the name of our Lord Jesus Christ may be glorified in you, and you in Him, according to the grace of our God and the Lord Jesus Christ...."

> 2 Corinthians 12:9: "My grace is sufficient for you [Paul], for my strength is made perfect in weakness."

> Hebrews 4:16: "Let us therefore come boldly to the throne of grace, that we may obtain mercy, and find grace to help in the time of need."

Paul's Conversion

Paul met the risen Christ on the Damascus Road. Although physically blinded in the encounter, he was spiritually illuminated, finding himself to be: the chief of sinners (1 Timothy 1:15), the murderer of God's people and the complete enemy of God! This devastating revelation birthed the amazing theology of the lavish grace of God.

> Since God was gracious to him, God's enemy, in this way, he came eventually to realize that this is the way God is toward all, Jew and Gentile alike, making no distinctions. Since all alike are sinful, all alike are potential recipients of God's grace (Gordon Fee).[4]

Significantly, Paul's conversion is mentioned three times in Luke's record: Acts 9:1-19 (historical account); 22:4-11 (Paul's address to the Jewish mob); and 26:13-18 (Paul before Agrippa and Festus).[5]

The conversion/commission transformed Saul the Terminator into Paul the disciple, a truly life-changing event ("old things are passed away; behold, all things have become new," 1 Corinthians 5:17). Four major concepts burst upon the new convert's mind: the Deity of Christ, the Grace of God, the Body of Christ (the Church) and World Vision.

Set free from dead religion and meaningless ritual, Paul was called to an undeserved ambassadorship. How could he allow such transforming grace to be imprisoned within the bars of a legal system? Impossible! Paul shouts it out for all to hear: "But by the grace of God I am what I am[6] and his grace to me was not without effect. No, I worked harder than all of them – yet not I, but the grace of God that was with me."

Did God Specifically Call Paul an Apostle?

Paul was not labeled as an apostle immediately, and no specific reference states that God addressed Saul/Paul as an "apostle." Colin Brown rightly says, "We would hardly expect Paul to be given the title of apostle at his conversion."[7] The seed of apostleship, however, is in Jesus' statement: "I will deliver you from the Jewish people, as well as from the Gentiles, to whom I now *send* you" (Acts 26:17, emphasis added). "Send," in this case, is the portentious verb *apostello*, laden with prophetic significance. Toward the end of his life, while incarcerated, Paul declared (Acts 28:28):

> Therefore let it be known to you that the salvation of God has been sent [*apostello*] to the Gentiles, and they will hear it!"

The messenger was chained, but the dynamic, *sending program* was in motion!

Defending himself to the Jewish mob, Paul abbreviated Jesus' statement to: "I will *send* you far from here to the Gentiles"

(Acts 22:21). This time the verb was *ekapostello* [*ek* = out of], which has an even heavier emphasis on being "sent out [cast out] of Judea with a commission to reach the Gentile world." Paul used that same Greek word while preaching in Antioch of Pisidia: "to you the word of this salvation has been sent [*ekapostello*]" (Acts 13:26). Paul was the messenger-become-apostle who delivered that word.

Paul did not become a recognized apostle over night, no short-cuts to apostleship existed. After conversion, he underwent a training program of approximately twelve years, taking him from Damascus to Antioch, immersing him in a number of preparatory experiences, synagogue confrontations, Scripture studies, visions and dreams, discussions with Peter, and so on -- all contributing to the maturity that was so apparent at the Council of Jerusalem.

A New Kind of Mentor

As he went forth to the nations, Paul's ambassadorial credentials gradually surfaced for all to see. "Apostle" appears effortlessly in epistles to those he fathered in the faith. Gradually his commission evolved into a recognizable, titled office, acknowledged by even the Twelve. Christ had truly added another apostle, one the Church would ever after acknowledge!

Following Jesus' example, Paul vigorously recruited apostolic assistants to assist him: carry epistles, interpret his meaning, reinforce his directions, preach, teach and work miracles, often as his representatives. In fact, Paul imbued all church members to get this message of life out to the people.

These younger adjutants quickly assumed the Spirit-empowered apostolic qualities, duties and responsibilities of their director. Without e-mails, cell phones and Skipe, they grasped the message and Spirit of their mentor and personally became his surrogate voice and ministry in multiplied, far-flung places, evolving from "proxy messengers" to *bonafide* apostles.

Let's Rethink the Conventional Requirements of an Apostle

Many church people do no think beyond the original Twelve Apostles and Paul, assuming no more apostles are expected, or no one since those days could meet the qualifications. The familiar references in the Gospels and Acts to "The Twelve" have cemented these outstanding men into our Christian consciousness, being fully confirmed by Matthew 19:28 and Revelation 21:14. We caution, however, that certain insights about additional apostles for our day should not be overlooked or ignored in our continued admiration of the original apostles.

A Legacy of Faith
The Ministry of T. L. Osborn

Imagine yourself in some far-off land, some developing nation whose name seems strange to you. The people are dark-skinned, but friendly, and you observe the sights and sounds of poverty. Outside the city limits you pause beside a vast, open field. In the distance you see workmen building a platform and setting up loud-speaker equipment. This is where in a day or so a great religious rally will take place. Very little advertising (by our standards) has taken place, but people are excitedly telling their friends of the upcoming meetings.

When the day arrives, you make your way to the great field, but lo! The empty field is now swarming with over 200,000 people. The sick have been brought, the deaf, the blind, the demonized – all in a state of hopeful expectancy. Each one desperately wants help.

It is hard to comprehend how – in our day of advanced media – hundreds of thousands of people could gather in a single location without attracting international attention. But this has been happening over the past six decades in the open-field crusades of T. L. Osborn in developing countries. His wife Daisy who worked at his side for 53 years, died in 1995. Osborn preaches and then prays for the masses, without laying hands on anyone. Astounding miracles take place, including the instantaneous healing of leprosy, blindness, crippled legs and demon possession. Many are saved, and tons, yes I said tons, of books are given away free to the eager masses.

One of the most impressive ministries that I have observed over the past sixty years has been that of T.L. Osborn. I don't know that he has ever called himself an apostle, but certain of his attributes, in my mind, would place him in the category of an apostolic-evangelist. Many people in America have not heard of this remarkable man, but he has preached to untold millions in some 90 countries. "Osborn and his family have conducted their ministry with no fanfare, no attempt to conform to the personality-driven culture of the American church, and little regard for their own personal safety or comfort."[8]

Going to India in the early days, the Osborns realized that they needed the miraculous to prove what they believed. The found they could do nothing with people who did not believe the Bible. Thus began their search which culminated in a personal appearance of Jesus to T. L., followed by their observation of healing ministries, and then an inspired, insightful reading of the Gospels "as if he had never read them before."

The simplicity of presentation is indeed heart-warming. T. L.'s faith is "in the seed of the Word of God ....that is the touchstone of everything about a successful gospel ministry.... And that's the reason for the books."[9] The Osborns have seldom used radio and TV, but they have fully embraced the Internet. Supporters can track their ministry at www.osborn.org, where they can download a series of e-books. In his mid-'80s, T. L. Osborn laughs at the idea of retirement, although he realizes how the rigors of extensive travel can affect a person. He is presently planning a significant writing project on the important elements of successful ministry.

Four Traditional Qualifications

These are the commonly believed qualifications for apostles of Christ.[10]

1. Has been called by Christ to this position (Galatians 1:1).
2. Has seen Christ, is a witness of His Resurrection (Corinthians 9:1, 2; Acts 1:8, 21-23).
3. Is evidenced by "signs, and wonders, and mighty works" (2 Corinthians 12:12).
4. Is not limited to a single church or locality, but is related to the world generally and to all the churches (Matthew 28:10; 1 Corinthians 11:28).

These "qualifications" easily developed in the institutionalized Church, particularly in the thinking of scholarly recluses not participating in apostolic activities. Unfortunately, such qualifications have tended to reduce the success of the Church's mission, almost silencing the voice of active apostolic Christianity. These qualifications certainly applied to the Twelve, but properly interpreted, do not have the same application for a continuing apostolate.

Rebuttal to the Traditional Qualifications

1. We cannot *Scripturally assume* that God has not called *additional* apostles. Although the title "apostle" has not been in common use, many outstanding individuals have answered the call to do apostolic ministry. Various lists of such individuals have

been suggested, undoubtedly with differences of opinion.[11] Ephesians 4:11 and 1 Corinthians 12:28 clearly state that this "number 1" ministry was intended to be in the churches *until* the perfection of the Church.

2. Since the Twelve's requirement was to have been observers and disciples of Christ from His Baptism to His Ascension (Acts 1:21-22), the idea of an apostle being a witness of His Resurrection was naturally assumed. Paul is usually considered an exception to the rule and left at that; after all, it is assumed, no one else would have an experience like his with the Resurrected Christ. Actually, Paul would not qualify to be one of the Twelve (not a disciple during Jesus' earthly ministry), and today's apostles cannot always qualify for the Twelve's standards or Paul's experience.

Some of today's ministers claim to have had visions of the risen Christ, but this experience in and of itself proves or disproves nothing. The point of the Twelve being credible witnesses of Jesus' resurrection was: they knew Him *before* His death, they knew him *after* His resurrection, they were contemporaries.

Such a vision may happen in our day, but anything visionary seems mystical, inconsequential and unscriptural; today's people give little credence to such a claim. The eyewitness testimony by those who saw Him before *and* after the Resurrection was certainly effective. Also, you need not have a vision of Jesus in order to proclaim His resurrection from the dead ("Blessed are those who have not seen and yet have believed," John 20:29). Paul apparently did not know Jesus before His death, although he was a contemporary of Jesus.

3. Miracles are not meant to compliment the apostle, rather authenticate the message preached. This thought challenges the traditional interpretation of 2 Corinthians 12:12 (NIV): "The things that mark an apostle – signs, wonders and miracles – were done among you with great perseverance." This translation does seem to say that signs and wonders authenticate the apostles. Jack Deere, however, casts some reasonable doubt:

> This translation . . . is inaccurate. A literal translation is, *"The signs of an apostle were performed among you in all endurance with signs and wonders and miracles."* In this passage Paul uses "sign" (Greek *semeion*)

> in two different ways. The first use of "sign" in the phrase "signs of an apostle" cannot refer to miracles, for then Paul would be saying that "the miracles of an apostle were done among you with signs and wonders and miracles."
>
> What would be the point of such a statement? Paul does not say that "the signs of an apostle" are miracles, but rather that "the signs of an apostle" are accompanied by signs, wonders and miracles. If Paul had meant that the signs of his apostleship were signs and wonders and miracles, then he would have used a different construction in the Greek language."[12]

The vindications of Paul's apostleship were not miracles but his suffering, his blameless life, his endless care of the churches and the many conversions among those to whom he preached (2 Corinthians 6:3-10; 11:22-33). *The miracles authenticated not the man but the message he preached.* This is also true in our day. Acts 4:10, 29-30; 8:6-7; 13:12; 14:3, 9.

4. The Twelve Apostles have assumed an international and eternal stature that makes their apostleship historical and global in nature, certainly true and how it should be. However, other apostles in Paul's time (as, Barnabas, Silas, Timothy) did not achieve such status, although they were clearly apostles.

Paul gradually related to the broader Church through his epistles, but during his missionary journeys, while founding and caring for churches, he was kept busy in local areas and had geographically limited recognition. Paul focused his efforts for a year and a half in Corinth (Acts 18:11) and three years in Ephesus (Acts 9:10, 26; 20:31). The care of his total church network was ever upon his heart, even though he always worked in local situations.

Demographics have changed drastically since then. The entire population of the Aegean Basin area, where much of Paul's ministry was centered, had less population than some of our present-day cities where pastor-apostles actually lead church memberships larger than the populations of some of those ancient cities.

Some Legitimate Questions

Grant R. Osborne, in The *Baker Encyclopedia of the Bible,* gives this conventional summary at the conclusion of an article on apostles:

> The grounding of the NT apostolic ministry in a personal authorization by the risen Christ *raises the question to what extent we can meaningfully speak of the apostolic office in our churches today.* In an important respect the position of those called apostles was unique, and *yet the church continues to expand and believes that it continues to be the body of Christ with him as Lord.* A final answer cannot be given here. Suffice it to say, the various ecclesiastical traditions and practices of church office and ministry are attempts to answer this question (emphasis added).[13]

The above statement raises legitimate questions pertinent to our discussion:

- Can we expect the apostolic office in our churches today?
- Does believing in other apostles discredit the unique standing of the original Twelve?
- Is the Church still the body of Christ with Christ as head? (And, apostles and prophets?)
- Are ecclesiastical traditions and practices adequately fulfilling the Scripture?

Yes, we can expect apostles in our day. This does not discredit the unique, eternal status of the Twelve, but rather enhances the work they founded. They would be delighted to know that presently an apostolic emphasis is taking place across the world. There is no jealousy there!

The fourth question raises the question about ecclesiastical traditions and practices. Every church body should realistically evaluate dead-wood tradition that is hindering the purpose of their Church; we must seriously seek to make the necessary changes that produce Spirit-filled, apostolic churches. Using Scriptural titles certainly has merit, but the main thing is *actual apostolic function.*

Has the Body Lost an Important Member?

The third question above leads us directly to Scripture. Of course, the Church is the Body of Christ, and Christ is Head. The problem does not lie with the Head, but rather with whether or not the members are functioning, including apostles and prophets.

Paul's great revelation (unique to his writings) was that the Church is the body of Christ, with each Christian being an individual member, and *apostles being very significant members*.

> For as the body is one and has many members, but all the members of that one body, being many are one body, so also is Christ.... For in fact the body is not one member but many.... But now God has set the members, each one of them, in the body just as He pleased.... Now you are the body of Christ, and members individually. And God has appointed these in the church: first apostles..." (1 Corinthians 12, 14, 18, 27, 28).

Today's churches and leaders frequently use Paul's metaphor of the Body of Christ, giving attention to spiritual gifts and ministries. This is important, but why delete apostles and prophets? The Bible's statements about functioning apostles and prophets seem clear enough. We must conclude, therefore, that the lack of these key ministries is due to misunderstanding, neglect, lack of know-how or the deliberate attempt by authorities to eliminate a controversial ministry from church life.

The Aegean Mission: Follow the Bouncing Ball!

The next two chapters recall some of the exciting adventures in Paul's Second and Third missionary journeys. Following Dunn's suggestion, think of the Second and Third Journeys as one: "The Mission to the Aegean Basin."

> What we actually have is the account of a sustained mission around the coasts of the Aegean sea. Luke presents it as a coherent and integrated unit. It has a clear beginning....And it has a clear end. [14]

Paul was like a bouncing ball as he covered this virgin territory, preaching the gospel, planting churches. The Aegean mission was the main focus of his missionary work. In this area were the cities where he planted churches and sent letters: Philippi, Thessalonica, Berea, Corinth, Ephesus and finally Colosse (100 miles from the Aegean coast). Although today's situation is much, much different, we can glean lessons from the accounts given in Acts. These concepts can help us concentrate on the important aspects of today's global mission.

The colorful description (in the next two chapters) of Paul's adventure in Macedonia and Asia is quite compelling, giving some idea of the impact his person and ministry had on his associates and the people of that time. Keep in mind "Paul's Commission Objectives" (given in Acts 26:18):

- Open people's eyes
- Turn people from darkness to light
- Turn people from the power of Satan to God
- Enable others to receive forgiveness of sins
- Enable people to receive an inheritance among those who are sanctified by faith in Christ

These objectives should not be for apostles only, but every sincere believer, even if our accomplishments are not as grand as those of Paul. When people experience such apostolic objectives, they are candidates to be members of an apostolic church!

Chapter 9 Endnotes

[1] F. F. Bruce, *Acts,* 1970 reprint, p. 406.
[2] Second Corinthians has been the subject of much scholarly debate; it has been said, "Second Corinthians describes the anatomy of an apostle" (*The New Open Bible Study Edition,* p. 1363).
[3] Gilbert Bilezikian, "Grace," Elwell, Walter A., ed., *Baker Encyclopedia of the Bible,* Vol. 1 (Grand Rapids, MI: Baker Book House, 1988), p. 899.
[4] Gordon D. Fee, *The First Epistle to the Corinthians (The NICONT)* (Grand Rapids: Eerdmans, 1987), pp. 734-5.
[5] Any apparent differences can be traced to the different audiences and circumstances in each situation. See Goodwin, *Harmony,* Appendix 1.

[6] Kistemaker: "Note that he writes 'I am what I am,' not 'I am who I am.' Paul is interested in looking at himself not as a person but as an instrument in God's hand to further the cause of the gospel." *1 Corinthians*, p. 537.

[7] Colin Brown, "Note on Apostleship in Luke-Acts," *The New International Dictionary of NT Theology, Vol. 1,* p. 136.

[8] Chad Bonham, "He Dared to Touch the World," *Charisma* (January 2007): 58-62, 82-83.

[9] Ibid., p.82.

[10] S. D. F. Salmond, "Ephesians," *The Expositor's Greek Testament*, p. 329. Qualifications taken from an 80-year-old commentary have remained basically the same.

[11] C. Peter Wagner says: "I have no doubt that apostles have been present in the Church throughout its history…. Who could deny that great men such as Gregory Thaumaturgus, Martin of Tours, Patrick of Ireland, Benedict of Nursia, Boniface, Anselm of Canterbury, Savanarola, John Wyclif, Martin Luther, Francis Xavier, John Knox, John Wesley, William Booth, William Carey, Hudson Taylor, and others throughout the centuries were true apostles?" *Apostles Today,* p. 7.

[12] Jack Deere, "Anatomy of a Deception," *MorningStar Journal* 4:2 (1944), 42-43.

[13] Grant R. Osborne, "Apostle, Apostleship," Walter A. Elwell, gen. ed., *Baker Encyclopedia of the Bible*, p. 133.

[14] Dunn, *Acts,* Part IV, p. 212.

Chapter 10
The Macedonian Crusade

In This Chapter:

- *Macedonia, here we come!*
- *Whoa! A "Python spirit"?*
- *Paul's most receptive "target group"*
- *Lessons from the Macedonian adventure*

The travelers were apostles of Jesus, kingdom ambassadors on assignment to Macedonia (Northern Greece), an area where no Christian Churches had previously existed. The two men were trudging westward on the Egnatian Way, the overland Roman military highway stretching some 530 miles from the Adriatic coast across Macedonia to Neopolis, and then farther yet to Byzantium, their passage transforming this main overland route between Asia and the West into an important bridge for the early spread of the gospel.

The immediate journey of some 100 miles was taking them from Philippi to Amphipolis, then on to Apollonia (a military station), finally arriving in Thessalonica -- the capital and most important and populated center in Macedonia at that time. The inlaid-stone road was sturdy and well kept, and Paul and Silas eagerly counted the passing roadside milestones installed by the Romans. For them, "The highways of [the Roman] Empire became the highways of the Kingdom of Heaven."[1]

The men moved cautiously with their stiffness,[2] not fully recovered from being beaten with wooden rods, spending half a night with hands manacled, feet thrust forward into wooden stocks.[3] Ah, that night in the Philippian jail was a night to be remembered!

The Commission: Penetrate Macedonia

The appointment came to the apostles in Troas, a port town on the Asian side of the Aegean Sea, southeast from Macedonia.[4]

Two others were part of the apostolic team: Luke the physician of Syrian Antioch and Timothy the young man from Lystra.

The assignment was disclosed on three occasions, two parts seeming strange -- like trying to solve a mystery when you don't have all the information.

1) *the Holy Spirit* forbade them to preach in the cities of Asia[5]
2) *the Spirit of Jesus*[6] did not permit them to go northward into Bithynia
3) Finally, *a night vision* in Troas called them forward into Macedonia.[7]

Like an unexpected news bulletin on TV, the vision burst upon Paul: *"A man of Macedonia stood and pleaded with him [Paul], saying, 'Come over to Macedonia and help us,'"* Acts 16:9. Imagine the excitement!

The journey to Troas had been hard. They by-passed Bithynia and the Asian cities, hurrying forward over the vast country (modern Turkey), finally ending their arduous trek at Troas, ready to fulfill the Lord's immediate purpose at the right time. Ramsay comments:

> [Paul] was led across Asia from the extreme south-east to the extreme north-west corner, and yet prevented from preaching in it; everything seemed dark and perplexing, until at last a vision in Troas explained the purpose of this strange journey.[8]

From Troas they took ship across the North Aegean, happy that both the wind and the Spirit were with them, they were eager and ready! They landed in two days at Neapolis, the seaport eight miles from Philippi, a leading city of Macedonia. This journey may have been but one of many to Paul, but it was one of the turning points of history -- the challenge to the Western world to accept Christ.

The City of Philippi

Christian apostles set foot on European soil, for the first time! Their arrival in Philippi occurred some twenty years after the church at Jerusalem was founded by the Pentecostal outpouring of the Spirit (Acts 2). No Christian churches yet existed in Macedonia, but the first was now in process!

Paul, Silas, Timothy and Luke busied themselves scouting out Philippi, asking in vain for the Jewish synagogue, finding instead a mighty city overwhelmingly filled with Romans and the temples of the Greek gods. Philippi was more a military city than a commercial center: few Jews, no synagogue!

The team surely considered the one unmistakable sign of Jews, closed shops and booths on the Sabbath. The shop of Lydia, for instance, the rich dealer in purple-dyed cloth from Thyatira, usually bustling with customers during the week, closed tight. A few other shops were also closed.

A Riverside Prayer Meeting

Finding out that on the Sabbath certain women (Jewesses and God-fearers) prayed outside the city walls at a secluded riverbank of the River Gangites,[9] the four men hastened to the place, introduced themselves, engaged in friendly conversation, finally announcing their good news: the Messiah has come, salvation is available to all!

The electrifying announcement of Jesus the Messiah, unbelievably good news, grabbed their attention. The Lord opened Lydia's heart to Paul's message, and she and her household quickly responded, being baptized in the nearby river. The household was not only immediate family members, but also her servants who resided under her roof. The apostolic team was invited to stay at her home, and Lydia's household is portrayed "as the core of the emerging church of Philippi."[10] G. Campbell Morgan describes this open heart of Lydia as the first "vantage ground" that the team gained,[11] and the second, soon to come, again involved a woman, but a very different type.

Later, as Paul and Silas walked on from Philippi toward Thessalonica (Luke and Timothy remaining in Philippi), they must have laughed, cried, and praised the Lord as they remembered their stay in Philippi: prayer times, public evangelizing, and particularly that next unforgettable episode.

Confronting the Python Spirit

The second "vantage ground" in Philippi was a demonized slave girl, physically owned by ruthless men and controlled by "a spirit of divination" to tell fortunes. The demonic power is best named "Python spirit" (*pneuma pythona*), constituting an insidious challenge to the apostolic team. As a python snake crushes its victim in tightening coils, so the designing demon moved the girl to follow the apostles and scream constricting, distracting statements to all within hearing, attempting to smother the message. Naturally, the team was irritated by the unwanted (but effective) advertising.

> Demons are inveterate liars, but not everything they say is a lie. Whether they speak the truth or falsehoods, however, their ultimate goal is to deceive. Sometimes they deceive by first building false credibility. The Python spirit spoke true theology and told true fortunes, enchanting people much as a spider would invite a fly in its web (Wagner).[12]

The owners and the girl were well-known in the marketplace by many customers, indicating the python spirit had secured an influential hold upon the populace. The situation presented "a direct, high-level power encounter" between God's ambassadors and this local satanic authority. Increasingly annoyed, Paul waited for the right moment. Several days passed, exasperation reaching a high level, then, God's time arrived! Paul boldly addressed the spirit: "I command you in the name of Jesus Christ to come out of her" (Acts 16:18). The woman squealed and the spirit came out, like air from a popped balloon. The glazed look in the girl's eyes disappeared, her voice returned to normal, the gravelly sound gone! Of course, the fortune telling immediately stopped.

Songs in the Night

Led by the furious owners (their income now gone), Paul and Silas were dragged by a howling mob to the city's two magistrates in the marketplace -- accused of sedition! Without proper trial, they were remanded to the licktors (police officers who carried the Roman symbols of law, a bundle of rods and an ax). In the presence of the mob, they were stripped and severely beaten with rods like common criminals. Then, more dead than alive, they were thrown by the brutal jailer into the innermost prison, the lightless inner *tullianum* or dungeon. Ah! Truly, what a night that was!

At midnight they prayed and sang hymns, backs bleeding and bruised, muscles groaning with pain, feet clamped in stocks. But...the Spirit of God moved upon them, inspiring exaltation and praise: the heavenly songs broke like shafts of light into the dark gloom of the hellish dungeon.

The astounded prisoners listened intently to the continuous, soaring words of gratitude and thankfulness to the one true God. Never had such things been heard in this place. Suddenly, accompanied by a rolling, thunderous sound, an *Intelligence-driven* earthquake struck, shaking the jail's foundations, springing open prison doors, crashing lock bars to the floor, breaking chains off, busting stocks loose -- and no prisoner attempted to escape or was hurt! The overwhelmed prison keeper, his family and household, suddenly awakened from sleep and gripped by the fear of God converted to Jesus the Messiah and were baptized. Another "group conversion," like that of Lydia's household! [13]

The next morning, notified of their release, Paul and Silas boldly declared that their Roman citizenship had been violated, and the magistrates must personally release them. Terrified, fearing for both jobs and lives, the magistrates ran to comply, begging the apostles to leave.

Some say that when the apostles, beaten but not bowed, proudly but lamely, walked out of the jailhouse accompanied by the two embarrassed magistrates, a large crowd had gathered out of curiosity and possibly fear. The crowd was possible, considering the publicity: ejection of the Python spirit, riotous marketplace altercation and thunderous earthquake.

And, the prisoners! Given the enormity of the occasion, the jailbirds probably reacted in typical fashion: clapping, mocking the magistrates, shouting, and even praising the Lord! The apostles taking their time, walked proud, making the most of the moment, then going on to Lydia's house for refreshment.

The powerful coils of the *Pneuma Pythona* had gone limp and helpless ....

The fledgling church had grown quickly: Lydia's family and servants, the jailer's family and servants, some women of prayer (possibly Euodia and Syntyche, Philippians 4:3), "the brethren" (probably recent converts, Acts 16:40), perhaps some of the prisoners, community people who saw the deliverance or the riot in the marketplace, and those who saw the prisoners released. Christians became front-page news, embarrassment preventing any immediate reprisals from the officials. One of Paul's favorite churches was launched.

> If Lydia came from the top end of the social scale and the slave girl from the bottom, the Roman jailer was one of the sturdy middle class who made up the Roman civil service; and so in these three the whole range within society was complete (Barclay).[14]

Paul and Silas left the promising, new church plant in the capable hands of Luke,[15] Timothy (for a short while), Lydia and others. It was time to head for the capital of Macedonia -- what better place to proclaim Christ and fulfill the vision?

The Church at Thessalonica

Walking for several days, Paul and Silas passed through Amphipolis and Apollonia (Gentile cities: no synagogues), finally arriving at the inmost bay of the Thermaic Gulf (now called the Gulf of Salonica). There, like a queen, sat Thessalonica, capital and chief seaport of Macedonia and naval station of the imperial fleet,[16] a proud, free city and extremely loyal to Rome. About 200,000 people,[17] including numerous Jews and other religious groups, lived in this great, walled commercial and administrative center. As Lenski says, "It shared the commerce of the Aegean Sea with Corinth and with Ephesus. Politically it ranked with Antioch in Syria and Caesarea in Palestine."[18] Such activity attracted Jewish merchants from the Diaspora, accounting for the presence of a well-established synagogue.

A Brief Stay

The casual reader may think they stayed only three weeks in the city: "Then Paul … for three Sabbaths reasoned with them [people in the synagogue] from the Scriptures…"(Acts 17:2). Actually, this time frame only indicates Paul's teaching time in the synagogue -- before he was ejected!

Thoughtful commentators agree that additional ministry in the community could easily have taken several months.[19] The time was short, but the apostles expended amazing missionary effort:

1) teaching Jews the fulfillment of Messianic prophecies in Christ
2) declaring idol worship to be evil and foolish in the marketplace
3) teaching the new Christians to lead godly lives
4) doing secular work to support themselves.

The Primary Focus

Paul had a simple strategy in a new city: *make the synagogue the primary focus of mission.* Why? Shouldn't Paul, apostle to the *Gentiles,* go after Gentiles?   After all, the Jews always gave him a hard time in the synagogues![20]

The reason is actually quite simple: *Paul focused his efforts on the most receptive people*, concentrating on where the harvest was ripest, just like a farmer.[21] In Philippi there was no synagogue, but the next-best thing, a women's prayer meeting of devout Jewesses and God-fearers (like Lydia) proved successful.

Were the Jews the most receptive? Comparatively few were, yet they rightly deserved to hear first that their expected Messiah had come. The God-fearing, sympathetic Gentiles who frequented the synagogues were actually the most responsive. These were people who had not totally converted to Judaism, finding circumcision, dietary restrictions, Sabbath laws and social ostracism a considerable challenge. At the same time, these devout people wanted to believe in the one supreme and invisible God, being fully dissatisfied (even disgusted) with pagan immorality, foolish idolatry and unreasonable forms of worship. The God of the Jews, the Hebrew Scriptures and pure family life were all fascinating and appealing, so they frequented the local synagogue.

These Hellenistic Greek people in the synagogues became the immediate focus, being the most receptive audience for the apostles. In addition to the beauty of the gospel of Jesus Christ, Paul's message appealed to Gentiles because upon accepting Jesus as the Messiah and being baptized, they were treated as acceptable to God, just like Law-abiding Jews, but without the traditional restraints. Undoubtedly, the reading of the letter from the elders in Jerusalem (Acts 15), requiring the four restrictions based on Noachian revelation (from Noah's time), must have been very impressive and perfectly reasonable.

> They had turned to Judaism because it brought them the doctrine of one God; but they were without the Jewish prejudice and pride, and when the great Word came to them, the Word of the one God, and the one God manifest, and the one God winning victory by death, some of the profoundest secrets of their own mysteries were drawn into the light and redeemed (Morgan).[22]

A second promising group was found in the central marketplace: the Gentile working class and their clientele. Since Paul and the team earned their living in this neutral location, making and selling tents and other coverings, they had great opportunity to confront the pagan population with the foolishness of idolatry, the wonderful satisfaction of the message of Jesus, and deliverance from evil spirits and sorcery.

> nor did we eat anyone's bread free of charge, but worked with labor and toil night and day, that we might not be a burden to any of you, 2 Thessalonians 3:8.

Some of the leading Greek women attended the synagogue in Thessalonica, a real plus for the Jews; the leaders appreciated having these important citizens attend services, give offerings, show interest in the Hebrew Scriptures and be friendly with their people. The sympathetic God-fearers actually became a buffer between the Jewish synagogue and the pagan community. Say! Can you imagine these dignified ladies, shopping at the agora, finding the visiting rabbi diligently making and selling cloth there?

Unrest in the Jewish Communities

Generally, this was not a good time for the Jews, for deepening unrest in the Jewish communities was happening throughout the empire. A militant, political messianism was springing up, not the Messianic message of Jesus, but rather an aggressive Jewish political belief that the time had come for the hoped-for Messiah to appear and put down the Romans. Because of this, a nervous Claudius Caesar commanded all the Jews to leave Rome (Acts 18:2).

Since "Christianity was indistinguishable from Judaism in the time of Claudius,"[23] many Romans did not know the difference between Jews and Christians; even a magistrate did not understand that certain Romans could also be Jews and Christians at the same time.

Hard-line Resistance

Paul's presentation of the Scripture might seem strange to an English audience, but was stimulating to eager Jewish minds, his approach being to "reason" from the Scriptures. Paul, the scholarly rabbi, would lay out Hebrew Scriptures that foretold the ministry, suffering, death and resurrection of the long-expected Messiah. Then, with excitement and joy, he would announce and show how this awaited Messiah – Jesus of Nazareth -- had already come, meticulously fulfilling all Scripture.

> Paul follows the example set by Jesus, who opened the Scriptures for the two men on the way to Emmaus and for the disciples in the upper room. Jesus showed them from the Law, the Prophets, and the Psalms that the Christ had to suffer and rise from the dead (Luke 24:25-27, 44-46). The term *explaining* comes from the Greek verb meaning "to open." Paul opens the Word and sets the explanation of the messianic prophecies before his listeners. By appealing to the Scriptures, he has a common basis to prove that the Messiah has come in the person and work of Jesus Christ of Nazareth (Kistemaker).[24]

Listening to Paul, a few of the Thessalonian Jews were won over, but most were hard-line skeptics and unbelieving, feeling their foundations of established order and custom were threatened. In contrast, "a great multitude of the devout Greeks, and not a few of the leading women, joined Paul and Silas" (Acts 17:4). This positive response infuriated the unbelieving Jews, making them "mad with jealousy" (M). Losing potential proselytes to the apostles stirred the Jews to violent action. Evil characters loafing around the marketplace were paid to foment a riot. Unable to lay their hands on Paul (probably warned of possible arrest), the mob surged to the house of Jason where some of the Christians were, dragging them to the city officials, accusing them of the militant messianism rampant elsewhere, asserting that the Jews had a king other than Caesar. The accusation was: "These who have turned the world upside down have come here too" (NKJ). This was not a positive statement (as some have made it), but rather a charge that these messianic agitators were practicing "subversive and seditious activity" (F.F. Bruce).[25] Ralph Martin says:

> They distorted the apostles' assertion that Jesus was king of human lives....to imply that Paul's message was political, and that he was advocating a treasonable opposition to the Roman *imperium.*[26]

Such political indictment alarmed the authorities, so they acted quickly to get the troublemakers out of town. Under pressure, Jason and friends posted heavy bail and pledged to have Paul and Silas out of town right away.

> The wonder is that in spite of it all the Christians of Thessalonica stood firm and actually began to propagate on their own initiative the message which they had believed. A few weeks later, when Paul wrote them a letter, he was able to say that the gospel had sounded forth from them throughout all Macedonia and Greece, and that their steadfast faith in God was a matter of common talk in other churches (F. F. Bruce).[27]

The church at Thessalonica was a great church of New Testament times. Combining 1st and 2nd Thessalonians with Acts 17, the reader finds a truly dynamic church body composed of Jewish believers, God-fearers and former idolaters. Wagner says,

> Paul had an outstanding nucleus for one of the most significant churches that he and his group would plant. Further affirming that they were largely Gentiles, Paul later writes that they had "turned to God from

idols to serve the living and true God" (1 Thess. 1:9). Jewish conversion would not have involved turning from idols.[28]

Leaving the Highway for the Byway

Bail was paid and the promise given to silence the preachers, so Jason and others lost no time in finding Paul and Silas, setting them on their journey that very night, thereby extinguishing any fiery opposition. The reluctant apostles (jubilant but sad) marched on to Berea, an out-of-the-way town[29] some 50 miles distant in a southwesterly direction. Although six miles off the main highway, the small town had a synagogue! Timothy soon rejoined Paul and Silas there. Two verses tell of the enthusiastic reception in Berea:

> These [Jews] were more fair-minded than those in Thessalonica, in that they received the word with all readiness, and searched the Scriptures daily to find out whether these things were so. Therefore many of them believed, and also not a few of the Greeks, prominent women as well as men (Acts 17:11-12).

> The Bereans "were more open-minded...and they listened eagerly to Paul's message. They searched the Scriptures day after day to check up on Paul and Silas, to see if they were really teaching the truth" (NLT).

The atmosphere, attitude, and activity in the small town provided almost an idyllic retreat atmosphere for the apostles, and their stay probably lasted several months. A quorum of ten Jewish men was required for a town or city to have a synagogue, so this small-town community of Jews was surprisingly large when contrasted with Philippi and Thessalonica.

> The implication is that the synagogue in Beroea functioned as a house of study, where the scrolls were kept, and where members of the Jewish community could attend daily (not just on the Sabbath) for scripture study (Dunn).[30]

The startling announcement that the Messiah had already come was almost beyond belief. Overnight, it appears, the synagogue was transformed into a busy library where manuscripts were studied daily and a resident librarian-apostle was handy to answer questions, all this taking place because only a few people owned copies of the Greek Old Testament (the *LXX*). The Thessalonians and Bereans were excited to learn that Jesus would return; having missed Him the first time, they must not miss Him the second time! (This was later addressed in 1st and 2nd Thessalonians and was probably read by the Bereans as well.)

The three apostles diligently worked and prayed with the people, and "Many of the Jews believed, as did also a number of prominent Greek women and many Greek men" (NIV). Possibly the Jews gathered with the apostles every day, after the evening *Shema,* reading the Holy Script with Paul interpreting. Paul was elated, the situation seemed too good to be true, but he remained concerned about Thessalonica (1 Thessalonians 2:8).

Then they arrived, angry rabble-rousers from Thessalonica, "agitating the crowds and stirring them up" (NIV). Paul, of course, was the main target of hostility, so the believers acted swiftly. Leaving Silas and Timothy in town, some of the Berean believers hurriedly escorted Paul to the coast and on to Athens.

The text does not say a church was established at Berea, but James D. G. Dunn suggests it was possible:

> The reference to Sopater of Beroea in 20.4 (= Sosipater in Rom. 16:21?) *indicates that the church became established,* even though it is mentioned nowhere else (emphasis added).[31]

Later, when Paul wrote to the Thessalonians of his desire to visit them, he mentions how "Satan hindered us" (1 Thessalonians 2:18), probably referring to the riots, accusations and persecutions – and the ban that the city magistrates had placed on his ever returning.

Apostolic Lessons from the Macedonian Story

The Macedonian Crusade illustrates key apostolic principles, arranged in the following chart under four headings: God's Guidance, Ministry Approach, Things Anticipated and General Procedure.

The next chapter presents Paul's amazing adventure in planting the church of Ephesus and reaching all Asia. His 16

Chapter 10 Endnotes

[1] F. F. Bruce, *Acts*, p. 324.

[2] Kistemaker could be right: "[W]e assume that Paul and his fellow travelers covered the distance (about thirty miles) between Philippi and Amphipolis in one day to find lodging for the night. We conjecture that they rode instead of walked, because Paul and Silas were still nursing their wounds from the beating they had received in Philippi." *Acts*, pp. 611-612. If they used horses, they would have been supplied by Lydia and the others.

[3] They could neither stand nor lie down. Lenski says: "[the stocks were] both a fetter and an instrument of torture, for the feet were locked wide apart and held in that painful position…. Bleeding, bruised, sore, without anything to assuage their wounds, Paul and Silas lay in the black dungeon in this painful position." *Acts*, p. 672.

[4] "A large seaport city of Mysia in northwest Asia Minor, 16 km (10 mi.) S of ancient Troy. In NT times it was the gateway from Asia to Macedonia and Thrace": G. L. Borchert, "Troas," *The International Standard Bible Encyclopedia, Vol. 4* (Grand Rapids: Eerdmans, 1988), p. 922.

[5] The exact way in which the Holy Spirit communicated with them is not known, but both Paul and Silas were sensitive to spiritual guidance. Silas was a prophet accustomed to giving spiritual directives (Acts 15:32).

[6] The expression is synonymous with "the Holy Spirit."

[7] Not uncommon for Christians: Acts 9:10, 12; 10:3, 17, 19; 11:5; 12:9; 16:9, 10; 18:9.

[8] Ramsay, *Paul*, p. 200.

[9] Possibly the place was determined by the Roman authorities who would not allow foreign religious practices within the city limits, tolerating them outside the city.

[10] Kistemaker, p. 590.

[11] G. Campbell Morgan, *Acts*, p. 380.

[12] C. Peter Wagner, *Acts*, p. 402. His explanation of the event as "strategic-level spiritual warfare" is worth reading.

[13] Ibid. "Presumably, the household group that was baptized included not only the relatives, but also the slaves, whom in all probability they would have owned, p. 410.

[14] Barclay, *Acts*, p. 147.

[15] Luke joined Paul at Troas (16:10-ll), and went with him to Philippi (16:12). The narrative continues in the first person till 16:40, resuming again in 20:5-6, when Luke is with Paul at Philippi and leaves with him for Troas. Luke is with Paul for the remainder of Acts: in Jerusalem (21:15), leaving for Rome from Caesarea (27:1), and arriving with him in Rome (28:16).

[16] Glenn W. Barker, William L. Lane, J. Ramsey Michaels, *The New Testament Speaks* (NY: Harper & Row, 1969), pp. 150-151.

[17] Robert L. Thomas, "1 Thessalonians," Frank E. Gaebelein, gen. ed., *The Expositor's Bible Commentary,* Volume 2 (Grand Rapids: Zondervan, 1978), p. 229.

[18] Lenski, p. 690.

[19] Reasons: 1 Thessalonians shows: Gentiles turned from idolatry, the team worked in the local marketplace, persecution occurred and the gospel spread; also, they stayed long enough to receive two financial gifts from the church at Philippi (Philippians 4:6).

[20] As in Antioch, Iconium and Lystra: Acts 13:45; 14:4; 15:19.

[21] "Focus on the responsive" was introduced by Donald McGavran, *Understanding Church Growth* (Grand Rapids: Eerdmans, 1970). Also, see Wagner's practical insights in *Acts*, pp. 416-417.

[22] Morgan, p. 407.

[23] F. F. Bruce, *New Testament History*, p. 297.

[24] Kistemaker, p. 613.

[25] F. F. Bruce, *Paul Apostle*, p. 225.

[26] Ralph P. Martin, *New Testament Foundations: A Guide for Christian Students, Volume 2* (Grand Rapids: Eerdmans, 1978), pp. 159-160.

[27] F. F. Bruce, *The Spreading Flame*, p. 114.

[28] Wagner, pp. 418-19.

[29] Cicero described Berea as an "out-of-the-way town"; i.e., one not on the main highway. *Against Piso* 36.89.

[30] Dunn, *Acts*, p. 229.

[31] Ibid. Kistemaker agrees: "Luke leaves the impression that a flourishing church arose at Berea. Nonetheless, he never indicates that Paul revisited the place." *Acts,* p. 621.

Chapter 11
The Word to All Asia

In This Chapter

- *Alone in a decadent Asian city!*
- *All superstition and demonism was concentrated in Ephesus*
- *Why so many Jews in such a worldly place?*
- *Check out Paul's amazing advice to the Ephesian elders*

Escorted by Berean friends, Paul headed for the Aegean Sea and southward, his destination Corinth. Whether taking ship or walking the southward 200-mile land route, Paul reached Athens. Now, he was alone: Luke was in Philippi, Timothy and Silas in Berea. What would a lonely apostle do in this pagan city? What kingdom business could be done here?

Paul did some sight-seeing, for he mentioned later the idols of Athens. Acts 17:17ff records his reasoning with the Jews and the Gentile worshipers in the synagogue, witnessing daily in the marketplace, and addressing the Epicurean and Stoic philosophers at the Areopagus. Amazingly, some token converts were won there, but the poor response undoubtedly was troubling to him. The restless apostle moved on to Corinth, and from this more familiar setting probably sent epistles to Thessalonica and Philippi by trusted messengers; these fellow workers could elaborate if necessary, speaking into the local situation with apostolic authority.

It is tempting to discuss the happenings in Athens and Corinth, for both places produced converts, churches and challenging lessons. Regretfully, we skip over that year and a half of activity in southern Greece, and now join Paul, after crossing the Aegean, as he makes a short, first-time stopover visit in Ephesus. Presently en route to Jerusalem, Paul will finally return to his home base in Antioch, completing "The Second Missionary Journey of Paul the Apostle." Consider now his time in Ephesus.

Background of the Great Ephesian Crusade

Our concern in this chapter will be the events and spiritual happenings which caused all Asia (modern Turkey) to hear the Word of the Lord, an exciting three-year period of "Paul's Third Missionary Journey" (c. A. D. 53-57), occurring while Paul made his headquarters in Ephesus.

The initial boat ride from Corinth to Ephesus (en route to Jerusalem) must have given time for serious prayer and reflection. Paul would recall how the Holy Spirit had forbidden them to preach in Asia and in Bithynia (Acts 16:6-7), but called them to Macedonia. Now, having completed the assignment to Macedonia in the north of Greece and Corinth in the south, he would stop briefly in Ephesus, the greatest commercial city of Asia Minor.

The Jewish community in Ephesus was probably the largest in the Hellenistic Diaspora, certainly having a synagogue. How could God use him in such a place? To work in Asia had been a long-time aim of Paul, and Ephesus could be both his biggest challenge and crowning achievement. As the seat of secular government, the city could also become the spiritual center for impacting the whole province of Asia for the kingdom of God.

Ephesus would not be easy pickings, being the hub for every nefarious activity of the magical arts and practices, functioning as the capital of satanic control over the Asian territory. Inevitably the teachings of Jesus and His kingdom will seriously clash with the dark principalities and territorial spirits: thunderous repercussions will issue from this coming battle of the titans!

Ephesus, Home of Every Foul Spirit

Strategically located to catch both land and sea trade, Ephesus was on the main road from Rome to the east, located near the mouth of the Cayster River which emptied into the Aegean Sea. Being the capital of the province of Asia, Ephesus was a proud, free city, having its own Senate and Assembly.

The city was extremely religious, being the guardian of the elegant temple of Artemas which allured pilgrims from throughout Asia Minor as well as other countries. The worship of Diana[1] was the spirit of the city, producing a hotbed environment for every foul, idolatrous spirit and belief. Also rampant were immorality, sorcery, demonism and superstition – an inferno of demonic fire fanned by the astrologers, the magicians, soothsayers, fortunetellers and idolatrous healers.

Further corruption was encouraged by mixing the profane business life of the city with the devout and religious, for "the great merchantmen made the temple of Artemis their banking house" (Morgan),[2] functioning like a commercial clearing house for the flow of cash in the city, adding credibility to the immoral activity. Barclay points out that "Ephesus had become the home of the criminals of the ancient world," since the Temple of Diana could grant asylum to any criminal reaching the safety of its area.[3]

In short, everything repulsive to a dedicated Jew or Christian were woven together, standing like an impenetrable stockade against apostolic invasion. The Jewish population, huddled together in their quarter of the city, valiantly tried to maintain their lifestyle and belief system, venturing cautiously out into the great commercial activity as dealers or hand-craftsmen. Many Jews were drawn to Ephesus by the special privileges granted them by both the city and the Roman government.[4]

Whetting Their Appetite in Ephesus

Paul's quick stopover in Ephesus was to appraise the situation, like a spiritual reconnaissance, an exploratory reconnoiter of enemy territory before the major assault. Priscilla and Aquila, close friends and co-workers, traveled with him, providing support, comfort and spiritual insight.

Paul depended on the guidance of the Lord; so, although it appeared that God was getting ready to breach the spiritual gates, the battle would not yet be joined. Eager-beaver missionaries should learn from Paul's prayerful preparation.

Paul's visit to the local Synagogue was brief but impressive. He "reasoned with the Jews" (Acts 18:19), a mysterious Jewish Rabbi with unusual appearance and style: shaved head (because of a vow[5]), scared face (because of stoning[6]), his urgency to be at the Jewish feast in Jerusalem (dedication), awesome knowledge (fluent grasp of both the Hebrew and Greek Scriptures) and his authority (strong teaching presentation). They urged him to stay! With mixed feelings, however, Paul declined, leaving his under-cover agents, Priscilla and Aquila, to prepare the hearts for the coming harvest.

He would return, Paul announced, and he did – about a year later. First, however, he visited his converts and churches in "the upper parts" (i.e., "the Galatian and Phrygian region"). This waiting period was not wasted time because the spiritual condition and needs of Ephesus had to reach "the tipping point" for God's purposes. Undoubtedly great prayer for the city was begun by Priscilla and Acquila during this time.

Prayer escalated in Paul's own heart, and increasingly he knew the city ripened for his message. Walking long stretches through central Asia, headed for Ephesus, provided an ideal opportunity for personal, fervent prayer. The city locked into his first concern, so he advanced with focused intent toward this immediate assignment. As Jesus had "steadfastly set His face to go to Jerusalem" (Luke 9:51), Paul "steadfastly set" his face toward Ephesus.

Preparation in Ephesus

The return to Ephesus is introduced abruptly in Acts 19:1, implying the beginning of the Ephesus adventure. Morgan wisely suggests, however, a better start for chapter 19 would be Acts 18:24.[7] This change allows the introduction of an exciting man of learning and great ability ("somewhat on the edge of mainline developments"[8]) who actually prepared the way for Paul.

Apollos, the eloquent Jewish preacher from Alexandria, came to the synagogue in Ephesus (some months after Paul's departure) with a burning but incomplete message: *the Messiah is about to come!* This was headline news for a Jewish audience, just as it had been when preached by John the Baptist in Israel.

Possibly Apollos had some knowledge of Jesus, but his information was prior to Jesus' death and resurrection, so his puzzle had missing pieces! He ran hard like a messenger should, but brought an indistinct or incomplete message. His golden oratory and grasp of Scripture held most of the Jewish audience transfixed. Sitting in the synagogue, however, two concerned people knew quite well that the Messiah had already come: *it would not do to have the Pauline message – the gospel of God – compromised at this point!*

Quickly taking Apollos aside, Priscilla and Acquila enlarged his understanding (Acts 18:26): the Messiah, Jesus of Nazareth and Son of David, had already come, been crucified, raised from the dead, ascended back to God and sent the Holy Spirit. To his credit, the great academic (later considered an apostle by Paul) accepted and believed the humble tentmakers. Shortly thereafter, equipped with high recommendations *and an upgraded Messianic message,* Apollos went to Corinth on the Greek mainland, preaching now the whole story: "The Messiah you are looking for is Jesus!"

A Man with the Message

Arriving in Ephesus, Paul did not accidentally stumble onto twelve disciples of John the Baptist. As Lenski says, "Luke's brevity need not imply that the 'disciples' were found in Ephesus immediately upon Paul's arrival...."[9] Paul's first action would have been to go to the Jewish quarter and find Priscilla and Acquila, learning from them what was happening and where potential converts might be found. Twelve Jewish men, he would be told, are anxiously awaiting the arrival of the Messiah, keeping their lives pure and dedicated, their hearts well watered by the preaching of Apollos.

Quickly finding the twelve, Paul delivered heaven's message:

• The Messiah's coming was not imminent as they supposed – He had *already* come, the time of waiting was ended. He died on a cross, and was raised from the dead! He ascended bodily to the right hand of God in heaven, and He will return again.

• John's water baptism had been one of *preparation,* now there was a new baptism, one of fulfillment, in the name of this glorious savior -- Jesus the Messiah and Lord.

• Furthermore, the baptism with the Holy Spirit foretold by John had also been given to the Church, sent by Jesus in heaven, available now to all who would believe.[10]

Paul's message ignited their hearts, and faith and assurance were born in each man. They believed, sealing confession with water-baptism in the name of the Lord Jesus Christ. "And when Paul laid hands on them, the Holy Spirit came upon them, and they spoke with tongues and prophesied" (Acts 19:6). Now, they possessed both saving Christ and empowering Spirit!

This marvelous charismatic manifestation, appearing 20 years after Pentecost, assures us that the basic pattern of initiation given in Acts 2:38 was still functioning (i.e., conversion + water baptism + the baptism or empowering of the Holy Spirit).[11] These men were now enlisted among the core believers of the great church at Ephesus.

From Synagogue to Schoolhouse

Although his synagogue welcome was usually cut short, surprisingly Paul spoke boldly in the Ephesian synagogue for three months, "reasoning and persuading concerning the things of the kingdom of God" (19:8). Undoubtedly, the golden-tongued Apollos had softened many hearts for Messiah's advent. Paul, however, was not the conciliatory Apollos, as the Jews soon discovered.

Once again, hard-liners thrust the apostle from the synagogue. Paul lost his teaching center! Making a daring relocation, he transferred his excited followers to the lecture hall of Tyrannus -- during the mid-day siesta time of the Greeks (when school was not in session).

> The Western text adds, 'from the fifth hour to the tenth,' meaning eleven o'clock in the morning until four in the afternoon. If this is correct, Paul took advantage of the hottest hours of the day when most people rested after the midday meal. The hall would normally be vacant, and perhaps rent cheaper, after Tyrannus, or whoever the teacher was, lectured in the cooler morning hours....This would allow Paul to work at his own trade during business hours....Then, instead of resting, he engaged in mission work and apologetics when those in trades and business were at leisure to hear him....Paul's regular and unmolested use of the room for two years, with such a wide hearing, indicates his exclusive use of a spacious, well-situated room for a period of each day.[12]

Missing siesta in a hot climate was hard, but hungry people came and responded to his daily teaching, "for they were prepared to forgo their own siesta in order to listen to Paul."[13] Paul's iron-man dedication must have been inspiring to his new converts. "And this continued for two years, so that all who dwelt in Asia heard the word of the Lord Jesus, both Jews and Greeks" (Acts 19:10).

Why Such Spectacular Church Growth?

The marvelous proliferation of the gospel throughout Asia occurred because certain factors combined to create "The Tipping Point" for Ephesus and Asia. Malcom Gladwell's best-selling book explains the process in a societal setting:

> THE TIPPING POINT is that magic moment when an idea, trend, or social behavior crosses a threshold, tips, and spreads like wildfire. Just as a single sick person can start an epidemic or the flue, so too can a small but precisely targeted push cause a fashion trend, the popularity of a new product, or a drop in the crime rate.[14]

Apply this concept to the spiritual explosion of dynamic Christianity in decadent Ephesus. Like a burning match touching off a roaring inferno, a handful of dedicated servants tipped the scales, releasing a healing epidemic of the kingdom of God that swept through the Proconsular Asia of ancient Rome. Let's review what happened.

• Twelve Spirit-filled Jews began witnessing to the lost, praying for the sick and demonstrating the power of the Holy Spirit.

• The students trained in the Hall of Tyrannus (both Jews and former pagans) began to put their lessons to work. Although Paul himself was somewhat restricted, his students and their converts took the message and ran.

• Paul concluded that God wanted to plant more than one church in Ephesus and Asia: He wanted to have the whole of Asia region planted with churches![15]

• Believing Jews, God-fearing Greeks (in the synagogue), and idolatrous pagans (in the marketplace) were converted and recruited with zeal.

The Apostolic "Missions Addiction"

David Shibley, in my estimation, is a remarkable, special type of apostle (although he may not call himself such). He is the founder-overseer-spiritual father of Global Advance, an organization that specializes in training and equipping church-planting ministers and Christian business people in underdeveloped nations. Founded in 1990, GA has trained over 500,000 frontline leaders in 80 nations! They have procedures in place to manage 100 conferences and training events internationally on an annual basis.

The Spring 2009 edition of Global Advance Frontline Update tells of some of their activities. "Dr. Shibley recently led a team to northwestern India, near Pakistan, where they were able to encourage and train over 600 pastors and church planters. God impressed it upon his heart to have a special call to any who had been persecuted in the past year. Over 80 came forward...and the team were able to personally pray over each one. Tears flowed and hearts were renewed...."

Eric is an example of those trained. He started his first church in an Indian village under a tree with three people. He had no outside support and no Bible school training. God began to work through his ministry as many Hindus and Sikhs were healed and delivered. Eric was beaten by radical Hindus on several occasions but pressed on to advance the Gospel in his region. Since 1994 Eric has helped plant 47 churches through the discipling of young leaders.

Efforts to train business leaders in underdeveloped nations is having phenomenal success. Marketplace Missions is a unique way in winning community business people to the Lord. This approach shows how apostolic insight can change communities.

David sends out a little e-mail called "Missions Minute." One of his messages so capsulates the heart of an apostolic person that I include it here. After mentioning his book *The Missions Addiction,* he said:

Naturally, people ask, "What do you mean, a missions addiction?" Well, a missions addiction is a willful fixation on God's purpose in history, which is the enthroning of Jesus Christ in every culture and people. It is a voluntary, magnificent obsession. Those with the missions addiction have their faith and their focus on what is final – the Father's hot resolve that Jesus will reign over all the earth and receive worship from every tribe, people and nation....The missions addiction is a willful addiction, one which we enter with eyes wide open....We are suddenly sensitized to the flow of events as they relate to God's grander scheme....The missions addiction brings laser focus and empowers us as transformation agents for individuals, whole cultures, even entire nations. This is one addiction we should not run from, but run to. So, capture God's passion for the world and catch the missions addiction. Lift up your heart to Jesus, and lift up your eyes to the harvest. [16]

• Local people and visitors were challenged thoughout the city to exchange foolish idolatry for the good news of Jesus Christ. Some converts returned to their home towns with the message, and new churches were planted. We can easily imagine that sailors coming to Ephesus expecting hilarious living were accosted, converted and returned to the sea to carry the message even farther abroad. Undoubtedly, the criminal element was impacted as well.

• Weaving, working leather and selling in the marketplace, Paul converted people to Christ. And, although handicapped to pursue personal visitation of the sick and needy, "handkerchiefs or aprons were brought from his body to the sick, and the diseases left them and the evil spirits went out of them" (Acts 19:12).

Pieces of cloth material, having been in contact with Paul, brought healing to the needy, just as healing came to those who touched the fringe of Jesus' garment (Mark 5:27-34; 6:56). Some commentators believe that the aprons were worn by Paul while working in the marketplace, and the handkerchiefs were sweat cloths. These proxy pieces of cloth conveyed Paul's prayers, faith and concern to distant places, ejecting evil spirits from demonized people when applied in Jesus' name. Consider this translation of Acts 19:11-12:

> God accomplished mighty works of no ordinary character through Paul. Sweat-rags and aprons which had been in contact with his body were actually taken from him and applied to those who were sick, so that their diseases left them and evil spirits were expelled (F. F. Bruce).[17]

• Some foolish Jews attempted to cast out evil spirits by invoking "the Jesus whom Paul preaches." The superstitious populace had special faith in Jewish exorcists because they used the names of Israel's strange, invisible God. The motives and spirituality of these young men were certainly suspect: obviously, they could not assume Paul's spiritual mantle.

A stirred-up evil spirit in one of the exorcist's candidates suddenly reacted! Speaking through the demonized man, the evil spirit caused the man to leap on the exorcists, inflict bodily injury, and strip off their clothes (19:16). This action, initiated by God Himself, openly challenged the authenticity of the city's soothsayers, magicians and exorcists, now making them all become suspect. God Himself was doing some "tipping"!

> This became known both to all Jews and Greeks dwelling in Ephesus, and fear fell on them all, and the name of the Lord Jesus was magnified (Acts 19:17).

• The God-imposed fear, the miracles, the conversions, the loss of interest in the cult of Diana and other gods, the proclamation of Jesus as Lord – the glorious combination brought a startling awareness of the true God to Ephesus, and the dark cloud of Satanic oppression began to lift, allowing the sunlight of God's message to break upon hungry hearts.

• Confessing their sins, many came, bringing their magic, incantation books, idols and other paraphernalia (valued at "several million dollars"[18]) to be burned in a great public bonfire. Attracting city-wide attention, the display possibly lasting for several days (probably orchestrated by Paul). These people were converts who realized the horrible error of idolatry. Selling the expensive objects to obtain offering money was not appropriate: the destruction of idols and magic by fire was a necessary, clear public announcement terminating idolatry in a person's life, openly repudiating all things satanic and magical. "As the potency of spells resides largely in their secrecy, their disclosure would be regarded as rendering them powerless" (F. F. Bruce).[19] The idolatrous spirits were like underground creatures paralyzed by blazing sunlight.

A personal note: While pastoring in San Jose, CA, some years ago, we had a large contingent of young adults from the Hippie culture and also the local university. Because of the witchcraft, drug use and other demonic things associated with that culture, our church took a public stand and held our own conflagration. Admittedly, not as grand as that at Ephesus, the fire still drew the interest of the local newspaper, and required a fire permit to use a metal barrel on the church parking lot.

I couldn't believe the trash that surfaced, as well as the feeling of cleansing that took place. The news of the fiery occasion (from no effort on our part) was broadcast near and far with various reactions. I was particularly proud of letters from three Church of Satan pastors (one being in Japan) who soundly denounced our happening (we must have done something right to get *them* so stirred up!). I know first hand the good and the advertising that such a biblical occasion generates. Overseas, where idolatry is more prevalent, converts often publicly burn their idols before water baptism.

• A dynamic Holy Spirit energy radiated throughout Asia from Ephesus! Other cities were reached by eager evangelists, and churches were established. Probably at this time churches were founded in Smyrna, Pergamos, Thyatira, Sardis, and Philadelphia. The three cities of the Lycus Valley (Colosse, Laodicea and Hierapolis) were evangelized by Epaphras, one of Paul's associates (Colossians 1:7-8; 2:1; 4:12-13). Stationed at the nerve center, Paul incited and encouraged his missionary troops to invade every community with the good news of Jesus Christ.

Thus, the message of Light penetrated the dark world of demons, immorality and idols.

> *"So the word of the Lord grew mightily and prevailed"* (Acts 19:20).

Bruce comments: "The province was intensively evangelized, and remained one of the leading centers of Christianity for many centuries."[20]

• The sale of idols and assorted goods fell dramatically, threatening the income of the local idol makers! The craftsmen retaliated by creating a citywide riot, causing frenzied citizens to run to the amphitheater shouting their allegiance to Diana.

Time for Paul to move on! The prayers of the saints gradually prevailed, the controlling "territorial spirits" were overcome, and the church grew in size and influence.

Paul departed for Macedonia, first going to southern Greece, visiting the churches, and encouraging his spiritual children. Returning to Macedonia, he sailed from Philippi to Troas where he preached all night in an upper room to the newly formed church. A young man, sitting on the ledge of the third story, overcome with sleep, fell down and died. Praying for him, Paul restored him to life, causing the believers to rejoice!

Paul and the Ephesian Elders

Rather than visit Ephesus again and risk delay, Paul called for the elders of the church to meet him in Miletus (some 40 miles south). Delivering a forceful, masterful farewell exhortation, he reviewed his ministry and warned of the future. That message is summarized in sixteen points on the following chart, marvelous principles for aspiring apostles and other shepherds. Kneeling, Paul prayed with them.

Paul's Personal Creed to the Ephesian Elders
(An abbreviation of Acts 20)

1. Do the Lord's work with great humility and tears.

2. Lay your life on the line, serving the Master no matter what.

3. Keep back no spiritual secrets, telling all things helpful.

4. Teach publicly and from house to house.

5. Preach the message of repentance to all ethnic groups.

6. Go where you are sent, even though chains and tribulations await.

7. Be unmoved by warnings; resolve to finish your divine assignment.

8. Know that one day you will finish your course, saying good-bye.

9. Be innocent of any wrongdoing toward anyone.

10. Do not avoid declaring the whole counsel of God to His people.

11. Take heed to shepherd the flock of Jesus carefully.

12. Stay constantly alert, because after my departure, savage wolves will come to destroy, and ambitious elders will attempt to lead away people after themselves.

---

13. Warn the church night and day with tears.

14. Commend the people to "the word of His grace."

15. Covet no one's money or possessions.

16. Be an example by laboring to support the weak.

God's Final Word to the Church at Ephesus

The church at Ephesus is mentioned in Revelation 2:1-7, giving some of the developments in that great church during the intervening years. The Lord made these positive comments: good works, strong patience, intolerance of evil people, tested self-proclaimed apostles, patiently persevered, labored hard (ignoring weariness), and hated the deeds of the Nicolaitans.

They did receive a challenging reprimand: "But, you have left your first love." How is it possible that this great church could leave the empowering grace of God and their zeal for souls?

Possibly, this is the reason that John the Apostle of love was eventually sent to be their bishop. May we all take the Lord's closing admonition to heart: "Remember therefore from where you have fallen; repent and do the first works, or else I will come to you quickly and remove your lampstand from its place – unless you repent."

The Lord extended a gracious invitation to the repentant and overcoming "to eat from the tree of life, which is in the midst of the Paradise of God" (Revelation 2:7). May we all be part of that great company!

Following next will be, "Part IV. Ministry of Apostles." This question deserves a straightforward answer: "What Do Apostles Do?" You will learn about their attributes, functions, spheres of influence, and have some biblical and historical illustrations. These subjects will benefit all ministries, and particularly emphasize the amazing dynamic of apostolic churches.

Chapter 11 Endnotes

[1] Artemis and Diana were the same personality, Artemis a Greek name, Diana being Latin.

[2] Morgan, *Acts*, p. 349.

[3] Barclay, *Acts,* p. 164.

[4] F. F. Bruce, *Acts* with Greek Text, p. 349.

[5] Dunn: "He made a vow which demonstrated his willingness to follow the Torah in matters of personal spiritual discipline in order to demonstrate his good faith to the Torah conservatives in Antioch (and Jerusalem) and to heal any continuing rift with them....it is wholly consistent with his own pastoral strategy laid down in 1 Cor. 9:20...." Pp. 246-7.

[6] At Lystra, Acts 14.

[7] Morgan, p. 435.

[8] Dunn, p. 250.

[9] Lenski, *Acts,* p. 779.

[10] As Jews, these men would have heard of the Holy Spirit. The meaning, taken in context of John's message, would be that they were not aware that the Spirit-baptism promised by John had happened. They waited for both Messiah and Spirit-baptism; Paul announced both were available – and they experienced both!

[11] For full coverage of what I call "the Peter Pattern," see my book *The Glorious Disturbance: Understanding and Receiving the Baptism with the Spirit.*

[12] A. M. Ross, "Tyrannus," Merrill C. Tenney, gen.ed., *The Zondervan Pictorial Encyclopedia of the Bible,* Vol. 5 (Grand Rapids: Zondervan, 1975), p. 832.

[13] F. F. Bruce, *Acts, Revised,* p. 366.

[14] Malcom Gladwell, *The Tipping Point: How Little Things Can Make a Big Difference* (NY/Boston: Little, Brown and Company, 2000/2002). Quotation from cover.

[15] Terry Virgo, while telling the story of New Frontiers International, describes how David Devenish of Bedford, UK, felt the Holy Spirit began to speak to him about planting a whole region of churches. He called this the "Hall of Tyrannus" principle, and found great success in gathering leaders in a region and then working together with them to plant new churches. Terry Virgo, *No Well-Worn Paths: Restoring the Church to Christ's Original Intention* (PO Box 2626, St. Louis, MO: Newfrontiers USA, 2008), chapter 24, "Church Planting."

[16] David Shibley, *Missions Minute from David Shibley* (update@globaladvance.org): March 15, 2006.

[17] Bruce, *Acts, Revised,* p. 366.

---

[18] NLT: "*Greek* 50,000 pieces of silver, each of which was the equivalent of a day's wage."

[19] F. F. Bruce, *Acts* with Greek text, p. 359.

[20] Ibid.

Part IV – Apostolic Ministry Today

Chapter 12 – Leadership in Christ's Body

Chapter 13 – Spheres and Callings

Chapter 14 - Definitions and Illustrations

Chapter 15 – Activation and Motivation

Chapter 12
Leadership in Christ's Church

In This Chapter

- *Is Paul our example of what an apostle should be?*
- *Four charts help explain how apostles lead*
- *How one church is reaching its city*
- *Find how the Church has a fivefold expression*

If apostles are to be an important part of today's church life, must their performance be identical to, similar to, or possibly in contrast to Paul? This is a reasonable question since most of our extant material about apostles is based on Paul's life. This book argues for present-day apostleship, so we must also ask: "Is Paul a suitable model for succeeding generations and our own society?"

Is Paul Our Example?

All agree that Paul did an outstanding job as a Christian Jew and Roman citizen, functioning in a pagan, Greco-Roman world and planting Christian churches where none existed -- the classic example of the successful pioneer church planter in a foreign society.

Unfortunately, we do not have the complete history of Paul or the original Twelve, where they went, and how they functioned. Many unusual situations and happenings occurred that were unique to a given moment, including many experiences that we cannot even imagine. The Bible itself does not tell the whole story.

We regret the lack of historical data, but God does provide us in the New Testament with seventy-nine occurrences of *apostolos* (twenty-nine times in Paul's epistles and Luke thirty-four times), and the Acts provides special insights on how apostles of that day functioned. "We also have the use of the verb *apostello* which provides the special emphasis of a 'commissioned sending,' being stronger than *pempto,* the common word for 'send.'"

> Thus Paul and his disciple and fellow-traveller [sic] Luke provide four-fifths of the examples and most of the material for studying the meaning of the word" (Rengstorf).[1]

Could this paucity of information be by divine design? God knew from the beginning how people movements and societies would develop. God was not inclined to foretell all the coming problems and predicaments we would face. He knew that unexpected things would increase our dependence on Him, causing us to know and serve Him better.

The Playing field Has Changed

Although similarity exists between Paul's methods of church planting and today's efforts in undeveloped countries, we must recognize the great population shift away from farms to the cities. If the world is the field, then the people in the cities have become the major part of that field. The burgeoning cyber-space communications revolution has made our world a global village. Everything is uprooted and updated by the surge of societal reformation.

Planting a church in a modern city requires special ingenuity and the abundant grace of God. Some modern cities have a bigger population than all of Macedonia in Paul's day. Modern apostles and apostolic churches still provide the winning edge, but such people must have both the power of God and the savvy for today's generation.

Sub-cultures exist within the modern city which are not usually the focus of today's ministerial training. We must know these groups and their unique needs, and discover how the kingdom of God can impact them.

Today's apostle will not always look and act like our predisposed Pauline image. Such people may be younger than we imagine Peter and Paul to have been! Modern day, younger apostles must lead apostolic SWAT teams into great intensity and high density situations; such people must be unafraid of sacrifice, demonic opposition or serious persecution. Every major city could have dozens of these sub-culture groups (some large, some small) with multitudes of people. A quick random sampling illustrates our point:

- Inner-city people, burdened with crime, fear and want
- High tech professionals, too busy for family life and church
- University students, filled with doubt, rebellion and political upheaval
- Minority groups, striving for success in a difficult environment
- The disenfranchised, needing shelter, food and clothing
- The entertainment industry, making new demands on time and effort
- Ethnic groups with their language and culture problems

So things have changed quite a bit, and functioning apostles and apostolic teams from the local churches must make reasonable adjustments. However, the principles of Jesus, the Twelve and Paul still remain with us, functioning like the city building code that safeguards any ongoing construction projects. No one is going to be just like Paul, but his personal dedication and spirituality are a grand example for all of us, including any church members who are not in a leadership capacity.

Why We Need to Discuss Apostles Today[2]

- A present emphasis in the body of Christ
- A ministry that God wants to function in the Church (Ephesians 4:11-13)
- A ministry that is prone to misunderstanding -- many definitions – many views on authority – tendency to elevate or exalt
- Some claim to be apostles and they are not (Revelation 2:2)
- We want true apostles, not the false (2 Corinthians 11:13)

Six Signs of an Apostle

Apostles, both past and present, can be recognized by common signs.

1. Dynamic and relevant message
2. Authority and the miraculous
3. Spiritual fruit and results
4. Acceptance and response (by both spiritual leaders and churches)

     5.   The call and direction of Christ
     6.   Compassion and insight

Paul established the idea that an apostle is an authorized representative of Jesus Christ Himself. He developed the theology of apostleship, literally keeping the concept alive. His mission to the Gentiles breathed new life into the Great Commission and raised the lagging vision of the original Twelve and the early Church. His example has been an inspiration to every Christian since then.

Apostles Are Leaders

Four charts in this chapter summarize how apostles lead (some points over-lap a bit). Not tedious explanations, these charts simply give categories and succinct statements that apply to apostles, regardless of personality, sphere or specific assignment. These leadership characteristics are helpful to review.

The charts are based on: Scripture, church history, personal observations of apostles I have known and suggestions from contemporary apostolic leaders. Since our subject is relatively new and quite challenging, keep in mind that some of us are making a sincere pioneer effort to awake a slumbering Church world. At this point, the heart and vision of an apostle is more important to our discussion than how-to, technical methods.

Local apostolic churches are like cities within a city, a biblical culture within a secular culture. For apostles and apostolic Christians to fulfill our calling, there must be a heavy dose of God's wisdom to make the necessary impact.

How An Apostle Leads:	
1. Word & Example	• *Inward signs: character & servant attitude* • *Outward signs: Changed lives, miraculous happenings* • *Suffering: models self-sacrifice & dedication* • *Humility: wears the title with humility*
2. Service & Care	• *Serves, shepherds & protects* • *Fathers the children, youth, and adults* • *Establishes leaders who care* • *Attracts people—calls, equips & releases* • *Propagates & populates*
3. Communication	• *Initiates faith response, generates vision* • *Proclaims & protects sound doctrine* • *Helps make important decisions* • *Casts out devils, challenges the demonic* • *Performs miraculous signs* • *Disciplines the unruly* • *Contends for unity*

Many seminaries *and churches* these days are wisely offering degrees in leadership training. This focus is good and represents an upgraded approach in ministerial training; nevertheless, I can't help but be sympathetic with Don Atkin, when he says,

> I am convinced that focusing upon the technical tends to draw us away from the spontaneous inspiration of the Holy Spirit....My heart is to see Spirit-led apostolic ministry replicated.[3]

An ideal balance is needed: wise leadership principles, spiritual gift activity and a loving shepherd's heart. Such ministry is truly profitable.

Apostles Lead in World Harvest

Biblical apostles are ambassadors of the kingdom of God. The burning passion to reach the peoples of the world through church growth, church renewal, culture penetration, and world harvest is a mandate of Jesus and an expression of God's heart.

The Great Commission of Matthew 28:18-20 is clear: Go to all the nations, make disciples, baptize and teach the ways of God.

Leading in World Harvest	
1. Expands Kingdom Borders	• *Maintains the goal of reaching the nations* • *Envisions and leads missionary expansion*
2. Penetrates New Territories	• *Reaches new language/ethnic/cultural groups* • *Concentrates on strategic centers*
3. Prioritizes Cultural Outreach	• *Is concerned about the secular market-place* • *Sees the bigger picture: impacting society*
4. Challenges Cultural Barriers & Demonic Powers	• *Prays* • *Preaches* • *Declares*
5. Marshals Resources	• *Produces kingdom funding* • *Helps the needy* • *Teaches Faith and Provision*
6. Rallies the People Of God	• *Presents a shining vision* • *Shows the way* • *Speaks for God*

This last-day harvest is portrayed in a prophetic vision the Lord gave me.

I saw wretched people, languishing in the murky obscurity of dark caves. Unlike dungeon cells, the caves had no restraining iron gates to hold the pitiful creatures within. The enshrouding darkness acted in the place of iron manacles and leg irons; the prisoners' were totally convinced that escape was impossible. Constant groaning mingled with the total darkness.

Then I saw *the ambassadors of light!* God's servants boldly approached the hell-holes armed with intense, flaming torches. The extreme light dispersed the horrible night as the torches were thrust into the cave openings! The messengers of God declared freedom – and as the good news resounded in the dark corridors, men, women and children began staggering forth.

Their miserable rags and filth dropped off and they became clothed in raiment of white. These delivered ones became a great, marching column of redeemed souls, singing as they headed toward the distant mountain of light where God dwells.

Apostles Lead in Planting and Building Churches

Planting churches was a specialty of Paul the apostle. There is no higher adventure than invading a community (group, sub-culture, city, country) held captive by Satan, then see the Word and the Spirit of God break forth. This is best accomplished when an apostolic team is utilized, even if most of the people are not actual apostles – but, as explained before, they are apostolic!

Diverse opinions about apostleship are expressed on the Internet these days, and sometimes the discussion becomes somewhat heated. I was surprised to read one author's statement that "nowhere in the New Testament does it say that apostles are to plant churches." A simple reading of 1 Corinthians 3:5-17 easily disproves his point. Verse 6 says, "I planted…." This means that Paul, the "wise master builder" (v. 10) was involved in designing and building spiritual foundations for churches. God used Paul to establish the groundwork for churches in Galatia, Syria, Crete, Asia Minor, Macedonia and Greece.

Paul and associates build up the churches on the foundation of Christ and His teachings. Paul, perhaps taking a cue from the Jewish synagogue system, realized the importance of Christians gathering in a local community to form a tangible base for extending the kingdom of God.

Leading in Planting & Building Churches	
1. Facilitator	*Initiates and networks for church renewal & restoration*
2. Explorer	*Pioneers new territory, plants churches in virgin territory*
3. Architect	*Makes plans, lays foundations, builds churches*
4. Farmer	*Ploughs, plants, waters*
5. Parent	*Nurtures, protects (to insure survival)*
6. Mentor	*Trains, equips, appoints leaders*
7. Authority	*Ordains elders and deacons (Acts 14:23; 6:1-6; Tit 1:5)*
8. Shepherd	*Tends, feeds, protects, heals*
9. Manager	*Develops strategies, executes plans*
10. Role Model	*Imparts the character of Christ the Chief Apostle*

The Importance of the Church

> *The Church: visible and invisible, eternal, composed of many members, joined to her Lord by bonds of love, devotion and mission. Every true, practicing follower of Jesus and His teachings is a member of the great Church of God. Various descriptions and metaphors give us insightful snippets: Body, Temple, Habitation of God, Army, Bride.*

When the Church invades satanic territory, delivered captives will certainly result. These new babes in Christ need care, nourishment and protection. Every new Christian needs baptism into the Body of Christ, followed by fellowship, help and encouragement from fellow Christians; this requires pastors, elders, teachers and cell leaders. All these "gathered-together-ones" make up the various segments of the local church in a given area, and they are also part of the total Church which fills the earth and heaven itself.

The concern of apostles in Bible days was to plant, grow and multiply local churches. Paul's emphasis on dynamic local churches was a brilliant insight for strengthening and retaining peoples' faith. The unified Spirit-filled Christians in a given area became the tangible expression of Christ and His kingdom to that community. "Local" refers to the community where a Christian lives and works, an area where Christians can gather at their meeting places within a reasonable walking or driving distance. This should be our focus also!

Pastor-Apostle Cho of Korea has communicated well his passion for church growth and soul winning to his workers and people. As an example, some workers live in high-rise buildings where the occupants quickly get on the elevator and then barricade themselves in their rooms; church planting seems impossible. One worker, finding no success in just knocking on doors, stationed herself at the elevator entrance and began helping people with their burdens, riding the elevator with them, and even entering the apartments with these hitherto unknown neighbors. Gradually a cell of believers developed; branch churches have actually been formed by this method: a local church in a large apartment building! When you are handed a lemon, make some lemonade!

The Fivefold Expression of the Church

1. *The Universal Church:*
   Composed of all saints of all ages, living and dead. All Christians now living on earth are numbered with that great heavenly host of redeemed spirits whose bodies await the resurrection of life; the believers on earth join their worship with that of heaven. Matthew 16:18; Ephesians 1:22; 3:21; Colossians 1:18; Hebrews 12:23.

2. *The Global Church:*
   All believers in Jesus Christ now alive and active throughout the whole earth who come from every tribal, ethnic, national and people group. This great international Body comes from a multitude of Christian groups, denominations and movements; they are the people who truly accept and proclaim Jesus as divine Savior, anointed Christ, risen Lord and Head of the one eternal and world-wide Church. Romans 16:4; 1 Corinthians 1:2; 7:17; 14:33; 2 Corinthians 11:28.

3. *The Local Church:*

The Christians of a given area who band together to form a tangible expression of Christ's Body, the Church on a neighborhood level. This is the fellowshiping, worshiping, serving followers of Jesus who join their talents and ministries to express New Testament Christianity in a given population or specialization area; their combined membership and activities bring the good news of Christ to that area. This is the familiar, personal level, and it is made up of individuals of all ages in various stages of spiritual development, who gather together weekly for spiritual edification. Hebrews 10:24-25; 1 Corinthians 1:2; 5:4; 11:18, 20, 33-34.

4. *The Cell Group:*

This is a dozen or so local church believers who form a circle of friends for personal, intimate fellowship, enrichment and outreach. They are a band of brothers and sisters who gather frequently to encourage and enable one another in Christian living as well as to introduce non-Christians to Christ. Such groups meet at various locations and times and often have a common interest or activity. They make up a small specialized congregation within the local church. Such groups form one of the most effective bridges for bringing new converts into the local church fellowship. Acts 2:46; 20:20.

5. *The Individual Believer:*

The smallest component of the Body of Christ. Sometimes this member finds him/herself the only believer present in a workplace, school classroom, etc. When alone in the secular society, the single Christian becomes both a witness for Christ in word or deed and a representative of the Body of Christ. Acts 1:8; 1 Corinthians 12:27; Romans 12:4-5.

The Building Is Not the Church

Previously, some Christians have equated the local church with religious buildings and architecture; however, today's race to build bigger and better church buildings has turned off many serious believers.

I believe the season for larger and larger houses of worship is coming to an end, as is the *Field of Dreams* ministry strategy that says if we build it, they will come. The idea that bigger is better, especially as it relates to bigger buildings, may be an approach to ministry that is about to transition into history (Kenneth Ulmer).[4]

"Church" in the New Testament always refers to the people of God. The building where Christians may meet is secondary to the people, they are the highest objective in Scripture. The religiously used building is primarily (to put it bluntly) "a sheep shed" and "house of prayer." The church itself (the people) is to be an energetic ministry juggernaut that impacts a given population area with the power of Christ's kingdom. The local church, in its various forms and outreaches, should engage, impact and even transform today's emerging culture. A church building is a reference point, a gathering place for the body of Christ -- it is *not* the church.

The Activity of Apostles

The final chart in this chapter distils the previous information into seven key categories of activity, accompanied by the appropriate objectives. In all categories one senses the burning zeal, the unashamed testimony, and the abounding confidence of heaven's ambassadors. Such leaders imbue the church members with apostolic vision and passion, transforming the people into a spiritual, inexorable force, crushing the demonic opposition before it.

Reaching a City
By Barbara Wright, Associate Pastor of Adult Education, City Church

When Wendell Smith, his wife, Gini, and their two teenage children left Bible Temple in Portland, Oregon, in the summer of 1992 to plant a church in Seattle, they were armed with three ingredients of divine strategy: the wisdom and insight gained through twenty years of faithful service to Pastor Dick Iverson and Bible Temple (now City Bible Church); a personal Word from God with prophetic confirmation; and a list of directives from the Lord that established the church's mission and vision.

Those directives (later synthesized into the Twelve Covenants of The City Church) became the spiritual foundation stones for The City Church and established the vision and mission of the church. As the church grew numerically and spiritually, all decisions were filtered through the twelve "covenants" to see if the new proposal fit the church's vision and mission so that the fledgling church was not being driven by the latest church-growth whim. Without yet realizing their full significance, the covenants served as solid bedrock—a firm strategy.

In addition, the Lord told Smith that The City Church wasn't his church—it belonged to the Lord. Thus, an apostolic strategy of waiting on God and then obeying explicitly His instructions became the hallmark of his ministry.

From the beginning, one word that described Smith's approach to pastoring was "strategic." Early on he developed The City Church TRAKS—an acronym for Training Routes and Kingdom Strategies—a five-step process of assimilating new believers and seasoned believers alike into The City Church's DNA, using the emphases of the fivefold ministry.

Not only has this strategic approach to pastoring raised up a strong local church in the Seattle area, it has also helped countless leaders plant, establish and strengthen their own local churches. The five courses, with the written manuals, are designed as disciple-building venues which will produce strong, committed believers who, in turn, become leaders who build generation-enduring churches.

The strategy is simple, but effective. God has blessed it and it works! So much so that the group of 40 who began holding church services in a hotel conference room in the summer of 1992 has now grown to nearly 7,000 meeting weekly on six different campuses around the greater Seattle area. In addition to dynamic church services, over 700 small groups are held each month. The church hosts several conferences each year; has a social service ministry to feed and clothe those in need; has built 22 cottages to house parents and their foster children; holds four separate summer camps for those from age six through college; and has strategic ministry to all of its members. Numerical growth is relative, however, as the greater Seattle area alone contains a population of roughly three million—scores of souls to be won to Christ.

Wendell Smith could be called an Apostolic Pastoral Strategist as he has produced numerous resources for the Body of Christ that are instrumental in forming disciples into believers and believers into leaders. In addition to preaching and teaching, he has written books and manuals that deliver full doctrinal treatments on the subjects of faith, prayer, prosperity with a purpose, and the ministry of women. Through these tools, pastors and leaders around the world have been further encouraged, strengthened and equipped and are building their own churches.

One of Smith's first responses when diagnosed with Multiple Myeloma in 2004 was to produce teaching materials on healing. The gift of Apostolic Pastoral Strategy once again was put into action, producing tools for the Body of Christ in the area of divine healing—tools of blessing and tools of warfare to "fight the good fight of faith," "overcoming the evil one."

In September, 2009, after much prayer and deliberation, Pastors Wendell and Gini transitioned into the role of Founding Pastors and their son and daughter-in law, Judah and Chelsea Smith, were installed as the new Lead Pastors. Although this was a prayerful and careful strategic decision, still transitions can be difficult seasons in a church. But the strong blessing of God has rested upon The City Church during the season of leadership transition and they have seen an increase in every area of church life—salvations, water baptisms, rededications, volunteer involvement and financial growth. The preaching is strong, the people are at peace, and a new excitement about the Kingdom of God is in the atmosphere.

Local pastors are anointed of the Spirit to do such things in the local setting. If leaders can keep vision fresh and anointed of the Spirit, great things are possible. An unabashed pride in sharing responsibility with team leaders will both mentor them and make them excited, participating, burden bearers.

Apostles Are God's Generals

Apostles see the bigger picture, casting a wider vision as generals of the Church. Illustrations come from the second world war. Many fine line officers fought on the front, but generals were responsible for the bigger picture.

General George C. Patton led his tank corps through Northern Africa, Sicily and France into Germany. A drive to win the war boiled inside of him. He felt born to lead men into battle.

Over him, however, General Dwight D. Eisenhower had the bigger responsibility of the Allied Invasion of France. As Patton wielded an iron-fisted, hard-driving assault against the enemy, Eisenhower worked a bigger plan using his authority, diplomacy and patience for an even greater accomplishment.

Ike deliberately side-lined Patton for a while, waiting to use his friend's intense military genius at a later, more strategic time. The big picture won the war, but both generals were needed in their own spheres. Meanwhile, those with lesser responsibility also served well.

A special edition book published by *US News & World Report* (2009), gives exciting episodes from the lives of famous

American generals. Amy D. Bernstein makes several statements that very well apply to apostle-generals of the Church.

> The secret of many a great general lies in having extraordinary mental and physical stamina, plus a willingness to endure significant hardship alongside his men...." For instance, Washington was described by a fellow officer: "He maintained full possession of himself; is indefatigable by day and night." "...the best generals seem to share an intuitive sense of how, where, and when to engage the enemy to their own advantage" (emphasis added).[5]

Pastors will certainly love their people and minister effectively to them, but an apostle additionally has *a general's restlessness that cannot be stilled*, a drive to see God's kingdom advance, a determination to reach new towns and cities, new cultures, new peoples. Apostles want to plant the flag of Christ in people groups that have long been captive to the prince of darkness. They cry out with Patton, "My God, I was born for this hour!"

Of course apostles and pastors are not doing all of these things every day, but sooner or later these things are done. More timid souls, will shrink from battle with its casualties and fatigue, but those who have been to the mountain and seen the vision will not be content. They will mount, rally the troops and lead the charge.

They will know, like Jesus, that they have been sent on a mission, and their churches will have flaming vision, consumed with the Great Commission of Jesus. Deity has ordained the apostles and churches to be ambassadors of heaven's kingdom. We are to love not our lives to the death. The kingdom will advance when the church wakes up! If martyrs must hang on a stake and a torch put to the wood, they will sing as the choking smoke engulfs them; their voices will be joined by a heavenly choir declaring all is well and that the Christ has prevailed again against insurmountable odds. And, when it is finished, like Paul, they will say, "...my departure is at hand. I have fought the good fight, I have finished the race, I have kept the faith!" (2 Timothy 4:6-7).

How Apostles Lead in Church Growth, Church Renewal, Culture Penetration, & World Harvest	
What Do They Do?	*What Are Their Objectives?*
1. Set in order	• *Establish and strengthen churches.............. ....1 Cor 3:10* • *Lay doctrinal foundations ....Heb 6; 2 Tim 3:16; Titus 2:1* • *Develop leaders/release ministries ....…....2 Cor 12:17-18* • *Ordain elders ....…........…........ Ac 14:23; Titus 1:5* • *Unmask false apostles and teachers.............2 Cor 11:13; Phil 3:2* • *Advise on problems/address concerns.........…...........1 Cor 7-16* • *Help churches achieve "candlestick status"............ Rev 2 and 3*
2. Preach	• *Communicate like a kingdom ambassador...................2 Tim 4:2* • *Speak boldly on major doctrines, select issues.…...........1 Th 2:13* • *Address local church matters (reinforce leadership)..2 Cor 2:7-11* • *Promote world missions...............…....…....Acts 1:8; Lk 24:47* • *Declare a theology of restoration…....Ac 3:19-21; Lk 4:18; Ac 13:41* • *Minister (preach, teach, impart) in gatherings.Ac 19:9-10; 10:7,17*
3. Teach	• *Teach the Scripture.................. Heb 5:12; 2 Pet 3:1-2; 1 Tim 4:11* • *Combat false doctrine......................................Titus 1:13; 2:1, 8* • *Encourage Christian conduct/practical living..Eph 4:1,17; 2C 7:1* • *Be a joyful, skilled theologian..........................…........Ac 20:30-31* • *Write and propagate spiritual truths.............…...Ac 20:27; Gal 6:11*
4. Demonstrate	• *Release Holy Spirit power – bring awakening!..........1 Thess 1:6* • *Display and impart spiritual gifts.…......Rom 1:11; 12:6-8; Ac 28:8* • *Discern and cast out evil spirits, heal the sick.Mk 16:17; Ac 16:18* • *Feed the hungry, care for the needy..…............Gal 2:10; 2 Cor 8:4* • *Bring prophetic insights........... 1 Cor 14:29; 1 Th 5:20; 1 Tim 4:14* • *Exercise and generate faith...........…................Jude 3; Col 1:23*
5. Be Present	• *Set an example of godliness..................1 Th 4:1; 1 Tim 3:2; 4:12* • *Live among and associate with the people......1 Th 5:12; Titus 1:5* • *Inspire faith and confidence..................…..............2 Tim 2:15* • *Lend authenticity to the doctrines taught.............…......Ac 20:31* • *Provide spiritual impetus..............…....…........Ac 13:1-3; 15:36* • *Promote church growth.............….....…..............Ac 19:10; 16:5* • *Demonstrate unique authority...................…...........Ac 28:28*

6. Pray	• Set a personal example................Ac 10:9; Eph 1:15-21; Col 4:12 • Lead in spiritual warfare..........Ac 13:9-12; Eph 6:18-19; Col 4:2-3 • Make public declarative prayer.......................Ac 4:24-31; 14:10 • Mobilize and promote prayer gathering............Ac 1:14; 3:1; 12:5
7. Strategize	• Pray, advise and strategize with church leadership........Ac 14:23 • Cooperate with community leaders........................Rom 14:6-7 • Initiate spiritual breakthrough & church growth............Ac 19:10 • Bring clear direction and leadership..........Ac 15:25-28; 20:188-36

Chapter 12 Endnotes

[1]   Rengstorf, *Apostleship*, p. 25.
[2] The five thoughts from "Apostolic Ministry" teaching notes by Bill Scheidler, missionary to South Africa.
[3] Don Atkin, *The Heart of Apostolic Ministry* (www.Kingdomquest.Net), p. 6.
[4] Kenneth Ulmer, "Ministry Paradigm Shift," *Charisma* (May 2010): 92.
[5] Amy D. Bernstein, "Glory and Honor," *Secrets of America's Best Generals* (US News and World Report, Collectors Edition, 2009), p. 6.

Chapter 13
Spheres and Cultures

In This Chapter

- *Paul uses "sphere" to explain ministry placement*
- *God's continual reaffirming of Paul's call and mission*
- *Note the parallel in ministry of Peter and Paul*
- *The importance of knowing your "sphere"*
- *Culture is a "many splendored" thing*

Consider the legendary Lawrence of Arabia. Although an officer in the English army, he was not only able to communicate with the Arabs but also become their friend, even leading them into battle. He, of course, was not a Christian leader or influence, but he illustrates how a person must have a sense of purpose and how he must identify with a given culture or group in order to influence them. (As, Hudson Taylor in chapter 2.)

"Dress as an Arab does," T. E. Lawrence advised his English military associates. "As long as you dress like an Englishman, you may be more comfortable, but you will always be the foreigner." Lawrence realized that he could not achieve his objectives acting as a staid British officer; he must identify with the requirements of the Arab desert people's "sphere" and expectations of their culture if he would be successful. Let's take this tip from Lawrence: every Christian minister needs to understand how to interact with sphere and culture. This concept is not only true of apostles and pastors but also for every Christian.

Part I. Spheres

Know Your "Sphere"

Usually "sphere" is defined according to its popular meaning: a ball, a round body or a globe; however, a second meaning for this word is applicable here: *domain, realm, area, scope, territory, province, bounds, beat.*

In his first epistle to the Corinthians Paul gave a firm, but courteous, statement of his apostleship, but this attitude changed in his second epistle: Paul strongly defended his apostleship "sphere," sternly denouncing parasitic "false apostles"[1] that would lead his congregation astray. Out of his frustration came the clearest statement on ministry spheres in the New Testament, which we will consider in a moment.

True-Life Illustrations

Spheres abound in our society: a third grade teacher in her class room, salesman working his territory, sergeant commanding a platoon of men, captain navigating his ship, driver of a bus, judge in his courtroom, mother with her children, athlete in a running lane, governor of a state, plumber fixing a pipe. Animals have their territories, like lions and hyenas, and so do franchised companies and military forces. Youth gangs, girl scouts and school districts have boundaries.

Joseph's Sphere

Spheres can outwardly change and mature, but behind a person's life is that invisible, determined will of God for your success if you will cooperate and be in the right place, at the right time, with the right attitude. Joseph, son of Jacob, is an interesting study in God's gifting and purpose; he was born to be one of God's champions and leaders.

Trace his life story through various "spheres": home, dungeon, Potiphar's House, Pharaoh's Court, and finally savior of his family and the known world (Genesis 37-50). Divinely blessed, Joseph's destiny and fulfillment nevertheless required finding and accepting the will and placement of God. Joseph found that he must cooperate with and allow the divine calling to materialize in the "sphere" ordained of God (Psalm 105:19).

Ambassador to the Inuit People

There are important (but lesser known) people all over the world that function in varying degrees of apostolic authority. I remember well how Kayy Gordon of Vancouver, BC, Canada, at the age of 22 headed for the Arctic Circle to be a missionary among the Eskimos. Eyebrows were raised by her pastor and other friends as they wondered how this young woman could undergo the rigors of the far North and challenge all the social problems and spiritual bondage of the native peoples. During her first year in the Arctic, Kayy lived in a tent with the reindeer herders. There she adapted to the land of the midnight sun, sharing with the Eskimos their camp life and winter storms, following the caribou and eating whale meat. She made 400-mile treks by dog sled and snowmobile to minister to the caribou hunters. For a number of years she was the postmistress of Cambridge Bay to partially support herself and contribute to the ministry.

She preached a message of deliverance from sin, sickness, drunkenness and evil spirits, and the Lord confirmed His word with signs following! Now, some fifty + years later (after many confirming miracles and efforts that would be daunting to Paul the apostle) there are churches and Bible schools established in that frozen land: a truly marvelous accomplishment of God's grace. Her story is told in *God's Fire on Ice*.[2] Kayy does not call herself an apostle, but everyone who knows her would certainly think she is. Here is an example of a young white woman crossing cultural and ethnic boundaries to bring the gospel to the Inuit people in the power of the Holy Spirit. Paul would be proud of the vision that brought her to the Arctic: "an Eskimo church that would be Bible-taught and totally self-sufficient, ministering to its own people across the desolate wastes of three quarters of a million square miles of ice, snow and unmarked tundra."[3] When anyone says, "A woman can't be an apostle!", I smile and think of Kayy Gordon.

Another clear illustration is the human body, seemingly Paul's favorite metaphor. The different types of cells, organs, systems, and members illustrate both the importance of organic unity and also individual ("spherical") organic responsibility. A blood cell cannot replace a muscle cell, and so on. So obvious! Yet, we sometimes fail to apply the same principle in our spiritual giftings and ministries. Every member has a spiritual sphere, a place to function fruitfully!

Understanding Spheres

The key text for understanding spheres (*ministry authority, assignments and boundaries*) is 2 Corinthians 10:12-15. The Greek text, unfortunately, is probably one of the most difficult to translate and interpret in the New Testament! C. K. Barnett's cryptic comment seems appropriate: "the very difficult Greek of an extremely complicated passage."[4]

Two Greek Words: Metron and Kanon

The word "sphere" appears five times in our English text, being three times the translation of *metron* (highlighted below in the New King James Version). *Metron* is translated in various ways, but always with similar meaning, a word meaning "that which is measured, a determined extent, a portion measured off" (W.E. Vine).[5] Our English word "metric" comes from this Greek term.

The translation of the text becomes more complicated by the addition of *kanon*, a second measurement word. This word originally meant "a cane" or "reed," like a measuring stick or our "yard stick." A. Sand says, "as a 'straight' staff it took on the meaning 'standard,' 'measure' [and eventually] a rule of conduct, a standard for making judgments."[6] For instance, Bible believers refer to "the canon of Scripture" which means the books of the Bible measure up to the approved standard. In the New Testament *kanon* also means "*prescribed range* of action or duty, 2 Co. 10:13, 15, 16; met. *rule* of conduct or doctrine, Gal. 6:16; Phi. 3:16."[7]

Scholarly debate has ensued because of Paul's use of *kanon*. Some claim that the word has such a strong *geographical* sense about it that Paul must have felt his area of ministry had physical boundaries. Paul, of course, knew that his ministry would take place in literal areas – he was not, after all, just a spirit flitting about. He understood also that Peter and others would be preaching in Greece, but he was determined to be faithful to *his assignment* from God.

> Paul advances here a canon for his own apostolic ministry. It lies in *his pioneering work under God's direction*. This probably does not mean that he has in view either a measuring line of God or the allocation of a geographical district giving him exclusive rights. The point is rather that *it has been divinely granted to him historically to come to Corinth and then to press on when his ministry is successful.* He will not stop where

the gospel is already known; this would involve boasting beyond limit in the labors of others (v. 16). (H.W. BEYER, EMPHASIS ADDED).[8]

Paul's calling was to reach people, and people lived in places. Paul realized a strong sense of ownership for those in the area to which he was called and those who responded. He had the consuming desire to reach every person he could (who did not know Christ), and this involved visiting Jewish synagogues and even proselytizing any responsive members!

2 Corinthians 10:12-16
Here is Paul's full statement:

12 For we dare not class ourselves or compare ourselves with those who commend themselves. But they, measuring themselves by themselves, and comparing themselves among themselves, are not wise.

13 We, however, will not boast beyond measure **[*metron*]**, but within the limits of the **sphere** **[*metron tou kanonos*]** which God **[*o theos* *metrou*,** God of the measure] appointed us – a **sphere** **[*metron*]** which especially includes you.

14 For we are not extending ourselves beyond our **sphere** (thus not reaching you), for it was to you that we came with the gospel of Christ.

15 Not boasting of things beyond measure **[*ametra,* immeasurably]**, that is, in other men's labors, but having hope, that as your faith is increased, we shall be greatly enlarged by you in our **sphere,**

16 to preach the gospel in the regions beyond you, and not to boast in another man's **sphere** **[*metron*]** of accomplishment.

Other Versions: • NIV -- "the field God has assigned," • NLT – "the boundaries of the work God has given us" • Interlinear – "the measure [*to metron*] of the rule [*kanonos*] which the God of measure (*ho theos metrou*] distributed to us"• Amplified – "the limits [of our commission which] God has allotted us as our measuring line."

Paul meant the area of activity and authority where a person will *function at his/her best and be most successfull by the grace of God* – the place of God's calling. The text means that Paul (and the rest of us) are expected to be *where* God wants us to be, to do *what* God wants us to do, *when* He wants it done! The idea is pure genius and very clear: *be in God's will, and you will have great success.*

Geographical Boundaries

As already mentioned, some scholars feel that Paul, in discussing "spheres," was speaking of geographical boundaries. Religious groups have always seemed to gravitate toward this *exclusive control syndrome* as they grow bigger. Several church organizations have felt that if one of their churches was planted in a city, they would not condone another church of their fellowship to be planted in that same city. So much for church growth!

The truth is that today's larger towns and cities need more than one church of a certain type. The fields are vast, the harvest is great . . . and the workers are few! Jesus reminds us, "Therefore pray the Lord of the harvest to send out laborers into *His harvest*" (Matthew 9:38, emphasis added). Actually, if the vision is to multiply souls won, there must be the multiplication of churches, *for this is one of the best ways to win souls!* Also, let us be realistic: even if our doctrine is right, people of our denomination may still not relate to our particular church!

The secret of multiplying churches is not merely gathering leaders around a map, and sectioning of parcels for certain presbyters to watch over. This has some merit, but there must above all be the call and direction of the Holy Spirit as well as dynamic apostolic leadership.

Paul Defines His Sphere, His Christian Job Assignment

Paul knew he was called as an apostle, selected by God, to be an ambassador for the kingdom of God to the unreached Gentiles. He was "directly commissioned by the risen Christ to undertake pioneer evangelism and to plant churches" (F. F. Bruce).[9] With time, maturity, and aging, this calling gradually did become more refined. Basically, Paul's active ministry was to virgin fields, a "sphere" based on Isaiah 52:15 and quoted in Romans 15:20-21:

> My ambition has always been to preach the Good News where the name of Christ has never been heard, rather than where a church has already been started by someone else.
> I have been following the plan spoken of in the Scriptures, where it says, *"and those who have never heard of him will understand."* In fact, my visit to you has been delayed so long because I have been preaching in these places (NLT).

There was also a "specificity" to Paul's activities. This is clearly shown in the decisions initiating his missionary journeys. That is, Paul was not only motivated by the Holy Spirit, he was also *directed* by the Spirit.

- Prophetic guidance launched the waiting Paul from Antioch (Acts 13:1-3)
- A clear prophetic vision directed him to Macedonia (Acts 16:9-10)
- "[T]he Lord spoke to Paul in the night" to confirm his stay in Corinth (Acts 18:9)
- While in prayer, the Lord told Paul to quickly leave Jerusalem (Acts 22:18)
- God clearly directed him to go to Rome (Acts 23:11)
- The angel of the Lord assured him that he would be brought to Caesar (Acts 27:24)

These examples seem quite dramatic, and they are, but much of his guidance was not so. For instance, when he was in Galatia, his guidance and impressions to go to the various towns did not necessarily require visions, dreams or a voice. But he did use wisdom and keep conscious of the Spirit's impressions.

Paul found his sphere, and although we might find the idea challenging in today's world (especially in populated megacities), we also can find our spheres and placements.

A Tragic Error: Measuring Yourself by Yourself

2 Corinthians 10:12, *they measure themselves by themselves.* The false teachers who invaded Corinth behaved as though there was no standard of comparison higher than themselves. In contrast

Paul boasts only in the Lord (see vv. 13-18; cf. 1 Co 1:31). He knew his job, and God worked through him to see it accomplished. He boasted only of God's commendation upon his ministry.

A Striking Comparison

Luke tells the story of the Church (in Acts) in a refreshingly straightforward way, describing the triumphant spread of the gospel from Jerusalem to Rome, the great Gentile capital of that day. He particularly stresses the activity of the Holy Spirit working through Paul, Peter and others in the Gentile cities.

Luke presented Paul in the best possible light so that both Jews and Jewish Christians could appreciate all that God had done through him and his associates, settling forever that Paul was indeed a *bona fide* apostle, ordained by Jesus Christ, and comparable to the Twelve. Such acceptance held the door ajar for the development of other post-Ascension apostles.

Luke accomplished this portrayal in part by presenting the striking similarity between Peter the lead apostle in Judea and Paul among the Gentiles. One commentary rightly says of Paul: "The parallelism with Peter's experience appears to be more than coincidental."[10] The miraculous ministry in Peter's life among the Jews is matched by that of Paul among the Gentiles.

Apostolic Similarities between Peter & Paul

Description of Event (in Acts)	Peter	Paul
1. Impulse of Spirit at beginning of mission	2:4 (Jerusalem)	13:2 (Antioch)
2. Followed by extensive sermon	2:124ff "	13:16ff (Pisidia)
3. Healing a lame man (in vicinity of a temple)	3:1ff "	14:8 (Lystra)
4. Persecution	5:17 "	14:19 "
5. Miraculously delivered from prison	5:19; 12:6ff "	16:25ff (Phillipi)
6. Hands laid on people, received Holy Spirit	8:17 (Samaria)	19:1ff (Ephesus)
7. Special cures and exorcisms	5:15 (Jerusalem)	19:11-12 "
8. Evil-intentioned people humiliated	8:18 (Samaria)	13:10 (Paphos)
9. Wrote epistles to God's people	2 epistles	13 epistles

Although these two had different spheres of ministry, a common denominator was clearly the power of the Holy Spirit at work in each of them.

Part II. Culture Is a Many-splendored Thing

I live in San Jose, California, the tenth-largest city in the United States. In this city of over a million people nearly half of the names in the phone directory are Hispanic. We also have a huge Asian population with over 100,000 Vietnamese alone.

When I first arrived over 50 years ago, to start a church, I was interested in what was occurring in several of the churches that functioned in a cultural milieu. I noticed that a certain Italian church that was doing quite well at the time, conducted their services in the Italian language only. This was also true of one of the larger Hispanic churches that insisted on only Spanish language in their services.

Defining "Culture"

"the sum total of ways of living built up by a group of human beings and transmitted from one generation to another" (*Random House Dictionary*).

"the particular state or stage of advancement in which a race, a people, a nation, a specific class, or an integrated group of these finds itself at a given period (Webster's Book of Synonyms., p. 159).

Naturally, the older immigrants wished to retain their comfortable language and customs, especially their religious habits and Bible translation. But, their children began to grow and attend public school and learn American English. After a time the youth became teenagers, and became embarrassed by the language and customs of their church.

Eventually, this created an inability to communicate religious convictions to their Americanized children – and their inability to draw English-speaking Americans into the church. Eventually those churches had to close their doors. It is only natural for new immigrants to retain language, dress, food, and traditions, but if they want to keep their youth, the church must adjust to the culture and language where they live.

The Cultural Challenge

Change is taking place in the whole world, in our immediate community, and in the personal world of every individual. With this rush of technology, youth explosion, racial tension, massive calamities, the internet, and so forth, the church cannot sit still and not do what we do best: bring people into meaningful contact with God. Culture shift in both the secular world and the religious world, brings the greatest challenge the Church has ever faced.

Consider this simplistic illustration. Craftsman Tools in a TV ad announced: "Craftsman wrench, going where traditional wrenches cannot go." Then it showed an exposed modern automobile motor. The bolt to be tightened was located in an awkward place, inaccessible to a standard wrench. The new wrench, however, had a swivel head, so the hard-to-reach bolt was easily tightened. The basic job still had to be done without compromise, but it was easily accomplished with a tool prepared for the situation.

The churches must keep our biblical perspectives and principles, but we must work with what God is doing in our particular communities. With our traditional mindsets, we cannot fix our communities, but with God's adjustments we can. The Church must not be defined by culture, but it must understand worldly culture shifts; our churches must be distinctive because of the Holy Spirit culture which we enjoy. Our church leadership and people can do this, and we must! Consider today's secular culture.

Five Cultural Trends Facing the Western Church

Both leaders and followers in our churches need wisely to understand what is happening in secular culture as well as in church culture.

1. Transition from Modernity to Post-modernity

"Post-modern?" Whatever happened to modern? Things are moving fast, like getting on a San Francisco Cable Car: jump on the running board and hang on for dear life! The man in charge has only one objective: stop and start that trolly at the right places, and let people do what they do. Either way, things are in motion, and the train lurches on.

Today's culture questions the modern age, and it doesn't trust the Church. The Bible is laughed at in the universities, and biblical morality is exchanged for whatever seems right at the moment. The newly emerging churches tend to be anti-institutional, moving away from hierarchy. There is a reemphasis on Calvin's teachings with unexpected and unwarranted consequences: Calvinism (I don't have to worry) and Grace (I'll never be judgmental).

2. Transition from Industrial to Information Age

Things have become quite competitive. The Internet has exploded our world knowledge beyond belief. First graders know more about their computers than their parents do! People get more health information from the Internet than they get from their own doctor!

Faith in big, established companies is gone. Entrepreneurialism is in confidence and the necessity of doing things yourself. An enormous desire for networking and team function is occuring. In the industrial world, control power from the top down, and this attitude seems to have taken over America's government!

3. Transition from Christendom to Post-Christendom

Because of Constantine, the Church once had privileges and position. The Church does not now speak for the people, established words don't count. No voice is to be muted, everyone has a say in things. Dr. Dobson's child and family advice clashes with the post-modern mindset. No church has automatic influence in the city; influence will come by service (bowl and towel). The Ten Commandments have become the Ten Preferences.

4. Transition from Produce and Initiative to Consumerism

There is a drive for marketing, that is, take a product and make it look a lot better. Market to people's taste and make quality secondary. Companies can fix things that are broken, but they cannot help people.

5. Transition from Religious Identity to Spiritual Exploration

People are not identifying with church names, but they are open to spiritual exploration. They care about people and Christ more than church connection.

Building a Spiritual Culture

Today we see many church cultures evolving, and each of them is based on how that church approaches "doing church." Our emphasis, and that of any true apostolic ministry and church, will attempt to build a biblical, spiritual culture rooted in beliefs, behaviors, values and convictions drawn from the Scriptures and blessed with His presence. I like this statement by Frank Damazio:

> The blending of Spirit-filled values into a relevant, vibrant church that connects with today's culture is the challenge the strategic leadership team must wisely and successfully achieve. ... Relevant church culture should be biblical, spiritually powerful, expand the kingdom of God, reach people for Christ and disciple them. Design a culture that has strong roots with flexible methods.[11]

The only church culture that will survive and prosper, I believe, is that culture where people truly encounter God's presence. This is the greatest possession of the Spirit-filled church. This will be a church culture that not only believes in Christ and the Holy Spirit, but one that has personal relationship with the Son and the Spirit of God.

Values of a Spirit-Driven Church[12]

- **A Prayer Culture:** Front and center, no apology, every member involved
- **A Worship Culture:** Free-flowing, Psalmic/Davidic, heart-felt, Spirit energized
- **A Spiritual Gifts Culture:** Every member gifted and participating
- **A Holy Spirit Presence Culture:** A total dependence on the Holy Spirit's help
- **A Prophetic Presence Culture:** Active prophecy and prophetic awareness
- **A Personal Holy Spirit Encounter Culture:** A dynamic awareness of the Spirit
- **A Supernatural Miracles and Healing Culture:** The impossible is possible
- **An Outreach Culture:** A focus on meeting people needs, spiritual and natural

Chapter 13 Endnotes

[1] "Parasitic" seems an ideal word for the uninvited teachers. Defined by *Webster's* as: "a person who exploits the hospitality of the rich and earns welcome by flattery... something that resembles a biological parasite in dependence on something else for existence or support without making a useful or adequate return." 10th Edition, p. 843.

[2] Her fascinating story: Kayy Gordon with Lois Neely, *God's Fire on Ice* (Plainfield, NJ: Logos International, 1977). Her book has a map of the Arctic showing 21 of the settlements (30 years ago) reached with the gospel. Also see "God's Fire on Ice" by Matthew Green in *Ministries Today* (November/December 2004): 31.

[3] Ibid, p. viii.

[4] C. K. Barrett, *The Second Epistle to the Corinthians* (Peabody, MASS: Hendrickson Publishers, 1973 reprint [1987], p. 255. Perhaps the best explanation of Paul's discussion and use of Greek terms in 2 Corinthians 10:12-18 is given by Paul Barnett in *The Second Epistle to the Corinthians (The New International Commentary on the New Testament)* (Grand Rapids: Eerdmans, 1987).

[5] W. E. Vine, *Expository Dictionary of New Testament Words* (Westwood, NJ: Fleming H. Revell Co, 1966, 17th pub.), Vol. 3, p. 52.

[6] Balz, H. R. and G. Schneider, eds., A. Sand, "KANON," *Exegetical Dictionary of the New Testament* (Grand Rapids: Eerdmans, 1993), 2:249.

[7] *The Analytical Greek Lexicon* (NY: Harper & Brothers), p. 213.

[8] W. Beyer, "Kanon," Gerhard Kittel and Gerhard Friedrich, trans. By Geoffrey W. Bromiley, *TDNT,* abridged on one volume (Eerdmans, 1985), p. 596.

[9] F. F. Bruce, *Paul*, p. 278.

[10] Glenn W. Barker, William L. Lane, J. Ramsey Michaels, *The New Testament Speaks* (NY: Harper & Row, 1969), p. 300.

---

[11] Frank Damazio, *The Strategic Church Leadership Conference 2011* (Portland, OR: Ministers Fellowship International), p. 9.

[12] Seven of the stated culture titles (but not the definitions) also from Damazio, p. 9.

Chapter 14
Definitions and Illustrations

In This Chapter

- *God doesn't make cookie-cutter apostles*
- *Apostles facilitate momentum*
- *How are apostles acknowledged?*
- *Definitions and descriptions of modern apostles*

Apostles are not cookie-cutter ministries, all taken from the same background, yet all are recognizable for their accomplishments in reaching, establishing and inspiring people and churches. They share a contagious zeal for God's program: they are ambassadors of a heavenly kingdom, they love the Church, they are obsessed with the Great Commission.

All did not graduate from seminaries or religious institutions – but they are all endued with the Holy Spirit; some outstanding apostles are without higher education – but all apostles are radical students of the Bible! They come from varied backgrounds with different personalities and ministerial expressions. All possess a unique calling and a great passion, but they are not necessarily gifted in the same ways. Some are experienced, polished and practiced in their performance, and some are rough-shod and primitive in their ways. Some are well advertised; others are tremendously successful at doing God's will, but go unheralded, unheard of. These differences were true in Bible times as well.

Apostles possess a "spiritual gift" [*charism*], but each also is a special gift [*doma*] of Christ to the Church (Ephesians 4:11), and an inner fire burns that cannot be ignored! Successful apostles have one thing in common: they hear from God and act on behalf of His kingdom; they are ambassadors!

Doug Beacham's observation is true:

> When you meet strong apostolic leaders you sense the divine fire that has burned for 2,000 years as the Lord has called forth and anointed people in every generation. You sense a passion for the lost, a vision for the local church that is greater than a local community, a spiritual authority over geographical areas, a profound sense of the Word and faith, and a life radically transformed and conformed to the person of Jesus Christ by the power of the Spirit."[1]

Primitive Christianity

A number of years ago, I participated in a conference of Christian workers in Mindano, Philippines (sponsored by World MAP). We used the facilities of a rather run-down Boy Scout Camp, and the participants were primitive church workers from Catholic and various Protestant backgrounds, many of whom were filled with the Spirit. We slept on hard, porous mats (which facilitated crawling-insect movement), and I discovered with some anxiety that a large tarantula spider occupied the space where the soap was kept in the make-shift shower facility (I first saw him when my hand was about 4" from the soap!).

But, these petty things that caught my immediate attention, soon paled before the awesome, rag-tag army of workers that descended on the conference. They came from the towns, jungles and mountains. Some had no shoes, but their soles looked tough as leather. Everyone's spirits were high -- their faith and expectation must have thrilled the heart of God.

I'm not saying all of these workers were apostles, but some were. I saw church planters in the raw, people who experienced the miraculous. They were getting the job done in jungles and villages in ways the average American could not imagine -- all without the publicity, creature comforts and hype. Some of the workers were highly successful, yet some probably could not function outside their element (sphere?). I sweated my way through the conference -- teaching, preaching, praying, wondering – but left with more than I brought, having seen primitive church-planters for the first time.

Apostles Facilitate Momentum

Apostles are able to lay biblical foundations and keep the New Testament pattern at work among the churches. They strengthen and encourage pastoral leaders, mobilize churches for action and present the global vision of Christ and his Church. They inspire greater faith and empower workers to reach the secular marketplace. Apostles present the big picture in an impressive way, often with miraculous confirmation. They hold fast the standard for members to be saved, water baptized, and filled with the Holy Spirit.

> After an apostle visits a local church, the leadership says:
> - "Why didn't we think of that?"
> - "Why haven't we presented that important truth so clearly?"
> - "Wow! The Lord surely brought the answer we needed!"
> - "That was a miracle!"

Our churches need to have apostles and prophets in on their strategic planning (this will be more apparent in chapter 17). Apostles wear a mantle of authority and experience, easily perceived and acknowledged by fellow Christians. An apostolic visit is like having your grandfather visit the family, or the president drop in on a gathering, or a coach meeting with team members; as Ron Myer says, fivefold ministers "are coaches who equip and train God's people for works of service." [2]

Apostles Need Assignment

Like any member of the body of Christ, the apostle will be fruitfully productive when obeying his/her own *commissioned assignment*. A well-known example is the contrast between Paul and Peter:

> … for He who *worked effectively* in Peter for the apostleship to the circumcised also *worked effectively* in me toward the Gentiles… (Galatians 2:8, emphasis added).

Unfortunately, Peter and Paul and their "spheres" do not always translate well into today's thinking, so the average church member does not consider that apostles are needed today or that *every* Christian has a personal sphere of authority. In that place a person will be blessed with amazing power and success. Outside that ordained sphere, the Christian has limited authority and success.

Christ Himself calls and gives assignments. He creates the situation to communicate with His servant: audible voice, heart-burden, prophetic insight, spiritual impression, appearance in vision and so on. We may have our preferences for placement, but ultimately we know that the best direction is God-given and Spirit-empowered.

How Can Modern Apostles Be Acknowledged?

Acknowledgement logically follows proficiency and peer approval. This is a life-principle that is true in both the business world and the ministry. A person truly called has fruitfulness that confirms the call, and this requires a reasonable amount of time. Premature public announcement has a way of turning people off.

A Proven Track Record

Those who run in the Olympics have won some preliminary track meets. A law firm uses the experienced attorney to argue the year's most important case. A teacher is not made a school principal without a teaching credential, a master's degree and high recommendations.

There is a natural progression that should be expected of all five of the Ephesians four ministries. The apostle Paul went through this process: he matured and functioned for some nine years before he was called by Barnabas to come to Antioch to help establish that great church. Also, a period of local church proving and ministry in Antioch passed before the Lord announced the time had come for him to launch out on the first missionary journey (Acts 13:1).

A Logical Sequence

Apostolic status is earned by degrees (although the call of God may come suddenly and before confirmation), finally culminating in the approval of ministry by peers and local church. Consider this sequence:

1. *Christian growth:* become grounded in Bible fundamentals and church function
2. *Proven record:* live the Christian life, maintain good testimony in a local church
3. *Active service:* humbly serve the Body of Christ and actively seek the lost
4. *Diligent servant:* achieve deaconship (servant) & eldership (shepherd) in local church
5. *Profitable function:* function with unction in local church, particularly in outreach
6. *Gradual promotion:* Be pleased with incremental promotion from local church leaders
7. *Authorized affirmation:* let there be public affirmation by peers after proving ministry

Apostolic calling finds assurance through these seven practical steps, and these steps work well for most Christians. The enthusiasm and dedication of such people will be a joy to behold. Also, these steps do not require that a person become a senior citizen before they can minister; young adults can qualify!

Misdirected Excitement

The dream of apostolic possibilities will sometimes cause a person to jump ahead of God's will with a premature announcement. Too hasty!!! Preparation is essential – the title can wait – approval by peers is essential -- ministry will prove itself -- become a servant of all!

About 60 years ago, I was a young minister in a meeting with about 200 older ministers who were all extremely excited about God's new restoration of spiritual gifts and ministries. The meeting was a gathering from scattered-out places, so leadership and protocol was somewhat lacking. The chairman asked for all the apostles present to please stand. To my amazement almost everyone stood up! In the excitement of the moment nearly all were convinced of personal apostleship. Needless to say, very little constructive action came from that meeting: *lots of steam but no power.* Many of us have learned better since then!

Some Practical Definitions

Paul did not spell out a detailed definition of "apostle"; however, he did furnish helpful, descriptive insights of apostolic activity. Both Paul and Luke were more interested in describing the Holy Spirit at work than coming up with titles and definitions.

C. K. Barrett, who wrote one of the older, non-charismatic books on apostleship, said "there is no simple, rigid definition of an apostle."[3] To say one is "sent" hardly seems to do justice, too simple and bland. A more expandable and functional definition seems appropriate, one allowing more latitude for defining today's areas of ministry. I prefer the bottom line to be, as you already know, "an ambassador of the kingdom of God." This means a person is commissioned to establish God's kingdom in some arena of human need, and bring the responsive people into local churches.

Older definitions seem more pertinent to the pioneer missionary church planter, and this is because most of our material comes from the New Testament. Some of my vignettes scattered through the book and illustrations later in this chapter fit this type of apostle. We do need, however, to give consideration to the modern setting and the challenges of culture changes. Let us not cancel apostles from today's ministry roster, but rather adjust our thinking to realize that multitudes of hungry people await the experience of an apostolic church.

This is my *expanded* definition for both biblical and modern apostles:

> An apostle is an ambassador of God, an emissary appointed and sent by Christ Himself, to establish people in the kingdom of God and fulfill the Great Commission. Such a person is uniquely equipped and gifted by the Holy Spirit to build and strengthen the Church, having authority and ability in a certain spiritual sphere of responsibility confirmed by peers and associated churches. An apostle is a primary church leader whose mission is to promote and oversee church planting, world harvest,

church renewal and culture penetration; this occurs principally through the founding of new churches, cultural outreaches, and providing oversight and strength to those already in existence.

The following list gives the definitions of eleven authors who not only believe in modern apostles but are personally active apostolically. Their efforts have contributed greatly to the insight for such ministry in our day.

Definitions of "What Is an Apostle?"

Apostles and prophets exist today as gifted persons sent by the Holy Spirit to equip the church to accomplish the Christ-mandate (Doug Beacham).[4]

[O]ne who is called and sent by Christ to have the spiritual authority, character, gifts and abilities to successfully reach and establish people in Kingdom truth and order, especially through founding and overseeing local churches (David Cannistraci).[5]

An apostle is a Christian leader gifted, taught, commissioned and sent by God with the authority to establish the foundational government of the Church within an assigned sphere of ministry by hearing what the Spirit is saying to the churches and by setting things in order accordingly for the expansion of the Kingdom of God (C. Peter Wagner).[6]

Apostles are God's builders [*architekton*] of the glorious church (Jonas Clark).[7]

The basic function of the apostle seems to be that of founding and establishing local churches. ... not merely...evangelization, but ... setting up church governments, organization of elders with ordination, and delegating authority. Often signs and wonders accompanied....Many times the apostles were sought after to settle disputes in teachings, doctrines or practices (Dick Iverson).[8]

One of the fivefold ministries of Ephesians 4:11....a foundation-laying ministry...that we see in the New Testament establishing new churches...correcting error by establishing proper order and structure...and acting as an oversight ministry that fathers other ministries....The New Testament Apostle has a revelatory anointing....Some major characteristics are great patience and manifestations of signs, wonders and miracles (Bill Hamon).[9]

[A]n apostle is one who is sent by God; a delegate, messenger, military officer; the leader of an elite group with the mission to conquer a territory for his King (Guillermo Maldonado).[10]

Working alone, prophets develop prophetic expressions, teachers develop teaching centers, evangelists keep getting people "saved," and shepherds and administrators struggle to maintain the status quo. Apostles are to be the strategists who weave together these gifts, and facilitate the emerging of corporate expressions of Christ's anointed body...(Don Atkin).[11]

...the ministry of the apostle can be defined as: a spiritual architect [based on *architekton,* architect, master-builder] who through their understanding of the beginning things of God are...able to lay a foundation for a community of believers to build upon to become a household of God. ...an apostle is a spiritual technician ... able by divine grace to communicate a spiritual technology within the framework of the community of believers that will develop and grow into God's building. ...an apostle travails and gives birth to the visionary seed of God within him, and transmits this vision into manifestation through the community of believers (T. L. Lowery).[12]

In the New Testament the apostle is an ambassador of the gospel, officially a commissioner of Christ, with miraculous powers. Every apostle has a specific commission, and is sent to do the Father's will... . ["Apostle"] was used by Christ as the designation for those He was appointing to represent Him in building and governing the church. They were to take charge of the advance of the kingdom of God under the leading of the Holy Spirit (John Kingsley Alley).[13]

In its verb form...means, "to send" and could be applied fairly generally to anyone or anything that was sent....in its noun form, an apostle, or a "sent one," was a specific title that referred to a specific function....The focus of the word "apostle" was on two things: the purpose and the sender....a clearly commissioned and authorized agent of a higher power...fully accountable...for the results of the mission that originates from the power (Bill Scheidler).[14]

Descriptions of Modern Apostles

Admittedly, restoration of this ministry has been slower in development that we would like, so we have no highly polished examples accepted by everyone. Consider that if Paul the apostle presented his credentials to some mission's boards today, he would not qualify! Let's be open-minded, generous and hopeful. The pros and cons are forcefully articulated on today's Internet, but prayerfully look beyond the debate to the Scripture and future.

Diversity in Personalities and Ministries

The four personality types (sanguine, melancholy, phlegmatic and choleric) illustrate how several types can blend to the betterment of a person. Few people would be a pure, single strain of just one personality type.

Correspondingly, you will find that a person whose primary gifting is that of an apostle can also have other strong abilities and spiritual gifts. This is true of all spiritual gifts. A person with a primary gift of teaching, for instance, may also be gifted prophetically, and so on.

C. Peter Wagner, following this insight, refers to "hyphenated apostles" who have several other gifts and offices, which he includes in his distinguishing four different kind of apostolic ministries.[15]

1. *Vertical Apostles*: senior or lead apostle over a given sphere or network
2. *Horizontal Apostles*: authority over other apostles during a particular assignment[16]
3. *Hyphenated Apostles*: when an apostle has other gifts and offices[17]
4. *Marketplace Apostles*: ministry mainly outside the Church community[18]

"Hyphenated apostles" is a practical suggestion, and Paul himself was an example of this. His dominant ministry was that of an apostle, but he was also a teacher and preacher (1 Timothy 2:7; 2 Timothy 1:11).

Some Suggested Apostle Types

Out of all the various combinations and various possible spheres of ministry, I would suggest that apostolic "types" possibly could be boiled down to the following seven general categories. Let us remember, regardless of category, an apostle must be a father and servant to the people, a vibrant person of spiritual power, a visionary, a person of prayer and sacrifice and an able exponent of Scripture.

The following descriptions are not set in cement, but they represent personal observations of ministerial people whom I think function as apostles. These are not meant to be absolute categories, and some people who function in such apostolic ways may not be actual apostles. Apostleship is a multi-faceted ministry, so there tends to be over-lap:

1. *Planters:* hands-on missionary work, starting churches in virgin territory
2. *Growers:* establishing doctrine/church structure, ordaining elders, strengthening
3. *Encouragers:* providing encouragement to far-flung weary ministers
4. *Expanders:* visionaries to take the work to the next level of outreach or new fields
5. *Supervisors:* mentoring, training, encouraging, administrating the growing force
6. *Overseers:* spiritually mature bishops with wisdom, proven ministry and vision
7. *Invaders:* Impacting nations, cultures, ethnic groups and societal strongholds and bringing spiritual and cultural change

1. Planters

We have all been so impressed and enamored with the fantastic Paul that to consider any other type of apostle almost seems sacrilegious. There were, of course, in his time a variety of apostles, but Paul was clearly given center stage in the New Testament. He epitomizes the heart and drive of early Christianity and the dynamism of those early churches. The fire in his heart must also flame in the hearts of today's apostles and Christians as well.

• Paul was a church-planter and epistle-writer that gradually became the father-figure, apostle-overseer of a great network of churches in the Aegean Basin (the land area surrounding the Aegean Sea). He was also used by God to be a sterling example of dedication and perseverance, gradually assuming a partriarchal-like status. Every true apostle – regardless of type, style or location – carries Paul's basic, influential imprint (like a spiritual DNA). Paul and his churches are a living example of the empowering presence of the Holy Spirit.

F.F. Bruce summarizes the basic "Church Planter-Apostle":

> The work of an apostle was to preach the gospel where it had not been heard before and plant churches where none had existed before. When those churches had received sufficient teaching to enable them to understand their Christian status and responsibility, the apostle moves on to continue the same kind of work elsewhere.[19]

Paul and other church planters go to the unreached with the message of Christ, establishing churches of fervent Christians in every possible community. He then turned these churches over to pastoral leaders to continue the work of outreach, shepherding and directing while he went on to new fields.

Consider Paul's drive to reach the Aegean Basin. He preached and planted strong churches in strategic centers which disseminated the gospel message: *Thessalonica* for Macedonia, *Corinth* for Achaia and *Ephesus* for proconsular Asia. No Christians existed in these areas before He came! Paul ever looked for new opportunities, and as his ministry approached the end, his heart was increasingly drawn to Spain, the oldest, farthest Roman province in the West. He was determined first to visit Rome; writing to the Christians there, he spoke of visiting them *en route* to that Latin-speaking, stronghold of Roman civilization, Spain. Possibly Paul did go to Spain, we do not know for sure, but we applaud *the apostolic determination to reach new areas for Christ.*

• Sometimes a church planter moves into an area to get a church started (not necessarily an apostle), a person who has a zeal for souls and is gifted at gathering people. This leader may have a support team, or sometimes just go do it alone! Often such a person is gifted to start churches -- but not necessarily gifted to stay indefinitely and pastor them. In such a case the church will grow for several years and then begin to plateau — until the church-planter moves on to plant another church! This, of course, necessitates bringing in a more pastoral person and raising up elders to lead, and it does point out the need of apostolic oversight. Nevertheless, a church was started!

• An apostle could be an active member of a local church who is sent forth from time to time to assist, help plant or expand other churches or the work of the Lord elsewhere. We had a couple in our San Jose church that helped plant two other churches in different cities. He finally retired from being an airline pilot, and he and his wife now travel all over the world teaching, preaching, praying for the sick, ministering the gifts of the Spirit. They have gone to places where few visiting ministers go; you can imagine how warmly they are received!

• Planting churches in "virgin" territory is an amazing feat. Stories I have heard of various Wycliff Translators are truly mind-boggling. For instance, two women translators going into a remote part of the world where the people have no written language. The translators painfully learn the language and transcribe the Bible into that language. Years go by, but gradually, as they teach, conversions and change occur, and a movement to God begins that converts the whole community. As I watched a film of this happening some years ago, I wept as I saw the huge parade of converted people march by to pay respects to the now elderly women who had brought the Bible and Christ to a "virgin" territory.

• Sometimes, an apostle planting or helping churches must derive livelihood from secular employment, something which Paul himself did on occasion (Acts 20:34; 1 Corinthians 4:12; 9:6; 2 Thessalonians 3:8-9). This should not be considered demeaning, but rather honorable when required. Worldwide, there are many of God's choice ministers employed in secular work, part-time or full-time. One of the great churches of the New Testament was at Thessalonica, started by working apostles (2 Thessalonians 3:8).

While starting two churches, I personally found it necessary to do secular work. My example seemed to be an inspiration to those who gathered into the church, and it personally was a hands-on education to be in the secular workplace. I did succeed in introducing two of my secular managers to Christ. I also discovered how essential it was for a church to be a team. As I helped the spiritual family, they in turn helped me, and our children experienced the camaraderie and excitement of serving the Lord.

When our local church in San Jose, CA, became large enough, we were able to send people and finances to launch other churches, actions which certainly speeded up outreach. Five of those church plants became churches (Gilroy, Hollister, Modesto, Salinas and Pleasanton) and two have launched new churches of their own. Also, missionaries to Brazil, Nigeria, India and Israel have gone forth! There is nothing like being part of an apostolic missionary movement!

2. Growers

Some apostles profitably spend their time working with churches already planted (but still fanning the flames of global outreach) that need spiritual and practical input from knowledgeable leaders. As a movement of God gets under way, churches can proliferate with amazing rapidity. In such cases apostles are needed to work with churches already in existence, which in many cases will enable an existing local church to plant another church. In this chapter there is a vignette page of an apostle that I know personally. The page is written, however, by one of the pastors that he has personally mentored and encouraged through the years, and I am sure you will join me in appreciating the great input that this man of God has made in a number of churches (some of which I have ministered in and heard first-hand of the pastors' appreciation).

3. Traveling Encouragers

I think we Americans like apostles who have built large works and are super efficient and effective. Some more primitive types, nevertheless, are both necessary, perfectly legitimate, and very effective.

Once I was staying briefly in the home of a missionary in Mexico while speaking in some of the churches. Unexpectedly, a humble, traveling minister dropped in unexpectedly at the pastor's home for a visit of several days. The family was delighted to welcome him. This minister had been a great inspiration and help to them over the years, and the family repeatedly told of how he had encouraged them.

We slept in the same room and ate at the same table. He told me of his far-ranging travels in which he ministers in all types of churches and encourages the pastors. He traveled light, with a smaller suitcase (I had arrived with two larger suitcases). When he left I felt awed, humbled and inspired, like I had really been with a true servant of the Lord. Wherever this dear brother goes (some are really out-of-the-way places with few visitors), he brings joy, encouragement and faith. I know several such traveling apostles like this who walk by faith and travel the world bringing spiritual uplift to weary ministers and congregations. God bless them abundantly!

4. Expanders

This kind of an apostle may not actually be on the front lines, but his/her strategic planning and teaching may cause many churches to be planted and strengthened. My illustration here is Frank Damazio, chairman of Ministers Fellowship International, to which I belong. In his many years of pastoring (two successful, growing churches) here in the states, he has been responsible for also planting one church per year, for the past thirty years!

Now, as the key strategic planner of a great network of local churches, he is able to influence and direct a huge number of churches both at home and overseas in planting and maturing churches and winning people to Christ. He is not a cross-culture missionary in a foreign land, but his experience and expertise enable him to be a highly influential apostle.

5. Supervisors

Some apostles serve as pastors of growing, church-planting churches. As the mother church matures and the fellowship network develops, the apostle-pastor assumes the oversight of the churches that recognize his/her leadership.

If the pastor-leader of a local church is also an apostle, this is reflected in the active, global advance of that church. Such ministers usually supervise impressive local churches, and underlying every program and instilled in every church member is a drive to take the message to the whole world.

David Cartledge's amazing book on modern apostleship documents "The Apostolic Revolution" in the Assemblies of God in

Australia. He says that churches whose pastors are also apostles will have the following seven characteristics:[20]

- The Church Is Set in Order
- Spiritual Breakthrough Occurs (and Rapid Growth Happens)
- Ministries Are Released
- Primary Concerns Are Addressed
- Faith Is Generated
- Spiritual Impartation Takes Place
- "Candlestick Status" Comes

Wagner has an hypothesis that "pastors of dynamic, growing churches of more than 700 to 800 members should, for the most part, be regarded as having the offices of pastor-apostle, or in some cases apostle-pastor."[21] He also feels that the average pastor with decent leadership skills can take a church to the 700-800 range, "but not far beyond unless the gift of apostle kicks in."[22]

6. Overseers

An apostle can be a person that oversees a network of churches in a full-time capacity of supervision, itinerating and spiritual input. This activity will find somewhat different expression in a modern society than in a primitive society. Sometimes such a person has actually planted the churches, or has found that the pastors of certain needy churches want apostolic oversight. The apostle then becomes a dynamic source of inspiration, wisdom and direction to that church.

The Apostolic Ministry of David Minor
By Doug Sherman, Pastor of Grace Harvest Church, Moses Lake, WA

I first became acquainted with David Minor in 1989 when he became involved with our church in Moses Lake, Washington. We heard through the "grapevine" that David was an apostle who oversaw a number of pastors, preached the word of God with authority and had keen prophetic insight. David began to consult with our church through a very difficult leadership transition and was a tremendous help. In 1990, David took the Senior Minister role at our church and

I served alongside him as the pastor to the church. During this time, David mentored me in pastoral ministry while continuing to provide apostolic oversight and input into a number of churches in the Pacific Northwest. During the 22 years that I have walked with David Minor, I have noticed a number of things about his apostolic ministry that define it clearly.

A FATHER'S HEART – Having come out of a number of abusive authority relationships, I was very wary of David Minor when I first met him. My understanding of the apostolic ministry often focused on the spiritual authority aspect of an apostle and not the relational side. David was first and foremost relational. He approached me gently, yet firmly and provided a father's wisdom in my life, and in the church. He often spoke to my wife and I, our elders, and the church body in a way that provided security and confidence. He was willing to address difficult issues, doctrinal error, and moral failure in a way that was both strong and gentle. During this time, God used David to bring healing to my own wounded heart and help our church through a very difficult season. David has walked with all of the pastors that he relates to in a very similar way. He has helped guide the pastors and churches through seasons of loss, division, marital and family problems and church discipline issues. In every situation he has acted with the highest integrity, care and a servant's heart. Some of the men in our group did not have healthy relationships with their own natural fathers and David Minor has been an instrument of healing in their lives.

AN APOSTOLIC WORD – Over the years, David Minor has often brought timely, apostolic messages of authority to our churches. Often these words have been foundational, present-truth messages that have been catalytic in moving the churches forward. Many times we would take the emphasis or topic and build upon it because we recognized it was a timely message from the Spirit of God. For example, these messages were often about the fivefold ministry, spiritual authority, the nature and person of God, the fear of the Lord, and walking strong and straight in difficult times. Many times David's messages to our churches have been foundational words that help to propel us into the future or protect us from potential errors that could lead the church astray.

PASTORAL AND LEADERSHIP TRANSITION – David Minor has been an integral part of the pastoral and leadership transitions many of our churches have experienced. He has helped us to define and clarify roles for elders, pastors, and others being considered for leadership. He has been a part of the ordination and the laying on of hands of new leaders and has offered poignant insight into potential candidates.

TROUBLESHOOTING – David Minor has been particularly gifted in helping our churches to troubleshoot difficult problems that we have faced. David has a unique ability to see and "smoke out" the essence of the problems many of us have faced in our churches. He has the ability to see the things that are out of order and to show us how to adjust them. He does not come off heavy-handed or authoritative but he does speak forthrightly, honestly, and boldly when he sees a problem.

EMPOWERMENT AND ENCOURAGEMENT – David has never forced himself upon our churches or us but has always taken the role of a servant. However, David has often spoken over our lives in a way that made us feel empowered and encouraged to be able to continue and fight the good fight of faith. There have been a number of times through a simple phone call when I have hung up feeling built up and able to deal with the difficult situations at hand.

Every apostle embraces God's heartbeat: the nations. Each accepts apostleship as a ministry demanding focused attention: the call burns, drives and seeks fulfillment. The elders of a local church will be wise if they will bring such a person from time-to-time for consultation and strategic planning to share insight about church operation and outreach. This blesses the whole church with apostolic covering.

Religious organizations have tended to appoint administrators and teachers as their leaders. This usually results after the organization has been started by charismatic, dynamic leaders that have a vision. At that moment of development the need (as in business) is to get the product on the market and develop an active sales force. The sheer enthusiasm of the strong natural leader carries the day.

Alas, however, as momentum is created and more people are involved, the need to organize soon becomes apparent. At that time the administrators and teachers step forward, and rightly so. Unfortunately, this step sometimes eliminates the enthusiasm and spontaneity that brought the organization or church into existence! The charismatic vision-setters are pushed aside in favor of traditional, administrative thinkers.

Businesses, denominations and religious fellowships all need a combination of these two elements: keep both the visionary charismatics with their boundless enthusiasm, but also keep the rather staid, but efficient, organizers and planners. Religious organizations need gifted organizers, but they must not neglect the on-fire visionaries – the apostles and prophets. When organizations capitalize on both giftings, amazing things will happen.

7. Invaders

Subcultures. In every modern city there are many sub-cultures with hungry hearts and bodies waiting to be set free. I am aware of bold messengers of the Lord that have planted themselves in positions to challenge racial tensions, sex-slave situations, hungry orphans, crime and poverty. The list is endless, but the Lord is raising up apostolic, bold servants to invade the dens of iniquity and bring light to the dark places of the earth. What a way to challenge and utilize today's youthful enthusiasm!

Marketplace. The marketplace in underdeveloped countries is probably the most exciting place in town! I have visited marketplaces in Mexico, Peru, Brazil, the Philippines, India, Jerusalem, Nigeria (and elsewhere) and farmers markets in the USA. In some countries the people have no refrigeration, so a daily visit to the marketplace is a necessity for milk, meat and other perishables. It is a social event as friends, relatives and community residents greet and talk.

Paul not only preached in synagogues and taught in homes, but he also ministered in the marketplaces. As was mentioned in chapter 5, he was born in Tarsus, a center for the manufacture of *cilicium,* a goats' hair fabric so durable that shoes, mats, and coverings of all kinds were made of it. Apparently the boy Saul was taught this local handicraft. This training supplied Paul with a craft that he could perform wherever his ministry took him, supplying his scanty needs.

Today's mall, shopping center or business center may seem a far cry from Paul making tents in the primitive marketplace. The principle is the same, however: working with people to gain their confidence, diplomatically sharing the gospel, boldly praying for people's needs and inviting them to informal home meetings where such people will find a bridge into the local church.

The Business World. Some business people have so positioned themselves in the flow of commerce that they meet and fraternize with important, influential people. Truthfully, the average minister is not always equipped to touch these people, but there are those that can win the confidence of business people and reach them for Christ. Our churches must learn the enthusiasm and skill to touch these untouchables! Such an outreach may demand gatherings outside of the local church setting and strategy meetings in office buildings, and so on, but we must do whatever we can to reach every level of society. The people in today's fast-moving society still represent fish for the kingdom, and they should not be neglected because they have become disillusioned with the traditional church.

People who are reached in the business sector have families and homes. They have the same basic needs that church members' families have. The ultimate goal, therefore, should be to use marketplace outreach to channel these people into the local church of the believers, without destroying their zeal to reach the business community.

Specialized Professionals. These people work in the fast-moving world of money, marketing, development and secular life. They will know more about reaching their contemporaries than many long-established church members.

Chapter 14 Endnotes

[1] Doug Beacham, "Apostolic characteristics," *The Vision* (Vol. II, 1): 10.

[2] Ron Myer, *Fivefold Ministry Made Practical* (Lititz, PA: House to House Publications, 2006).

[3] C. K. Barrett, *The Signs of an Apostle* (Philadelphia: Fortress Press, 1970), p. 85.

[4] Doug Beacham, *Rediscovering the Role of Apostles & Prophets* (Franklin Springs, GA: LifeSprings Resources, 2004), p. 131.

[5] Cannistraci, *Apostles,* p. 91.

[6] C. Peter Wagner, *Dominion!* (Grand Rapids: Chosen Books, 2008), p. 31.

[7] Jonas Clark, *Advanced Apostolic Studies* (Hallandale Beach, FL: Spirit of Life Publishing, 2002), p. 8.

[8] Dick Iverson, Dick Benjamin and Jim Durkin, *The Master Builder* (South Lake Tahoe, CA: Christian Equippers Int., 1985), p. 76.

[9] Bill Hamon, *Apostles, Prophets and the Coming Moves of God* (Shippensburg, PA: Destiny Image Publishers, 1997), p. 279.

[10] Guillermo Maldonado, *The Ministry of the Apostle* (Miami, FL: ERJ Publications, 2006), p. 61.

[11] Don Atkin, *The Apostles' Role among the Priesthood of All Believers* (Self published, 2008), p. 20.

---

[12] T. L. Lowery, with Craig L. Ervin, *Apostles and Prophets: Reclaiming the Biblical Gifts* (Cleveland, TN: T. L. Ministries, International, 2004), p. 32.

[13] John Kingsley Alley, *The Apostolic Revolution: The Reformation of the Church* Surprise, AZ: Selah Publishing Group, LL.C, 2002), pp. 45, 47-48.

[14] Bill Scheidler, *Apostles: The Fathering Servant*, pp. 13-14.

[15] C. Peter Wagner, *Apostles and Prophets,* Chapter 3.

[16] Ibid, p. 45-52. Wagner uses James (Acts 15) as an example because he feels that James had the ability to call together the apostles, elders and members of the Jerusalem church to address and settle the matter of Gentiles coming into the church uncircumcised. Wagner feels James' "horizontal" influence made him non-threatening to all participants. I do believe James had the final spiritual authority "delegated by the Holy Spirit" to declare the verdict without any spoken opposition.

I respectfully disagree that James was a "horizontal apostle." As explained in Chapter 8, the delegation was not summoned to Jerusalem, but the Antioch leaders saw the situation with the Jewish legalists as a local church situation, so they sent a delegation to Jerusalem church to settle a problem that Jerusalem church members initiated. Also, James did not have the authority to proclaim a decision of this nature without first having a consensus of the apostles' opinions. James *did* give a word of wisdom accompanied with prophetic power, but it had already (I believe) been superseded and controlled by the wisdom of the Holy Spirit working in all the apostles.

[17] A concept that was first articulated, I believe, by Bill Hamon, *Apostles, Prophets and the Coming Moves of God* (Shippensburg, PA: Destiny Image Publishers, 1997), Chapter 14.

[18] Wagner, p. 54: "Marketplace apostles minister mostly *outside* the Church, although all of them need to be rooted in and covered by a local church in order to minister effectively." Wagner assumes that marketplace apostles that will function in all the segments of society will "move Christ's kingdom through the warp and woof of society in general."

[19] F. F. Bruce, *Paul Apostle,* pp. 314-315.

[20] David Cartledge, *The Apostolic Revolution,* p. 268 (or 208?),

[21] Wagner, p. 53.

[22] See Wagner's discussion of "The Hypothesis of 'Pastor-Apostles'" in *Apostles of the City* (Colorado Springs, CO: Wagner Publications, 200, pp. 48-49.

Chapter 15
Motivation and Activation

In This Chapter

- *The Apostle's number one priority*
- *How should an apostle relate to a local church?*
- *Should local churches be under hierarchal control?*
- *Should an apostle be a father, a servant – or both?*

No minister, regardless of talent, can challenge, energize and inspire a congregation like a person clothed with the mantle of an apostle. We are talking now about a program very different from the typical church scene where teachers and administrators run the church operation. An apostle, functioning properly in a divinely assigned sphere of influence, has *a delegated authority of the Holy Spirit* -- and will operate with prophetic insight and spiritual empowerment that is awesome.

Bill Hamon said it well:

> **God's supernatural power should be manifest in the apostle's ministry regardless** of what type of apostle a minister may be. Apostles have been described for years as administrators, concerned about church structure, practical Christianity and ruling over others. Apostles have been so busy trying to live up to that job description that they have forsaken their greater ministry, the ministry of giving themselves to prayer, study of the Word and manifesting the miraculous.[1]

Apostles Move the Church Forward!

Apostles who give themselves to prayer, the study and proclamation of the Word and the manifestation of the supernatural will automatically motivate and activate the people of God. Such as:

- *Encourage and direct* local churches without dominating; they are to help provide wise counsel and strong direction from

God to the local church. Their person, their message and their spiritual confirmation charge the people with new enthusiasm!

• *Help the church see the big picture* of what God is doing and how He wishes to work locally and globally. They will have been places and seen things that will inspire the local church people. This opens the windows of the church to see what God is doing world-wide and what he wants done locally.

• *Lead into green pastures* without demanding subordination, making extravagant demands (especially about money) or insisting on the use of self-exalting titles; they come to serve not rule; they come as spiritual fathers and servants. Apostles should have no other agenda than to lift and inspire the people in God. Like generals they have a built-in authority to guide the people to fulfill their destinies.

• *Give spiritual oversight, help and practical solutions* when requested and sought out (i.e., help when invited by the local eldership or when they perceive suggestion is needed);[2] they are to give their lives for the churches. There should be no ulterior motives or agendas. The attitude of servitude enables them to give unprejudiced advice and sincere direction.

• *Relate and coordinate* with the pastors, elders, evangelists and teachers of the local church, allowing the local leadership to carry their own administration and pastoral ministry. Like an experienced and well-known coach that knows how to play the game and win, apostles must humbly yet forcefully work with local church leadership, particularly in their strategic planning.

• *Function as:* a loving parent, dedicated servant, powerful preacher, wise master-builder, eye-opening Bible teacher, global visionary and miracle worker. Such ministers greatly facilitate apostolic function in the local church body – they maintain our global momentum. The amazing thing is that "the sphere" of God's calling makes an apostle productive, even if there is an educational or professional lack. People respond to this awareness of God's call and the proficiency of His servant.

• *Serve the people.* Eddie L. Hyatt says:

According to Matt. 20:25-26, apostles are not rulers over God's people, but servants to God's people. Jesus presented this new and radical model of leadership to the 12 apostles when they were vying for, what they thought would be, positions of authority in the kingdom. Jesus explained that in His kingdom leadership would be characterized, not by governing, but by serving. The Greek word used is *diakonos* and it referred to one who served or "wait on" another. John G. Lake, a modern apostle to South Africa, said, "the modern conception of an apostle was not to be a big boss; he was to be like his Lord—a servant of all."[3]

• *Set an example of faith* for people ground down by their circumstances and lacking hope and expectancy for the future. Congregations at times need to be lifted by those not loaded down with the negative problems of the local people. A case in point would be the people in Joppa who sent for Peter. A leading woman of the congregation had died, and the women stood around Dorcas' dead body weeping and reminiscing (Acts 9:39). When Peter arrived, he put them all out of the room – and went to God in prayer! Perceiving the will of God, he commanded her to come back to life, and she did! A wave of excitement and renewed faith swept through the whole church, in fact throughout the whole town of Joppa.

In the following chapter, Cornelius the Roman centurion sent for Peter to explain what God was doing. As Peter addressed the household of expectant people, the Holy Spirit fell upon them. The apostle again came into a setting that He alone could not handle, but operating in his "sphere" he functioned powerfully and impressively.

• *Lead in taking a stand against satanic encroachment.* Some situations demand fasting and prayer to bring spiritual breakthrough. When the Council at Jerusalem took place (Acts 15; Chapter 8 in this book), a situation was handled by the apostles that could easily have split the church.

Paul's frequent mention of his intercessory prayer for the churches under his care indicates his perception of satanic oppression. Indeed, his insightful knowledge of the adversary (given in Ephesians 6)[4] indicates that "spiritual warfare" (and the instruction of the churches about it) is of primary concern to apostolic leaders.

Apostles and the Local Church

The local church, for its highest fulfillment, must be *independent* of outside hierarchal control, but very *dependent* on helpful "parental" insight, spiritual input, impartation, direction and participation from apostles and prophets both within and outside the local church. The relationship in ministry (with local elders and ministry) must be mutually beneficial and based upon productive service and genuine relationship (not demanded obedience or financial obligation). It certainly appears that the churches of Paul's day were not bound by an institutional type of oversight, guided rather by dedicated fathers. As Paul said, "Not that we have dominion over your faith, but are fellow workers for your joy..." (2 Corinthians 1:24).[5]

Those early churches were "indigenous" in the sense they were self-governing, self-supporting, self-propagating and self-esteeming. That having been said, the degree that a local church will respond to authentic apostolic and prophetic guidance will determine and assure that church's future success.

Chapter 15 Endnotes

[1] Hamon, *Apostles, Prophets,* pp. 227-228.
[2] An apostle who lays the right foundation will not need to "rule" the church.
[3] Eddie Hyatt, *Apostles: 5 Popular Misconceptions in the Church Today* (Ft. Worth, TX: Hyatt International Ministries).
[4] Chapter 11 describes the satanic presence in Ephesus. Small wonder that Paul reminded the Christians of Ephesus about the importance of spiritual warfare in Ephesians 6.
[5] Bill Scheidler's book, *A Fresh Look At ... Apostles,* is the best available to show the fatherly characteristics of an apostle.

Part V – Apostolic Church Function

Chapter 16 – The Metamorphosis of "Church"

Chapter 17 – Full Coverage for the Local Church

Chapter 18 – The Ministry of Apostolic Women

Chapter 16
The Metamorphosis of "Church"

In This Chapter:

- *Find out what the LXX is and where it came from*
- *Discover why the "church" at Ephesus got in an uproar*
- *Examine an unusual chart showing all the local churches*
- *Why did the people of Antioch coin the nickname "Christian"?*

As a teen-aged Christian I attended Pentecostal churches that frequently sang with great gusto the four stanzas of a marvelous gospel hymn, "A Glorious Church." I still love that opening refrain:

> Do you hear them coming, brother,
> Thronging up the steeps of light,
> Clad in glorious shining garments,
> Blood-washed garment pure and white?

The chorus really reverberates! My, how those words boom out!

> 'Tis a glorious church without spot or wrinkle,
> Washed in the blood of the Lamb;
> 'Tis a glorious church, without spot or wrinkle.
> Washed in the blood of the Lamb.

This chapter introduces the basic meaning of "church" by using two scenes from long ago. The next chapter, longer and practical, will concentrate on the "local church" and the ways in which it can function in powered-up ministry; hence, this section is called "Apostolic Church Function." The charts are not meant to be tedious, but instead impressive. When you realize how quickly the early Christians planted churches in the towns and cities of that day, you will have a new appreciation of the apostolic church planting that took place. We would like to see strong local churches planted in every community around the world. These microcosms of the great Universal Church are by God's design the best way to win new people to Christ and also strengthen, train and mature those who do become believers. The books of the New Testament are actually letters to local churches – informative, inspired epistles to educate and mature the Christians of that day, all of whom were in local churches.

The People of God, the *Ekklesia*

The story of the Bible is the story of God desiring to have a people as His own, similar to a man wishing to have a wife and family. The account of Moses leading Israel out of Egyptian bondage is one of the greatest in the Bible, and it illustrates the concept of God "calling out" a people to follow Him – and then "calling together" those "called out ones" to be a people, congregation or nation called by His name (belonging to Him).

Most of us are generally familiar with certain Greek words from the New Testament that have found their way into Christian conversation. For instance, *koinonia,* is used interchangeably with "fellowship." Some words, like "baptism" (from *baptisma*) are transliterated. Many of us have learned that the Greek word used for "church" in New Testament times was *ekklesia.* Usually, however, the full import of the word is not fully understood.

In Bible days the word *ekklesia* referred to the people of God in a very special way. Buildings were not considered "the church," but in those early, formative times it was commonly understood that the people were "the church," and in a local area the congregating or gathering of the followers of Jesus to worship and serve God under apostolic covering was considered "the church" of that community.

Ekklesia was actually a secular word, whose basic meaning fit the Christian concept of assembling/congregating/serving God so well, that it became popular usage. It was a word that had technical use in the Hellenistic world of Jesus and the apostles; this secular meaning had *such literal application,* that the word was easily coined by the early Christians. Although not commonly used in the Gospels, Jesus is quoted twice as having used the word (Matthew 16:18; 18:17).

In a moment we will discuss the Greek Old Testament (the *LXX*) and how it originated, because this Greek edition of the Hebrew Scriptures became like a Living Bible translation for the many Greek-speaking Jews as well as the Hellenistic Gentiles. In the *LXX* the translators used *ekklesia* to translate the Hebrew word *qahal,* but there was no ecclesiastical significance to it. The Hebrew word was used to describe the gathering of the people, their congregating together, as when Israel gathered at Mount Sinai (Acts 7:38).

Consider where this *LXX* came from, and how the early church adopted it for their own use. Two scenes from history throw some light on the subject.

Scene 1: Secluded on an Island: 70 Elders Produce the LXX

The arrival of an Egyptian embassy in Jerusalem caused no small stir. The ambassador bore a letter of unusual request to Eleazar the Jewish high priest from Ptolemy II Philadelphus (284-247 B. C.), the reigning Egyptian monarch residing at Alexandria. The king, as a precaution to insure a favorable response (it was told), had already purchased the freedom of more than one hundred thousand Jewish captives.

The request. The high priest was surprised by Pharaoh's request: the king asked for seventy-two Jewish elders, six out of each tribe, to come and translate the sacred books of the Jews into Greek. The priest finally agreed – undoubtedly remembering that there were more Jews in Alexandria than in Jerusalem, and they all spoke Greek! Seventy-two scribes were dispatched on a holy mission to Alexandria, carrying with them a copy of the law written in letters of gold on rolls of skin. Given a magnificent reception by the royal Egyptian court, the elders were then provided a secluded retreat on the island of Pharos to do their translation undistracted.

Alexandria. After Alexander the Great had conquered Egypt, he founded the jewel-city of Alexandria (331 B. C.) – "a place where the Greek language, although by no means in its purest form, was the medium of written and spoken communication amongst the varied population there brought together."[1] As

Alexandria became influential in the Mediterranean world, the city became home to a major Jewish colony (occupying the whole eastern part of the great port) -- and a center of scholarship with a world-renowned library.

E. M. Blaiklock comments: "It was in this spiritual and mental context that the Hellenistic Jew first became a phenomenon of culture."[2] The Alexandrian Jew spoke Greek, a prerequisite for citizenship and participation in trade, business and social intercourse. Blaiklock adds: "The Jew of Alexandria, like any Jew of Tarsus, was truly the intellectual citizen of two worlds of culture; hence the urge to translate the Hebrew Scriptures into their other tongue."

The Library. The cultured Ptolemy favored the idea of adding to his vast and famous library a collection of the translated Jewish laws. So it was that he invited the translators and they did their job, supplying what has become a monumental (if controversial) translation of the Hebrew Scriptures. It became known as the "Septuagint" (Lat. *Septuaginta,* meaning seventy, hence the abbreviation in Roman numerals, *LXX*) because of the tradition that it was the work of seventy (some say seventy-two) Jewish elders.

New Testament Usage. The *LXX* had been current about three centuries before the time when the New Testament books were written, so it is not surprising that the Apostles used it frequently in making citations from the Old Testament.

> They used it as an honestly-made version in pretty general use at the time when they wrote….After the diffusion of Christianity, copies of the Septuagint became widely dispersed amongst the new communities that were formed; so that before many years had elapsed this version must have been as much in the hands of Gentiles as of Jews.[3]

For our immediate purpose, the *LXX* used two words, *apostolos* (apostle) and *ekklesia* (church) that came to have significant meaning.

Our present focus: ekklesia. Various comments, both positive and negative, could be made about the quality of the *LXX* translation, but our immediate interest is the translated word *ekklesia* and how it greatly affected the future use of "church." The *LXX* usage of *ekklesia* became significant because it embodied both the Hebrew and Greek meanings which were appropriate in describing the gathered Christian community.

Ekklesia occurs about 100 times in the *LXX*, some 70 times the preferred translation of the Hebrew *qahal* which means "gathering," "coming together," "assembly," "an assembled community."[4] This translation of *qahal* (with its general meaning) into *ekklesia* coupled with the literal Greek meaning ("called out ones," the recognized citizens of a Greek city) made *ekklesia* an ideal word to describe the Church of God, both local and world-wide.

Archbishop R. C. Trench, in his well-known *Synonyms of the New Testament,* discussed how the Alexandrian translators handled two constantly recurring words in the Hebrew Scriptures, *'edah* and *qahal,* both of which referred to assemblies. Usually, the two words were rendered into the Greek language by *sunagoge* and *ekklesia* respectively, which then later evolved into synogogue and church. As the Christian churches developed, "the greater fitness and dignity of the title ekklesia" prevailed.[5]

Scene 2: Riot at the Stadium: The Ekklesia in an Uproar!

An urgent summons was made for "the church of Ephesus" to gather, and the city's large amphitheatre (seating 25,000) quickly filled with anxious citizens. Soon this enraged "church" of Ephesus transformed into a frenzied mob shouting: "Great is Diana of the Ephesians!" (Acts 19:28). Even those with slight interest were drawn irresistibly into the chaos. No semblance of order remained.

The roar of the vast crowd continued for two hours! This great assemblage was the "church" at Ephesus. These were the registered citizens of the Greek city-state of Ephesus. They were "the called out ones" who comprised the governing body (to which no slave or outsider could belong).

The volatile situation had begun to develop as converted citizens ceased to purchase the idols of Diana sold at the marketplace. When the tense atmosphere of the city had reached critical mass, some of the silversmiths loudly accused Paul and the

Christians of denouncing their silver idols devoted to the city's goddess. The immediate reaction was like a lighted match tossed on gasoline. Out of hand, the city's rioting citizens shouted uncontrollably.

It seems strange to call such a mob "the church at Ephesus," but that is exactly what they were. Not, of course, the Christian "church," but rather the "called out" *ekklesia* or "citizen body [of Ephesus] in its legislative capacity" (F. F. Bruce).[6] As Luke recorded this great disturbance, his intentional use of *ekklesia* (three times in the Greek text) is not at all out of line, for he properly uses this secular word in its technical sense, "returning to its earlier significance" (Trench),[7] Acts 19:32, 39, 41.

Paul's Use of Ekklesia

Paul, writing later to the Christian church in this *same* city of Ephesus, used *ekklesia* nine times in reference to the universal Church of Jesus Christ.

This word was tailor-made for the Gentile Christian churches in the Hellenistic culture of that day. Paul, and Luke particularly appropriated and adopted this meaningful word; so it appears 111 times in the Greek New Testament, referring either to the local church(es) in various communities or the universal church of Jesus Christ.[8] Karl Ludwig Schmidt, the author of the article on "*ekklesia*" in Kittel's prestigious *Theological Dictionary of the New Testament,* confirms this:

> What is the significance of the fact that Greek-speaking Jews and early Christians chose this particular expression? ... The derivation is simple and significant: the assembled citizens are the *ekkletoi* (called out), i.e. those who have been summoned by the herald. This naturally suggests that in the Bible the reference is to God in Christ calling men out of the world.[9]

The Importance of the Local Churches

As you will see in the following charts, a great deal is said in the NT about the Church and churches of Jesus Christ. Ephesians particularly points out the glories of the *universal* Church (capitalized when we so use it). Paul and Luke, in their writings, specialized in the *local* churches (not capitalized when used); that is, the churches existing in various cities, towns, and communities. These churches were the cities of the Christ-believers within the secular cities -- the tangible, visible representatives of the kingdom of God, the light in the darkness, the city on a hill that cannot be hidden. The churches are the practical, observable, working force of the kingdom of God in a world of darkened unbelief. Their gatherings were notable for the wonderful peace and power of the Holy Spirit and the miraculous workings among them.

Notice in the following chart that churches in 26 cities and 11 provinces are mentioned in the New Testament, indicating a much larger distribution of apostolic Christianity, a ubiquitous presence of Christ throughout the Empire. You will also notice that the NT refers to the universal Church 14 times. The Church and churches are described in a number of colorful ways, as you will see in the last chart: saints, army, bride, workmen, temple, and so forth.

Why stress local churches so much? Very simply, because the local church is the key messenger of Christ to the secular community. The people of a local church become the heart, the hands and the voice of Jesus Christ. This brilliant strategy is God's way of maintaining active spiritual life in His saints, and then, through them, impacting the secular world. When the people of a community see the members of the local church body, they (hopefully) will see Christ.

Local Church Locations in the NT
*Indicates the word "church" not used but is strongly implied (12 times)

26 Cities Recorded/Implied	References
Antioch	Acts 11:26; 13:1; 14:23, 26-27; 15:3, 30; Gal 2:11
Antioch of Pisidia*	Acts 13:52; 14:23
Caesarea	Acts 18:22
Cenchrea	Rom 16:1
Colosse*	Col 1:2; 4:16
Corinth	1 Cor 1:2; 6:4; 10:32; 11:18,22; 14:23, 28, 35; 2 Cor 1:1

Damascus*	Acts 9:19
Derbe*	Acts 14:21
Ephesus	Acts 20:17, 28; Eph 1:1; Rev 2:1
Hierapolis*	Col 4:13
Iconium	Acts 14:23
Jerusalem	Acts 2:47; 4:31; 5:11; 8:1,3; 11:22; 12:1,5; 15:4,22
Joppa*	Acts 9:36-43
Laodicea	Col 4:15-16; Rev 3:14
Lydda*	Acts 9:32-35
Lystra	Acts 14:23
Nicopolis*	Tit 3:13
Pergamos	Rev 2:12
Philadelphia	Rev 3:7
Philippi	Phil 1:1; 4:15
Rome*	Rom 1:7
Sardis	Rev 3:1
Smyrna	Rev 2:8
Thessalonica	1 Th 1:1; 2 Th 1:1
Thyatira	Rev 2:18
Troas*	Acts 20:7
11 Provinces Recorded	
Achaia*	2 Cor 1:1
Asia (Minor)	1 Cor 16:19; Rev 1:4, 11, 20, 20
Cilicia	Acts 15:23, 41
Crete	Titus 1:5
Galatia	1 Cor 16:1; Gal 1:2; 1 Th 2:14; 2 Th 1:4
Galilee	Acts 9:31
Judea	Acts 9:31; 12:5; 15:4, 22; Gal 1:22; 1 Th 2:14
Macadonia	2 Cor 8:1
Phoenicia*	Acts 15:3
Samaria	Acts 9:31; 15:3
Syria	Acts 15:23, 41

Other Descriptions of Local Churches	
All the churches	Rom 16:4; 1 Cor 7:17; 14:33; 2 Cor 8:18; 11:28; Rev 2:23
Church(es) of (living) God	Ac 20:28; 1 Cor 1:2; 10:32; 11:16, 22; 15:9; 2 Cor 1:1; Gal 1:13; 1 Th 2:14; 2 Th 1:4; 1 Tim 3:5
Churches of (in) Christ	Rom 16:16; Gal 1:22

Churches of the Gentiles	Rom 16:4
Churches of the saints	1 Cor 14:33
House churches	Rom 16:5; 1 Cor 16:19; Col 4:15; Phlm 2

General References to the Local Churches

Mt 18:17, 17; Ac 16:5; Rom 16:23; 1 Cor 4:17; 7:17; 14:4, 5, 12, 19, 34, 35; 2 Cor 8:18, 19, 23, 24; 11:8, 28; 12:13; Phil 3:6; 4:15; 1 Tim 3:5, 15; 5:16; Titus 1:5; Ja 5:14; 3 Jn 1:6, 9, 10; Rev 2:7, 11, 17; 2:23, 29; 3:6, 13, 22; 22:16

Local Gathering: 1 Cor 5:4; 11:18, 20, 33-34 – Come together in the church
14:26 – when come together
Heb 10:25 – Do not forsake the gathering
Jas 2:2 – your assembly
Acts 15:30 – gathered multitude together

14 References to the Universal Church

Mt 16:18	"…and on this rock I will build My church…."
1 Cor 12:28	"And God has appointed these in the church: first apostles…."
Eph 1:22	"…and gave Him to be head over all things to the church."
Eph 3:10	"…now the manifold wisdom of God might be made known by the church to the principalities and powers in the heavenly places."
Eph 3:21	"to Him be glory in the church by Christ Jesus…."
Eph 5:23	"…Christ is head of the church…."
Eph 5:24	"…as the church is subject to Christ…."
Eph 5:25	…as Christ also loved the church and gave Himself for her."
Eph 5:27	"that He might present her to Himself a glorious church…."
Eph 5:29	"…as the Lord does [nourishes and cherishes] the church."
Eph 5:32	"This is a great mystery, but I speak concerning Christ and the church."
Col 1:18	"And He is the head of the body, the church…."
Col 1:24	"…for the sake of His body, which is the church."
Heb 12:23	"to the general assembly and church of the firstborn…."

Illustration of Local and Universal, 1 Cor 1:2:

"To the church of God which is **at Corinth**, to those who are sanctified in Christ Jesus, called to be saints, with **all whom in every place** call on the name of Jesus Christ our Lord, both theirs and ours."

27 Descriptions of the Church	
Description	*References*
Army	Eph 6
Assembly	James 2:2 (Heb 2:12)
Body	1 Cor 12; Eph 1:23; Col 1:18, 24; 3:15
Brethren, Faithful	Col 1;2
Bride	Eph 5
Building	1 Cor 3:8
Children	1 Jn 2:18; 3:1
City	Rev 3:12
Circumcision, The	Phil 3:3
Citizens, Fellow C with the Saints	Eph 2;19
Dwelling Place (for God)	Eph 2:22
Elect	Col 3:12
Fellow Workmen	1 Cor 3:8
Field	1 Cor 3:8
Firstfruits (of his creatures)	James 1:18
Flock	Ac 20:28; Heb 13:20; 1 Pet 2:25; 5:1-3
Fullness (of Him)	Eph 1:23
Generation, A Chosen	1 Pet 2:9
Habitation of God	Eph 2:22
House, A Spiritual	1 Pet 5:2
House (of God)	1 Tim 3:15; 1 Pet 4:17
Household of God	Eph 2:19
Man, One New	Col 2:15
Nation, A Holy	1 Pet 2:9
People (His Own Special)	1 Pet 2:9
People (of God)	1 Pet 2:10
Priesthood (A Royal)	1 Pet 2:9
Saints	1 Cor 6:1; Eph 1:1; Col 1:2
Sojourners (and Pilgrims)	1 Pet 2:11
Temple	1 Cor 3:16-17; 6:19; Eph 2:21; Rev 3:12
Workmanship, His	Eph 2:10

Through the Church Age, various splinter groups have occurred; that is, sincere people dissatisfied with the *status quo* of their mother church, break off to start a church more in line with their understanding of apostolic Christianity. People being people, they naturally found it necessary to put a name on their religious movement or building.   So we have some calling themselves "Brethren," or "Saints," or "The Church of God," or "The Assemblies of God," or hundreds of other names.   Sometimes the break-away group chooses to identify themselves by a certain methodology; such as, Episcopal, Presbyterian, Baptist.

Like many of you, I would like to see the Church and churches return to New Testament Christianity in the fullest sense of the word. But, with all our enthusiasm, we dare not forget Paul's great statement in Ephesians 4:2-6:

> With all lowliness and gentleness, with longsuffering, bearing with one another in love, endeavoring to keep the unity of the Spirit in the bond of peace. There is one body and one Spirit, just as you were called in one hope of your calling; one Lord, one faith, one baptism; one God and Father of all, who is above all, and through all, and in you all.

The early Christians were first called "Christians" in Antioch (Acts 11:26). Although the secular residents of Antioch had often heard this name used, *"Xristos"* (Christ) meant nothing to unbelieving Gentiles. Actually, the Christians themselves did not call themselves by that name, and the Jews would certainly not use that name. They were simply the people of the Christ, whoever that might be. Barclay says,

> The title began as a nickname. The people of Antioch were famous for their facility for finding sarcastic nicknames. Later, the bearded emperor Julian came to visit them, and they nicknamed him "the Goat". The word-ending *–iani* means *belonging to the party of;* for instance, *Caesariani* means *belonging to Caesar's party.* Christian means *these Christ-folk.* It was a contemptuous nickname; but the Christians took it and made it known to all the world. By their lives, they made it a name not of contempt but of respect and admiration and even wonder.[10]

In the Next Chapter

The term "apostolic" has been used a great deal through this book to describe ministries, doctrine and churches. And, I am well aware that there are various religious groups that use "apostolic" in their name. I do not mean it to describe any particular fellowship or denomination.

I am writing about literal apostles, first of all; then I am interested in what those apostles actually taught; and finally, I wish to promote the kind of people and vision that those apostles and their doctrine produced. To be "apostolic" in the full sense of the word is to accept both the original apostles and their message and their scriptural teaching as appropriate for today's churches.

I suggest that the fivefold ministries of Ephesians 4 can have a unique, practical application in making our churches truly "apostolic" – and that is what the next chapter is all about.

Chapter 16 Endnotes

[1] *The Septuagint Version of the Old Testament* (Grand Rapids: Zondervan, 1976, 8th ed), from the Introduction, i.

[2] E. M. Blaiklock, "Septuagint," Merrill C. Tenney, gen. ed., *The Zondervan Pictorial Encyclopedia of the Bible*, Vol. Five, (Grand Rapids, Zondervan, 1975), p. 343. This six-page article is an excellent review.

[3] Ibid., p. iv.

[4] "In the LXX *ekklesia* has no ecclesiastical significance….The nature to the gathering depends entirely upon the nature of those who compose it." Karl Ludwig Schmidt, trans. and ed. by J. R. Coates, *The Church* (London: Adam and Charles Black, 1950), p. 51. This is Kittel's article published as a small book or manual.

---

[5] Richard Chenevix Trench, *Synonyms of the New Testament* (Grand Rapids: Associated Publishers and Authors, Inc., reprint with no date given), p. 5. Also, for a complete detailed analysis of *'edah* and *quhal* in terms of *ekklesia,* see Lothar Croen, "ekklesia," Colin Brown, gen. ed., *Greek Dictionary of New Testament Theology,* Vol. 1, 291-305.

[6] F. F. Bruce, *The Spreading Flame* (Grand Rapids: Eerdmans, 1973 [1958]), p.71.

[7] Trench, p. 2.

[8] It seems remarkable that it does not appear in Peter's epistles, but as Schmidt points out (p. 5), although the word is missing, the thought itself is still present in the special emphasis on the OT community and its meaning and the use of OT expressions.

[9] Schmidt, p. 24.

[10] Barclay, *The Acts of the Apostles*, p. 105.

Chapter 17
Full Coverage Ministry
for the Local Church

In This Chapter

- *A good way to monitor church ministry*
- *Are we mobilizing the church to do the important things?*
- *Can our church really be apostolic and prophetic?*
- *How Can we be more evangelistic?*
- *Key questions help monitor the functions*

Some years ago, I accepted a car ride from a fellow minister at a conference, and was pleasantly surprised: the car *talked!* The car had a built-in electronic voice alert system. Impressive! So, guess what? The next time Joy and I bought a car, it too had a "message center" with a computer controlled warning system which monitored ten input sensors on the vehicle.

With the engine running, the system detected and reported conditions such as: "A door is ajar," "Your parking brake is on," "Your washer fluid is low," and "our fuel is low." Some of the statements were startling: "Your engine oil pressure is low, Prompt service is required" (delivered two seconds after the Engine Warning Light came on). Other warnings urged "prompt service."

My favorite was "All monitored systems are functioning," giving a sense of confidence about the car -- although I knew there could be other problems not covered by the warning system. At least we knew that certain key functions were being monitored!

All Monitored Systems Are Functioning

This chapter suggests that your local church's ministry can also have a built-in warning system that will monitor five major activities that make local church function effective. This does not mean, of course, that simply *knowing* about a problem or situation automatically fixes it! The system must be tended with the care of a loving gardener, despising weeds and loving fruit.

> "To monitor": *to watch, keep track of, check up on – to see if a special purpose is being achieved"*

Sometimes the pastoral staff, trustees, elders, or leadership team (those responsible for leading) spend their time with auxiliary issues: money problems (as trifling as buying pencils or toilet tissue) and counting bodies (numbers do not always indicate organic success). Of course, don't neglect the finances and attendance, but realize your best time is spent monitoring the welfare of the people and doing strategic planning for the church.[1] Become familiar with the FIVE sensors described in the "owner's manual" that comes with every church.

This chapter urges church leaders to monitor (keep tabs on) the spiritual development of the local church by regular oversight of the five key sensors listed in Ephesians 4:11: apostles, prophets, evangelists, pastors and teachers. Extremely helpful as individuals, the fivefold ministry can have a *broader* application for church operation.

Make the nouns into adjectives – think of them as descriptive titles of the five main pistons that drive the church: *apostolic, prophetic, evangelistic, pastoral, and teaching.* Plug in and monitor the information of this chapter – and see if an upgrade in congregational health doesn't occur.

Full Coverage Ministry for the Local Church
Monitoring the Fivefold Function in Our Churches

Are We Mobilizing the Church To Do the following?

1. **Apostolic:** Plant and foster churches at home and abroad through team ministry and financial aid; equip and mobilize the entire church so that all function in their ministries and are engaged in church growth and planting; develop and encourage apostles.

2. **Prophetic:** Maintain the atmosphere in our church which allows the Holy Spirit to manifest the inspiring presence of Jesus and His prophetic voice; encourage congregational prayer and biblical worship which creates the atmosphere for spiritual manifestations; identify each person's ministry; develop and encourage prophets.

3. **Evangelistic:** Present the Good News of Jesus Christ to the non-Christians of our area so that they will be caused to repent, be baptized, and be assimilated into the local church; win the lost to Christ by every means possible as quickly as possible; develop and encourage evangelists.

4. **Pastoral:** Give spiritual oversight (leading, feeding, tending, guarding, counting) to all the people composing the local church so that there will be healthy growth in each of them; know and care for the spiritual health and welfare of each person in the entire flock; develop and encourage pastors.

5. **Teaching:** Present an over-all, balanced instruction of the entire Bible so that the people may know the ways of God and rejoice in His acts; help people live lives that are based on biblical principles; develop and encourage teachers.

At the end of four of the five sections, there will be questions that leadership should ask themselves about their local church operation. In addition think up your own questions as well.

Certainly pray over the deficiencies you find in the church, and seek to correct them; strategize to improve. At the same time, *favor focusing on your strengths, identifying and building upon those things the church and elders to well.* We must spend time and energy on identifying and developing strengths, doing what we can do, positioning the church to capitalize on the opportunities that God brings.

All the various ministries in a church will not be mentioned in every leadership discussion, but "the fivefold function" will have dynamic application for everything from ushers, nursery and worship leaders to the dozens of other jobs. Keep these five functions in the forefront of pastoral concern, the subject of continual, dedicated prayer.

Leadership Responsibility

Recognition and identification of church leadership is important. These are the people who must stay cognizant of the "state of the flock" and its health, initiating the necessary procedures that maintain a healthy condition in the total flock. The idea of God's people being like sheep and their leaders like shepherds is an ancient-but-good concept, particularly meaningful to an agrarian economy. Jesus called himself "the good shepherd" (as opposed to a hireling that does not care for the sheep), John 10:11-15.[2]

More will be said about pastoral participation under the heading, "The Pastoral Function of the Local Church," but for now, consider the overall leadership concerns of the churches of Bible times. Remember that apostles and prophets in some way must be an effective part of helping the churches maintain "apostolic" function (in the fullest sense of the word) in the local church.

I. The Apostolic Function of the Local Church
"The Church is a missionary enterprise"

Matthew 28:18-20; Acts 2:42; 14:14; 15:36, 41; 16:4-5; 1 Corinthians 4:9, 15; 15:1-2; 2 Timothy 3:16-17; Titus 1:5; Ephesians 2:19-20; Galatians 3:2-3; Jude 3

An "apostolic church" is the local expression of the Church in proclamation -- transformed from a slumbering, banking institution or tired, business enterprise into a militant, missionary, apostolic movement that flings kingdom seeds throughout the world, reaping harvest locally and globally.

"Apostolic" describes *the "ambassadorial function"* of the local church, moving outward *from* the local setting, planting churches near and afar, reaching the nations as well as the local marketplace, impacting culture. This kind of local church experiences remarkable local renewal and growth. Today's churches can choose to stay ingrown and self-satisfied (and gradually die), or they can follow the vibrant example of the church of Antioch (Acts 13) with its visionary activity of going, sending and staying vibrant.

Five Types of Apostolic Ministry

1) *The Original Twelve,* Matthew 10:2-4, described in chapter 4. Long-gone, their message and ministry remains in dynamic force – and will throughout eternity (Matthew 19:28; Revelation 21:14). We must emulate their zeal and dedication, finishing the job they started!

2) *Paul the Extraordinary Apostle,* discussed in Chapter 5. The writings and example of this post-Ascension apostle remain our guiding light.

3) *Other apostles* mentioned in Scripture, listed in Chapters 6 and 7. They inspire the continuing traditions of the NT Church (as, James, Barnabas, Jude, and Titus). Modern apostles fall into this category of post-Ascension apostles.

4) *Apostolic Team Ministry* produces powerful effects! Twelve teams are mentioned in Acts, eleven in the Epistles. See Appendix C for a chart of those teams and additional ideas about team ministry.

What Is an Apostle?

The apostle is an ambassador sent from God to introduce and establish the principles of the kingdom of God. My definition plus eleven other definitions by various authors are given in chapter 14.

279

Several times they are correctly called architects or master builders, based on Paul's referring to apostles as "master builders" [*architekton*]. An apostle is given the gift to plant and grow churches, and by dedication and spiritual gifting, lead God's people in church renewal, church growth, culture penetration and world harvest.

What Do They Do?

Apostles are innovative sparkplugs for the life of the churches. They speak for God with divine confirmation. They serve, shepherd and protect the churches. They cooperate with the local church leaders and people to make the local church stronger and more productive. They rally the people of God for action. They expand kingdom borders, confronting cultural barriers and demonic powers. They model self-sacrifice, dedication and suffering. They serve the local churches in whatever ways that will benefit.

Apostles impart vision to a local church, inspire the membership and encourage the leadership. Their job is not to take over a local church, but rather to impart spiritual direction and input when requested, and to be a spiritual "covering" in the sense of keeping the church going in the right direction.

Monitoring the Apostolic with Key Questions

1. *Is our church truly built on an Apostolic foundation?*
2. *Is our church helped and influenced by a modern apostle(s)?*
3. *Can our people recognize and relate to a true apostle?*
4. *Are the church people trained and sent to minister in community, secular marketplace and other places at home and abroad?*
5. *Is strong prayer support maintained for apostolic activity?*
6. *Have we planted another US church recently – or ever?*
7. *Do we encourage "team ministry" at home and abroad?*
8. *Is there some type of ministerial candidate program?*

9. *Have we considered an outreach to foreign students at local universities?*
10. *Is at least 10% of church income used in world outreach?*
11. *Do we have an annual missions conference?*
12. *Do we have any potential candidates for apostleship in our church?*

II. The Prophetic Function of the Local Church
"The Church is the habitation of His Presence"

Isaiah 56:7; Acts 2:17-18; 11:27-28; 13:1; 15:32; 21:9-11;
1 Corinthians 11:5; 12:28; 14:1, 24-25,:29-33; Ephesians 3:5; 4:12

A "prophetic church" is characterized by an awesome awareness of the Holy Spirit in its gatherings, an awareness fostered by the prophetic activity that takes place. This kind of church believes that the Holy Spirit speaks today through spontaneous prophecy, the gift of prophecy and the ministry of prophets. This amazing prophetic activity is made possible and workable by the atmosphere of expectant faith in the congregation, which is driven in turn by sincere prayer, passionate intercession and truly biblical worship.

The local church is meant to be a habitation of His presence and voice. Such God-awareness is particularly encouraged and enhanced by the inspiring ministry of prophets. Seek His face – hear His voice – discern His will!

What Is a Prophet?

The New Testament prophet (male or female) is a leadership ministry that the Lord Jesus Himself has set in the Church. The prophet brings prophetic direction and edification, working closely with other church leadership. Prophets are to be a voice of God to the people, sometimes bringing simple impressions and edification. At other times the prophet, working in conjunction with others in leadership, brings significant direction or prediction for the local church, a group of churches or the Church worldwide.

What Do They do?

Prophets are to seek His face, hear His voice and discern His will. They are called to edify, comfort and exhort the churches -- to inspire, direct and inform in the ways and purposes of God. They function most successfully in conjunction with church leadership and apostles. Prophets enable your church to experience divine direction and spiritual insight.

Prophets are to build up churches, not control or take-over. Prophets have special gifting to discern demonic attacks, reveal Divine strategies, recognize callings and gifting and impart prophetic gifts. They preach as well as prophesy, declaring at the moment what God is saying to specific churches and individuals. Prophets will help work with the people of the church to bring them into a higher level of prayer activity and prophetic expression.

Monitoring the Prophetic with Key Questions

1. *Are the three types of prophecy commonplace in our church: general prophecy, the gift of prophecy and the ministry of the prophet?*
2. *Is prayer a regularly emphasized and scheduled part of congregational life? Are special prayer/worship/fasting services ever scheduled?*
3. *Is biblical worship high priority in our congregational meeting?*
4. *Is there communication between Pastor and worship leaders in both pre-planning and post-evaluating the worship service flow?*
5. *Is there teaching about the provision for the manifestation and evaluation of spiritual gifts, especially prophetic protocol? How is misguided prophecy handled?*
6. *Is the prophetic voice active in our church, and do we have a way to recall what God has already said to us?*

7. *Are the sacraments of our church performed in an orderly, disciplined, biblical manner that enhances the historic significance and also allows a present manifestation of Christ's presence?*
8. *Is there a training program for musicians and singers to produce a more excellent worship atmosphere?*
9. *Does our church ever invite outside prophets for ministry and input?*
10. *Are there prospective prophets in our church?*

III. The Evangelistic Function of the Local Church
"The Church seeks to find and save the lost"

Matthew 18:11; Mark 16:15-16; Luke 9:1, 56; 10:1; Acts 1:8;
2 Timothy 4:5

An "evangelistic church" is one with a "harvest mentality." The objective of such a church is: *win the lost to Christ by every means possible as quickly as possible.* This kind of church has a driving passion to present the Good News of Jesus Christ to the lost and dying people of their area so that they will repent, be baptized, and assimilated into the local church. *The local church is a harvesting combine that utilizes every member to reap the harvest of a given area.* The local church can be described as a great net, secured by many hands, pulling in a great draught of fish.

An evangelistic church realizes the importance of evangelists. Some active members in every local church will be gifted as evangelists. In addition there are traveling evangelists with higher visibility, greater resources, and more experience to teach and lead the local church in successful outreach. Although everyone in a local church is not an evangelist, every Christian should be evangelistic. Every Christian winning people to Christ!

What Is an Evangelist?

A gift to the Body of Christ – a leadership ministry – a herald to the secular community with the ability to gather people to Christ and into the local church. An evangelist is "the bearer of good news," one whose primary role is to persuade nonbelievers to become believers. This is done by declaring the "Good News" of the kingdom of God.

What Does an Evangelist Do?

Leads the way in evangelistic outreach – models compassion – proclaims good news – seeks to convert sinners – invites the community to Christ and the church – operates spiritual gifts, such as healing – mobilizes local evangelists – organizes public outreach – helps plant churches – equips the saints.

All this, when accompanied by the miraculous, brings results. We must not underplay our spiritual equipment in outreach. As Evangelist Rheinhardt Bonnke says: "Signs and wonders are biblical . . . they authenticate the gospel."

Win More People to Christ

Mobilize for soul-winning, make it hard for anyone in the community to die without Christ. Win the lost – train evangelists – influence neighborhoods!

If a church can at least mobilize the evangelists and the evangelistically inclined within the congregation things will start to move. It is estimated by church growth experts that at least 10% of every local church are evangelists. Add to that all the rest of us doing the work of an evangelist -- what a powerful expression of the kingdom that would be!

Unfortunately, as Scott Boren has said: "Too many churches are going outside the walls when what is happening inside the walls is not worth the cost of a printed invitation." That's why these challenging questions in each section should be reviewed periodically by the church leadership, strengthening every weak area, moving ahead with confidence in strong areas.

Think of the local church as a great building with few doors, each door representing an appealing way of drawing some type of people. Realize, then that *the more entrances we make into the building, the more people can come in!* Multiply the doors opening into the church!

A few of the many ideas about reaching people:
1. Invite an evangelist to come, train people, show them how, and hold special meetings.
2. Help improve the community, be interested in upgrading the schools and parks, feed the hungry, care for the needy.
3. Befriend neighbors (the hook and line approach).
4. Cast the nets (support groups, marriage seminars, food distribution, cell groups).
5. Sponsor mass meetings (saturation evangelism).
6. Tract distribution, church website, etc.

Monitoring the Evangelistic with Key Questions
1. *Is there a training program on soul winning in the church?*
2. *Are the evangelism outreaches tied to the philosophy of ministry of the church?*
3. *Are there target areas of ministry available to the people?*
4. *Is there an immediate assimilation process for new comers and converts?*
5. *Is the home meeting "cell" program evangelistic?*
6. *Does the pastor make an appeal for souls in the public church services?*
   Note: Some people will not bring others to a decision, but they will bring those people to a church service if they know the invitation will be given by the pastor.
7. *Does the church ever sponsor some form of an evangelistic crusade?*
8. *Do we emphasize that God answers prayer and He heals and delivers?*
9. *Do we have potential evangelists in the church?*

IV. The Pastoral Function of the Local Church
"The Church gives pastoral care to its members"

John 21:15-17; Acts 20:28; 1 Timothy 3:1-7; 1 Peter 2:25; 5:2-4;
Titus 2:5-9

A "pastoral church" is supervised by mature, caring leaders called by various names:

- elder (*presbuteros*) because of experience
- bishop (*episcopos*) because of supervision
- pastor (*poimen*) because they functioned like shepherds[3]

All church members were to be part of the total church team, helping in any possible capacity, but some were also singled out and given additional authority to lead and work in designated areas with the eldership. Such people were called deacons (*diakonos,* helpers). Acts 6:1-7; Philippians 1:1; 1 Timothy 2:8-13.

Description of an Elder?

When Paul and his associates appointed elders in local churches (as, Acts 14:23; Titus 1:5), what kind of people were they? Well, they were quality people, if these listed qualifications are any indication: *blameless, monogamous, temperate, sober-minded, well behaved, hospitable, able to teach, not excessive drinkers, not violent, not money-hungry, gentle, not quarrelsome, not covetous, having godly homes, experienced, having good testimonies in the community* (1 Timothy 3:1-7; Titus 1:5-9). They would, of course, be committed, wise, baptized Christians who were filled with the Holy Spirit.

What Did They Do?

The terms "pastor" and "shepherd" are synonymous. These responsible elders are called to *lead, feed, tend, guard and count (keep track of)* the people of God (John 21; Acts 20:28-29). The local church size and the need will dictate the number of pastor-elders needed. Every successful church will have an experienced lead pastor-elder as the senior pastor-leader gifted for the setting of vision and supervision with a group of spiritual, capable elders to share the care of the people and the strategic planning for the church's growth and success.

An Elder

It was not unusual for an elder of a local church also to be one of the fivefold ministries of Ephesians 4, that is an apostle, prophet, evangelist, pastor or teacher. Such gifted local ministries would work humbly and cooperate with fellow local elders, concentrating on a particular area of strength.

I knew a man who was a gifted prophet, who would be called on to minister in various churches, but he was also considered a resident local church prophet. Tom Edmondson earned his basic living as an employee of the local church, doing menial maintenance tasks around the church building, thoroughly enjoying his life. In that church he was a very profitable prophet (praying a lot while working around the church building).

Also, outside fivefold ministers should visit the local church to bring their inspiration to the local people and for special input and help (for local eldership) in strategizing for natural and spiritual growth. Each local church should be in fellowship with a network of other local churches, but each sovereignly sustained and internally lead, staying open to wise and prophetic input from apostles and prophets.

How Were the Local Elders Selected?

At times in our modern churches, people are ordained to ministry, selected for leadership, voted in as trustees or elders – and their qualifications are based mainly on popularity, position, wealth, friendship, and so on. This is an unfortunate approach for supplying the spiritual leadership of dedicated, Spirit-filled people. A possible candidate may be a highly trained professional in the community, but this alone would not qualify him in Bible days. The qualities of righteousness, godliness, honesty, spirituality, etc., were paramount.

When a church is started from scratch, a wise apostle or pastor will understand that although people may gather into a newly forming church, many will need biblical teaching and time to improve their quality of life. As an example, after Paul had ministered on Crete, they still had no elders in the churches. But Paul had to leave, so Titus one of his adjutants was left "to set in order the things that are lacking, and appoint elders in every city as I commanded you" (Titus 1:5). Both Titus and Timothy, both acting as younger apostles, were urged to always keep in mind the standards and qualifications of those who would be guardians of the flock.

Confirmation

Whether a lone founding pastor or an established church with existing elders, it is always good to give the people an opportunity to confirm an elder's appointment. The spiritual leader(s) must seek God first, then make the recommendation to the congregation for approval. There should then be a public acknowledgement or ordination with prayer and the laying on of hands.

Things are considerably different when an established church wishes to call in a new pastor. It does happen sometimes that the established leaders (trustees, elders, board) really do not want another leader, they just want some one to follow their orders. It takes time to understand this kind of a situation, and can hardly be decided by a prospective pastor preaching one trial sermon.[4]

The most ideal situation is in starting a church and working with those that God brings to you. Those who are responsive to your message and style of operation should be the ones discipled and mentored. When the time comes for elders such people will work easily and harmoniously with you. Honestly, if a voting member of a leadership board does not agree with your philosophy of ministry or doctrine, you will have nothing but trouble.

V. The Teaching Function of the Local Church
"Experience Biblical Education with Teachers"

Acts 13:1; 19:9-10; Romans 12:7; 1 Corinthians 12:18; 14:26;
Ephesians 4:11; 1 Timothy 4:6; 2 Timothy 2:2; 3:16-17; Titus 2:1

The "teaching church" presents an over-all, balanced instruction of the entire Bible to help the people live lives that are based on biblical principles. Teachers enable your church to be a school of biblical education where people learn the ways and acts of God. We all value prayer, worship, preaching, etc., but we must also contend for each church, in whatever format is used, to be an effective teaching center.

What Is a Teacher?

Teachers in the body of Christ are gifted in research and presentation; they take biblical information and make it interesting, enjoyable, and understandable. The church teacher has the marvelous opportunity to teach and explain the Bible, emphasizing what Hudson Taylor once said: "The Bible is intended to teach us what God would have us do."

Teachers come in great variety – matching the various ages, groups, and needs that make up a local church. Some are particularly adept at teaching teachers. Others instruct children extremely well, but do not do well with adults. Every church should develop an inspiring team of teachers with a varied education program that will upgrade all the people. The senior pastor must set the pace by presenting the Bible clearly and forcefully, being the shepherd's voice to the congregation.

The education program can be enhanced and given new emphasis by bringing in well-known teachers or teaching videos; new perspective will lift the people's admiration of God and His Word to a new level.

When commenting on the fivefold ministry, R. T. Kendall said, "The office of the teacher… is the least controversial, but possibly the most neglected and needed of the five."

What Does a Teacher Do?

I would like to have Susan Boyer and her mother answer the following questions. While visiting their church in Federal Way, Washington, some years ago, I felt prophetically moved to tell Susan to pursue the vocation of a public school principal; I was surprised as she was! This, however, she has diligently done, and become quite successful, now with two master's degrees and working on her doctorate. I asked her several years ago to answer the question, "What does it mean 'to teach'?" She told me this, and I think it is worth repeating.

> Teaching is trying to impart a skill, an idea, or a concept that enables people to be equipped with tools or knowledge that will enhance their lives in some way. Teachers teach more than subjects; they also teach who they are (attitudes, beliefs, convictions, personality). In the case of Bible teaching, the teacher should not teach personal ideas but rather the ideas, concepts, or beliefs that come from the Bible. I also believe that teaching means that you give your students the tools to continue learning without you…it is important that they are not dependent on the teacher to learn but that they are inspired and taught to continue learning – to be a life-long learner.

What Does It Mean "To Learn"?

> Learning occurs when a person takes the ideas, skill, or concept that someone else has taught and makes it his/her own. Learning means that we have realized that we don't know everything and there are still things that others have to share with us. And, to really learn one must be willing to make mistakes (Susan Boyer).

What Should Bible Teachers Accomplish?

> This was the hardest of the three questions and really made me think….Bible teachers need to give their students the skill to be able to read their Bibles with understanding and depth, and I don't mean that they should necessarily be just showing them how to use a Bible dictionary or concordance….They should also show their students how the Bible reflects the nature of God so that when they read it they are pointed towards the one that we have a relationship with - God"(Susan Boyer).

> [T]his question (#3) again leads to the idea that teachers give more than knowledge – they give tools (pathways, skills, connections) to improve, deepen, strengthen their relationship with God and to live, from the heart, in a way that conforms them to an outcome…the image of Christ. I think Bible teachers need to be "outcome driven" – teaching with a specific, usable goal. At least in theory, "outcome" based education gives students skills for successful life. For the Christian, this means a life that is successful and prosperous (as God defines success & prosperity) as well as pleasing to God….Bible teachers should not just be teaching facts or rules, but showing the applications and uses for those

things, always...with the goal of revealing the love and goodness of God and the value of a viable relationship with God (Dorothy Mouracade, Susan's mother).

The Church Must Teach!

Every church needs an inspiring group of teachers. Also, the input of outside teachers will bring new perspective to life in the people's admiration of God and His Word and to make the Bible practical and relevant.

To maintain itself and also move forward, every church should strive to have a pipeline of supplying new workers in the church. This means a vital church must make new converts and then train them to assume spiritual responsibility. To do this effectively, every age level must receive factual Bible training as well as understanding how to live the Christian life and enjoy the ministry of Christ in His Church.

Our church teachers should be the best we can find, and they must teach with joyful enthusiasm, clarity, and with the best teaching aids possible. Every teacher should love the students, be filled with the Spirit, and know what they are talking about. Explain the Bible – equip disciples – enable successful lives!

What Should Teachers Teach?
1. Biblical world view
2. The ingredients for living a successful Christian life
3. God's covenants
4. Old Testament teachings
5. Life of Christ
6. The Early Church
7. New Testament Theology

Monitoring the Teaching with Key Questions
1. *Is there on-going Bible instruction available for the church family?*
2. *Are the children being taught basic Bible truths and given opportunity for expression?*
3. *Is the teaching of the church character-forming as well as factual and topical?*

4. *Is there a method of catechizing people in the major doctrines of the church?*
5. *Are potential men and women being trained for leadership?*
6. *Is there an avenue for older women to teach younger women to live godly lives?*
7. *Does the church ever bring in top-notch teachers who address key doctrines or major subjects?*
8. *Do people have a reason to bring their Bibles to the church services?*

Chapter 17 Endnotes

[1] One of the best books on leadership unity and focusing on the important issues is Larry W. Osborne's *The Unity Factor: Getting Your Church Leaders to Work Together* (Dallas: Word Publishing, co-published with *Christianity Today,* 1989).

[2] Two excellent books on shepherds, written by Phillip Keller, a preacher who was a world-class shepherd: *A Shepherd Looks at Psalm 23* (Grand Rapids: Zondervan, 1970) and *A Shepherd Looks at The Good Shepherd and His Sheep* (Grand Rapids: Zondervan, 1978). When pastoring, I frequently reviewed Keller's principles as applied to local church operation.

[3] W. E. Vine, *Expository Dictionary of New Testament Words,* p. 167, says of *poimen:* "a shepherd, one who tends herds or flocks (not merely one who feeds them)...Pastors guide as well as feed the flock...this involves tender care and vigilant and superintendence."

[4] John C. Maxwell gives an amusing but serious illustration in *The 21 Irrefutable Laws of Leadership,* Chapter 5, "The Law of E. F. Hutton: When the Real Leader Speaks, People Listen." After graduating from college at 22, John went to pastor his first church in rural Indiana. The average age in the church was about fifty. Assuming that he was the appointed leader he opened his first meeting, quickly finding that "Claude" was actually the untitled leader of the board. He realized that any of his suggestions must first pass with Claude. When he accepted this, he was amazed to see how quickly the board OK'd everything. A week before the next board meeting, John went to see Claude and asked his opinion about a series of things that needed to be done. When the board met, everything passed easily, with Claude's spoken approval. Maxwell advises:

You're a leader only if you have followers, and that always requires the development of relationships — the deeper the relationships, the stronger the potential for leadership. Each time I entered a new leadership position, I immediately started building relationships. Build enough of the right kinds of relationships with the right people, and you can become the real leader in an organization. P. 50.

Chapter 18
Women in Apostolic Ministry

In This Chapter

- *The amazing roll call of women in Scripture*
- *Seven approaches to women ministry. Which is right?*
- *The Church's "Magna Carta" verse on freedom*
- *The success secret of the world's largest church*

This chapter is about releasing and recognizing women to serve in whatever function God has called them. Leading churches in the world successfully utilize women in leadership -- and their loyal stewardship is legendary. *A wise church does not dismiss or ignore 50% of the workforce!*

This study does *not* show that apostleship – or any other leadership ministry -- is open to just anybody who is interested, man or woman. The question is not one of discrimination, favoritism or gender. Apostles do not commission themselves, and neither does any other ministry in the body of Christ. God chooses and calls us all, individually, for whatever ministry.

The Role of Women

From the beginning of time, God has ordained that both men and women bear the responsibility of living and procreating. God said in Genesis 2:18 that the first woman was created to be a helpful companion to the first man created.

Notable Women in the Old Testament		
Reference	**Name**	**Description**
Genesis 3:20	Eve	Adam's wife, and the mother of all living
Genesis 11:29; 17:15-16; Hebrews 11:11	Sarah	Abraham's wife, the mother of faith
Genesis 16:1-16;	Hagar	Maidservant of Sarah, the mother of

21:9-21;25:12-16; Galatians 4:21-31		Ishmael
Genesis 24:58-67	Rebecca	Wife of Issac
Genesis 29:21-25	Leah	Jacob's first wife
Genesis 29:28	Rachel	Jacob's second wife
Genesis38:26; Matthew 1:3	Tamar	A righteous woman
Exodus 1:15	Puah	Israelite midwife
Exodus 2:21	Zipporah	Moses' wife
Exodus 6:20	Jochebed	Moses' mother
Exodus 15:20-21	Miriam	Moses' sister, prophetess and musician in Israel
Exodus 38:8, NIV 1 Samuel 2:22	Servants of the Tabernacle	"assembled at the door of the tabernacle of the congregation." Heb. Wd. For "assembled" (*tsaba*) can mean "to serve it, perform, wait on"
Numbers 6:2-27	Nazarite Women	Separated unto God for sacred purposes & ministry to the Lord
Numbers 27:7	Daughters of Zelophehad	Claimed an inheritance from Moses reserved for men
Joshua 2:1-3; 12-21; Hebrews 11:31	Rahab	Woman of faith who saved the spies and her household
Judges 4:4-9	Deborah	An authority figure, a prophetess & judge. Appointed Barak as general & prophesied his victory
Judges4:12-22; 5:6,24-31	Jael	Assassinated Sisera, & was highly commended
Judges 9:52-54	A Certain Woman	Dropped a millstone on Abimelech's head
Judges 11:34-40	Jephthah's Daughter	Sacrificed to keep her father's vow
Ruth 1-4	Ruth	The Moabitess who married Boaz
1 Samuel 1-2	Hannah	The praying mother of Samuel
1 Samuel 25:3; 23-35	Abigail	Woman of great wisdom that spared David's judgment and became his wife
2 Samuel 11:2-27; 12:1-25	Bathsheba	Wife of Uriah, then wife of David. Mother of King Solomon
2 Samuel 14:2-19	The Wise Woman	Of Tekoa, intervened for Absalom to David
2 Samuel 20:15-22	Another wise woman	Delivered her city

1 Kings 4:8-37; 8:1-6	Shunammite Mother	Miracle birth of a son; son raised from dead
1 Kings 10:1-13	The Queen of Sheba	Came to honor King Solomon
1 Kings 17:8-14; Luke 4:25-26	Widow of Zarephath	Helped Elijah and received provision and her "dead raised to life again"
2 Kings 22:14; 2Chronicles 34:22	Huldah	A prophetess who advised Hilkiah & King Josiah when they sought her out
Esther 4:14	Esther	The queen who saved a nation
Job 42	Daughters of Job	Famous throughout the land
Psalms 68:11-12	Great company of women	Published good news and divided the spoil
Proverbs 1:20; 7:4; 9:1-6	Wisdom	Wisdom is personified as a woman
Proverbs 31	The Virtuous Woman	A description of her fine qualities
Isaiah 8:3, 18	"The Prophetess"	Wife of Isaiah, who bore two sons for signs and wonders in Israel.

Humankind has proceeded to develop into families, communities, and nations, filling all the earth. The people of God, the Church, are male and female.

In the community of Israel the best of family structures evolved, and women were an honored part of that community. Both Israelite men and women also functioned in the larger society outside the home, but the woman particularly devoted herself to the welfare of home and family. This has also been true during the Christian era.

Women of the Old Testament

Men did occupy a more prominent place in the Old Testament record, but an Israelite woman in that time was in a much better position than her counterparts in heathen nations. She was honored, respected, often working closely with her husband (note Proverbs 31). Sometimes God raised up women as judges and prophets to guide Israel (as Miriam, Deborrah, Huldah), but women were not priests or kings. Esther the Jewess was used as queen in Babylon to save the Jewish people. Notice how the prophetic blessings on the offspring given to Sarah (Genesis 17:15-

16) and Rebekah (Genesis 24:10) were on a par with those given to their husbands.

Women with Jesus

Jesus elevated women to a higher status than that experienced in any other society, treating them with a courtesy they had never known before. That policy continued in Christian circles. The following chart lists about two-dozen women. Some of them were disciples simply because of the love, compassion, joy and the welcoming message that Jesus shared; some had been miraculously healed or delivered from demons. Women knew that they were not just tolerated, but rather they felt the genuine concern that made the message of the kingdom of God so real and vital. Jesus healed, forgave, encouraged and made no personal discrimination concerning a woman's acceptability before God.

Jackie Pullinger: Chasing the Dragon

In her book, *Chasing the Dragon,* Jackie Pullinger tells of being called by God to Hong Kong to work among the prostitutes and drug addicts living in the notorious walled city. Though fearful for her own safety, daily she would try to make contact with people who lived in some of the worst conditions one could imagine, but after six months little had been achieved and despair set in.

She agonized, "If God has called me to be here why aren't people responding?" One morning she realized she's been telling people of God's love, and that Jesus loves them and wants to forgive them, but she'd not been loving them in any practical way. The next three months she spent, "soaking herself in scripture and prayer – and being drenched by the Holy Spirit!"

Her new and very practical approach yielded a remarkable response. Providing food, shelter and healthcare, visiting prisons and speaking up for victims; these became the ingredients of her everyday life. This approach so transformed her situation, that even the drug barons watched out for her safety. She's still there after 41 years, and so is the church that grew from her work. The "Walls" of the city were finally torn down ten years ago.

Her call: "My mission was to help the walled city people to understand who Christ was. If they could not understand the words about Jesus, then we Christians should show them what He was like by the way we lived. I remembered He had said, 'If someone forces you to go one mile, go with him two miles.' So this was the beginning of what I called 'walking the extra mile.'

There seemed to be a lot of Christians who did not mind walking one, not many who could be bothered to walk two, and no one who wanted to walk three. Those in need that I met seemed to need a marathon."[1]

When the large crowds gathered, ailing women were healed as readily as men. Women sat and listened on the hillsides with the men and felt no discrimination (as in the synagogues). Suddenly women had a purpose in living! The disciples carried bread and fish in baskets to feed the multitudes, and the women shared equally.

A woman disciple was not chosen to be part of the Twelve Apostles because of the social stigma attached in Jewish culture and the immediate demands made; they were, however, just as dedicated in serving Jesus and His cause as the men were. Jesus apparently did not take offerings, but the support of the Twelve and His additional disciples was sustained by the generous donations of wealthy women (see references below).

Jesus had a sense of orderliness and efficiency as well as the ability to do miracles. When the 5,000 + people were hungry, Jesus had the disciples seat the people in groups of fifty so the Twelve could efficiently distribute the bread and fish (Luke 9:14) *to all without discrimination.*

Luke records that Jesus not only sent out the Twelve, but on at least one occasion, the group swelled to 70 evangelists.

the Lord appointed seventy others also, and sent [*apostello*] them two by two before His face into every city and place where He Himself was about to go" (Luke 10:1).

The entourage traveling with Jesus included women who served the needs of the team and did personal work with the needy. In addition to the neophyte apostles, the total group at various times must have included servants, guards, food handlers, crowd controllers, messengers (no cell phones!), and children. They would often camp out for the night on the ground (there were no adequate motels!), cooking their meals. The Galilean crusade reached all the cities, so Jesus and followers were on the move ministering in synagogues, open fields, and in homes. These two references give some idea of the women's participation (emphasis added).

> Luke 8:1-3. Now it came to pass, afterward, that He went through every city and village, preaching and bringing the glad tidings of the kingdom of God. And the twelve were with Him, and *certain women who had been healed of evil spirits and infirmities* – Mary called Magdalene, out of whom had come seven demons, and Joanna the wife of Chuza, Herod's steward, and Susanna, *and many others who provided for Him from their substance.*

> Matthew 15:40-41. There were also women looking on from afar, among whom were Mary Magdalene, Mary the mother of James the Less and of Joses, and Salome, *who also followed Him and ministered to Him when He was in Galilee; and many other women who came up with Him to Jerusalem.*

Notable Women in the Gospels		
Reference	Name	Description
Matthew 1:20-21 Luke 1 & 2	Mary	The Virgin Mary, mother of Jesus. Occupied an esteemed position in the church.
Matthew 9:20-22	Hemorrhaging Woman	She touched the hem of His garment!
Matthew15:22-28	Syro-Phoenician Woman	Prevailed on Jesus for her daughter.
Matthew 16:9; 27:56- 61; Mark 16:9; Luke 8:2	Mary Magdalene	Healed of demons; follower and helper of Jesus; first to see the resurrected Jesus.
Matthew 20:20-24	Salome	Mother of James and John.
Matthew 27:55-56; Mark 15:40-41; Luke 23:49, 55	Women at the Cross	Women followed Jesus when the men had forsaken Him.
Matthew 28:8, 10	The Two Marys	The first to "go tell" of His resurrection
Mark 1:30	Peter's Mother-in-law	Healed of a fever, she served Jesus.
Luke 7:36-39	A Sinful Woman	Washed the feet of Jesus
Luke 1:5, 13	Elizabeth	Mother of John the Baptist
Luke 2:36-38	Anna	Elderly prophetess, first to proclaim Jesus after His dedication

Luke 7:12-15	The Widow of Nain	Jesus raised her son from the dead
Luke 8:3; Matthew 15:40; 27:55	Many Women Disciples (as, Joanna & Susanna)	Ministered of their time and money, two mothers whose sons were apostles
Luke 10:38-42	Mary and Martha	Friends of Jesus; sisters of Lazarus
Luke 13:11	The Bent-over Woman	Set free from an 18-year old affliction
Luke 21:1-4	The Benevolent Widow	This poor woman gave her all
John 4:4-42	The Samaritan Woman	Convinced by Jesus at the well, she became the first evangelist of Samaria
John 8:3	The Adulterous Woman	Forgiven and urged to sin no more.

How Did Women Function under Paul?

A careful reading of the Acts and Epistles leads to one conclusion: women were a vital part of the workforce of the early Church. Paul, our leading apostolic example, recognized and encouraged the dynamic contribution of women. F. F. Bruce, a leading New Testament scholar, made this appropriate statement:

> The most incredible feature in the Paul of popular mythology is his alleged misogyny [hatred of women]. [Actually] He treated women as persons: we recall his commendation of Phoebe, the deacon of the church in Cenchreae, who had shown herself a helper to him as to many others (Rom 16:1f), or his appreciation of Euodia and Syntyche of Philippi who worked side by side with him in the gospel (Phil 4:2f). The mainstream churches of Christendom, as they inch along towards a worthier recognition of the ministry of women, have some way to go yet before they come abreast of Paul." (footnote 8: "Even if he asks them to keep their heads veiled when praying or prophesying, the veil is the sign of their authority to play a responsible part in church life.")[2]

Women in All Major Activities

We must not downplay women's equal opportunity to become Christians *and also* active participants in the local churches. The Gospel of God that Paul proclaimed (our Magna Carta) had an astounding open-door policy for anyone who wished to come and take part (Galatians 3:26-28, emphasis added):

For you are all sons of God through faith in Christ Jesus. For as many of you as were baptized into Christ have put on Christ. There is neither Jew nor Greek, there is neither slave nor free, there is *neither male nor female*; for you are all one in Christ Jesus.

Women heard and responded to the Gospel just as men did, perhaps even more readily! Their joyful reception of God's Word was communicated with great zeal throughout the communities of that day. The Scripture was literally being fulfilled: "The Lord gives the word [of power]; the women who bear *and* publish (the news) are a great host" (Psalm 68:11, AMP).

Consider Women's Participation

Women did share and perform ministry in the early churches; their commanded "silence" referred to appropriate behavior, not the silencing of all public utterance in the assemblies (see Appendix B).

1. Men and women prayed together to receive the Spirit on Pentecost, Acts 1 & 2.
2. Multitudes of "both men and women" were added to the Lord, 5:14. It is significant that women are mentioned.
3. Women believers, considered a threat by Saul the persecutor, received the same harsh treatment as men, 8:3; 9:2; 22:4-5. This indicates that women were a strong force in the growth of Christianity.

Notable Women in Acts and Epistles		
Acts 1:13-15	Women at Pentecost	Prayed with the men
Acts 2:3-4	" " "	Spoke in tongues & prophesied
Acts 5:1	Sapphira	Lied to Peter and the Holy Spirit
Acts 5:14	"Multitudes of both men & women"	Added to the Lord in the early Church
Acts 8:3: 9:2; 22:4-5	Men & Women Believers	Saul imprisoned both men and women (considered equally dangerous)
Acts 8:12	Men & Women	Baptized by Philip the evangelist
Acts 9:36-42	Dorcas (Tabitha)	Woman of great influence; helped others; first person raised from the

		dead in early Church.
Acts 12:6-17	Mary, mother of John Mark	The church which met in her home prayerfully executed Peter's release
Acts 12:13-15	Rhoda	Girl at the prayer meeting at Mary's house
Acts 16:1-3; 2 Timothy1:5;3:14-15	Lois and Eunice	Mother and grandmother of Timothy, highly regarded by Paul
Acts 16:14, 15	Lydia & Women	Paul's first converts in Europe (Philippi)
Acts 17:4	Leading Women	Responded to Paul's preaching in Thessalonica
Acts 17:12	Leading Women	Devout Greeks who joined Paul and Silas in Berea
Acts 17:34	Damaris	A Woman of Athens who believed Paul and joined his group
Acts 18:1-3; 18, 26; Romans 16:3; 1 Corinthians 16:19; 2 Timothy 4:19	Priscilla	Worked with husband in Ephesus; a "sunergos" (co-laborer, companion in labor, workfellow in Christ Jesus) of Paul
Acts 21:9	Four Virgin Daughters	Of Phillip the evangelist; known for their consistent use of the gift of prophecy
Romans 16:1, 2	Phoebe	"a servant (*diakonos*) of the church which is at Cenchrea." Sent to Rome to preach; "A helper of many"
Romans 16:1, 3, 6, 12, 15	Seven devoted Women: Prisca (Priscilla), Mary, Tryphena, Tryphosa, Persis, Julia, & the sister of Nereus.	Among the 29 people that Paul greeted in this chapter; his fellow workers: Mary "labored much," Tryphena & Tryphosa "labored in the Lord," Persis "labored much in the Lord"
Romans 16:7	Junia	Commended as an apostle. Was a Christian before Paul.
1 Corinthians 1:11	Chloe	Alerted Paul of division in Corinthian Church
1 Corinthians 11:5	Women in Corinth	Prayed & prophesied publicly
Philippians 4:2, 3	Euodias & Synthche	Paul's fellow workers in the Gospel, in leadership at Phillipi
Colossians 4:15	Nymphas	Leader of the church in her home at Colosse

Titus 2:4, 5	Older Women	Told to teach the younger
1 Timothy 5:2	Women Elders, *presbutera*	To be honored as mothers
1 Timothy 5:9	Registered widows	Special ministry for offering assistance[3]
2 Timothy 1:5	Lois and Eunice	Mother and Grandmother of Timothy
2 Timothy 4:21	Claudia	Christian at Rome
Philemon 2	Apphia	Beloved sister in the Lord to Paul & Timothy
2 John 1	Elect Lady	A "house leader" pastor.

4. Philip the evangelist baptized men and women, 8:12.
5. The first person raised from the dead was a woman well-known for her testimony and charitable works, 9:36-42.
6. Women were Paul's first converts in Europe, 16:14-15 the core group that started the church at Philippi.
7. A woman of Athens believed Paul and joined his group, 17:34. This was a challenging step in that society, requiring defiant, aggressive attitude.
8. Leading women in Berea joined Paul and Silas, 17:12.

Consider These Women Leaders

In his *Leadership Bible,* John Maxwell makes this comment about Romans 16:1-21 (emphasis added):

[W}e see the warm, relational approach this tough leader practiced. Note that the first few people Paul greets are women: Phoebe, Priscilla, Mary. *Many pillars of the early church were faithful ladies who ministered and gave strong leadership.* Jesus' life began with a woman named Mary and ended at his resurrection with a woman at the tomb.[4]

1. Priscilla: a "sunergos" (co-laborer and workfellow), 18:1-3, 18, 26; Romans 16:3. Possibly a "marketplace" apostle; see Chapter 7, p. 9.
2. Four Daughters of Philip: known for their gift of prophecy, 21:9. They must have exerted strong influence on the church of Caesarea.

3. Pheobe: a preacher sent to Rome; a servant of the church
    at Cenchrea, and a helper [*prostasis*] of many, Romans
    16:1,2. Patricia Gundry calls attention to the meaning of
    prostasis in this text: "a woman set over others" which
    indicates supervision and high authority.[5]

Let the Little Children Come

The story of Amy Carmichael leaves a person amazed, awe-struck – and
weeping. In a day in which sex-slavery and child prostitution has increased
world-wide, we do well to reflect on one of the greatest lives ever lived. Amy
would never classify herself as an apostle, but she was drawn nevertheless into
an apostolic sphere of ministry which could never have occurred without the
power of the living God working through this dedicated, called-of-God woman.
Other godly people were drawn to help and serve under her leadership in a
cause most important to God.

Amy Carmichael was born December 16, 1867, in Ireland and died January
18, 1951, in Dohnavur, South India. Daily for fifty-five years, Amy laid down her
own life to save abused children in the most appalling of conditions. She said:

> The significance of this work depends upon its background – the
> existence, I mean, of that evil of which the lotus pool may be taken
> as a symbol. The waters of that pool are not clean but mirey; its
> depths are very deep.

The long and painful story of her first years in India are heart-rending and
need to be read on their own. Suffice it here to say that after much investigation
on her part she discovered and verified the sale and gifting of small girls to
become wards of the temples, religious prostitutes even at the age of five. The
stories uncovered and the children discovered by Amy broke her heart, but fired
her determination to save these unfortunate ones. (Fortunately, social reformers –
British, American, Indian alike – fought to bring an end to child prostitution in
India, and a law was passed in 1947 making it illegal to dedicate a child to a
temple.)

The story of Amy's endeavors to find and save these children ("jewels") is
one that every Christian should read. Here is a story that would amaze the
Apostle Paul and that must have thrilled the heart of Jesus. Such great, unsung
apostolic women heroes of Christ's missionary force must surely shine in heaven
as the brightest luminaries of the followers of Jesus.

Read: *Amy Carmichael: Let the Little Children Come* by Lois Hoadley Dick
(Chicago: Moody Press, 1984).

4. Paul's fellow workers: 10 of the 29 people greeted in Romans 16 were apostolic women who had served with Paul in various places, and now were in Rome.
5. Junia: an apostle with commendation, Romans 16:7. See my comment in Chapter 7, pp. 130-131, and also this endnote.[6] If Junia was not an apostle, she was certainly an acknowledged, active leader.
6. Chloe: a concerned worker and confidant of Paul who alerted him to division in the church at Corinth, 1 Corinthians 1:11.
7. Women at Corinth: active church participants who prayed and prophesied, 11:5. Such people are influential, spiritual leaders.
8. Euodias and Synthche: leaders at Philipi, fellow workers, Philippians 4:2, 3.
9. Nymphas: home church leader in Colosse, Colossians 4:15.
10. Older women: to teach the younger, Titus 2:4, 5
11. Claudia: a notable Christian in Rome, 1 Timothy 4:21.
12. Older men and women: treat as fathers and mothers, 1 Timothy 5:2.
13. Lois and Eunice: Grandmother and mother of Timothy, who were so influential in his Christian heritage, 2 Timothy 1:5.

Ministry Options for Women

How proactive should women be in today's churches? Various attitudes and approaches exist, challenging the strong examples of women leaders given in the Scripture.

How Women Are Presently Used in Ministry

1. No ministry is allowed women except teaching children.
2. Allowed to lead a public function is an *exception*, not the rule.
3. *Minor* leadership roles are allowed -- when supervised by men.

4. Women, if under male leadership, may teach men.
5. Permitted to serve as deaconesses, pastors, evangelists and teachers – but not as elders.
6. Women can serve as deacons, pastors, evangelists, elders, and teachers -- but not as apostles.
7. Any position open to men is open to women, but they must qualify just as men do, and they must be subject to supervision, evaluation, and acceptance just as men are. Also, the family role and responsibility must be carefully guarded by husband and family.

Number 7, in my estimation, is the only reasonable, viable option for today's churches. Taking all Bible references into consideration, this approach seems the most logical. A number of studies have been done on this subject, but unfortunately strong disagreement exists and feelings run deep.

Dan Kimball shares this advice on the subject:

> In the emerging culture, the role of women in the church is a huge issue. People in the emerging generations think of churches as male-dominated and oppressive of females. So whatever your theology may be about the role of women in the church, I would still highly encourage you to have females in up-front roles as much as possible, whether it is teaching, giving announcements, leading worship, sharing testimonies, or reading Scripture. This is critical for the emerging church.[7]

A Surprising Secret of the World's Largest Church
By Loren Cunningham[8]

Many have heard of the world's largest church pastored by Dr. Cho Yonggi in Seoul, Korea. Dr. Cho has been a friend for many years. When I first went to Korea thirty years ago his church was a struggling pioneer work of "only" six thousand. Now Dr. Cho has 763,000 members in his church. Much has been written about the phenomenal growth of this church, but one secret has been overlooked. I have Dr. Cho's permission to tell this story.

Thirty years ago, as we were seated in his office, Dr. Cho said, "Loren, I have a problem. My mother-in-law, Mrs. Choi, is an outstanding Bible teacher and preacher. But in our culture, we can't have her teach or preach. What should I do?"

I said, "Put her in your pulpit!"

He cringed. "Loren, as an American, you don't understand what that means to a Korean!"

"Okay, I have an idea. Get my mom over here to preach for you." Dr. Cho knew my folks. When he first went to the United States as a young, unknown preacher, he stayed in my parents' home. Dr. Cho told how my mom, Jewell Cunningham, taught him from the Word of God at the breakfast table.

"Since my mom is from another culture, they'll accept her preaching," I said. "Then as soon as she finishes, put Mrs. Choi in your pulpit. Your people will see the connection. They'll see it isn't a matter of culture but a matter of ministry."

Dr. Cho did invite my mother to preach in his church. Following Mom's visit, Mrs. Choi emerged as an outstanding leader and preacher. She was the first of thousands of women who became ministers under Dr. Cho's leadership. Several years later I saw him at a large event in the Olympic Stadium in Berlin where we were both speaking. He told me about a certain country he had just visited where the work of God has struggled for many years. He said, "All their churches are so little! And all of them are holding back their women, not allowing them to do what God calls them to do. I've told them to release their women, but they insist that's not the problem. They ask me, 'What's the key to your church?' I tell them again, 'Release your women,' but they just don't hear me!"

God has given this man the largest church on earth to pastor. He has seven hundred senior pastors on his staff, including many women. He also has thirty thousand cell groups; the vast majority of these are led by women. Do you think God might be trying to tell all of us something?

Women with Families and the Ministry

A woman called to lead and minister must balance this calling with a strong home life. This requires an understanding and sympathetic husband and children. It requires family team effort, and also a husband that is not jealous of his wife's gifting.

One of the most esteemed woman ministers in our day is Joyce Myers whose ministry in home crusades, overseas ministry, TV and publishing projects are well known. Joyce herself admits that without her husband and children's cooperation she wouldn't be able to accomplish what she is doing.

Many homes these days require two incomes to make it, so often the mother has full-time or part-time employment as well as the husband. A woman should not be criticized for her gospel service but encouraged in every way possible. In the home, there should be unity in every decision, but if there is a disagreement (and if there has been much prayer and thought), the man must exercise his God-given authority wisely and carefully lead in a united decision. A husband's home authority should not be violated by the woman's church ministry, but unity and cooperation must reign or the woman's ministry will become impossible. The principles of Ephesians 5:21-25 must not be violated.

Can a Woman Be an Apostle?

Although an increasing trend in churches is to accept women as pastors, apostleship seems to be an entirely different question. A difference of opinion exists, even among those who believe that women can be prophets, evangelists, pastors and teachers (an interesting twist is that sometimes women are accepted as pastors, but not as elders).

Two key thoughts must be addressed on feminine apostleship. First, is there anything in the Scripture that forbids a woman to be an apostle? Second, if no biblical argument exists, would God actually call a woman to apostleship?

No Member of the Twelve Was a Woman

The primary argument is easily made that Jesus chose only men to be the original Twelve Apostles; and, therefore, any additional apostles would also need to be men.

This is *very shallow* thinking. What seems to be a strong argument against women apostles, actually falls apart upon examination. A syllogism would state it like this:

> *Jesus chose Twelve Apostles.*
> *Those twelve apostles were men.*
> Therefore, any additional apostles must be men.

The syllogism is faulty, because it assumes certain information! First, Jesus chose not just any men. They were young men, Jewish men, and all but Judas came from Galilee. They were called to do *a specific task at a specific time;* only a few disciples could meet the qualifications. Paul, James and Barnabas would not have qualified, because the original Twelve were required to have associated with Jesus' ministry from His baptism until the Ascension. The Twelve were heavily involved with Jesus' ministry as the Jewish Messiah to the nation of Israel.

The above syllogism assumes that Jesus had only Twelve apostles, and no additional apostles – Jew or Gentile -- were called after the Ascension. Paul taught that there would be more apostles (1 Corinthians 12:28; Ephesians 2:20; 3:5) called after the Ascension (Ephesians 4:11). These new apostles would not qualify or function entirely like the first Twelve: they would not necessarily be Jewish, young men or those who had been present to observe Jesus' earthly ministry.

James D. G. Dunn correctly points out that the Twelve were ordained for the universal Church, Paul and others to specific spheres of mission:

> [Paul] was not an apostle of the universal Church, one whose authority would be recognized by all churches [at that time]. His authority was confined to his sphere of mission....[9]

Revelation 21:14 says that the 12 foundations of the walls of the New Jerusalem had the names of the Twelve Apostles written on them, thereby indicating that the original Twelve were foundational to the Universal Church. Certainly true, but does not justify the belief in *only* Twelve Apostles, which cancels any additional apostles to the nations of the world.

The Importance of a Call

One does not simply decide to be an apostle – regardless of gender! This is not a vocational choice or a matter of social discrimination. *A divine call initiates this ministry: apostleship is a gift of Christ to His church.* A talented successful male minister is not automatically a candidate for apostleship, and neither is a woman with matching talents. Men or women, not so talented, might have the right emotional, mental and spiritual aptitudes that would be a delightful gift of the Lord to His people.

A comparatively small percentage of men and women are called to apostleship, so we cannot argue that the gate is now open for *any* men or women who want the job. Our argument is simply that a man or woman is called by God to fulfill any ministry that Jesus so selects. Please remember my section in chapter 14, pp. 242-244, on 'How Can Modern Apostles Be Acknowledged?' Also, as said previously, *every* Christian should be apostolic, even if he/she is not an apostle.

Chapter 18 Endnotes

[1] Jackie Pullinger, *Chasing the Dragon* (Servant Books: 1980), p. 53.

[2] F. F. Bruce, *Paul Apostle of the Heart Set Free,* p. 456.

[3] The Message

[4] John C. Maxwell, ex. Ed., *The Maxwell Leadership Bible*, p. 1386.

[5] Patricia Gundry, *Woman Be Free!* (Grand Rapids: Zondervan, 1977), p. 102.

[6] Although there is disagreement among some scholars about the gender of Junia in the Greek text, John Chrysostom (337-407), bishop of Constantinople, and Origen of Alexandria (c. 185-253) both believed Julia to be a woman. Leonard Swidler cites Jerome (340-419) and others as concurring. *Biblical Affirmations of Women* (Philadelphia: Westminster Press, 1979), p. 299. Swidler states: "To the best of my knowledge, no commentator on the text until Aegidus of Rome (1245-1316) took the name to be masculine."

[7] Dan Kimball, *The Emerging Church,* p. 158.

[8] Cunningham, Loren and David Joel Hamilton with Janice Rogers, *Why Not Women?* (Seattle, WA: YWAM Publishing, 2000), pp. 67-68. Used by Permission.

[9] Dunn, *Unity,* p. 111.

Appendices

Appendix A – Use "Apostle" Appropriately

Appendix B – Should Women Be Silent in Church?

Appendix C – Apostolic Team Ministry

Appendix A
Use "Apostle" Appropriately

The title "apostle" should be used, because apostles did exist, exist today and more are yet to come. Although in greater use, "Apostle" as a title is not commonly used today. Sometimes it is used inappropriately and sometimes misappropriated. "When is it appropriate to use?" The subject merits attention.

Three Views

Three views about the use of "apostle" exist among those believing in contemporary apostles.

1) Some feel the term lofty, super-spiritual and lacking in humility; great care is taken, therefore, not to directly grace a qualified person with such a grand title; this approach allows referencing a qualified person as an apostle, but not in direct communication.

2) Some claim the title, demanding to be addressed as "Apostle so-and-so," seemingly concerned their authority or position will be overlooked. Of course, when referred to publicly, they feel the term "apostle" should always be attached to the person's name.

3) Some choose a moderate approach, choosing to recognize the title as appropriate when it is done without ostentation or when it would not make an uncomfortable situation. This recognition would be justified if a person is so acknowledged by the religious fellowship to which that person belongs.

A scriptural use of the title should be possible -- one that humbly acknowledges position without promoting pompous pride or over-riding the opinion of others. The apostles of Bible days (our best examples) taught and practiced the humility of Jesus, yet were recognized as *bona fide* apostles.

Thankfully many ministers today model this balance. Using, claiming or deserving the title "apostle," should result from a proven track record and solid endorsement from a legitimate church fellowship. God calls apostles, but people verify that calling.

Do Apostles Actually Need Recognition and Affirmation?

Some leaders feel that "recognition and affirmation must begin with the apostles themselves."[1] Functioning as a duly recognized apostle, a person must claim and use the title. This openness to use the title supposedly enables the apostolic movement "to gain and sustain its vitality" -- which in turn causes the teaching to be credible to the Church at large.

A strong argument is used that "pastor" as we know it only emerged after the Protestant Reformation, and "evangelist" was not recognized until the time of Charles Finney. Since it took time for these terms to be used comfortably, the term "apostle," being newly used, will take time for acceptance as well. "We should not be surprised, therefore, if some choose to argue against the contemporary office of apostle."[2]

The present emphasis on recognizing apostles and prophets can be beneficial. This is a time of divine restoration, and the implementation of the Ephesians 4 ministries is an important key. Our desire, however, should be more than the publicizing of another renewal movement. We need to restore a biblical concept that has been in consideration for a number of years, a belief that should be a solid part of Christian ecclesiology.

The Importance of a Title

A successful person knows his/her job assignment and the title or designation attached to it. A title identifies a position, responsibility or function and is understood by associates and customers. A title is not *always* used (certainly not flaunted) except in more formal situations or when a task requires it. Friends may respect a person's title, but not necessarily use it.

An illustration would be my personal CT scan. Since I had not experienced this procedure, I was a little nervous, wondering about the man and woman in the hospital room. Both wore badges, but it was comforting to have the woman give her name and nursing position; the man introduced himself as the technician that operated the machine. A doctor came into the room, introducing himself as "doctor so-and-so," the head of that department. After introductions, titles were not mentioned: I was just happy to know they were competent! The titles confirmed years of preparation and experience, but were not needed in personal conversation.

Public Acceptance

A person functions best with public acceptance and recognition of his/her job position. Group confidence increases as fellow workmen observe that the requirements connected with the title are being met, especially if the person is a manager. High school basketball players don't mind calling their teacher "coach" when real leadership is given. Good leaders inspire confidence.

Religious titles are more challenging, because the function takes on a spiritual dimension of honor, power and respect that can be misunderstood or misused. Such titles can assume an unchallengeable status that defies any form of correction or suggestion. Leaders must remember: "Absolute power corrupts absolutely." Jesus taught His disciples to be servant-leaders.

Mark Sanborn's book *You Don't Need a Title to Be a Leader* gives inspiring examples of title-less leaders in the secular world. He says, "little actual power exists in a title alone….a title is not a job description….influence and inspiration comes from the person, not the position."[3] Group confidence confirms a job title; a person's ability to perform secures the necessary recognition and acceptance.

John Maxwell says, "Leadership is positive influence," and this can be present with or without a title; usually, however, a title goes with the flow of dynamic leadership and can be inabtrusively worn, like a well-fitting suit. Lynn Anderson says: "Trust is *earned,* not demanded, and it is built *over time.*"[4]

Authority Invested in a Title

A person needs respect for personhood and accomplishment. A title confirms and compliments the quality of the life that bears it. Authority is invested in a title, and hopefully the title commands the respect needed from the followers. Consider the policeman's badge. Only a person with the goods to back up the claim can use the authority of a title or badge.

Christians appreciate a title clothed in humility. Those with "apostle" on a fancy T-shirt or on slick business cards will soon lose respect. Anderson says: "The authority of an elder grows, not out of a title emblazoned across a church letterhead, but out of the quality of the elder's life."[5] Paul's defense of his apostleship to the Corinthians is a classic expression of both humility and authority (2 Corinthians 10 and 11).

It really is not necessary for a person to demand the use of "Apostle," correspondingly it is not necessary for others to show distain or disrespect for a title used in a discreet and appropriate way. Perhaps this is why the New Testament records "Paul, the apostle" rather than "the Apostle Paul."

Jesus' Attitude about His Titles

Jesus bore leadership titles graciously without flaunting them. Sometimes called "teacher" and "Lord," He calmly replied, "...and so I am" (John 13:13-14). He was not ashamed to own his position and titles. He walked the walk and lived the life. The titles came naturally, and were used honestly by people who had viewed His qualifications.

Jesus actually referred to Himself as "Lord" (Matthew 21:3; Mark 11:3; Luke 19:31) and called Himself "the Teacher" (Matthew 26:18; Mark 14:14); He acknowledged to Pilate that He was "King of the Jews" (Matthew 27:11).

Jesus visited Nazareth, His hometown, and spoke in the synagogue jam-packed with excited, curious friends and relatives who came to see what He would say and do. He read the well-known Messianic text in Isaiah 61, a popular portion that had been read many times in every synagogue. Naturally, the Jewish listeners longed for that day when the Messiah would fulfill these words of Isaiah. What would the carpenter-turned-Rabbi say?

Jesus quickly ended speculation by declaring: "This Scripture has come true today before your very eyes!" (Luke 4:21, NLT). In other words, "I am the Messiah!" The Message says:

> Every eye in the place was on him, intent. Then he started in. "You've just heard Scripture make history. It came true just now in this place."

This was probably a typical "synagogue sermon" (i.e., given in a variety of places,[6] perhaps every synagogue visited). Jesus boldly declared His ministry, title and intentions throughout the land -- but done in appropriate settings and backed with observable credentials. His humble but assured manner was in stark contrast to the ostentatious manner of the religious leaders.

During Jesus' last day of teaching in the Temple (just before His crucifixion), the religious authorities challenged His claim to Messiahship (Luke 20). Jesus calmly drew attention to the more basic question: what is real, spiritual authority (using John the Baptist as an example)? The question disoriented His opponents, and His humility and title remained intact.

Jesus' Advice about Titles

A superficial reading of the Gospels gives the impression that Christian leaders should not use titles, but solid references disprove this.[7] Actually, *hypocrisy* was the real issue of Jesus' concern. In Luke 12:1, for instance, He referred to "the leaven of the Pharisees" (Luke 12:21) by which he meant hypocrisy, the trait of pretending to be something one is not.

Confrontation

In Matthew 23:1-12, Jesus seemed to place a taboo on three common titles: Rabbi, father and teacher. Actually, Jesus was not against these titles *per se,* but rather the flagrant manner in which these titles were *called out* and flaunted publicly -- making the common folk look insignificant. This deplorable habit often occurred in the synagogues *in front of the congregants* just before services began. How Jesus loathed such hypocrisy.

> *...do not do according to their works....*all their works they do to be seen by men....They love the best places at feasts...greetings in the marketplaces, and to be called by men, 'Rabbi, Rabbi.' ... *he who is greatest among you shall be your servant. An whoever exalts himself will be abased, and he who humbles himself will be exalted* (vss. 3-12, emphasis added).

Jesus' Emphasis on Humility

Jesus once observed how people chose the best places, so he gave a parable about "The Ambitious Guest." He advised taking a seat at the lowest position, and then possibly the host might invite to a better position. "For whoever exalts himself will be abased, and he who humbles himself will be exalted" (Luke 14:7-14).

Let us not become modern Pharisees – ostentatious, proud, foolish – flaunting religious titles to gain self-glory, trying to impress those of supposedly lower spirituality.

The appropriate use of titles, when couched in the attitude of humility and service, is both powerful and impressive.

Opinions about Using the Title "Apostle"

Because of differing opinions about the use of "apostle," it seems appropriate to share some thoughts by well-known ministers active in today's spiritual renewal.

Eddie L. Hyatt: "At no place in the New Testament is 'apostle' placed in front of someone's name as a title....Paul refers to himself numerous times...always by his name, 'Paul.' ... In Acts, Luke mentions Paul by name more than 120 times and not once does he say 'Apostle Paul,' but merely 'Paul.'"[8]

Bill Hamon: "If the title is not relevant then why do pastors call themselves pastors? ... When you receive a prophet in the name of a prophet, you get a prophet's reward...God has respect for positions....We are all on the same level with Christ but there are positions of honor and respect...and that doesn't make one greater than another it's just positions."[9]

Jack Hayford: "[I]n successive efforts at 'renewal' of the New Testament apostolic office, an exaggeration of authority has repeatedly done damage to otherwise valid awakenings….I have no particular opposition to people who feel it is important to use the title, but I confess—I don't believe the title is that important. What is important is that each apostle…functions in the spirit that Jesus demonstrated by His apostleship."[10]

David Cannistraci*:* "To escape the discomfort of the actual term 'apostle,' have we arbitrarily retired it and replaced it with the more sanitary title of 'missionary' (a term not found in Scripture)? It is hard to understand why we are so inconsistent….Why then has it been so hard for us to clarify the subject of apostleship and to see it exercised and implemented…."[11]

Larry Keefauver*:* "What we don't need is self-promoting, titled grandstanders who seek media limelight and financial gain from positions named and claimed. What we do need is to esteem the humble, holy examples set by sacrificial servants of the lord who faithfully follow Paul's example [1 Cor. 11:1]…in being called by Christ as an apostle and sent out to pioneer…."[12]

Doug Beacham*:* "The opposite of the reluctance to recognize apostles and prophets is the tendency…to insist that they be called by such titles. If the body can find a way to recognize and affirm such gifts … then our …attitudes are molded by the humility that comes when we realize others have affirmed something …that God has given rather than …having to toot our own horns."[13]

C. Peter Wagner: "I believe that the biblical *office* of apostle carries a dimension of power with it that the *function* alone cannot attain."[14] "I am not sure I agree that the use of the title 'apostle' should be considered optional in this day and age….Let us overcome our inhibitions and take our lead from role models such as Paul and Peter who begin epistles with "Paul, an apostle of Jesus Christ" or "Peter, an apostle of Jesus Christ."[15]

Wayne Grudem: "If any in modern times want to take the title of 'apostle' to themselves, they immediately raise the suspicion that they may be motivated by inappropriate pride and desires for self-exaltation, along with excessive ambition and a desire to much more authority in the Church than any one person should rightfully have."[16]

David Cartledge (Australian Assemblies of God): "The restoration of apostolic and prophetic gifts has stirred controversy about the way these ministries are to be addressed and recognized…. Almost all Australian apostolic ministries are quite emphatic that they will not use the title 'apostle'. While they are usually recognized … as apostles and are frequently referred to as such by the churches they visit I do not know of one who personally uses 'apostle' as his or her personal title. In fact most…prefer to be known by their first name."[17]

Marcus Yoars (editor of *Ministry Today*): "God has not called us to lead so that we can glory in what precedes or follows our names, but so we can stoop lower than others to serve them."[18]

Conclusion and Personal Opinion

The following principle has good application to our discussion: *"The Law of Unintended Consequences."* This means: "When we change things, we cannot easily predict the ramifications."

Today's Church is undergoing many changes, and already some changes have had unintended consequences, both good and bad. The worldwide Church is coming alive with new possibilities and problems.

Apostolic authority is gaining such widespread hearing and response that many are claiming that a major reformation of the Church is underway. This is good news if the reformation includes apostles and prophets that are biblically grounded enough to lay true foundations for today's generation. Used improperly, the title "apostle" can generate far-reaching, unforeseen, *unintended* affects.

The idea of modern apostles came to the forefront in the United States during the 1990s. The subject of apostles, however, has been given serious consideration for some 175 years (that I know of) among various charismatic groups. It would be a shame if the unbridled use of "apostle" would now discourage many well-meaning and otherwise interested people.

My Biggest Concern

"Unintended consequences" could result from widespread, inappropriate use of "apostle." Perhaps these suggestions might be helpful:

1. We lead by serving ("service leadership"). Every leader must keep in mind -- before any title -- that we are all "prisoners of the Lord" and "servants of God" and the people.

2. Any call from God will mature gradually during a time of ministry development. A title, properly used, is appropriate when that ministry has been proven before one's home church and bestowed by ministry associates. If deacons must be first "proven"

or "tested" (1 Timothy 3:10), how much more the apostles! A person who demands a hearing or entitlement without proof is dead wrong. A person with a ministry will find that the friends in the church, the family and one's spiritual leaders are not blind and deaf to spiritual calling. Their confirmation is essential.

3. In conferences and conventions it seems appropriate that a visiting speaker with a known ministry be recognized for his/her position. I would, however, suggest we refrain from announcing people by using "apostle" as a title in front of the name. Such as, "Apostle Jim Jones," or "Prophet Phil Smith."

More in keeping with the spirit of ministry would be something like: "Jim Jones is an apostle, and we are delighted that he is here. Jim, please make yourself at home among us!"

An apostle may be approved by some, but not outside his/her area of jurisdiction; when addressing the whole world, it would seem that *some* restraint is in order. Isn't it logical to concentrate on the identification of that person's sphere of influence, their proven record and perhaps a demonstration of what they have to offer? Personally, I like to know what a person's ministry sphere is – and honestly I like to hear them called by their first names (I don't find this distracting).

4. Let us not be too quick to dispense with the title "Pastor." Actually, all fivefold ministries (Ephesians 4:11) function best when based on a shepherd's heart. Of all the religious titles used, "pastor" seems the least threatening to people, the one that conveys humility, the one that expresses a loving relationship. "Pastor" means shepherd, and this is an appropriate, complimentary, endearing, non-intimidating, comfortable title for use. The word avoids undue exaltation, and helps us maintain better balance.

5. Anderson says: "A church leader who has to *assert* his authority doesn't have much." Most parents realize that when they resort to the words, "Because I said so," they have already lost this relational round with their child.[19]

Let others confirm your title. Like a tree, you will produce the observable fruit that you have to offer. Younger brethren in Nigeria honored me with the flattering title: "grandfather," and that has been my personal favorite.

Appendix A Endnotes

[1] C. Peter Wagner, *Apostles and Prophets* (Ventura, CA: Regal, 2000), p. 61.

[2] Ibid, p. 63.

[3] Mark Sanborn, *You Don't Need a Title to be a Leader* (NY: Doubleday, 2006), pp.5,6,7.

[4] Lynn Anderson, *They Smell Like Sheep* (West Monroe, LA: Howard Publishing Co., 1997), p. 25.

[5] Ibid, p. 128.

[6] I. Howard Marshall, *New International Greek Testament Commentary*, p. 180.

[7] For instance, these examples show that the early Church did use the titles of Apostle, Prophet, Evangelist, Pastor, Elder and Teacher: Acts 13:1; 14:14, 23; 21:8; Ephesians 2:20; 3:5; 4:11.

[8] Eddie Hyatt, article on *Apostles: 5 Popular Misconceptions in the Church Today* (Ft. Worth, TX: Hyatt International Ministries).

[9] Bill Hamon, *The Voice,* Vol. III, Issue 2 (April 2006): pp. 41-42.

[10] Jack Hayford, "The Apostolic 'Right Stuff,'" *Ministries Today* (Nov/Dec 2004): 96, 98, 97.

[11] David Cannistraci, *Apostles*, p. 78.

[12] Larry Keefauver, "Acts of the Apostles," *Ministries Today* (Nov/Dec 2004): 84.

[13] Doug Beacham, *The Vision* (Vol. 2, Issue 1): 10, 11.

[14] C. Peter Wagner, Forward, John Eckhardt, *Moving in the Apostolic* (Ventura, CA: Regal, 1999), p. 15.

[15] Wagner, *Apostles and Prophets*, p. 62.

[16] Wayne Grudem, *Systematic Theology* (Grand Rapids: Zondervan, 1994), p. 911.

[17] David Cartledge, *The Apostolic Revolution,* Chapter 56, "No Need for Titles Down Under."

[18] Marcus Yoars, "The Charismatic Name Game," *Ministry Today* (November/December, 2009): 10.

[19] Anderson, pp. 33-34.

Appendix B
Should Women Be Silent in the Church?

Two texts are frequently quoted in discrediting women's participation and leadership in church work, both mentioning women being "silent." The two references at first seem very restrictive – and yet all Scriptural and historical evidence indicates that women actively participated in the life and ministry of the early churches. This Appendix makes an honest effort to evaluate context, historical setting and meanings of the original words. Each text will be approached separately as we search for Paul's intended meaning.

The Two Scriptures
1 Timothy 2:11-12

"Let a woman learn in **silence** with all submission. And I do not permit a woman to teach or to have authority over a man, but to be in **silence**."

1 Corinthians 14:34-35

"Let your women keep **silent** in the churches, for they are not permitted to speak; but they are to be submissive, as the law also says. And if they want to learn something, let them ask their own husbands at home, for it is shameful for women to speak in church."

The Context of 1 Timothy 2:11-12

Honest, inductive study of a given passage requires that the paragraph surrounding the given verse(s) be examined thoroughly. A good approach is to read and reread a given paragraph until the basic thought is crystallized in your mind; then, write a capsule statement that describes that particular "block of thought" in the book. Reducing a paragraph to one summarizing sentence takes concentration, but the effort is rewarding. Try doing this with 1

Timothy 2:11-12. After discussion I will give you my capsule statement.

Silence . . .

is our main word in verses 11 and 12. The Greek word (*hesuchia*) does not refer to women being uncommunicative, mute or speechless (we know this because of 1 Corinthians 11:4); the verse means "to be restful, at peace, tranquil." This is easily proved by the use of the same word in verse 2 ("lead a quiet and peaceable [*hesuchia*] life").[1]

Submission ("Subjection," KJ) . . .

in verse 11 comes from *hupotasso* (*hupo* = under; *tasso* = to arrange). This term is used in describing the marriage relationship (Colossians 3:18; Titus 2:5) where one chooses not to assert personal rights but rather yield to another's preference.

The Man . . .

in verse 12 is misleading. Although the original text says "a man," some translations unfortunately imply that this refers to all men, thereby substantiating the theory that women cannot teach a group of men. Two samples would be the Living Bible: "I never let women teach men"; and, the Amplified Bible: "keep silence (in religious assemblies)." Neither translation is warranted here.

The Greek word "*aner*" is better translated in this case as "husband." This rendering suggests that Paul is speaking of the marriage relationship. Is this interpretation warranted?

The Pauline epistles use *aner* 59 times, 34 of which the KJ translates "husband." Of the remaining 25 occurrences, 18 are cases where the text is clearly speaking of a husband. *Aner* should be translated "husband "in this case.[2]

To Have Authority over a Man . . .

is the translation of *authenteo* (v. 12), which is translated variously: to usurp authority over" (KJ), "exercise authority" (NAS), "to have authority over" (NCV, NIV, NLT, Rhm), "to rule over" (Alf), "to domineer over" (Ber), "tell men what to do" (CEV),

323

"dictate to" (Mof), "issue commands to" (Knox), "Lord it over" (LB). Jack Hayford makes this interesting comment:

> In this spirit, the woman is not to 'usurp authority,' i.e., **not to be domineering** *authentew)*. This verb occurs but this one time in the entire New Testament. The intent of the instruction here is against an overbearing, demeaning control of her spouse. If the idea intended had to do with authority in the divine structure of the church, other terms more consistent with New Testament usage would have been employed.[3]

The Williams Translation confirms this translation: "I do not permit a married woman to practice teaching or domineering over a husband." Our conclusion is that 1 Timothy 2:11-12 is talking of the proper husband-wife relationship and their respective testimony to the world.

The men are unashamedly to take the leadership in prayer, and the women are to dress moderately and maintain a demeanor that is modest and serious. Women have the need and right to learn (at that time women were not given educational and vocational opportunities like men), and they will do so if they maintain a contented, peaceable spirit, free of strife and discord, as they listen to the instructions and explanations of their husbands. Paul forbids the wives to dominate their husbands.

A further proof that the man and woman mentioned in this text refer to husband and wife is given in verse 15 where it speaks of the wife being saved in childbirth *if "they" continue* in proper life style.

My capsule statement for this paragraph (after reading it dozens of times in various translations) is: *"Sound, saving advice for husbands and wives."*

The Context of 1 Corinthians 14:34-35

Our first Scripture addressed a woman's quiet, respectful nature ("silence") in the marriage relationship. Now, let us shift to our second Scripture which applies the same principle to her behavior in public church services.

Our context for these two verses (i.e., chapters 11-14) is particularly concerned with proper conduct in the public church gatherings. The present paragraph on talkative wives deals with only one of several disruptive influences in the assembly meetings. The apostle desires the services to flow smoothly and in a meaningful fashion.

The broader context involves eight chapters (7:1 through 14:40). Listed below are the basic issues that Paul tried to clarify. He apparently was attempting to answer questions that the Corinthians already asked him (7:1).

1. To be or not to be married? (7)
2. Should Christians eat food offered to idols? (8)
3. Should ministers receive salaries? (9)
4. Can we overcome temptation? (10)
5. How should men and women dress and act in church? (11)
6. What is proper conduct and attitude at the Lord's Supper? (11:17-34)
7. What are the spiritual gifts? (12:12-31)
8. What is real love? (13)
9. How should prophetic gifts be exercised in services? (14:1-3)
10. Should talkative wives be allowed to disrupt service (14:34-35).

Women are an important part of Paul's teaching in chapters 7, 11 and 14; the latter two chapters clarify the proper conduct of women, or specifically, wives.

How 1 Corinthians 11:2-16 Blends with 14:34-35

1 Corinthians 11:5 states that women may pray or prophesy in church, yet Paul says later that women should be silent in church (14:34). When a discrepancy like this appears in the Bible, it is well to investigate both the customs of that time and also the words used. Actually, Paul is not contradicting himself, and he certainly is not angry with women in the church -- but he is laying down two restrictions to insure the good testimony of the Christian women. They may speak at appropriate times and ways in the church, and their appearance must not violate the common customs everyone follows.

Christian Women Were To Wear Veils

Christian women were to follow the custom of that society (in the Grecian churches) and wear veils as a sign of proper relationship to their husbands. Henry H. Halley, in his popular Handbook says:

> It was customary in Greek and Eastern cities for women to cover their heads in public, except women of immoral character. Corinth was full of temple prostitutes. Some of the Christian women, taking advantage of their newfound liberty in Christ, were making bold to lay aside their veils in church meetings, which horrified those of more modest type. They are told not to defy public opinion as to what was considered proper in feminine decorum.[4]

Some of the verses in 1 Corinthians 11 pertaining to veils need special comment.

Verse 2, "Keep the traditions." "Traditions" in the NKJ is better and more understandable than "ordinances" (KJ translation). The NIV uses: "holding to the teachings"; the NLT: "you are following the Christian teaching I passed on to you;" The Message: "keeping up the traditions of the faith I taught you."

Verse 4, "Having his head covered." A literal translation would be "having something hanging down from his head." This part of Paul's teaching for men was more shocking to the Jews of that day than the teaching of women's veils is to us or the people of that time. A Jew accustomed to the ways of the synagogue would find Paul's teaching strange and challenging. Greek scholar M. R. Vincent gives this insight:

> Referring to the **tallith,** a four-cornered shawl having fringes consisting of eight threads, each knotted five times, and worn over the head in prayer. It was placed upon the worshipper's head at his entrance into the synagogue. The Romans, like the Jews, prayed with the head veiled....The Greeks remained bareheaded during prayer or sacrifice, as indeed they did in their ordinary outdoor life. The Grecian usage, which had become prevalent in the Grecian churches, seems to have commended itself to Paul as more becoming the superior position of the man.[5]

Verse 6, "Shorn or shaven." This means "to have the hair cut close, or to be entirely shaved as with a razor" (Vincent). Paul was concerned about the testimony of the church women. If the Christian woman (in her new liberty in Christ) "cast off her veil" (Concordant Version), this action would have the same effect on her acceptability as if she adopted the socially repugnant sign of the courtesan – close cropped hair or shaven head. The New Bible Commentary says: "In a woman this was at that time a sign of disgrace indicating that she was an adulteress."[6] Lamsa's translation from the Aramaic says: "For if a woman does not cover her head, let her also cut off her hair; but if it be a shame for a woman to be shorn or shaven, let her cover her head."

Verse 10, "A Symbol of Authority." This translation is more understandable than "power on her head" (KJ). Phillip's Translation says: "For this reason a woman ought to bear on her head an outward sign of man's authority."

The covering of the head by a woman in church services grew out of the Jewish social custom. It was a custom too ingrained in the social life of Christians in Palestine and Syria to be lightly dismissed by the Christian women in Asia Minor and Greece. Even as it was, Paul's liberation of men to go bareheaded in a religious gathering challenged the Judaizers. Lamsa comments:

> ...in the East it would be difficult for men to worship at places where women were unveiled during preaching or prayers. The men would be looking at the women instead of worshipping. This is because men do not see women's faces on other occasions. Thus to see the face or arms of a woman is unusual. [then Lamsa adds: "If Paul were living today he would never have made such recommendations."][7]

Paul's teaching is not in conflict with Galatians 3:28. Compare the wording of that verse with 1 Corinthians 11:11-12 (from the Lamsa Translation). It seems that Paul is saying the same thing:

> "there is neither male or female: for ye are all one in Christ Jesus."
> "Nevertheless, in our Lord there is no preference between man and woman, neither between woman and man...but all things of God.

If God uses a woman or man in some charismatic manifestation, the effectiveness of such ministry could be destroyed, distracted or diluted by the outward appearance of the person so used. Paul did not hate women, he simply respected the laws and customs of the land (verse 16); actually, his letters indicate that Paul treated the women of the churches as real friends and highly esteemed co-workers. These customs still prevail in some countries, but not in the USA. Our situation dictates that men and women dress appropriately, moderately, and wisely to give the very best impression possible on the average person in our social environment.

Women Are Not to Chatter in Church

Services should be free of distraction caused by unnecessary talking. This is the basic thought of 1 Corinthians 14:34, 35.

Examining the society of that day suggests the proper interpretation. Public services had the men separated from the women. Graham Truscott in his study on Women's Ministry, comments that this custom is still true in most parts of India today. George Lamsa says that in the East, "During the services they stand or sit by themselves, in a portion of the church reserved for them." Jim Beall makes this comment:

> In those days, custom dictated that men and women be separated in public services. This was true in the Jewish synagogues and Greek gatherings as well. Women were usually confined to a side room or a screened-off balcony where they could barely hear what was being said. Consequently, attention would soon lag and they were on their way talking and chattering. In some buildings, the men and women were separated by an aisle.[8]

The problem is not difficult to see. Christian women are eager to learn spiritual truths, so the frustration of being unable to read and even hear the teaching clearly, must have provoked some wives to call out to their husbands or their women friends for answers and clarification. Also, poor ideas or comments proposed by some men (or husbands) would be irritating to thoughtful women. Paul's solution (although not perfect for every setting) tolerated the social custom of that day and still placated the women's curiosity.

Fortunately, we do not have this problem in the USA. Our women are equally as educated, informed and spiritual as our men. They sit comfortably in our public gathering without discrimination. Nurseries handle the small children and babies. No need exists in our services for men or women to practice inappropriate chatter or disruptive utterances. Consider the words used: *Verse 34, "Keep silent…not permitted to speak."*

A woman is to listen quietly in the services and not call out questions (that could be answered at home by her husband) or make disruptive, "frivolous chit-chat."[9] C. K. Barrett says that "to speak" (from *lalein*) in this case refers to uninspired speech, and like the verb in Classical Greek can mean "to chatter" (although the verb "does not normally in this chapter have this meaning").[10]

It should be mentioned here that "silent" used for both the prophets and women in 1 Corinthians 14:28, 30, 34, is *sigao*, a different Greek word than the *hesuchia* which occurs twice in 1 Timothy 2:11,12. The meaning of both words, however, is similar; they both refer to controlling speech – not the forbidding of speech. Paul emphasizes in both texts quietness of spirit and tongue control;[11] he had no intention to forbid a woman to speak, but rather to be sensitive to her setting and circumstances and maintain a peaceful heart.

Verse 34, "Your women." Since verse 35 says that they are to ask questions of their husbands at home, this must refer mainly to wives.

Verse 34, "Be submissive." This refers to the wife's relationship to her husband, a thought from Genesis. A logical place to display proper husband-wife behavior would be public church gatherings. Talkative wives must not disrupt public service and embarrass the church, husbands – and even angels.

Verse 34, "As the law also says." This expression is controversial. Some commentaries list Genesis 3:16 as the source, but this reference is clearly not intended. In fact, nothing in the Old Testament suggests the silencing of women; this, therefore, must refer to the Jewish Oral Law. The Talmud said that it was "a shame for a woman to let her voice be heard among men."

Paul apparently was reinforcing his teaching by an appeal to a non-biblical source, one which carried weight with his audience. Today, we recognize the clear teaching of both Old and New Testaments and interpret the principles taught in the most direct and meaningful way possible in our society. In this case, it was appropriate to use the Oral Law, because it addressed itself to disruption of public services, not the public ministry of women.

Is There a Conflict between 1 Corinthians 11:4 and 14:34-35?

Some scholars feel that Paul was inconsistent when he said in 11:5 that women could pray and prophesy in public (if the head was covered), and yet in 14:34 women are told to be silent in the church. Is there an unresolved tension in Paul's teaching? No, Paul would hardly contradict himself in the same epistle![12]

The silence imposed in 14:34 does not eliminate all vocal activity! Women are encouraged to minister, pray, worship and prophesy (11:5; Acts 2; Romans 16). Paul did not exclude women's meaningful contribution. Ralph Martin says:

> Paul remains committed to social egalitarianism in the gospel (Gal. 3:28), and there is the undeniable evidence of the role he accorded to women colleagues (Phoebe, Prisca, the women of Philippi [Phil. 4:3], and the several women coworkers in Rom. 16). It is *prima facie* unlikely he should state categorically "let your women keep silent" in worship.[13]

The silence apparently refers to "chattering," but Dunn offers an additional possibility: "interrupting the process of evaluating prophetic utterances by asking unnecessary questions"[14] Possibly, Paul had in mind the indiscriminate use of glossolalia in the church services (bursting forth in tongues and disturbing the meeting). Paul wanted the participation of both men and women in the congregational meetings, he wanted the church to be a charismatic community, and He wanted proper decorum.

> [Paul] does not impose an absolute ban on speaking but only issues guidelines to promote orderly worship at church (Kistemaker).[15]

Appendix B Endnotes

[1] *The Analytical Greek Lexicon* (NY: Harper & Brothers), p. 189, suggests: "rest, quiet, tranquility; a quiet, tranquil life, 2 Thes. 3:12."

[2] J. B. Smith, *Greek-English Concordance to the New Testament* (Scottdale, PA: Herald Press, 1955), p. 24.

[3] Jack Hayford, *On the Question of a Woman's Place in Church Leadership* (Van Nuys, CA: The Church on the Way publication), p. 7f.

[4] Henry H. Haley, *Halley's Bible Handbook* (Grand Rapids: Zondervan, 1965, 24th revised edition), pp. 596-7.

[5] M. R. Vincent, *Word Studies in the New Testament* (Associated Publishers and Authors: Wilmington, DEL, 1972, reprint of 2nd edition, 1888), p. 786.

[6] W. C. G. Proctor, "The Epistles to the Corinthians," F. Davidson, ed., *The New Bible Commentary,* (Grand Rapids: Eerdmans, 1953), p. 983.

[7] George M. Lamsa, *New Testament Commentary* (Philadelphia: A. J. Holman Co., 1945), p. 272.

[8] Jim Beall, *The Female of the Species,* p. 33.

[9] Ralph P. Martin, *The Spirit and the Congregation* (Grand Rapids: Eerdmans, 1984), p. 85.

[10] C. K. Barrett, *The First Epistle to the Corinthians* (NY: Harper & Row, 1968), p. 332.

[11] Hayford comments, "Had the verb *Phimao* been used (to silence, to muzzle, in effect, to produce muteness) a case for speechless-women-in-the-Church might be attempted." P. 8. We are happy to say that Paul had no such intent.

[12] One major problem that scholarly commentators have in trying to explain the function of the Pentecostal/Charismatic Corinthians, is that such commentators only work with the textual criticism and have never been a part of a charismatic community. To those of us who have done so for a number of years, Paul's teaching seems quite clear. This is also true of women wearing veils. Having faced this question in India, Brazil and Nigeria, I can assure you that Paul was working hard with a deeply entrenched social custom that required patient attention.

[13] Martin, Ibid.

[14] James D. G. Dunn, *Unity and Diversity in the New Testament* (Philadelphia: Trinity Press International, 1991, 2nd Impression), p. 130.

[15] Simon J. Kistemaker, *New Testament Commentary: 1 Corinthians* (Grand Rapids: Baker Books, 1993), p. 514.

Appendix C
Apostolic Team Ministry

Joy and I stared in amazement! We were visiting the waterfront area of San Francisco, and stood transfixed as a street musician performed. Not just one instrument, but he was simultaneously keeping more than a half dozen instruments going at once. He had a harmonica held in place near his mouth, cymbals attached to each knee, bells, guitar, horn and so on. The music was not the greatest, but keeping all those noise-makers going at once was a marvel to behold. This, unfortunately, is how some churches function!

The early Church understood that the "one-man band" ministry was not effective. Why wear one person out when we can have a whole symphony of participating ministries? Ten men working are better than one man doing the work of ten men!

The Teams of Jesus

Jesus knew the importance of help and support (both natural and spiritual), so He sent the disciples out by twos, as in Luke 22:8. Anyone who has done door-to-door visitation knows the value of one speaking and the other praying! Consider the progressive sequence of Jesus' approach:

1. Jesus began His ministry without help from others.
2. Jesus gradually gathered disciples and exposed them to His methods.
3. Jesus authorized twelve apostles to represent Him and follow His methods.
4. Jesus deputized seventy (or, seventy-two) more to help propagate the Good News, going only to the Jews, not to the Gentiles (Luke 10).[1]
5. All the villages, towns and cities of Israel received the Good News.[2]
6. Finally, having finished taking his message to every corner of the nation of Israel (stage 1 in reaching all nations), Jesus gave his

followers the Great Commission of Matthew 28, an open-ended mandate to bring His Kingdom message *to all nations.*[3]

There was a difference between the authority, commission and power given to the original Twelve and that of the Seventy (Luke 9:1; 10:1). Consider, however, that in the list of Hippolytus (A.D. 170-235), which supposedly lists the names of the Seventy that Jesus sent out, some of the Seventy were *at that later time* named apostles, and many became bishops in various places.[4]

Apostolic Teams in Acts and Epistles

Paul always seemed to travel with others, not just as companions but participating team members; he was always training and mentoring. He knew that *academic training* must be balanced by *operational activity*: tangible results are essential! Not all who formed these teams had the gift of apostleship -- nor held the office of apostle in the Early Church, but as part of a team that exercised apostolic function, each one was certainly "an apostolic person."

Comprised of people with various spiritual gifts and natural talents, the teams were all praying, local-church people, and some would not be categorized as full-time ministers. Sometimes a team was recruited from several churches for a short-term mission, just as it happens today.

A team or part of a team can be made up of professional and technical people who use their expertise for practical problems. Once our church sent some people to Brazil to help a church with their computer and other things. Their services were deeply appreciated and improved the church's effectiveness. A team of builders can go and construct a church building during the day, holding evangelistic meetings in the evening. This kind of activity keeps the missionary fire burning in the home church as well. Racial and sexual differences seemed unimportant at the time of Romans 16 and Galatians 3:28. Not a great deal of detail is given, but it is obvious that everyone pulled his/her share of natural and spiritual responsibilities. A functioning house church of that day would make up a unique local team.

Teams Mentioned in Acts	
References	*Persons*
1. Acts 3:1; 13:2, 13	Peter – John
2. Acts 8	Philip – Peter – John
3. Acts 10:23; 11:12	Peter and 6 Brethren
4. Acts 11	Men from Cypress and Cyrene
5. Acts 13-15	Barnabas -- Saul – Mark
6. Acts 15:22, 30-32	Paul – Barnabas – Judas – Silas
7. Acts 15:40f; 16:19	Paul – Silas
8. Acts 15:37-39	Barnabas -- Mark
9. Acts 16:9, 10ff	Paul – Silas – Timothy -- Luke
10. Acts 18:2, 24ff	Paul– Silas– Timothy– Luke-- Aquila–Priscilla -- Apollos
11. Acts 19	Paul—Silas—Timothy—Luke—Erastus—Gaius--Aristarchus
12. Acts 24	Paul—Silas—Timothy—Luke—Sopater—Aristarchus—Secundus—Gaius —Tychicus--Trophimus
Teams Mentioned in the Epistles	
1. Romans 16:21-22	Timothy – Lucius – Jason – Sosipater
2. 1 Cor. 16:17-18	Stephanas – Fortunatus – Achaicus
3. 2 Cor. 12:18	Titus, "and send our brother with him."
4. Ephesians 6:21	Tychicus, with others?
5. Philippians 4:21	"The brethren who are with me."
6. Colossians 4:7-9	Tychicus -- Onesiums
7. Colossians 4:10-12	Aristarcus—Mark—Justus—Epaphras—Luke—Demas (fellow workers)
8. 1 Thess. 1:1; 5:25; 2 Thess. 1:1; 3:1	Paul – Silvanus – Timothy
9. Titus 3:12	Paul – Artemas -- Tychicus
10. Titus 3:13	Paul -- Zenas – Apollos
11. Philemon 24	Mark – Aristarchus – Demas – Luke, "my fellow laborers"

Four Objectives of Team Ministry

John C. Maxwell calls this principal of sending out teams of leaders "The Law of Explosive Growth"[5] -- and that is exactly what happened.

1. Planting Churches

Acts 13:4-14:21. Apostolic teams were not exclusively for apostles; sometimes evangelists or other servants of the church with specialized spiritual gifts were used. Philip the Evangelist, for instance, brought the gospel message to Samaria (Acts 8), but the apostles Peter and John soon joined him and contributed the authority that Philip lacked. A team of fervent believers can impact a community more quickly than a lone individual.

2. Establishing Churches

Apostolic objective was to establish – in every community -- churches that were *indigenous* expressions of the Body of Christ, Acts 14:21b-26. Four concepts define "indigenous": self-governing, self-supporting, self-propagating and self-esteeming.

This statement by veteran missionary supervisor Ed Murphy is excellent:

> … a church is only truly indigenous when it sees itself as the people of God in its own community, a church culturally relevant and socially rooted in the culture in which it has been planted. Such a church not only governs itself, supports itself, and propagates itself, but does so in terms of its own culture, not in terms of foreign cultural patterns imposed by the planting missions.[6]

A team should be a group of paracletes (no, I didn't say parakeets!), *helpers* who come alongside the weary and lift them up. *Musicians* with the touch of God rejuvenate a church. Those with spiritual *gifts of healing and supernatural manifestations* lift the faith level. *Technicians* with know-how and bearing gifts of new equipment bring renewed pride and joy to a congregation. *Carpenters* that love God and share their testimony and also put a new roof on the church or orphanage are really appreciated. A *bookkeeper* helps with church finances, and a *team of givers* can generate a gift of money to help the church or local pastor at a critical time. *Prayer warriors* who back the other team members with prevailing prayer and joyful testimony are a significant part of such a team.

Older people need to be involved. In some countries you hardly see any people with grey hair, for life expectancy could be from 25-35 years old. Some of our older folks should get a passport and go. Most of these older saints have forgotten more than some of these dear foreign people have ever learned. *Young people* should also go and use their talents; witnessing with *drama and miming* has a strong appeal to the unsaved youth on the streets.

3. Teaching Churches

An example would be the #6 team (Acts 15) that went to the Gentile churches to teach the conclusions of the Apostles in Jerusalem (Acts 15). Also, the Pastoral Epistles of 1 and 2 Timothy and Titus illustrate how Paul urged his younger adjutants to teach strong doctrine to keep churches spiritually healthy. Doctrine was clearly articulated by Paul and maintained in the churches.

Once my wife and three daughters, a nurse, a son-in-law (who is my pastor) and myself went to Nigeria to hold a conference. My daughters are all prophetic, musical and good speakers. They ministered to pastors wives, while we two men spoke to the men. Sometimes we combined both men and women.

The meetings were excellent and having capable women speaking so well was a great encouragement; just having women speak in Nigeria was something new and exciting. Teachers can impart so much! One of my daughters had taken part in the Assemblies of God program in South Africa for AIDS prevention. I sat there in awe listening to her informative and excellent presentation; the native pastors and wives hardly blinked, giving their rapt attention. This strengthened and taught the churches and did so much good, but this type of teaching also did much to improve the whole community. People who are not necessarily ordained ministers can have impacting ministry.

In addition to preaching and teaching, one of my greatest thrills was to give complimentary books to each pastor. They were overjoyed to receive a new, informative book, for most of them barely could afford a Bible. Helping sponsor business ventures among needy people, especially single mothers, is another excellent effort.

4. *Correcting Churches.* Notice Paul's strong, corrective doctrine about godly living, advice to families, slave holders, slaves, and older people. 1 Corinthians 14 is a classic example of Paul bringing instruction to confusing local church problems. Churches need apostles to come and present *the better way of doing things,* solid explanation of the Bible and good living that is reasonable and irrefutable.

Husband and Wife Teams

Two husband and wife teams are noteworthy in the New Testament. First, Priscilla and Aquila who were Paul's "fellow workers in Christ Jesus, who risked their own necks for my life…" (Romans 16:3). One example of their work is found in Acts 18 and 19. They went to Ephesus with Paul, and while he hurried on to Jerusalem, they worshiped and fellowshipped in the Jewish synagogue and made tents in the city marketplace, preparing for Paul's return by establishing relationships with the non-Christians.

Upon his return, it seems that Paul inadvertently stumbled across twelve seeking men. Actually, the context indicates that Paul was directed to the disciples of John the Baptist because of Priscilla and Acquila.[7]

Secondly, consider Andronicus and Junia, whom Paul calls "my countrymen and my fellow prisoners, who are *of note among the apostles,* who also were in Christ before me" (Romans 16:7, emphasis added). I have already listed them under "Other Apostles;" in Chapter 7 I discussed the possibility of the wife Junia being an apostle.

Special Commissions (Short Assignments)

The following teams and commissions all involved people on apostolic mission (the verb is *apostello*). All were apostolic people, but not necessarily apostles. They were sent, prayed for, supported and encouraged by their churches. Each had a reason to go, a commission, and they were not all alike.

1. Peter and John summoned to Samaria: Acts 8:14.
2. Ananias sent to Saul: Acts 9:17.

337

3. Cornelius sent messengers: Acts 9:38; 10:8, 17, 20, 21; 11:11, 13.
4. Barnabas sent to Antioch: Acts 11:22.
5. Barnabas and Saul brought money to Jerusalem: Acts 11:30.
6. Judas and Silas (prophets) were sent with an epistle: Acts 15:27.
7. Paul sent two, Timothy and Erastus: Acts 19:22.
8. Tychicus sent to Ephesus: 2 Timothy 4:12.
9. 2 Corinthians 8:23; 12:17; Philippians 2:25.

Some church people and their leaders are not aware that the more we reach out, the stronger the local church will become. Giving people in service and starting other churches actually opens the channel for local expansion. What and how we sow, determines our harvest. As we learn to work with church teams, and then with fellowship churches, we are on our way to networking with other fellowships and organizations that will make the universal Church stronger and more unified. Together we stand, divided we fall.

Appendix C Endnotes

[1] Cannistraci, *Apostles*, p. 58: "The number 70 was special and symbolic in Israel. Seventy elders were present with Moses in the wilderness…and they became symbolic of the Spirit of Christ coming on His people. Seventy was the 'number' of the nations of the earth as found in Genesis 10….a symbol of the whole earth to which the 70 were sent."

[2] See Chapter 4, Endnote #59.

[3] Kevin Conner says, "The following Scriptures should be read together, for they give the complete 'Great Commission' of the Lord Jesus: Matthew 28:18-20; Mark 16:14-18; Luke 24:46-49; John 20:21-23; Acts 1:8." He suggests: "If we want to know how the

disciples interpreted the Commission of Christ, then the only Divine record we have is that found in the Book of Acts." *Acts*, p. 12.

[4] See David Cartledge, *The Apostolic Revolution,* pp. 251-254.

[5] Maxwell, *The Maxwell Leadership Bible*, p. 202.

[6] Murphy, *Overseas Crusades*, p. 33.

[7] Of the six times that the couple's names are mentioned together, four times Priscilla's name is mentioned first, possibly indicating that hers was the stronger ministry.

Bibliography

Allen, Leslie C. "Romans." F. F. Bruce, ed. *The International Bible Commentary.* Grand Rapids: Zondervan, 1986 (rev. ed.).

Allen, Roland. *Missionary Methods: St. Paul's or Ours?* Grand Rapids: Eerdmans, 1962.

*Alley, John Kingsley. *The Apostolic Revelation: The Reformation of the Church.* Surprise, AZ: Selah Publishing Group, LLC.

Analytical Greek Lexicon. NY: Harper & Brothers.

Anderson, Lynn. *They Smell Like Sheep.* West Monroe, LA: Howard Publishing, 1997.

Anderson, Ray S. "Apostle." Systematic Theology: Fuller Seminary, 1983.

Archer, Gleason L. and Gregory Chirichigno. *Old Testament Quotations in the New Testament.* Chicago: Moody Press, 1983.

Arndt, William and F. Wilbur Gingrich. *A Greek-English Lexicon of the NT and Other Early Christian Literature.* Chicago: The University of Chicago Press, 1957.

Asch, Sholem. *The Apostle.* NY: G. P. Putnam's Sons, 1943.

Atiya, Aziz. *A History of Eastern Christianity.* London: Methuen & Co., Ltd, 1968.

*Atkin, Don. *The Heart of Apostolic Ministry.* Self published 2002. Email: donatkin@kingdomquest.net

--------------. *The Apostles' Role Among the Priesthood of All Believers.* Self published 2008.

Barclay, William. *The New Daily Study Bible: The Acts of the Apostles.* Louisville, KT: Westminster John Knox Press, 2003.

Barker, Glenn W., William L. Lane, J. Ramsey Michaels. *The New Testament Speaks.* NY: Harper & Row, 1969.

Barna, George. *Revolution.* Carol Stream, IL: Tyndale House Publishers, 2005.

Barnett, Paul. *The Second Epistle to the Corinthians (NICONT).* Grand Rapids: Eerdmans, 1987.

Barrett, C. K. *The Signs of an Apostle.* Philadelphia: Fortress Press, 1970.

----------------. The First Epistle to the Corinthians. NY: Harper & Row, 1968.

----------------. *The Second Epistle to the Corinthians.* Peabody, MASS: Hendrickson Publishers, 1993 reprint [1987].

Barth, Marcus. *Ephesians, The Anchor Bible.* Garden City, NY: Doubleday & Co., 1974

*Beacham, Doug Jr. *Rediscovering the Role of Apostles & Prophets.* Franklin Springs, GA: LifeSprings Resources, 2004.

----------------------. *The Vision* (Vol. II, 1):10.

340

Beasley-Murray, George R. *Jesus and the Last Days.* Peabody, MASS: Hendrickson Publishers, 1993.

Bernstein, Amy D. "Glory and Honor." *Secrets of America's Best Generals.* US News and World Report, 2009.

Betz, Hans Dieter. "Apostle," *The Anchor Bible Dictionary,* Vol. 1. NY: Doubleday, 1992.

Bilezikian, Gilbert. "Grace." Walter A. Elwell, ed. *Baker Encyclopedia of the Bible, Vol. 1.* Grand Rapids: Baker Book House, 1988.

*Bittlinger, Arnold. *Gifts and Ministries.* Grand Rapids: Eerdmans, 1973.

Blaiklock, E. M. "Dalmatia." *Zondervan Pictorial Encyclopedia of the Bible,* Volume 2. Grand Rapids: Zondervan, 1975.

Bonham, Chad. "He Dared to Touch the World." *Charisma* (Jan 2007): 58-62; 82-83.

Borchert, G. L. "Troas." Geoffrey W. Bromiley, gen. ed. *The International Standard Bible Encycopedia, Vol 4.* Grand Rapids: Eerdmans, 1988.

Brown, Colin, ed. *The New International Dictionary of NT Theology,* Vol. 1. Grand Rapids: Zondervan, 1973.

Bruce, A. B. *The Training of the Twelve.* Grand Rapids: Kregel Publications, 1972 reprint [a classic which first appeared in 1871].

Bruce, F. F. *The Spreading Flame, Vol. 1.* Grand Rapids: Eerdmans, 1958 (1973).

--------------. *Paul: Apostle of the Heart Set Free.* Grand Rapids: Eerdmans, 1976 [1964].

--------------. "The Acts of the Apostles." *Exploring New Testament Backgrounds.* Washington, D.C.: *Christianity Today.*

--------------. *The Acts of the Apostles.* Grand Rapids: Eerdmans, 1970 reprint.

--------------. *The Book of the Acts, Revised Edition.* Grand Rapids: Eerdmans, 1988.

--------------. *New Testament History.* Garden City, NY: Anchor Books, 1969.

*Cannistraci, David. *Apostles and the Emerging Apostolic Movement: A Biblical Look at Apostleship and How God is Using It to Bless His Church Today.* Ventura, CA: Renew Books, 1996.

Carmichael, Amy. *Let the Little Children Come.* Chicago: Moody Press, 1984.

Carson, D. A. *Becoming Conversant with the Emerging Church.* Grand Rapids: Zondervan, 2005.

*Cartledge, David. *The Apostolic Revolution: The Restoration of Apostles and Prophets in the Assemblies of God in Australia.* Chester Hill, Australia: Paraclete Institute, 2000.

Christian History & Biography. "India's Apostle." 85 (Summer 2005): 3.

*Clark, Jonas, "Apostles & Spiritual Jurisdictions," *The Voice* (Vol.1, Issue 1, January 2004): 8-11.

-----------------------, *The Apostolic Equipping Dimension: Equipping and Deploying Every Believer.* Hallandale, FL: Spirit of Life Publishing, 2001.

*Conner, Kevin J. *The Book of Acts.* Portland, OR: City Christian Publishing, 1973.

Cunningham, Loren and David Joel Hamilton. *Why Not Women?* Seattle, WA: YWAM Publishing, 2000.

*Damazio, Frank, *The Strategic Church Leadership Conference 2011.* Portland, OR: Ministers Fellowship International.

Dayton, Edward R. and David A. Fraser. *Planning Strategies for World Evangelization.* Grand Rapids: Eerdmans, 1980.

Deere, Jack. "Anatomy of a Deception," *MorningStar Journal* 4:2 (1994): 42-43.

Dunn, James D. G. *The Acts of the Apostles.* Valley Forge, PN: Trinity Press International, 1996.

----------------. *Unity and Diversity in the New Testament.* Philadelphia: Trinity Press International, 1991.

Edersheim, Alfred. *The Life and Times of Jesus the Messiah,* Vol. 1. Grand Rapids: Eerdmans, 1950.

*Eckhardt, John. *Moving in the Apostolic.* Ventura, CA: Regal Books, 1999.

Fee, Gordon D. and Douglas Stuart. *How to Read the Bible for All Its Worth.* Grand Rapids: Zondervan, 1993.

----------------. *The First Epistle to the Corinthians (NICONT).* Grand Rapids: Eerdmans, 1987.

Findlay, G. G. "Paul the Apostle." James Hastings, ed. *A Dictionary of the Bible,* Vol. III. NY: Charles Scribner's Sons, 1902.

*Fleming, Stan. "Thomas: From Doubter to World Changer." *Gate Breaker News* (Vol. 2, Issue 1, Jan. 2008): 4.

French, Richard Chenevix. *Synonyms of the New Testament.* Grand Rapids: Associated publishers and Authors, Inc., reprint (no date).

*Gentile, Ernest B. *Awaken the Dawn!* Columbus, GA: The Eastwood Publications, 2001.

---------------------. *The Glorious Disturbance.* Grand Rapids: Chosen Books, 2004.

---------------------. *Your Sons & Daughters Shall Prophesy.* Grand Rapids: Chosen Books, 1999.

---------------------. *Worship God!* Portland, OR: City Christian Publishing, 1994.

Gladwell, Malcom. *The Tipping Point: How Little Things Can Make a Big Difference.* NY/Boston: Little, Brown and Company, 2000/2002.

Goodwin, Frank J. *A Harmony of the Life of St. Paul.* Grand Rapids: Baker Books House, 1953.

*Gordon, Kayy. *God's Fire on Ice.* Plainfield, NJ: Logos International, 1977.

*Green, Matthew D. *Understanding the Fivefold Ministry.* Lake Mary, FL: Charisma House, 2005.

*Greenslade, Philip. *Leadership, Greatness and Servanthood.* Minneapolis, MN: Bethany House Publishers, 1984.

Grudem, Wayne. *Systematic Theology.* Grand Rapids: Zondervan, 1994.

Gundry, Patricia. *Woman Be Free!* Grand Rapids: Zondervan, 1977.

Halley, Henry H. *Halley's Bible Handbook.* Grand Rapids: Zondervan, 1965 ed.

*Hamon, Bill. *Apostles, Prophets and the Coming Moves of God.* Shippensburg, PA: Destiny Image Publishers, 1997.

Harrison, E. F. "Apostle, Apostleship." *Evangelical Dictionary of the Bible, 2nd Edition.* Grand Rapids: Baker Academic, 2001.

*Hayford, Jack. *On the Question of a Woman's Place in Church Leadership.* Van Nuys, CA: The Church on the Way publication.

------------------. "The Apostolic 'Right Stuff.'" *Ministries Today* (Nov-Dec 2004: 96-98.

------------------, gen. ed. *Hayford's Bible Handbook.* Nashville: Thomas Nelson Publishers, 1996.

Hendriksen, William and Simon J. Kistemaker. *New Testament Commentary: Thessalonians, the Pastorals and Hebrews.* Grand Rapids: Baker Books, 1995.

Hendriksen, William. "1 Timothy," *New Testament Commentary, Thessalonians, the Pastoral and Hebrews.* Grand Rapids: Baker Books, 1995.

Higginson, R. E. "Apostolic Succession." Walter A. Elwell, ed. *Evangelical Dictionary of Theology,* 2nd ed. Grand Rapids: Baker Academic, 2001.

*Hyatt, Eddie L. *Apostles: 5 Popular Misconceptions in the Church Today.* Fort Worth, TX: Hyatt International Ministries.

Irenaeus. *Against Heresies,* III, 3; c. A.D. 180.

*Iverson, Dick, Dick Benjamin, and Jim Durkin. *The Master Builder.* South Lake Tahoe, CA: Christian Equippers Int., 1985.

*Keefaufer, Larry. "Acts of the Apostles." *Ministries Today* (Nov-Dec 2004): 84.

Keller, W. Phillip. *Rabboni…Which Is To Say Master.* Old Tappan, NJ: Fleming H. Revell company, 1977.

----------------------. *A Shepherd Looks at Psalm 23.* Grand Rapids: Zondervan, 1970.

----------------------. *The Good Shepherd and His Sheep.* Grand Rapids: Zondervan, 1978.

Kimball, Dan. *The Emerging Church.* Grand Rapids, MI: Zondervan, 2003.

Kistemaker, Simon J. *New Testament Commentary: Peter & Jude.* Grand Rapids: Baker, 1987.

--------------------------. *New Testament Commentary: Acts.* Grand Rapids: Baker, 1990.

--------------------------. *New Testament Commentary: 1st Corinthians.* Grand Rapids: Baker Books, 1993.

Küng, Hans. *The Church.* Garden City, NY: Image Books, 1976.

Ladd, George Eldon. *A Theology of the New Testament.* Grand Rapids: Eerdmans, 1974.

Lamsa, George M. *Gospel Light.* Philadelphia: A. J. Holman, 1936.

----------------------. *New Testament Commentary.* Philadelphia: A. J. Holman Co., 1945.

Latourette, Kenneth Scott. *A History of Christianity, Vol. 1., to AD 1500.* NY: Harper & Row, 1975.

*Layzell, Reg., compiled by B. M. Gaglardi. *The Pastor's Pen.* Vancouver, B.C.: Glad Tidings Temple, 1965.

Lenski, R. C. H. *The Interpretation of the Acts of the Apostles.* Minneapolis, MINN: Augsburg Publishing House, 1961.

Lewis, Robert and Wayne Cordeiro. *Church Shift.* San Francisco: Jossey-Bass, 2005.

Lockyer, Herbert. *All the Apostles of the Bible.* Grand Rapids: Zondervan, 1972.

----------------------. *All the Women of the Bible.*

*Lowe, Valerie G. "The Unlikely Ambassador." *Charisma* Magazine (November 2006): 22-23.

*Lowrey, T. L. *Apostles and Prophets: Reclaiming the Biblical Gifts.* Cleveland, TN: T. L. Lowrey Ministries, International, 2004.

MacArthur, John, author and gen. ed. *The MacArthur Study Bible.* Thomas Nelson, 1997.

---------------------. *Twelve Ordinary Men.* Nashville: Thomas Nelson, 2002.

*Maldonado, Guillermo. *The Ministry of the Apostle.* Miami, FL: ERJ Publications, 2006.

Martin, Ralph P. *New Testament Foundations: A Guide for Christian Students, Volume 1.* Grand Rapids: Eerdmans, 1978.

---------------------. *The Spirit and the Congregation: Studies in 1 Corinthians 12-15.* Grand Rapids: Eerdmans, 1984.

Marshall, I. Howard, ed. *The New International Greek Testament Commentary (Luke)* Grand Rapids: Zondervan, 1978.

--------------------------. *The Acts of the Apostles* (Tyndale New Testament Commentaries). Grand Rapids: Eerdmans, 1988 reprint [1980].

Maxwell, John C. *The 21 Irrefutable Laws of Leadership.* Nashville, TN: Thomas Nelson Publishers, 1998.

----------------------, Ex. Ed. *The Maxwell Leadership Bible.* Nashville, TN: Thomas Nelson Publishers, 2002.

McBirnie, William Steuart. *The Search for the Twelve Apostles.* Wheaton, IL: Tyndale House, 1973.

McGavran, Donald. *Understanding Church Growth.* Grand Rapids: Eerdmans, 1970.

Morgan, G. Campbell. *The Acts of the Apostles.* Fleming H. Revell, 1924.

----------------------------. Sermon: "Church Ideals: The Church Instituted." *The Westminster Pulpit,* Vol. 5. Grand Rapids: Baker Books, 1995 [orig 1906-1916] : Chapter XV.

Müller, Dietrich. "Apostle." Colin Brown, ed. *The New International Dictionary of NT Theology,* Vol. 1. Grand Rapids: Zondervan, 1975.

Münck, Johannes. *The Acts of the Apostles (The Anchor Bible).* Garden City, NY: Doubleday & Co., Inc., 1967.

*Murphy, Ed. *The Ministry and Organizational Development of Overseas Crusades as an Apostolic Team.* Overseas Crusades, 1973.

Meyer, F. B. *The Life of Love.* Old Tappan, NJ: Fleming H. Revell Company, 1987 reprint.

*Myer, Ron. *Fivefold Ministry Made Practical.* Lititz, PA: House to House Publications, 2006.

Nee, Watchman. *Spiritual Authority.* NY: Christian Fellowship Publications, 1972.

Osborn, Larry W. *The Unity Factor: Getting Your Church Leaders to Work Together.* Dallas, TX: Word Publishing/Christianity Today, 1989

Osborne, Grant R. "Apostle, Apostleship." Walter A. Elwell, gen. ed. *Baker Encyclopedia of the Bible.* Grand Rapids: Baker Book House, 1988.

Proctor, W. C. G. "The Epistles to the Corinthians." F. Davidson, ed. *The New Bible Commentary.* Grand Rapids: Eerdmans, 1953.

Pullinger, Jackie. *Chasing the Dragon.* Servant Books, 1980.

Ramsay, W. M. *St. Paul the Traveller and the Roman Citizen.* London: Hodder and Stoughton, 1907, tenth ed.

Rengstorf, Karl Heinrich. *Apostleship (Bible Key Words from Kittel).* London: Adam and Charles black, 1952.

Ridderbos, Herman N. *The Epistle of Paul to the Churches of Galatia (TNICNT).* Grand Rapids: Eerdmans, 1979 [1953].

*Rowe, W.A.C. *One Lord, One Faith.* Bradford, Yorkshire, England: The Apostolic Church, Australia, 1960.

Salmond, S.D.F. "The Epistle to the Ephesians." W. Robertson Nicoll, ed. *The Expositor's Greek Testament.* Grand Rapids: Eerdmans, 1951.

Sand, A., "KANON." Balz, H. R. *Exegetical Dictionary of the New Testament.* Grand Rapids: Eerdmans, 1993.

Sandborn, Mark. *You Don't Need a Title to be a Leader.* NY: Doubleday, 2006.

Schaff, Philip. *History of the Christian Church, Volume 1.* Grand Rapids: Eerdmans, 1950.

*Scheidler, Bill. *A Fresh Look At...Apostles.* Portland: City Bible Publishers, 2001.

--------------------. Teaching Notes on "Apostolic Ministry."

Schmidt, Karl Ludwig, "ekklesia," Kittle, Gerhard, ed., translated by Geoffrey W. Bromiley. *Theological Dictionary of the New Testament*, Vol. III. Grand Rapids: Eerdmans, 1965. pp. 501-536.

---------------------------- and edited by F. R. Coates, ed. *The Church (Bible Key Words from Gerhard Kittel's Theologisches Worterbuch Zum Neuen Testament).* London: Adam and Charles Black, 1950.

Shepherd, J. W. *The Christ of the Gospels.* Grand Rapids: Eerdmans, 1939.

Shepherd, M. H. "Apostle." George Arthur Buttrick, dict. Ed. *The Interpreter's Dictionary of the Bible, Vol. 4.* NY: Abingdon Press, 1962.

*Shibley, David. *The Missions Addiction* (update@globaladvance.org).

Smith, J. B. *Greek-English Concordance to the New Testament.* Scottdale, PA: Herald Press (Mennonite Publishing House), 1955. P. 116.

Smith, Wilbur. *Peloubet's Select Notes on the International Sunday School Lessons, 1939, 1942, 1961.* Boston: W. A. Wilde company, 1938, 1941, 1966.

Swidler, Leonard. *Biblical Affirmations of Women.* Philadelphia: Westminster Press, 1979.

Taylor, Howard. *Hudson Taylor's Spiritual Secret.* Chicago: Moody Press, 1989.

Tenney, Merrill C., gen. ed. *The Zondervan Pictorial Encyclopedia of the Bible.* Grand Rapids: Zondervan, 1975.

Thayer, Joseph Henry. *A Greek-English Lexicon of the New Testament.* NY: American Book Company, Corrected ed. 1889 [1886 Harper & Brothers]. P. 195-196.

The Analytical Greek Lexicon. NY: Harper and Bros. .

The New Open Bible Study Edition. Nashville, TN: Thomas Nelson, 1990.

The NIV Study Bible. Grand Rapids: Zondervan, 1985.

The Septuagint Version of the Old Testament. Grand Rapids: Zondervan, 1976, 8th ed.

Thomas, Robert L. "1 Thessalonians." Frank E. Gaebelein, gen. ed. *The Expositor's Bible Commentary, Volume 2.* Grand Rapids: Zondervan, 1978.

Thiessen, Henry C, revised by Vernon d. Doerksen. *Lectures in Systematic Theology.* Grand Rapids: Eerdmans, 1983 reprint [1949].

*Torres, Hector. *The Restoration of the Apostles and Prophets.* Nashville: Thomas Nelson Publishers, 2001.

Trench, R. C. *Synonyms of the New Testament.* Grand Rapids: Associated Publishers and Authors, reprint.

*Ulmer, Kenneth. "Ministry Paradigm Shift." *Charisma* (May 2010): 92.

Underhill, Evellyn. *Worship.* Harper & Bros, 1937.

Vincent, M. R. *Word Studies in the New Testament.* Willmingtn, DEL: Associated Publishers and Authors, 2nd ed., 1888.

Vine, W. E. *Expository Dictionary of New Testament Words.* Fleming H. Revel Company, 1966 [17th impression], first published 1940.

*Virgo, Terry, *No Well-Worn Paths.* St. Louis, MO: New Frontiers, 2008.

Von Campenhausen, Hans. *Ecclesiastical Authority and Spiritual Power in the Church of the First Three Centuries.* Peabody, MASS: Hendrickson, 1997.

*Wagner, C. Peter. *The New Apostolic Churches.* Ventura: Regal Books, 1998.

---------------------. *The Acts of the Holy Spirit.* Ventura, CA: Regal Books, 1998.

---------------------. *Apostles of the City.* Colorado Springs: Wagner Publications, 2000.

---------------------. *Apostles and Prophets: The Foundation of the Church.* Ventura: Regal Books, 2000.

---------------------, ed. *Pastors & Prophets: Protocol for Healthy Churches.* Colorado Springs: Wagner Publications, 2000.

---------------------. *Seven Power Principles That I Didn't Learn in Seminary.* Colorado Springs: Wagner Publications, 2000.

---------------------. *Changing Church: How God Is Leading His Church into the Future.* Ventura, CA: Regal Books, 2004.

---------------------. *Apostles Today.* Ventura: Regal Books, 2007.

----------------------. *Dominion: How Kingdom Action Can Change the World.* Grand Rapids: Chosen Books, 2008.

*Walker, Gordon. *Twentieth Century Apostleship.* Mt. Hermon, CA: Conciliar Press.

Walker, Ken. "European Church Fuses Faith, Politics." *Charisma* Magazine, November 2006): 22-23.

Watson, David. *I Believe in the Church.* Grand Rapids: Eerdmans, 1979 [1978].

Williams, Don. *The Apostle Paul and Women in the Church.* Van Nuys, CA: BIM Publishing Co., 1977.

Williams, J. Rodman. *Renewal Theology,* Volume Three. Grand Rapids: Zondervan, 1992.

Wood, A. Skevington. "Ephesians." *The Expositor's Bible Commentary, Vol. II.* Grand Rapids: Zondervan, 1978.

*Worsfold, James E. *The Origins of the Apostolic Church of Great Britain.* Thorndon, Wellington, New Zealand: The Julian Literature Trust, 1991.

Wuest, Kenneth S. *The New Testament: An Expanded Translation.* Grand Rapids: Eerdmans, 2002 reprint.

*Yoars, Marcus. "The Charismatic Name Game." *Ministry Today* (Nov-Dec 2009):10.

*Yoder, Barbara J., gen. ed. *Mantled with Authority: God's Apostolic* Mandate *to Women.* Colorado Springs: Wagner Publications, 2003.

Other Books by Ernest Gentile:

Awaken the Dawn!
Discovering the Joy and Power
of Early Morning Prayer

Numerous people have told the author, "This book changed my life!" The reason is really quite simple: these people learned how to unlock the secret of Jesus' prayer life (a clear explanation of Psalm 50), a practical way to implement such dynamic prayer in their lives and the amazing reality that comes with daily prayer.

The Final Triumph
What Everyone Should Know About Jesus'
Glorious Return

Here is a clear and comprehensive study of Jesus' return. Many have expressed their delight at the way in which the 453 New Testament verses (which produce 159 key ideas) are woven together, giving comprehensive meaning to this wonderful teaching on the Second Coming of Christ. If all the verses on the Second Coming seem to be like a pile of puzzle pieces, see how easily they can all fall into place!

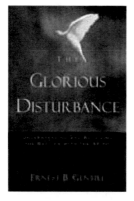

The Glorious Disturbance
Understanding and Receiving
the Baptism with the Holy Spirit

How can something be glorious and disturbing at the same time? Millions of people worldwide have come to find – like the early Church – that the presence of the Holy Spirit in a person's life can be just that! The secret power-source of the early Church is found in being filled with the Holy Spirit. The Church was launched – and is sustained by – the mighty outpouring on the Day of Pentecost. Find how you too can experience this Baptism with the Holy Spirit.

Worship God!

Exploring the Dynamics of Psalmic Worship

There is an exciting surge of interest and participation in worship in this generation! Of course there are many styles and expressions, and this is to be expected. This book gives the biblical foundation, especially emphasizing both heart-worship and also the nine modes of worship mentioned in the book of Psalms. The early Church incorporated David's secrets with the manifestations of the Spirit, producing amazing results. You will find, as many other have, that this book has an amazing content of worship statements by leading authorities of various churches. Used in a number of Bible Colleges.

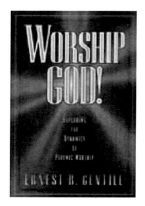

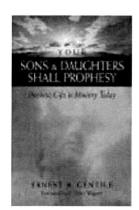

Your Sons and Daughters Shall Prophesy
Prophetic Gifts in Ministry Today

How amazing that God still speaks to His people through prophetic gifts! With those gifts, however, comes responsibility! Although prophets and prophecy may cause some concern, the checks and balances are given in the Bible. Dick Iverson has said, "this book is one of the most balanced and proven that I have read." Used in a number of Bible Colleges.

Adora a Dios

La adoración y la alabanza son temas de máxima actualidad en la iglesia del siglo XXI. El "boom" de la música cristiana, las grabaciones millonarias y los conciertos multitudinarios son exponentes de un interés creciente en el pueblo cristiano para adorar a Dios.

Pero, al mismo tiempo, son también una importante fuente de conflictos. A saber, la controversia entorno a las distintas formas de adoración ha sido siempre un

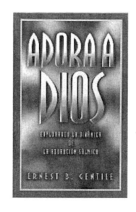

punto negativo que mina la unidad del Cuerpo de Cristo. . .

Y este libro aporta una guía universal invalorable para aclarar posturas. Fruto de la pasión manifiesta de su autor por la adoración, pero a la vez sazonado por su elevada preparación académica, analiza los principios y métodos de la adoración y presenta los fundamentos bíblicos y teológicos de la alabanza de tipo sálmico.

Así, los creyentes devotos adoradores, hallarán en sus páginas una fuente de inspiración; los ministros de música, un recurso de orientación y aliento, y los pastores y lideres, un manual teológico útil para establecer y mantener un equilibrio bíblico.